Adolf Keller

(1872–1963)

Adolf Keller, about 70 years old (archive Dr. Pierre Keller)

ADOLF KELLER

(1872–1963)

Ecumenist, World Citizen, Philanthropist

Marianne Jehle-Wildberger

Translated by Mark Kyburz with John Peck

CASCADE *Books* · Eugene, Oregon

ADOLF KELLER (1872–1963)
Ecumenist, World Citizen, Philanthropist

Copyright © 2013 Marianne Jehle-Wildberger. All rights reserved. Except for brief quotations in critical publications or reviews, no part of this book may be reproduced in any manner without prior written permission from the publisher. Write: Permissions, Wipf and Stock Publishers, 199 W. 8th Ave., Suite 3, Eugene, OR 97401.

Cascade Books
An Imprint of Wipf and Stock Publishers
199 W. 8th Ave., Suite 3
Eugene, OR 97401

www.wipfandstock.com

ISBN 13: 978-1-62032-107-2

Cataloguing-in-Publication data:

Jehle, Marianne.

Adolf Keller (1872–1963) : ecumenist, world citizen, philanthropist / Marianne Jehle-Wildberger ; translated by Mark Kyburz with John Peck.

x + 290 pp. ; 23 cm. Includes bibliographical references and index.

ISBN 13: 978-1-62032-107-2

1. Keller, Adolf, b. 1872. 2. Ecumenical movement—History—20th century. 3. World Council of Churches. Division of Inter-Church Aid, Refugee, and World Service. 4. Ecumenical movement—Biography. 5. Clergy—Switzerland—Biography. 6. Church and social problems—International cooperation. 7. Barth, Karl, 1886–1968. 8. Bell, George, 1883–1958. 9. Söderblom, Nathan, 1866–1933. 10. Macfarland, Charles S. I. Kyburz, Mark, 1963–. II. Peck, John. III. Title.

BX6.5 J4 2013

Manufactured in the USA

Contents

Introduction

THE AMERICAN THEOLOGIAN WILLIAM A. Brown, himself an ecumenist, hailed the Swiss theologian Adolf Keller as one of the eight most important pioneers of ecumenism in the decades prior to the founding of the World Council of Churches in 1948.[1] Keller (1872–1963) served as a pastor for the Protestant community in Cairo, for a church in his native canton of Schaffhausen and then in Geneva, and finally at St Peter's parish church in Zurich. Already from the outset of his career, he sought to promote social justice and world peace. After the end of World War I, the Federal Council of the Churches of Christ in America entrusted the well-educated, multilingual, and open-minded Keller with cultivating relations between churches in America and Europe. He retired from parish work at the end of 1923 to play a key role within the ecumenical Universal Christian Conference on Life and Work (hereinafter abbreviated as Life and Work), which was steadily evolving at the time. At its inaugural world conference, held in Stockholm in 1925, Keller was elected second associate general secretary, in which capacity he later became director of the International Christian Social Institute in Geneva. From 1930 on, his work focused on spreading ecumenism in the churches throughout the world.

In 1922, Keller founded the ecumenical relief agency Inter-Church Aid, which he headed until 1945. It became the cornerstone of his life's work. The agency supported churches in France and Germany that had suffered the effects of World War I. Keller placed particular emphasis on coming to the aid of Protestant minorities in Eastern Europe. In particular, he supported their efforts to recruit and train young ministers. Furthermore, he lent assistance to the hard-pressed Protestant and Orthodox Christians in the Soviet Union. Financial support for these ventures came chiefly from the United States and from the Swiss Protestant community.

1. Brown, *Toward a United Church*, see Index.

Like his friend Karl Barth, Keller adopted a clear stance toward National Socialism. He became actively involved in enlightening the English-speaking world about the Nazi regime, and was among the first theologians to tend to the needs of German refugees.

Among Keller's fellow ecumenists were Nathan Söderblom, Charles Macfarland, Henry S. Leiper, Eugène Choisy, Wilfred Monod, Marc Boegner, Adolf Deissmann, and George Bell. Together they aspired to the same overarching objective and shared the ideals encapsulated in Keller's book *Von Geist und Liebe: Ein Bilderbuch aus dem Leben* (1934).[2]

Keller wrote more than twenty books, dozens of brochures, and hundreds of articles. His copious, unpublished estate is housed in numerous archives, among other places, in Geneva, Bern, Basel, Zurich, Berlin, London, and Philadelphia. The present English version of the biography of Adolf Keller dispenses with an exhaustive appendix. It is an abbreviated version of the comprehensively researched German original, *Adolf Keller (1872–1963): Pionier der ökumenischen Bewegung* (2008).

2. Hereafter abbreviated as *Von Geist und Liebe*.

Abbreviations

APIDEP	Association Protestante Internationale De Prêts
AV	Assembly of Delegates
BAR	Schweizerisches Bundesarchiv in Bern (Swiss Federal Archives, Bern)
CH W	Winterthurer Bibliotheken, Winterthur Schweiz (Association of libraries in Winterthur, Switzerland)
ECLOF	Ecumenical Church Loan Fund
EPD	Evangelischer Pressedienst Zürich (Evangelical Press Service, Zurich)
ETH	Eidgenössische Technische Hochschule Zürich (Swiss Federal Institute of Technology Zurich)
EZA	Evangelisches Zentralarchiv Berlin (Evangelical Central Archives, Berlin)
Faith and Order	Faith and Order, ecumenical movement
Federal Council	Federal Council of the Churches of Christ in America (until 1952, now known as the National Council)
HEKS	Hilfswerk der Evangelischen Kirchen der Schweiz (relief agency of the Swiss Protestant Churches; official name: Swiss Interchurch Aid)
ICC	International Christian Committee for German Refugees
ICRC	International Committee of the Red Cross, Geneva
ILO	International Labor Organization, Geneva
Inter-Church Aid	European Central Bureau for Relief
KBA	Karl Barth Archive, Basel
KJV	King James Version of the Bible
Kirchenbund	Federation of Swiss Protestant Churches (SEK)
Life and Work	Universal Christian Conference on Life and Work
LPL	Lambeth Palace Library London

Abbreviations

NCC	National Council of Churches of Christ in America (since 1952)
NLAK	Estate of Adolf Keller, including documents on ecumenism (held in the private archive of Dr. Pierre Keller, Geneva)
NLDSK	Estate of Doris Stäuli-Keller, eldest daughter of Adolf Keller (archive Stiftung Sulzberg, Winterthur)
NLTK	Estate of Tina Keller-Jenny (held in the private archive of Dr. Pierre Keller, Geneva)
NSDAP	Nationalsozialistische Deutsche Arbeiterpartei (National Socialist German Workers' Party)
NZZ	*Neue Zürcher Zeitung*
Ökumenischer Rat	Ökumenischer Rat der Kirchen, World Council of Churches
PHS NCC	Presbyterian Historical Society, National Council of Churches Records, Philadelphia USA
Reformed Alliance	World Alliance of Reformed Churches (= World Presbyterian Alliance)
RGG	*Religion in Geschichte und Gegenwart* (encyclopedia)
SEK	Federation of Swiss Protestant Churches
StAZ	Staatsarchiv Zürich (State Archives of Zurich)
Stockholm	*International Sociocritical Church Journal*
TVZ	Theologischer Verlag Zürich
UTS	Union Theological Seminary, New York
WCC	World Council of Churches, Geneva
YMCA	Young Men's Christian Association
YWCA	Young Women's Christian Association
Zentralstelle	Central Bureau for Relief, Inter-Church Aid
World Alliance	World Alliance for Promoting Friendship through the Churches
WS	Winterthurer Sondersammlungen

1

From Village Boy to Pastor

CHILDHOOD, YOUTH, AND STUDENT DAYS

RÜDLINGEN IS A SMALL farming village in the Canton of Schaffhausen, situated in northern Switzerland. The village is surrounded by a beautiful countryside only a few miles downriver from the Rhine Falls. Fertile fields extend toward the river, and steep vineyards rise behind the village. The Protestant church sits enthroned high above the village. Almost all of the villagers belonged to the Protestant faith. Adolf Keller was born and raised in one of Rüdlingen's pretty half-timbered houses in 1872. He was the eldest child born to the village teacher Johann Georg Keller and his wife Margaretha, née Buchter. Three sisters and a brother were born to the Kellers after Adolf. A large fruit and vegetable garden contributed to the upkeep of the family.

For six years, Adolf Keller attended the primary school classes taught by his father. The young boy's performance so conspicuously excelled that of his sixty peers that the highly regarded village teacher decided not to award his son any grades. Occasionally, Keller senior involved his son in the teaching of classes. Both parents were ecclesiastically minded. Keller's father took his Bible classes seriously. Adolf was required to learn by heart countless Bible verses. His mother ran the village Sunday School. She was a good storyteller. Unlike her more austere husband, Keller's mother represented an emotional piety. She never missed attending the annual festival of the devout Basel Mission.

The village of Rüdlingen and the Rhine (old picture postcard)

The village pastor taught the young Keller Latin, and his daughter, who had traveled widely in Europe as a governess, taught him English and French. He also took piano and organ lessons with her. Keller attended secondary school in Flaach, a neighboring village situated in the nearby Canton of Zurich. He then entered the highly regarded Humanistisches Gymnasium, the classics section of Schaffhausen Grammar School. The college was also attended by students from further afield. Among these was Conrad Jenny, Keller's future brother-in-law, who attended the college a few years later and commuted there from Zurich.

Keller became one of the best students in his class. He enjoyed all subjects, with the exception of mathematics. He joined the Scaphusia student fraternity, where members not only drank beer but also recited poems, gave talks, and engaged in intense debate. His fraternity affiliation challenged the shy country boy and nurtured him immensely. At Scaphusia, he met Jakob Wipf, who became his first close friend. Upon graduating with flying colors, Keller enrolled in the Faculty of Theology at the University of Basel in 1892, together with Wipf. Founded in the fifteenth century, it is the oldest university in Switzerland. Keller moved into rooms in the Alumneum, a time-honored student house.

Upon his arrival in Basel, Keller suffered a profound shock: the Faculty of Theology was dominated by liberally minded theologians influenced by the Enlightenment, who approached the Bible using historical-critical methods and who took a critical stance toward Christian dogma. Such an attitude was alien to Keller, who had been raised in a theologically orthodox home. Rüdlingen's pastor was also orthodox. While liberally minded in private, Keller's Religious Education instructor at Schaffhausen Grammar School had steered clear of modern theological questions in the classroom.

Quite deliberately, presumably, Keller did not attend any lectures given by the purportedly extremely "modern" Franz Camille Overbeck, who achieved lasting fame. Although he realized that Bernhard Duhm, the moderately liberal professor of Old Testament, was an outstanding scholar, Keller felt more attracted to Conrad von Orelli, his orthodox counterpart. Some of Keller's fellow students shared this experience, including Paul Wernle, who later became one of the most important professors of theology in Switzerland. In the Schwizerhüsli (Swiss Cottage) fraternity, which had been founded by pious circles in Basel, Keller was lent an understanding ear. He discovered, however, that in some respects he was more open-minded than his fellow fraternity members. Much to their dismay, for instance, he advocated the admission of women to the University of Basel.

The Schwizerhüsli (Swiss Cottage) fraternity,
Adolf Keller sitting at the left (archive Dr. Pierre Keller)

In spite of his firm theological orthodoxy, the young Keller wrestled with his proposed calling. However, he sought to evade the "bitter struggles and doubts" over whether he had chosen the right profession by pursuing his study of the Bible in "his own way."[1] For a time, he consoled himself with the idea of being a "pagan . . . with a Christian heart."[2] Ultimately, he wrenched himself free from the "rigid doctrine of inspiration," that is, verbal inspiration of the Bible. He found some distraction from his personal problems by immersing himself in philosophy, attending courses in classical Arabic, and following the last lectures of the great art historian Jacob Burckhardt on the Renaissance and on the Baroque period. In the summer of 1894, he visited Paris and marveled at the paintings exhibited in the Louvre that Burckhardt had described in his lectures.

In late 1894, Jakob Wipf and Keller visited Salzburg, Vienna, and Prague on their way to Berlin, where the latter intended to continue his theological studies for two semesters. At the time, Berlin was shining in the imperial splendor of William II. In Keller's eyes, the university emanated even greater splendor.[3] In Berlin, he thus hoped to form a "unified theological outlook."[4]

Berlin's Protestant Faculty of Theology was renowned as the most outstanding of its kind in the German-speaking world. Among its teaching faculty was Adolf von Harnack, the leader of liberal theology at the time. Hundreds of students from across the world, including no less than forty Americans during Keller's period, attended von Harnack's lectures. Keller was fascinated:

> Here was the great Harnack, whose lectures on the history of dogma I attended. For the first time, I experienced a sovereign mastery of the subject, and such ease in shaping the delivery, like a work of art. Often, one did not feel like taking notes when he brought the great Church Father Saint Augustine to life, extemporizing and performing gymnastics while lecturing.[5]

He was also impressed by Hermann von Soden, the New Testament scholar, but even more so by Julius Kaftan, a systematic theologian, who placed great emphasis on ethics and a faith with practical consequences. Kaftan insisted that the roots of religious belief lay not in the intellect, but instead

1. Keller, "Curriculum vitae."
2. Ibid.
3. Keller, "Aus meinem Leben," 6.
4. Keller, "Curriculum vitae."
5. Keller, "Aus meinem Leben," 6.

in the "feeling and willing spirit."[6] One counterpoint to these liberal professors was Adolf Schlatter, the orthodox Swiss New Testament scholar. Conspicuously, Keller attended more of Schlatter's lectures than those of any other professor: "His classes were not only remarkably witty, but they also involved the profound exploration of the evangelical truth of the Bible."[7] While Schlatter to a certain extent applied the historical-critical method to exegesis, he arrived at conservative conclusions.

Keller also attended the lectures of Ernst Curtius and Heinrich von Treitschke on history, as well as those by Hermann Grimm on art history. Almost every day, he would spend his lunchtime at one of Berlin's numerous museums. He joined a choir to sing Bach's *St. Matthew Passion*, and often attended theater and concert performances in the evenings. He absorbed literally everything that Berlin had to offer by way of culture.

Adolf Keller as a student in Berlin
(archive Dr. Pierre Keller)

In 1890, German theologians of all stripes had founded the Evangelisch-Sozialer Kongress (Protestant Social Congress) to discuss the negative effects of industrialization and Manchester Capitalism. Keller became personally acquainted with many of the figures involved in the Congress. He also read the writings of Friedrich Naumann, a German liberal politician and Protestant pastor. Berlin's working-class districts provided abundant evidence of social misery. Together with Arthur Titius, adjunct professor of theology, Keller visited a range of welfare facilities maintained by the Innere Mission (Home Mission), including hospices, hospitals, orphanages, and homes for the blind. Later, on his return journey to Switzerland, he visited Bethel hospices near Bielefeld: "On this visit, I became personally acquainted with the elderly Bodelschwingh as an incarnation of Christian love. Whoever

6. Horn, "Berlin, Universität," col. 1053.
7. Keller, "Aus meinem Leben," 7.

had looked into his eyes, either when he was delivering a public speech or when he was attending to the sick, can never forget those loving eyes."[8]

In April 1896, Keller was awarded the second-highest honors by the Examination Board of the German-speaking Reformed Churches of Switzerland. What was his theological stance at the time? In his curriculum vitae, which he was required to submit at his final examinations, he maintains that the diversity of religious convictions is fully justified by the freedom and originality of each and every individual:

> I realized that religion rests upon individual personalities and human relationships, and not upon abstract ideas or teachings . . . I therefore understood that while there are presumably different kinds of dogmatists, *the* Christian Dogma can never be found . . . I became increasingly disinclined to systematize my Christianity into a theology as expediently as possible . . . On my path toward attaining these convictions, not only Schlatter but also von Harnack and Kaftan exerted a profound influence on me . . . Berlin afforded me the greatest possible stimulation, without, however, demanding that I swear an oath on the words of any single teacher.[9]

Thus, Keller's hope for a unified theological outlook had remained unfulfilled. His curriculum closes with the words uttered by the Apostle Paul in Philippians 3:12: "Not that I have secured it already, . . . but I am still pursuing it." From this point on, Keller was spared existential crises of faith. He joined a group of young Swiss theologians around Paul Wernle committed to mediating between orthodoxy and liberalism. This approach was also shared by the widely read *Kirchenblatt für die reformierte Schweiz* (Church Magazine of Reformed Switzerland), to which Keller later often contributed articles.

8. Ibid., 12–13. The theologian Friedrich von Bodelschwingh (1831–1910) founded Bethel in 1872 and was its director. Bethel was (and still is) a large complex of several hospitals and different homes for handicapped or elderly people and the working poor, as well as a faculty of theology and social work. His son Friedrich von Bodelschwingh Jr. (1877–1946), also a theologian, was his successor, and in 1933 for some months *Reichsbischof* of the German Evangelical Church, as such opposing Hitler. See below, pp. 81, 166–69.

9. Keller, "Curriculum vitae."

IN COSMOPOLITAN CAIRO (1896–1899)

In the autumn of 1896, Keller was appointed auxiliary pastor at the German Protestant parish in Cairo.[10] The congregation also included German- and French-speaking Swiss citizens. Presumably, Keller had negotiated his posting to Egypt while still in Berlin. During his time in Berlin, he had written his first book, *Der Geisteskampf des Christentums gegen den Islam bis zur Zeit der Kreuzzüge* (The Spiritual Struggle of Christianity against Islam until the Time of the Crusades). He undertook this treatise, which extended to approximiately a hundred pages, at the suggestion of the Reverend Wilhelm Faber, director of the German Oriental Mission. Keller later distanced himself from his fledgling work, since he had lacked the necessary critical judgment at the time. It is nevertheless worth examining.

Keller's reflections on his subject begin with a reference to Islam as an "arrogant religion."[11] While it had brought "relative morality" to the peoples of the world, he further observes, it had barely afforded them "life, freedom, and full satisfaction." It was a "humanitarian duty," particularly toward women, to acquaint Muslims with the blessing of freedom and with the gospel. Moreover, the Christian church had an "explicit, absolute Great Commission."[12] Islam had ossified, and therefore the point in time for missionary work was favorable.[13]

However, he continues, one should not underestimate the "truth content of Islam," since it originated in Judaism and Christianity, both of them revealed religions. Mohammed had also possessed "creative power."[14] The church had been mistaken in considering Islam its greatest enemy for centuries and in neglecting the "common elements of both religions."[15] Particularly the Latin West had remained uninformed about Islam, falsely branding Muslims as pagans.[16] Keller approvingly cites the medieval theologian Peter the Venerable: "Aggredior vos, non ut nostri saepe faciunt, armis, sed verbis, non vi sed ratione, non odio, sed amore."[17] Keller

---

10. See Acta 1896–1899 on the German Protestant parish in Cairo (EZA Bestand 5 3085/3086/3092).

11. Keller, *Der Geisteskampf des Christentums*, 4.

12. Ibid., 5–6.

13. Ibid., 8.

14. Ibid, 8–9.

15. Ibid., 4.

16. Ibid., 40.

17. Ibid., 7 and 54. The famous words uttered by Peter the Venerable (1092/94–1154), abbot of the Benedictine abbey of Cluny, translate into English as follows: "I

condemns both the "holy war" waged by the Muslims and also, albeit less explicitly, the Crusades. Often, however, the Muslims had been "more magnanimous and more tolerant than the Christians"; moreover, the Crusades had brought about the bankruptcy of Oriental Christendom.[18]

Presumably, Keller did greater justice to Islam, owing to his reading of the Koran and Jacques Paul Migne's sourcebook on patrology,[19] than those commissioning him had anticipated. Keller's booklet and his entry into the interreligious World Brotherhood, founded after World War II, were thus not miles apart. Significantly, he learned modern Arabic during his time in Cairo. Acquiring the language allowed him to engage in conversation with the bedouins on his journey to Sinai in 1898. While they too submitted to the will of Allah, he wrote, their submission was softened by their faith in His benevolence. "The naiveté and simplicity of Islam" were magnificent, Keller observed, even though all kinds of superstition clouded this religion in his eyes.[20]

And thus to Cairo! At the time, Egypt was under British rule. Cairo and Alexandria were cosmopolitan cities, whose populations, besides sizeable British contingents, included Greek, French, German, and Swiss nationals; along with the native Muslims, religious denominations included Jews, Copts, Anglicans, members of the Greek Orthodox Church, Catholics, and Protestants. Amid this rich panoply of nationalities and denominations, Keller acquired an extraordinary cosmopolitanism and learned to deal with a broad cross section of people. His Protestant parish included agronomists, apprentices, archaeologists, Arabists, artists, bankers, diplomats, doctors, engineers, geologists, governesses, historians of religion, lawyers, mechanics, merchants, university professors, watchmakers, and Swiss hotel proprietors. Most parishioners attended services only rarely. At Christmas, however, a large congregation gathered around the Christmas tree, which was traditionally imported from Europe.

Keller preached alternately in German and French, not only in Cairo but also in Heluan, a health spa where numerous German and Swiss tuberculosis patients spent the winter months. He also ran the Sunday school and visited the sick at the Hospital Victoria, run by deaconesses, in Cairo. He devoted most of his time, however, to the parish school, which was

---

attack you, indeed, but not, as our people often do, with weapons but with words, not with violence but with rationality, not with hatred but with love."

18. Ibid., 36–37, 23, 31, and 84.

19. Keller also familiarized himself with Joseph Assemani's *Bibliotheca Orientalis Clementino-Vaticana* and with the relevant secondary literature.

20. Keller, *Sinai-Fahrt*, 89.

attended by children of different nationalities. He taught German, religious studies, mathematics, Latin, natural history, singing, and drawing: the language of instruction was partly German, partly French. Fortunately, his father had introduced him to the art of teaching back home in Rüdlingen.

Adolf Keller bound for St. Catherine's Monastery near Mount Moses
(from Adolf Keller, *Eine Sinai-Fahrt*, 23)

He also spent time visiting the mosques and museums, enjoyed riding out to the pyramids with friends in the evenings, and joined the Cairo Music Society. He would often play four-handed piano with Felix von Müller, the German general consul. He organized two concerts, including a performance of Mendelssohn's *Elijah*, for which his German friend Carl Hasselbach provided the score.[21] A mixed choir was established for the occasion, and the performance was accompanied by the British Regimental orchestra. Keller conducted the whole affair "with the unconcerned impertinence of an inexperienced apprentice," as he later admitted.[22] Among Keller's best friends in Cairo were the von Bülows. Otto von Bülow, a lawyer by training, was a member of the international tribunal in Cairo. Following his death, Keller socialized with Elsa von Bülow for decades.[23]

In the spring of 1898, Keller was "deeply moved" when he set foot in the "Holy Land."[24] Under the supervision of Hermann von Soden, his

21. On Olga Hasselbach, the wife of Carl Hasselbach, see below p. 188.
22. Keller, "Aus meinem Leben," 19.
23. On Elsa von Bülow, see below p. 257.
24. Keller, "Aus meinem Leben," 25.

former New Testament professor in Berlin, he visited the Temple Square and the Garden of Gethsemane in Jerusalem, as well as Bethlehem und Galilee. And Keller was indeed enthralled by the prospect of spending several weeks doing research at St Catherine's Greek Orthodox Monastery. Located in the Sinai Peninsula, the monastery was still untouched by tourism in those days. In midsummer, and accompanied by bedouins, he reached the monastery on a camel. Commissioned by von Soden, two young theologians were already immersed in comparing texts based on old Bible manuscripts.[25] In the monastery's library, the three young scholars would sit hunched over the materials during the morning and evening hours. In the afternoons, they would retire for their siestas and spend the nights in a tent pitched beneath an olive tree in the monastery's garden. They climbed Mount Moses (Jebel Musa) several times:

> I remained . . . at the summit, alone, while the sun set in unforgettable glory and the moon rose above the thin strip of sea at Akaba. Only at the summit was there still light; the valleys and canyons below soon lay shrouded in black, silent darkness. At this moment, the many theories, hypotheses, and critical questions arising in connection with our work sank into the night. One forgets one's disputes over Moses and Israel, the Revelation and the Commandments, and the situation of the real Sinai. One wants to experience . . . what distinguishes the pure religious and spiritual content of the narratives of Moses, the man of God, who speaks to Yahweh as to a friend.[26]

"AUF BURG" AND GENEVA: ALBERT SCHWEITZER, KARL BARTH, AND PSYCHOLOGY

In 1899, Keller was appointed to serve the parish auf Burg beside Stein am Rhein, a small town on the River Rhine in the North of Switzerland (Canton Schaffhausen). The church "auf Burg" sits on a hill, amid the ruins of an ancient Roman fort. Medieval frescoes decorate its interior. The view from the adjacent rectory onto the Rhine and the small town lying opposite is magnificent. But the contrast to cosmopolitan Cairo could not have been greater. Most of Keller's parishioners were farmers. The congregation was very affectionate. One day, after the vicarage had been burgled, Keller

25. Von Soden revised the Greek New Testament. See above, p. 4 and 9–10, and below, p. 29–30.

26. Keller, *Sinai-Fahrt*, 67–68.

was presented by way of consolation with a mighty piece of gammon and veal roasted on the spit; he was also given a white Pomeranian to guard the rectory.

Keller filled his time by writing an account titled *Eine Sinai-Fahrt* (A Journey across the Sinai), playing the piano, and copious reading; among many others, he read the writings of Thomas Carlyle, the Scottish social critic. He taught religious studies at Schaffhausen Grammar School, and regularly contributed articles to the *Neue Zürcher Zeitung*, one of the most renowned German-speaking newspapers. Most important, however, he made important friends. These included the Curtius family in Strasbourg. Friedrich Curtius, a lawyer and the son of professor Ernst Curtius in Berlin, was the president of the Evangelical Lutheran and Evangelical Reformed Churches of Alsace-Lorraine, which was still German at the time. Curtius's wife was Swiss. Their son, Ernst Robert Curtius, later became a well-known scholar of Romance languages and literature (he translated T. S. Eliot's *The Waste Land* from English into German), with whom Keller corresponded until well beyond World War II. "The Curtius family home in Strasbourg was a bridge between countries and minds."[27]

At the Curtiuses', Keller met Albert Schweitzer, who paid the family almost daily visits. Schweitzer had been adjunct professor of theology in Strasbourg since 1902. Keller observed:

> If one had spent the afternoon sitting on the organ bench [at Saint Thomas] with Schweitzer, where he brought to life the idiosyncracies of the old Bach, in the evenings he acquainted one with the modern Bach, who bridged the old strict style with marvelous fioritura which . . . represented the full scale of human emotions . . . Schweitzer had something of Bucer's ecumenical and modern manners, the latter being the actual reformer and precursor of the ecumenical movement. It was in those days that he conceived the plan to travel to Africa.[28]

Thereafter, Keller and Schweitzer saw each other only seldom, but they corresponded from time to time. When Keller attended the large ecumenical congress hosted by Life and Work in Stockholm in 1925, Schweitzer wrote to him: "However, here I sit in Lambarene, where I treat boils, build huts, houses, and latrines, and steadily lose the use of my pen."[29]

27. Keller, *Geist und Liebe*, 191.

28. Ibid., 191–92.

29. Schweitzer to Keller, "Am Tage nach Johanni," June 25, 1925 (WS, MS Sch 153/48).

In 1904 Keller was offered a position at the "German Reformed Parish"[30] in Geneva. He accepted without hesitating, since he was attracted by the city's urban atmosphere. Keller was fortunate enough to belong to the *Vénérable Compagnie des Pasteurs*, the association of Protestant Genevan clergymen going back to the time of Reformation. There he met Eugène Choisy, who became perhaps his closest friend and a lifelong companion.[31] Keller held his services in the *Auditoire*, as Calvin's lecture hall was called, which is located adjacent to the cathedral. Much work awaited him. The parish extended across the city, and from 1908 across the whole canton. On paper, its membership totaled several thousand parishioners, but approaching them proved difficult. Membership fluctuated significantly, and those who remained became *Romands* (French-speaking Swiss) within a few years. Owing to his considerable efforts, including many house calls, Keller managed somewhat to pull the parish together. In 1907, at least sixty-nine male parishioners attended the parish assembly meeting. On public holidays, attendance was far greater so that services had to be held at the Madeleine, the old city church.

Keller received much support from Theophil Fuog, president of the parish council. Fuog greeted the proposals of his enterprising new pastor with great enthusiasm. Among Keller's ideas were the enrichment of the liturgy, the accompanying of church services with more singing, the founding of a church choir, the introduction of a parish bulletin, the establishment of group discussions on "the difficult questions of spiritual life,"[32] and the organization of concerts, exhibitions, parish evenings, and a lecture series. One of the cycles was devoted to the prophet Elijah, of whom Keller had grown fond on his ascents of Mount Moses during his earlier spell in Egypt. Another cycle focused on "The Image of Christ in Art."[33] Keller's most daring wish was for a parish hall, which was a new idea at the time. The parish council embraced the idea, and the investment proved worthwhile: the hall, which exists to this day, soon became indispensable.

Keller often resorted to humor to rouse his somewhat passive parish. In the parish bulletin, he published a piece titled "A Dream," which envisioned a gathering of the parish in the *Auditoire*:

30. The parish has been known since 1940 as the German-Swiss Protestant Parish of Geneva; see Göhring, *75 Jahre*.

31. Keller and Choisy were both active in the Federation of Swiss Protestant Churches, in the ecumenical movement, and in Keller's relief agency.

32. Minutes of the Church Council, February 1, 1905 (archive of the Geneva Church Parish).

33. Ibid., February 21, 1907.

All of a sudden, a noise descended from the gallery as if someone had banged their fist irately on the cornice. Look at how
everyone raises their heads—now would that not be the great
Johann Sebastian Bach himself, he who has blessed us with
such magnificent chorales . . . ? "What, is this supposed to be a
hymn *ad majorem Dei gloriam*, to the greater glory of God? If
this be the case, then the dear Lord will surely hold his hands
over his ears . . . True evangelical church singing is pure delight,
strength, and merrymaking emanating straight from the heart.
Sometimes, it must resound through the edifice like blaring
trumpets, . . . sometimes like affectionate shawms . . ." Then,
everything set in powerfully, and I, too, joined in the singing,
until I awoke from hearing my own voice, and realized that it
had only been a dream.[34]

The majority of parishioners were craftsmen, factory workers, or nannies.
For the first time since becoming a parish pastor, Keller was confronted
with poverty. He observed with great concern that many workers, disappointed by its lack of interest in their predicament, turned their backs on
the church. It was precisely at this time that a religious-social movement
began to emerge in Switzerland.[35] Keller was close to the movement. In his
sermons, he demanded higher wages and called upon the affluent to have
"a subtle conscience": he considered the divide between rich and poor "the
most pressing problem."[36]

The Geneva popular vote on the separation of church and state, held
in 1907, presented another problem: the motion was approved owing to
the votes of the free churches and of the secular part of the electorate.
Like the majority of his parish, Keller was disappointed. While he made
no qualms about his dismay, anger, and fear, he also sought to offer his
congregation encouragement: "If we can summon the feeling in such a
predicament that Jesus is with us, then we are safe."[37] Not only should the
church be "the Lord's home for all," but there was also a need for a "wide,
open church."[38]

34. Keller, "Ein Traum."

35. The movement was founded in 1906 by, among other theologians, Leonhard
Ragaz and Hermann Kutter.

36. Sermons delivered by Keller on the Day of Prayer and Repentance of 1904, and
on Mark:10,17–27, November 27, between 1904 and 1909 (NLAK A 3 Early Sermons).

37. Sermon on Matthew 8:23–27, delivered on July 7, 1907 (ibid.).

38. Sermon on the Parable of the Weeds among the Wheat, Matthew 13:24–30,
delivered on June 30, 1907, (ibid.).

Adolf Keller at the age of about 35 (archive Dr. Pierre Keller)

Notwithstanding his many duties, Keller resumed his attendance at lectures on theology and classical Arabic. Throughout his five years in Geneva, he attended all of Théodore Flournoy's lectures and seminars on psychology, in order to become a better pastor. Like Sigmund Freud and C. G. Jung, Flournoy had trained as a medical doctor.[39] One of his friends was William James, who was among the first to speak of the "unconscious mind."[40] James and Flournoy were among the founders of the psychology of religion. Flourney's lectures were always listed as *Psychologie experimentale* (experimental psychology), his seminars as *Exercices pratiques dans le laboratoire de psychologie expérimentale et recherches spéciales*

39. Edited by Flournoy and Claparède, the *Archives de Psychologie de la Suisse Romande* was the first journal of psychology to be published in Switzerland.

40. Keller, "Aus der Frühhzeit der psychoanalytischen Bewegung." William James is credited with founding American pragmatism.

(practical exercises in the experimental psychology laboratory and special research).[41] In his classes, Flournoy discussed current affairs, reflected on contemporary debates, and explored parapsychological and pathological phenomena. Like Freud, he considered dreams to hold the key to the unconscious. Keller was impressed by Flournoy, whom he described as "a warm-hearted and upright Christian with a liberal disposition," and who stood for a "theology of experience."[42] Noticeably, Keller's sermons all of a sudden included references to "Jesus, the doctor of the soul," or to Jesus as the one who had recognized man's "paralyzed soul."[43]

Then a highly significant event occurred: on September 26, 1909, the young Karl Barth took up his appointment as an assistant minister in the Geneva parish, a position that had been created to ease the burden on Keller.[44] For a few weeks, Barth thus officiated as Keller's curate. These few weeks were decisive, not least because Keller had met the young, "mercurial" violinist Nelly Hoffmann through Theophil Fuog, the acting president of the parish council. Keller and Nelly would often play music at her family's home.[45] After Keller left Geneva, Nelly attended the confirmation class taught by Barth, and a few years later she became his wife. The couple was married by Keller in Nydegg Church in Bern on March 27, 1913. Some years later, Keller observed that Barth had "exhibited a refreshing lack of respect for both what used to be and what had come to be," and had "started the world over from scratch." Furthermore,

> To him, the whole of famous Geneva, the center of Calvinism . . . , was no more than an international hodgepotch that lacked spirit and character. He added salt and pepper . . . The acting minister [Keller] introduced the curate to his duties and responsibilities as a parish pastor, to the impoverished attics of St Gervais, to undertaking social welfare and pastoral work . . . , that is to say, to a thoroughly well-defined position. In turn, the young curate soon introduced the acting minister to other affairs and concerns, including the social tensions that he had experienced far more strongly in Germany as a young adherent of the religious-social movement than we were accustomed to

41. "Programme des Cours de l'Université de Genève" (1904–1907; archive of Geneva University Library).

42. Keller, "Aus meinem Leben," 49.

43. Keller, "The Healing of the Paralytic."

44. See Marianne Jehle-Wildberger, "Karl Barth und Adolf Keller. Geschichte einer Freundschaft."

45. Keller, "Aus meinem Leben," 53.

> in Switzerland . . . Barth's sermons brought home to his listeners
> the urgency of his message, and they left no place for incidental
> considerations . . . He was capable of grasping an older colleague
> . . . by the scruff, and challenging him: "Where is your impetus?"
> . . . Today, I no longer know who was whose curate.[46]

Keller regretted that he was unable to continue his cooperation with Barth after assuming office in Zurich at the end of October 1909.[47] Conversely, Barth hailed Keller as "an immensely rich and multifarious spirit," and asserted that "we also had a good understanding in theological affairs."[48] Barth preserved Keller's humorous style in the parish bulletin; like his predecessor's, his contributions also made frequent reference to everyday experience. Following Barth's appointment as pastor in Safenwil, a blue-collar, working-class village, Keller wrote to him thus: "Your Safenwil sermon is well conceived, well structured, and persuasively formulated, but it is the work of a young man and an outgrowth of your study. I wonder how your folks are supposed to understand you."[49] Keller and Barth remained lifelong associates, even though their relationship was not always free of conflict.

It was with quite some reluctance that the Geneva parish allowed Keller to leave. He departed with mixed feelings, since the post had permitted his creative imagination to run free. On relocating to Zurich, at the age of almost thirty-eight, Keller was still young, and yet already highly experienced. His appointment to St Peter's Church in Zurich had astonished him, since the parish was a "citadel of liberal Christianity."[50] Keller, however, did not consider himself a liberal theologian. Jakob Escher-Bürkli, president of St Peter's Parish, came down firmly on his side, because he considered Keller "a strong personality," a pastor endowed with a vivacious and original mind.[51] And thus, Keller accepted the appointment. He was to remain at St Peter's until the end of 1923.

46. Keller, manuscript, presumably dating from after 1919 (NLAK A Folder Unpublished Manuscripts).

47. Keller to Paul Walter, Geneva, June 10, 1910 (BAR J.2.257, 1989/211).

48. Barth to W. Spoendlin, November 12, 1909; cited in Busch, *Karl Barth, His Life from Letters*, 53.

49. Keller to Barth, undated letter, presumably written in the spring of 1915 (KBA 9315.38).

50. Minutes of St Peter's Parish Council, July 16, 1909, vol. 1902–1920 (archive of St Peter's Parish).

51. Ibid., July 7, 1909.

MARRIAGE AND FAMILY LIFE

In the autumn of 1911, Keller was visiting Conrad and Albertina Jenny in Thalwil, a village situated on the Lake of Zurich. He had taught their son religious studies at Schaffhausen Grammar School. The younger Conrad Jenny, who had meanwhile entered law school, was enthusiastic about Keller's sermons at St Peter's. He arranged for Keller to visit the family, and also invited his older sister, Tina Jenny, who was aged twenty-four at the time. After supper, Keller sat down at the piano, as so often on such occasions.[52]

Keller thus entered an upper-class milieu. The villagers referred to the Jenny villa as the "castle." Tina Jenny's parents both came from families of textile manufacturers in the Canton of Glarus. "I was born in a Victorian-style home," she later observed in her autobiography.[53] As a young man, her father had spent several years in India and in England. While he modeled himself upon the English gentleman, her mother styled herself as a nineteenth-century lady.[54] Tina Jenny and her three younger siblings received private tuition at home. At the age of sixteen, she realized that she wanted to break out of the bourgeois "aristocracy" and belong to the common people. At the age of eighteen, she was sent to Cheltenham Ladies College in the South of England. One of the principal aims of the College was to awaken a sense of social responsibility among its students. Tina decided to become a nurse. In her autobiography, she noted that "my parents could not understand this."[55] At the age of twenty, she became a hard-working hospital nurse and discovered a hitherto unknown happiness. She went on to do an internship in a slum in the East End of London. She spent several weeks in shared accommodation in Saint Hilda's Settlements. The tenements had been established to systematically combat social misery and to provide purposeful poor relief.[56] Their resident staff were mostly young people, who often followed a religious calling and worked gratuitously. Every Monday, Tina Jenny visited twelve families, each of which had a disabled child. She looked after elderly people, often spending long hours with a "sweet elderly couple" who occupied a tiny room up many flights of stairs in a back alley. "Probably, the greatest misery occurs

---

52. Keller, "Aus meinem Leben," 70; see also Tina Keller, "In Memoriam."
53. Tina Keller, "Autobiography" (version of summer 1981), 1.
54. Sträuli-Keller, *Erinnerungen*, 7.
55. Tina Keller, "Autobiography," 5.
56. Tina Keller, "Soziale Arbeit in Ost-London," 23.

where illness exacerbates poverty . . . ; particularly where tuberculosis and infant mortality are rife." Tina Jenny entered a new world, and began contemplating the meaning and value of life.[57]

On the occasion of his first visit to the Jennys, Keller played a Beethoven Sonata. "I fell in love with my future husband while he played the piano."[58] She told him about London. He admired her ability "to empathize with the unfortunate and to embrace their distress,"[59] and suggested that she furnish a written account of her experiences among the poor. Tina, who was fifteen years younger than Adolf, lacked the confidence to do this, and so he offered to help her. The account was published in *Neue Wege* (New Paths), a religious-social journal. "As we were writing down these experiences, we entered each other's hearts so completely that the decision to ask for her hand fell into my lap like a ripe apple."[60] Adolf Keller and Tina Jenny were married in January 1912. "Far from being a large and glamorous wedding, we were married in Thalwil church; after the ceremony, there was a hearty reception for our dear friends at Castle Thalwil; we took off on our honeymoon the same day." The newly wed couple traveled to Egypt, where they enjoyed "unforgettable days and hours."[61]

Following her husband's death, Tina Keller wrote: "I was very happy in my marriage . . . I was nearly breathless as I stepped from such a very narrow home into such a wide space . . . Everything seemed so wide that I was bewildered for joy und excitement . . .There was something so healthy about my husband, everything was so natural. He was a spirited man, but his ideas and also his religion were natural."[62] At the end of 1912, their first child, Doris, was born. Two years later, Paul was born. "During the first three years we had two children that were a delight. My babies thrived and my pregnancies were among my healthiest times."[63] Over the years, two more girls, Margrit and Esther, were born, followed by another son, Pierre, in 1927. In the first years of her marriage, Tina Keller-Jenny attended almost exclusively to her children. Years later, her husband regretted not spending more time with his children. Nevertheless, family

57. Ibid., 33.
58. Tina Keller, "Autobiography," 60.
59. Keller, "Aus meinem Leben," 70–71.
60. Ibid.
61. Ibid., 71–72.
62. Tina Keller, "Autobiography," 6ff.
63. Ibid.

life had been warm and affectionate.[64] In her recollections, Doris wrote: "We were often embraced . . . My parents promised each other that their children could remain spontaneous . . . We talked about everything."[65]

Tina Keller-Jenny wanted to emulate her husband: "His knowledge, his tremendous commitment to work, and his concentration seemed to be like . . . a distant wonderland. I envied him."[66] Furthermore, "my husband's harmonious spontaneity demonstrated a more pleasant kind of life, which I wanted to acquire also."[67] "He worked with ease and joy, but he did not force himself . . . More and more I wished I could also find such creativity."[68] "Gradually I now came to the insight that I needed more education."[69] She earned her baccalaureate after only one and half years of study.[70] "Adolf received me with pride, with a Latin inscription he had written for my homecoming. He could show such joy and warmth."[71] Now, however, the mother of three wished to study medicine. At first, Keller "was angry, hurt, disappointed."[72] But he realized that Tina's idea was not a passing fancy; thus he needed to give her a free hand if she was not to become unhappy.[73] "True loyalty," he wrote later, "accompanies the development and transformations of our fellow human beings."[74]

While pursuing her medical studies, Tina Keller also ensured that her children suffered no lack of "emotional affection."[75] One of her teachers was C. G. Jung. She became one of the first female psychiatrists in Switzerland, and soon made a name for herself. She was now her husband's equal. But the hours they spent together were few, not least owing to Keller's increasing professional commitments. "I would like to add, that in spite of being often lonely, of having difficulties in accepting many absences of

64. Keller, "Aus meinem Leben," 76ff.

65. Sträuli-Keller, *Erinnerungen*, 8.

66. Tina Keller, "Zusatz" (supplement) to Adolf Keller's "Aus meinem Leben," 3 (NLTK).

67. Tina Keller, "Autobiography" (version of summer 1981), 84.

68. Ibid., 16.

69. Ibid., 17.

70. Tina Keller, "Zusatz," 3.

71. Tina Keller, "In Memoriam."

72. Ibid.

73. Keller, "Aus meinem Leben," 77; see also Tina Keller, "Autobiography," 17 and Tina Keller, *Wege inneren Wachstums*, 16.

74. Xenos (=Keller), *Auf der Schwelle*, 87.

75. Keller, "Aus meinem Leben," 80.

Adolf Keller

my husband, I was happy to be the wife of a man who was consecrated to a great humanitarian work."[76]

Adolf and Tina Keller with the children Esther, Doris, Paul, and Margrit (ca. 1924) (archive Dr. Pierre Keller)

SOCIAL COMMITMENT: ST PETER'S CHURCH IN ZURICH (1909–1923) ·

St Peter's was a proud, tradition-conscious parish. Seating over a thousand people at the time, the parish church—with its massive tower and enormous clock—is one of Zurich's landmarks. In the Middle Ages, St Peter's had been *the* parish church in Zurich. During the Reformation, Leo Jud, Huldrych Zwingli's friend and associate, had officiated there, while the late eighteenth century witnessed the appointment of Johann Caspar Lavater, who became famous for his *Physiognomische Fragmente* (Physiognomical Fragments) and for his friendship with Johann Heinrich Pestalozzi and Johann Wolfgang von Goethe. Upon his arrival, Keller took up residence in Lavater's rectory. His study was the so-called "Lavaterstube"; the growing Keller family soon filled the large house with cheerful life.

The parish consisted of two very different parts: the old-town parish, which consisted largely of ordinary people, and the so-called friends, who

76. Tina Keller, "In Memoriam." See below, chapter 3, p. 68–81.

lived outside the parish, either on the Zurichberg, a wooded hill over-looking the town, or in one of the neighboring villages on the Lake of Zurich. Consequently, Keller had more than one hundred confirmands in his charge. His preaching style was spirited and vivid:

> Faith is first and foremost a matter of trust, and without trust no human relationship and no human venture is possible. You board a train and travel overnight across vertiginous bridges, through thundering tunnels, and past deep abysses. You lie down on your bunk and are perfectly still . . . But do you know whether the engine driver is trustworthy, whether the switch man at his junction will do his duty, whether the stationmaster is at his post, whether the engineer has correctly calculated the tension of the bridge, whether the iron supplier has delivered good material . . .? You do not know this, but you believe it to be true . . . Without such faith, neither education, nor the art of medicine, nor indeed science, which all believe that the human mind can grasp reality, would be conceivable . . . Thus, it is good that we need faith, as an activity of the soul, already on our daily journey through life, and how much more we need it on the journey into a distant, unknown future! Thus, we feel safe in trusting that a higher power will watch over our journey, switch the points, and know the destination.[77]

Keller experienced the traditions of his parish as a brake on progress. Only owing to his sheer persistence did he succeed in introducing various changes. Among other achievements, he prized open the existing "stolid-ity and monotony"[78] of the liturgy, introduced a parish bulletin, initiated discussion evenings on theological issues, founded a parish association as well as two associations for confirmed youths. Yet a further accomplish-ment was the establishment of a Sunday School. Moreover, he submitted a plea for a parish hall for the four old-town parishes, a request that was received with incomprehension by them. However, the council of St Pe-ter's agreed to fund the building of a hall in the rectory to accommodate Keller's wide range of activities.

Keller made no secret of the fact that he socialized with "friends" of the parish, many of whom belonged to the local "high society." For in-stance, Jakob Escher-Bürkli, president of the parish council, was also a member of the town's leading social circles. Other "friends" included Max Huber, a renowned expert on international law, who was later appointed

77. Keller, "Der Glaube des Alltags," 14–17.
78. Keller, "Die heutige äussere und innere Lage des Protestantismus."

judge at the Permanent Court of International Justice at The Hague, and afterwards became president of the International Committee of the Red Cross (ICRC). Many years later, Escher-Bürkli, Huber, and other "friends" provided Keller's ecumencial and humanitarian work with much-needed moral and material support.

Keller, however, remained true to his social impetus. Thus, he reprinted the explicitly progressive "Social Creed" of the Federal Council of the Churches of Christ in America in St Peter's parish bulletin.[79] The document demanded the abolition of child labor, shorter working hours, and an old-age pension scheme for all workers, thus nothing less than the eradication of poverty. For Keller, such an endeavor meant placing the world under the sovereign principles of the Gospel. His duties at St Peter's included the supervision of prison inmates detained in his parish: "In my capacity as parish pastor, I have sat next to many young prisoners in their cells and listened to their predicament."[80] The question foremost on his mind was how and for which reasons a prisoner had blundered into committing an offense.[81] In contemplating these questions, he often cited unfavorable social surroundings and fateful circumstances. To assist those serving prison sentences in gaining a foothold in everyday life upon their release, he demanded that they receive proper supervision. Keller's social awareness also becomes evident in his stance on the national strike that engulfed Switzerland at the end of 1918, as a result of the deprivation suffered during the war years. With dismay, he listened to the shots fired by the military at the demonstrating workers: "Thus, there was bloodshed among brothers."[82]

Keller did not shy away from summoning his partly very affluent congregation to assume responsibility: "The leading and educated classes must realize that their culture, their intellectual property, . . . constitute a boundless obligation."[83]

From Albert Schweitzer, now a "jungle doctor" in Lambarene, Keller received word of the brutal consequences of colonialism. He was deeply shaken by Schweitzer's account and indignant at "how Christian peoples

---

79. *Gemeinde-Blatt* 2, no. 3 (June 7, 1913), 11. The "Social Creed" emerged in 1908 from the Social Gospel movement in the United States.

80. Keller, "Vom religiösen Jugendunterricht," 2.

81. Keller, *Vom Unbekannten Gott*, 49–50.

82. Keller, "Aus meinem Leben," 89.

83. Keller, *Von der inneren Erneuerung unseres Volkes*, 13.

have occupied the heart of Africa among its local peoples."[84] His criticism of social injustices, wherever they existed, concurred with that voiced by Leonhard Ragaz and Hermann Kutter, the two leading figures of the religious social movement in Switzerland. Karl Barth and Emil Brunner were also close to the movement.[85] Opinions, however, were divided on whether Christians could play a part in establishing the Kingdom of God promised by the Bible, that is, a kingdom of peace and justice. According to Keller, Barth was inclined to leave the establishment of the Kingdom of God alone to God, since man was weak; Ragaz, by contrast, placed too much confidence in man and depicted him as God's associate. In 1915, Keller wrote to Barth in this matter.[86] He distanced himself both from Barth's one-sided quietism and also from Ragaz's exaggerated activism. Not untypically, as his later life and career prove, he thus assumed the role of an intermediary. Keller's reflections on this fundamental theological problem were immensely significant for his later involvement in the ecumenical movement under the auspices of Life and Work, where this question played a pivotal role.

LIFE-CONCERN AS LIFE-STANCE: C. G. JUNG AND HENRI BERGSON

Barely after his arrival in Zurich, Keller joined the discussion group at Burghölzli psychiatric clinic that gathered around Eugen Bleuler, its director, and C. G. Jung: he immediately recognized the significance of psychoanalysis for the psychology of religion, pastoral care, and pedagogy.[87] "The question concerning the boundary between psychiatry and the ministry" had preoccupied Keller since his studies in psychology in Geneva.[88] Keller

84. Keller, "Von der Macht des Alkohols."

85. Along with Barth and Ragaz, Brunner was one of the most renowned twentieth-century Swiss theologians; see also Frank Jehle, *Emil Brunner*.

86. Keller to Barth, February 25, 1915, and April 23, 1915, KBA 9315.21 and 9315.47. In both letters, Keller maintains that he could only support the belief in the practicability of the Sermon on the Mount either by shifting its promise into the future or by declaring the tension between the proclamation made there and the real world not as meaningless but as willed by God, and by embracing it so that "he receiveth a perpetual thorn in his side" that would urge him on. In saying this, Keller continued, he did not mean that man could simply bide his time and leave everything to God, as Barth seemed to postulate.

87. Keller, "Aus meinem Leben," 58.

88. Keller, "Aus der Frühzeit der psychoanalytischen Bewegung."

and his fellow student Oskar Pfister were the only two theologians in the Burghölzli circle. Together with Bleuer and Jung, Keller attended the third International Psychoanalytical Congress in Weimar in 1911. There, he met Sigmund Freud, whom he described as a "scientific magician endowed with immense authority."[89] At the fourth psychoanalytical congress in Munich in 1912, Keller witnessed the break between Freud and Jung. He took sides with Jung, since he found Freud's claim that every neurosis stemmed from a sexual trauma too one sided.[90]

In 1913, C. G. Jung and his wife, Emma, founded the *Verein für Analytische Psychologie* (Association for Analytical Psychology), and then in 1916 the *Psychologischer Club* (Psychological Club). Keller often gave talks there, such as on the "Psychology of Great Mass Movements" (1924), a feverishly debated political issue at the time.[91] It perturbed him that for the "actual club members, psychoanalysis became a worldview. For me, however, it remained a method."[92] He sought to convince the "Jungians" of the merits of Christianity, for instance, by delivering an innovative talk on "The Gospel and Christianity,"[93] in which he referred to the Gospel as a life impulse that had broken out of the depths of the soul and the mind: "It is . . . a vital force, an incursion of new life forces, which pointed humanity's thoughts and aspirations in a new direction." The gospel, he argued, was at once both impetus and moral force. In its purest form, it was incarnated in the figure of Jesus Christ, who placed perfect humanity before the eyes of mankind:

> Already the boy was said to evince traces of beginning individu-
> ation. The boy leaves his home and family . . . He retreats into
> solitude, into the desert, and he opposes to collective constraint
> his sovereign "But I say unto you." . . . He died in solitude . . . If
> we [in psychoanalysis] speak of complexes, then we mean the
> same bonds that the Gospel expresses through the rule of the
> flesh, of the law, and of sin.[94]

89. Keller, "Aus den Anfängen der Tiefenpsychologie."

90. Oskar Pfister, pastor at the nearby Predigerkirche in Zurich and a friend of Keller's from their student days, favored Freud.

91. The titles are excerpted from the lecture lists of the Psychological Club (archive of the Psychologischer Club Zurich).

92. Keller, "Aus meinem Leben," 62–63.

93. Keller, "Evangelium und Christentum."

94. Ibid., 4ff. For the KJV, see Matthew 5:22, 28, 32, 34, 39, 44. The "I" of Jesus is stressed.

Keller was one of the first theologians who sought to understand the life and conduct of Jesus in terms of analytical psychology. However, he also pointed to the limits of such a reinterpretation: Jesus, he argued, had accomplished "a real detachment from man's inner bondage."[95]

Keller observed an increase in severe mental health problems, which he attributed to the spiritual upheavals of his time. In various articles on psychoanalysis and psychotherapy, he suggested that neurotic disorders, such as hysteria, compulsive obsessive behavior, anxiety, and inhibitions, were caused by psychic disorders, and therefore required "psychic treatment."[96] He argued that the methods of pastoral care and spiritual welfare employed hitherto had been inadequate to effectively treating these predicaments.[97] As a pastor, however, it was his duty to offer support, healing, and meaning to the suffering. For this reason, he ventured into dream analysis, which he conceived merely as a preliminary to the proclamation of Christ.[98] Many years later, Keller's wife, herself a trained psychiatrist, credited him for being "very successful with psychoanalysis."[99] One case in point was one of Keller's former confirmees, a violin student, who all of a sudden could no longer move her hand. Since the doctors treating the woman had been baffled by her condition, she sought Keller's assistance: "It looked miraculous that through dream-interpretation it was possible that a paralyzed hand could again function."[100]

One particular case of Keller's efficacious pastoral care was Edith Rockefeller McCormick, an American who arrived in Zurich in 1913. She was the daughter of John D. Rockefeller Senior and the wife of Harold McCormick, chairman of the Harvester Company in Chicago. Suffering from a neurosis, she underwent eight years of psychoanalytic treatment with C. G. Jung. Jung sent her to consult Keller: "One day, Rockefeller's daughter stood in the Lavaterstube [Keller's study] and said 'I would like to see human beings.'"[101] "For an entire year, she accompanied me on my visits to the small alleys in the Schipfe (a then-poor quarter in the parish of St Peter's), where I dragged her by the hand up putrid staircases and pas-

95. Ibid., 6ff.

96. Keller contributed the articles on "Psychoanalysis" and "Psychotherapy" to the first edition of the encyclopedia *Religion in Geschichte und Gegenwart* (1913).

97. Keller, *Von Geist und Liebe*, 42–43.

98. Keller to Ragaz, April 7, 1918 (StAZ W I 67 103.2).

99. Tina Keller, "Autobiography," 85.

100. Tina Keller, "In Memoriam."

101. Keller, *Von Geist und Liebe*, 44.

sageways, so that she was forced to take out her smelling salts on reaching the top; thus she became acquainted with the lives of 'other people' and with the phenomenology of poverty."[102] Keller hoped that these forays into low life would make it easier for her to break out of her ivory tower. Later, his acquaintance with Edith Rockefeller McCormick opened many a door for Keller in the United States.

Keller's relationship with Jung became increasingly ambivalent. As he observed in 1935, Jung spoke of God not as a metaphysical reality, but instead meant no more than religious experience. This, he further assert-ed, could not be equated with what Christian theology referred to as the Revelation. Religion, said Keller, was not a creation of the conscious ego.[103]

Every day he would spend one or two hours perusing new publi-cations in literature, theology, and philosophy. He was a member of the philosophical working group around Ernest Bovet, professor of romance studies at the University of Zurich. But he believed that philosophy so far had been overly determined by a fundamental rationalistic attitude. In his eyes, this would not afford a real understanding of life. He was therefore profoundly intrigued by the new approach to philosophy advanced by Henri Bergson, a professor at the Collège de France in Paris. Bergson's thinking struck a powerful chord with Keller. He published several ar-ticles on Bergson's philosophy in *Wissen und Leben* (Knowledge and Life), a journal edited by Ernest Bovet. In 1914, these essays were published in a book-length monograph titled *Eine Philosophie des Lebens* (A Philosophy of Life).[104]

Bergson called for a "return to life." He argued that immediate expe-rience stood at the beginning of knowledge.[105] Using terms and concepts, human reason attempted to classify experience according to certain sche-mata for the purpose of making inroads on cognition. The shortcomings of this attempt became most plainly evident, as Keller observed in *Eine Philosophie des Lebens*, "where reason seeks to grasp psychic life and to express it through its terms and concepts." Further, "these are the limits of the intellect per se, which fails whenever life, movement, and becom-ing are concerned." Bergson, said Keller, placed a "higher, more valuable" form of cognition alongside the rational, "pragmatic" kind. Finally, "it is

102. Keller, "Aus meinem Leben," 60.
103. Keller, "Analytische Psychologie und Religionsforschung."
104. Keller, *Philosophie des Lebens.*
105. Ibid., 7. For the citations appearing in the same paragraph, see 9ff.

not the intellect, but intuition that affords us knowledge." Life, movement, becoming, intuition rank among Bergson's keywords.

Artistic inspiration provided evidence for the existence of human intuition, or as Keller asked: "Do not Johann Sebastian Bach's *St Matthew Passion* or Michelangelo's *Pietà* accomplish a more immediate relationship to religious life than the concepts of dogmatic theology?"[106] The object of intuition is life, that is, organic matter, whereas it was precisely the essence of life that slipped away from reason. Intuition, however, readily grasps this. According to Bergson, the nature of human life was quintessentially spiritual: "Indeed, the soul is the actual 'impulse in life,' which urges forward in all rhythms of becoming . . . Only in free and creative life does life break asunder its chains, come to itself, and realize its essence."[107] Keller associates this "disquiet in life," or what Bergson called the *élan vital*, with Jungian psychology, according to which the "libido" is that living psychic energy that contains all growth and becoming.[108] He noted, furthermore, that until that period Bergson had scarcely commented on religion: "But it is not too difficult to recognize the value of the philosophy of intuition for religious thinking . . . The intellect corrodes religion, and where it alone approaches the religious phenomenon, it must destroy it; for it cannot tolerate the unconditional and absolute; religion, however, is anchored therein."[109] Bergson's philosophy pointed to a new metaphysics, which once again perceived depth, creative force, and new promises in life. Amid a world characterized by a sophisticated material and intellectual culture, Bergson's philosophy represented "a cry for the soul and for inwardness."[110]

Bergson felt understood by Keller: "I have long been meaning to tell you that I have read your penetrating and valiant study of my work in 'Wissen und Leben' with great interest."[111] Following Keller's review of Bergson's latest book, *L' Energie Spirituelle* (Spiritual Energy) in the reputed *Neue Zürcher Zeitung*, Bergson observed in a letter to Keller: "You have analyzed the selected chapters with extreme precision."[112] In January 1918, a year before the end of World War I, Bergson invited Keller

106. Ibid., 16. For the subsequent two citations, see 17 and 19.

107. Ibid., 24.

108. Keller, "Tiefenpsychologie," 54. On the "élan vital," see the same page (27) above.

109. Keller, *Philosophie des Lebens*, 31.

110. Ibid., 46.

111. Bergson to Keller, August 9, 1914 (WS Ms Sch 152/76).

112. Bergson to Keller, October 21, 1919 (ibid.).

to Paris to attend his inauguration ceremony at the Académie Française. Keller described the occasion as "a literary and political event" of the first rank. [113] Bergson, he noted, spoke before the "elite of France."[114] After the ceremony, Bergson invited Keller for supper at his home.

In the curriculum vitae submitted at his final university examinations, Keller had already suggested that religion was carried neither by abstract ideas or teachings nor by dogmas, but instead by individuals and their relations with life.[115] From this early statement, this theme runs through his preoccupation with Théodore Flournoy and C. G. Jung, and his interest in Bergson's philosophy, to his worldwide ecumenical activity.

113. Keller, "Aus meinem Leben," 84.
114. Keller to Bergson, October 23, 1939 (WS Ms Sch 152/3).
115. See above, p. 6.

2

Entering Ecumenism

Peacebuilding and Bridging Europe and America

A JOURNEY TO SCOTLAND (1918)

DURING HIS STAY IN Paris in early 1918, Keller was unexpectedly summoned to the British Embassy, where he was asked to travel to Scotland as a guest of the Foreign Office. Evidently, one of Keller's articles had attracted the interest of the British Embassy in Bern. In this article, he had discussed the role of neutral Switzerland, the spiritual and theological values that transcended national borders in the context of war, and the close affinity between Swiss Protestants and Scottish Presbyterians.[1] Keller was issued with a diplomatic visa and left Paris on the same day.

The English Channel was teeming with submarines, and the crossing was dangerous. But Keller arrived safely in London, where he stayed at the magnificent Savoy Hotel. A Zeppelin attack forced him to spend the night in the hotel cellar. The next morning, he realized that the house opposite had been completely destroyed during the bombing. Without further delay, he presented himself at the Foreign Office, from where he traveled onward to Glasgow, with a stopover in Oxford, to spend a week at the home of James Moffatt, a recognized New Testament scholar. Moffatt had translated the New Testament on the basis of the Greek version established by Hermann von Soden, a New Testament scholar from Berlin

1. Presumably, this article was published in the *Kirchenblatt für die reformierte Schweiz* in the autumn of 1917.

whose work Keller was very familiar with.[2] Moffatt introduced Keller to the leaders of the two Presbyterian churches and the head of the Glasgow Faculty of Theology, before accompanying him to Edinburgh to meet Joseph H. Oldham, a theologian and the later *spiritus rector* of the World Conference of Life and Work, which was held at Oxford in 1937.

Writing on Keller's account of his journey to Scotland, Adolf Deissmann, an internationally acclaimed New Testament scholar, a professor of theology in Berlin, and a professed pacifist, found it "unusually instructive and valuable."[3] Deissmann published several excerpts in his *Evangelischer Wochenbrief*:[4]

> February 2 [1918]. The beautiful and peaceful studies in Oxford, Glasgow, and Edinburgh are, thank God, not clouded by hatred. German books line the shelves. The Protestant sense and spirit, which also seeks to do justice to the enemy, has nevertheless found a home, amidst warfare, in so many studies and in so many hearts. How many people resist betraying the Gospel to the war-making nation, and instead preserve their Protestant faith, which can encompass humanity and thus also the enemy, and is working for a better future already now.—I see trains fully loaded with cannons standing at the station, and the colleges are crowded with the injured. But here I find hearts who endure their Gethsemane for this reason; people who are capable of believing in the future of the mind and of love notwithstanding all these horrors; men who continue to work on the great peace project that is the Gospel and who wrest from their hearts time and again faith in a future Christian family of peoples. Without penance and a change of mind, however, this will not happen.— Can peoples do penance? . . .
>
> February 9. The theological faculties in Edinburgh[5] have invited me to a reception, during which their wish for a stronger affinity

2. On von Soden, see chapter 1, p. 4 and 9–10.

3. Deissmann contributed a critical report to the *Evangelischer Wochenbrief* on the role played by Germany in the war. On New Year's Eve of 1915, before the entry into the war of the United States, he held a secret meeting with Charles Macfarland, the general secretary of the Federal Council of Churches of Christ in America, at Unter den Linden in Berlin. "Our personal talk, . . . here in Berlin," Deissmann observed, was pervaded "by a spirit of mutual and fraternal understanding" (Protestant Weekly Letter = English edition of the *Evangelischer Wochenbrief*, Berlin, October 1916, in PHS NCC RG 18 7/6).

4. Keller, "An der Schwelle des fünften Jahres," 3–4.

5. There were two Presbyterian churches at the time in Scotland (the state church and the free church), and hence two faculties of theology.

> with Swiss Protestants is pleasantly given expression. Most of
> these seriously minded scholars have studied in Germany, and
> are now speaking about individual [German] scholars and their
> academic accomplishments with love and appreciation. Both in
> scholarship and among Christians, there remains a feeling of
> community here that the war has not managed to suppress!—
> Thank God, invisible threads nevertheless continue to exist
> between the peoples of the Earth . . . The dean mentions that
> after the war, spiritual feeling will have to be re-established once
> again. Visiting enemy countries, however, will remain an impos-
> sibility for a long time. But Switzerland . . . is a country where
> this feeling could be regained.

Thus, the hope that the Protestant churches of neutral Switzerland could
serve as intermediaries after the war was the rationale underlying the invitation extended to Keller to travel to Scotland. Under the impression
of his journey, Keller identified three truly international spiritual forces:
scholarship, socialism, and Christianity. Scholarship sought the truth. His
journey to England and Scotland had convinced him that academics, or
at least theologians, continued to cooperate during wartime. Even though
the socialists had done little to prevent the war, at heart the socialist idea
remained international. But bolshevism had marked the fall from grace of
socialism. The nature of Christianity, finally, pointed toward an encom-
passing human community. The theology of war had betrayed the Gospel.
In its ideal conception, the Kingdom of God also expressed the sociopo-
litical objective of a community of nations: "The principal Christian commandment of love established principles that know no boundaries."[6]

Keller's discussions in Scotland affirmed his conviction—which he
had already expressed at the beginning of the war—that Switzerland was
destined in a particular way to contribute to international reconciliation.
The Swiss churches, he continued, could also "be considered the mother
churches of the whole of Reformed Protestanism."[7] Thus, we can now turn
to Keller's peacebuilding efforts during and after World War I.

6. Keller, "Der internationale Kitt," 209–10.

7. Ibid., 214ff. The founders of the "mother churches" of Reformed Protestanism
were Huldrych Zwingli in Zürich and John Calvin in Geneva.

Adolf Keller

WORLD WAR I AND THE LEAGUE OF NATIONS

Though Switzerland as a neutral country was not directly involved in Word War I, Keller was deeply shaken. Immediately after the outbreak of warfare, he contacted the French writer and peace activist Romain Rolland.[8] Keller observed widespread confusion, emptiness, fear, dismay, and a paralyzing sense of powerlessness.[9] Had God sent down to earth such horror and dread? Did he in effect bear the world in his arms or eventually leave it to its own devices, many people asked.[10] In his sermons, Keller told his congregation that God could be trusted, even if one failed to understand him: "But what we have understood about it, in the life of Jesus Christ . . . , was love, justice, benevolence, mercy, peace. What remains of this unfathomable will of God . . . we can safely leave to eternity and its secrets. Whenever we have felt close to God, then we have perceived His will as an overwhelming, benevolent power, as a giving love. The power of his benevolence and love will prevail, notwithstanding all evil and all misery."

Keller categorically rejected the initial euphoria that had gripped the warring nations: "The talk of fresh, cheerful warfare strikes me as outrageous."[11] He decidedly condemned the widespread appropriation of God by the warring parties; rather, he asserted, it was the will of mankind and of the nations that compelled the earth to "gulp down the blood of thousands and tens of thousands . . . Hell has broken loose, that hell that lies dormant in the depths of a wild, unbroken instinctual life. It has ascended with its hatred, with its cruelty, with all the demons of confusion. They blur the boundaries between good and evil, justice and injustice, culture and barbarism. They blind the nations, so that none sees the good in the other, but instead only the evil. They sneak into the hearts and confuse the piety that . . . seeks to entice God to take sides, to nationalize him, whereas in fact he is the Lord and Father of all mankind and of all nations."[12]

At the time, many French-speaking Swiss took sides with France, while many German-speaking Swiss pledged allegiance to Germany. Thus, a rift opened up between the two parts of the country. This troubled Keller profoundly, and he felt called upon to appeal for prudence and calm. On September 9, 1914, only a few weeks after the outbreak of the war, Keller

8. On Rolland, see Mattmüller, *Leonhard Ragaz*, 261.

9. Keller, "Die Rüstung des Herzens," 6.

10. Keller, "Einer trage des andern Last," 50.

11. Keller, "Die Rüstung des Herzens," 21.

12. Keller, "Dein Wille geschehe," 23–24.

conducted the first divine service ever conducted in both German and French in Zurich, together with William Eugène Cuendet, his young fellow minister from the French-speaking parish. The service was held at St Peter's to give ecclesiastical expression to national unity.[13] In his sermon, Keller made the following emphatic statement:

> God has placed our country amidst the world powers ... We are surrounded on all sides by highly ambitious nations, with which we have very close relations ... Our hearts are involved ... —But let us exercise caution! ... There is no Swiss race, and we do not want to enter into the squabbling over races. Instead, a common, strong will has brought us together, and it has shaped our history ... Through a rarely seen self-restraint, our country has summoned a spiritual force that is unique in Europe, to wrest itself from the grasp of the dull powers of blood and race, and also to bind together opposing forces into a higher unity.[14]

Already at that time, Keller opposed the invocation of "blood and race." On October 18, 1914, he also held a "Patriotic Address" in St Pierre Cathedral in Geneva, in which he invoked the common will of German- and French-speaking Swiss to coexist. Immediately after the outbreak of the war, only very few Swiss stood up for national cohesion and solidarity: "[Ernest] Bovet, [Paul] Seippel, Adolf Keller, [William Eugène] Cuendet, and [Leonhard] Ragaz established a climate in which Spitteler's famous reconciliation speech became at all possible."[15]

Although Keller reproached a part of the population for betraying the ideals of unity and neutrality, he nevertheless believed that Switzerland had a mission in Europe:

> Alas, if precisely this difference within our unity would mean that one country and its people among the warring parties could feel more profoundly and more justly with its neighbors and friends, so that it became Europe's conscience, the merciful Samaritan of a wounded world, the faithful friend who understands and helps bear not only the suffering but also the guilt of the nations ... Europe cries on our shoulder ... In the final instance, from Jesus Christ comes the wonderful capacity to unite

13. Keller and Cuendet, *Wir wollen sein ein einzig Volk von Brüdern*, Preface.

14. Ibid., 6ff. Nationalism, racism, and anti-Semitism were widespread at the time.

15. Mattmüller, *Leonhard Ragaz*, 70. On December 14, 1914, the Swiss writer Carl Spitteler delivered a rousing speech, "Unser Schweizer Standpunkt," which dealt with Switzerland's views on the war.

what is different and alien . . . We are allowed to love, that is our task, our prerogative.[16]

Toward the end of the war, trains carrying the wounded and evacuated passed through Zurich central station: "What a terrible loss these two nations [Germany and France], which could have been good neighbours, have suffered! We sensed a profound compassion for those who inflicted such savagery upon their fellows, and we realized how blessed we were as a people that we could be an island of peace and the work of love."[17] Keller served as president of the "Zurich Bureau for the Location of Missing Persons," which liaised with the International Red Cross in Geneva and assisted "many a missing person in finding their family."[18]

The logical consequence of Keller's commitment to peace and reconciliation during World War I was that he propagated the League of Nations, whose founding President Woodrow Wilson proposed in early 1918. Shortly after the outbreak of warfare, Keller had also envisaged such a community of nations: "Precisely the current battle of nations . . . places before our eyes, with clarity and pressing urgency, the need for a great human community . . . It becomes ever more apparent to all those with human feeling that war must be a matter of the past in a world that hears and wants to accept the message of Jesus Christ . . . As the great empires prepare to conquer the world, this makes us pray even more deeply: 'Thy Kingdom Come!'"[19]

A year later, Keller wrote: "We are standing at a turning point in world history. We must rebuild the world."[20] When the League of Nations was established after the war, he regarded it as "the greatest political project in world history."[21] "The weapons have spoken. Now it is time for the spirit to speak."[22] Keller was elected vice-president of the Swiss branch of the international League for the Protection of the Natives.[23] He also became a member of the League of Nations Society, a private Christian organization dedicated to lending "critical and helpful" support to the activi-

16. Keller, *Wir wollen sein ein einzig Volk von Brüdern*, 9–10.

17. Keller, "Aus meinem Leben," 88.

18. Ibid., 89 and personal communication to the author from the International Committee of the Red Cross, Geneva, January 7, 2008.

19. Keller, "Die Rüstung des Herzens," 21.

20. Keller, *Von der inneren Erneuerung unseres Volkes*, 7.

21. Keller, *Der Völkerbund und die Kirchen*, 3.

22. Ibid., 11.

23. Keller to Macfarland, December 5, 1919 (PHS NCC RG 18 12/8).

ties of the League of Nations, and to addressing the needs of minorities.[24] The Society totaled 500,000 members, with the majority living in Great Britain. At the beginning of each session of the League, the Society would convene a church service in St Pierre Cathedral of Geneva. In 1919, Keller was elected honorary member of the League of Nations Society.[25] He attended its conferences in Brussels and Munich, where the fate of religious minorities was debated. One minority affected by the war were Protestant Christians living in territories that, under the Treaty of Trianon, Hungary would be obliged to cede to its neighboring states.[26]

Like the Society, Keller also demanded that under no circumstances should diplomats and statesmen alone be allowed to determine the shape of the League of Nations. The aim of Christians should be to attain a human community of love: "The proclamation of the Kingdom of God set us this ultimate objective."[27] A few years later, Keller wrote: "The churches know . . . that the will of God is the will to peace." But since "opposing powers" existed, the Protestant and Catholic churches had to stand united as one "against the flush of victory that seeks to base the League of Nations once more upon the principle of power, against a narrow-minded nationalism that would prefer not to open the door to the League of Nations equally wide for all." Keller opposed the exclusion from the Council of Germany and of the young Soviet Union. The churches had to issue a "warning call" against violence, self-interest, and materialism in the relations between the nations. In short, "it is the task of the churches to give the League of Nations a soul."[28]

In 1920, the Swiss electorate was called upon to vote on the country's accession to the League of Nations. Keller appealed passionately to those Protestants who continued to waver: "Why should it be inopportune and premature to summon the spiritual forces of the Church without delay and no less imposingly, and to bring its influence to bear upon history?"[29] He argued further that the League of Nations concerned political idealism, which stood opposed to the "sacro egoismo," that is, the egocentric

24. Occasionally, the League of Nations Society was also referred to as the League of Nations Union.

25. The League of Nations Society to Keller, April 9, 1919 (NLAK C 23).

26. Annual Report of the Federation of Swiss Protestant Churches for 1921/1922, 19. See also Keller to Macfarland, February 23, 1922 (BAR J.2.257 1462/160).

27. Keller, *Der Völkerbund und die Kirchen*, 8ff.

28. Keller, *Die Kirchen und der Friede,* 77.

29. Keller, *Der Völkerbund und die Kirchen,* 9.

nationalism of nations.[30] Two of Keller's friends—Max Huber, the international law expert, and Leonhard Ragaz, a professor of theology—also
came out strongly in support of accession.[31] "I am pleased to concur with
your assessment on the League of Nations," Keller wrote to Ragaz.[32] "You
are indeed correct in stating that pastors are in effect a hive of resistance."[33]
Among the dissenting clergymen were the theologians Emil Brunner[34]
and Karl Barth. To the latter, Keller wrote as follows: " I realize how Ragaz
and you [the dialectitians]—of a similar provenance and pursuing similar
objectives—are so very far apart with regard to fundamental issues such as
the League of Nations."[35] Barth shared the anti-American stance common
among parts of the Social Democratic Party, of which he was a member.
At the time, it seemed as if the United States still wanted to join the League
of Nations. On May 16, 1920, the Swiss electorate narrowly voted in favor
of accession, following assurances that the country would "differentially"
preserve its neutrality, that is to say, with certain restrictions.

Keller believed that the United States were seriously mistaken not to
join the League of Nations. Writing to the Federal Council of the Churches
of Christ in America, he remarked: "It is with serious concern that we [the
Federation of Swiss Protestant Churches] take note of the announcement
of the United States to withdraw from European affairs, under the aegis
of its new policy, and thus also from the duties and tasks of the League of
Nations. We are grateful that the American churches united in the Federal
Council do not intend to participate in this withdrawal."[36] Charles Macfarland, general secretary of the Federal Council, praised the Swiss for set-
ting an example to Americans, since the following message to Woodrow
Wilson had been posted in many churches in Switzerland: "The citizens of
the oldest Democracy in Europe have been profoundly impressed by the
immortal words in which you have set forth the duties of a new humanity
and laid down the principles of a Society of Nations, based not on force,
but on Justice, Liberty and Right."[37]

30. Keller, "Der Idealismus als praktisches Problem," 256.

31. Mattmüller, *Leonhard Ragaz*, 545; Semmler, *Kirche und Völkerbund*, 55–56.

32. Keller to Ragaz, December 24, 1920 (StAZ W I 67 103.2).

33. Keller to Ragaz, undated, written in advance of the popular vote on Switzerland's accession to the League of Nations (ibid.).

34. Jehle, *Emil Brunner*, 154–55.

35. Keller to Barth, February 6, 1920 (KBA 9320.40).

36. Keller (on behalf of the Federation of Swiss Protestant Churches) to the Federal
Council of the Churches of Christ in America, November 10, 1920 (NLAK C 23).

37. Charles Macfarland, "Woodrow Wilson: Prophet of a new Era of Humanity,"

Keller fiercely criticized the Treaty of Versailles: "Those responsible for establishing order through the peace treaty have been unable to restrain the chaotic forces . . . , which not only the war but now also peace has unleashed more than ever."[38] Moreover, Keller grew increasingly disillusioned, not so much with the idea of the League of Nations itself, but with its practical work. The vision of a community of nations springing from religious roots had evaporated.[39] On behalf of the Federation of Swiss Protestant Churches, he served as an observer at the Disarmament Conference of 1932. What he witnessed and heard there troubled him profoundly:

> Gathered here are the philosophers of the League of Nations, who construe world peace in the abstract out in the blue sky. Gathered here are the conference's mongers, who regard disarmament as a market and as an opportunity for barter. Gathered here are the diplomats and strategists, who do not reckon with the possibility of what should be, but instead dabble in all the frivolous arts of what might be possible, particularly new wars. Gathered here are the advocates and jurists, who have turned the law increasingly into nonsense and reason into a plague, and who confuse law with justice in particular. Nor is the *advocatus diaboli* absent. Gathered here are also the clowns of history, and even the ghosts, who forever negate. To these men the fate of the world is entrusted, the bread of nations, the sleep of women and children . . . Sitting in the gallery is the press, the eye of the world, the megaphone of public opinion. Here such opinion is made. But here poison gas is manufactured, as well as the bombs that threaten the world.[40]

PIVOTAL EXPERIENCES (1919):
THE UNITED STATES AND CHARLES MACFARLAND

In 1916, at the height of the war, the idea of establishing an English-speaking library in Switzerland arose from within the circle around Ernest Bovet, professor of Romance studies in Zurich. Keller approached the Swiss Federal Council, which welcomed the idea, as did the United

June 3, 1924, 7 (PHS NCC RG 18 13/27, Macfarland correspondence).

38. Keller, "Ist Gott für uns, wer mag wider uns sein. Röm. 8,31," 8.
39. Keller, *Die Kirchen und der Friede*, 90.
40. Keller, "Abrüstung," 69–70.

States Embassy. In late 1919, the first consignment of books was shipped to Europe.[41] A few years later, Keller requested the Federal Council of the Churches of Christ in America to send specialist publications in the field of theology and religion: "It is . . . proposed to create in the interest of international relationship a religious Central Library which should include the most prominent American publications in the field of biography, historical and systematic theology, religious psychology, religious education, and social problems."[42] Keller's request was accepted. Albeit small and consisting entirely of American publications, the library was established and housed at the Central Library in Zurich.[43]

Shortly after the end of the war, Keller traveled to the United States upon the initiative of the Federal Council of the Churches of Christ in America. Established in 1908, the Federal Council united a large part of the Protestant churches of America. In March 1919, Charles Macfarland, its general secretary, requested the Swiss churches to dispatch a representative to the United States.[44] Macfarland wished to reestablish contacts with churches in Europe, which had broken off during the war. The churches of neutral Switzerland were to serve as intermediaries. Since Keller spoke several languages and was well-versed in the ways of the world, as well as one of the most distinguished Swiss clergymen, he was appointed delegate. Both Otto Herold, president of the Church Council of Zurich, and the American John L. Nuelsen, the Zurich-based resident bishop of the Methodist Church in Europe, were instrumental to Keller's appointment. Keller received a warm welcome at the seat of the Federal Council in New York. He experienced his acquaintance with Macfarland, the "mighty secretary of the Federal Council," as "almost fate-determining." He characterized Macfarland as a "dynamo machine," a man brimming with ideas who had turned the Federal Council into what it was. Already on his first visit, he became "a genuine friend."[45]

41. Keller to Macfarland, December 5, 1919 (PHS NCC RG 18 12/8, General Secretary 1919–1948).

42. Keller, "Theses about the creation of a Library of American books in Central Europe," presumably written in July 1924, 1 (PHS NCC RG 18 73/9).

43. Macfarland to Keller, December 26, 1919 (PHS NCC RG 18 12/8). Today the American Library forms an integral part of the Zentralbibliothek Zürich. Following Keller's initiative, the Library was expanded after World War II.

44. On Charles Macfarland, see "Personal and Confidential" (PHS NCC Rg 18 13/27).

45. Keller, "Aus meinem Leben," 93ff.; see also Keller, "Die Schweizerische Delegation an das Federal Council."

Charles Macfarland (archive Marianne Jehle-Wildberger)

On behalf of the Swiss churches, Keller's address to the administrative committee of the Federal Council of the Churches of Christ in America referred to the longstanding ties between Swiss Protestantism and various American churches, and also to the particular situation of Switzerland during the war, which had allowed the country to engage in broad-based charity. Switzerland was prepared to actively contribute to rebuilding the Christian community. Owing to its linguistic, geographical, and cultural diversity, it was particularly well-suited to this task. Conversely, Keller was informed about the Council and its activities: "The Federal Council gave me a clear insight into its various branches of activity." The Council, moreover, was committed to "fellowship" and "cooperation." Therefore, Keller concluded, "Upon this America—there is another—we set our hope. In this America a world embracing spirit of union is developing, which is attempting to bring harmony and fellowship through service—a kind of Protestant catholicism which we can visualize and which is trying to solve the greatest problem of the present time—the union of individual freedom with the strength of cooperation."[46] Presumably, he was one of the first Protestants ever to speak of a "Protestant catholicism," that is, a Christianity that while Protestant nevertheless takes seriously a Christian faith that encompasses all ages and nations.

Keller embarked on a lecture tour to Philadelphia, Washington, St. Louis, Chicago, Harvard, and various other places.[47] He also visited Union Theological Seminary (UTS) in New York. At UTS, he met "that man, who was doing more than any other American theologian in the academic field to establish a closer relationship between American and European Protestantism, namely, Professor William Adams Brown," a specialist in systematic theology.[48] This "scholar of the first rank" was not content "with an academic role detached from the pulsing life of the world." Specifically, "Dr. Brown's clear insight into the necessity for a greater Protestant unity soon led him to a concern for interdenominational cooperation that became a master passion of his life."[49] A few years later, Keller also entered into close contact with Henry Sloane Coffin, who taught "classical theology" at UTS, Princeton, and Yale.[50]

Keller's friendship with Arthur C. McGiffert, the then-president of UTS, also proved valuable. They negotiated an annual scholarship to be awarded to a gifted young Swiss theologian. This arrangement was highly significant, because while many highly motivated young American theologians had studied in Europe before the war, including William Adams Brown, barely any Europeans, let alone Swiss, had done so in the United States. In consultation with Leonhard Ragaz, Keller awarded the first UTS scholarship to Emil Brunner, who was serving as a minister in a small rural community at the time.[51]

46. Keller, "American Churches as Seen by an European," 4ff.

47. Keller, "Die Schweizerische Delegation an das Federal Council," 3.

48. Keller, "Aus meinem Leben," 94; Brown, "General War-Time Commission of the Churches. Its Organization and its Purpose."

49. "William Adams Brown, Servant of the Ecumenical Church," *Federal Council Bulletin* (January 1944), 4–5 (UTS Presidential Papers 47/36, 1914–1956); see also Keller to Ragaz, January 26, 1923 (StAZ W I 67 103.2).

50. Henry Sloane Coffin served as president of UTS from 1926 to 1946.

51. On Emil Brunner at UTS, see Jehle, *Emil Brunner*, 123ff.

In Washington, Keller visited his brother-in-law Conrad Jenny, who had since been appointed secretary to the Swiss Delegation.[52] In Chicago, he met Harold McCormick, the husband of Edith Rockefeller McCormick,[53] and in New York he met her brother, John D. Rockefeller Jr. The latter had been overseeing the affairs of the Rockefeller Foundation since 1917. Presumably, Keller told Rockefeller Jr. about his vision of an interdenominational relief organization to assist destroyed churches in Europe, as discussed in greater detail below.[54]

Upon his return to Switzerland, Keller found a letter from Rockefeller awaiting him: "It was a great pleasure to have the opportunity of meeting you at luncheon, and I thoroughly enjoyed our talk together, only regretting that it could not have been longer. Please give my affectionate greetings to my sister, whom I have to thank for the privilege of having come to know you. Hoping to see you at some future time, either in Switzerland or in America, I am, very sincerely, John D. Rockefeller Jr."[55] Some smaller publications were enclosed with the letter, including a brochure entitled "The Christian Church—What of Its Future?," written by Rockefeller Jr., as well as reports on the Rockefeller Foundation for the years 1917 and 1918.

Keller made a most favorable impression on the Federal Council. Upon his return to Switzerland, he wrote to Macfarland: "Hoping that the coming days may deepen the personal relationship formed with you so delightfully."[56] In reply, Macfarland wrote that "Your visit here received a very wide publicity after you left in both the religious and secular press which is really the more important."[57] Reflecting on Keller's visit, the annual report of the Federal Council for the year 1919 remarked:

> The Rev. Adolf Keller . . . remained with us several weeks and rendered a most significant service to our churches . . . Pastor Keller made a sympathetic study of our religious institutions, especially of our cooperative and federative work, and the report has been translated . . . and distributed to the members of the Council because of its national value to us, coming from one, who, in a sense, views us objectively. Pastor Keller has made recommendations to his own churches and also to our

52. Keller, "Aus meinem Leben," 94–95; see further Keller, "Die Schweizerische Delegation an das Federal Council," 2.

53. See above, pp. 25–26.

54. See below, pp. 87–88.

55. Rockefeller to Keller, June 5, 1919 (NLAK C 23).

56. Macfarland to Keller, August 15, 1919 (PHS NCC RG 18 12/8).

57. Macfarland to Keller, September 8, 1919 (Ibid.).

> Administrative committee which are of the highest importance,
> not only in our particular relations with Switzerland, but also in
> connection with the religious bodies of other nations.[58]

Keller's first encounter with the United States completely changed his life, as he later recalled: "On this journey, I became one of the pioneers of the later ecumenical movement."[59] From then onward, he would spend two to three months in the United States almost every year, mostly at the request of his American acquaintances. It is no exaggeration to state that Keller became one of the most important bridge builders between churches in the United States and in Europe. Among other things, two of his most important books, *Dynamis* and *Protestant Europe*, bear witness to his steadfast commitment in this respect. Since their writing and publication took time, the next section considers the immediate upshot of Keller's first stay in the United States, namely, the founding of the Federation of Swiss Protestant Churches.

THE DRIVING FORCE BEHIND THE FEDERATION OF SWISS PROTESTANT CHURCHES

The idea was in the air. Already during World War I, many Swiss churchmen had realized that a body cultivating relationships with churches abroad was missing. Further, they were perturbed by the lack of cohesion among the Swiss Protestant churches. In earlier times, particularly during the Reformation, a different situation had held: at the time, Switzerland had been a confederation of states. Each canton (that is, state) decided whether it would remain Catholic or instead join the Reformation, which several cantons chose to do (Zurich, Bern, Basel, and Geneva). In the latter cantons and also in some others, Protestant state churches were founded. In 1559, the Consensus Tigurinus led to the establishment of a common Evangelical-Protestant denomination within Switzerland. Moreover, loose institutional relations between the cantonal churches emerged. While manifold contacts were established with Reformed churches abroad, over time these lapsed somewhat. The French conquest of Switzerland in 1798 put an end to the confederation. A period of political vicissitude ensued, during which the Swiss cantonal churches were severely isolated both within the country and beyond. In 1848, Switzerland became a federal

58. "Annual Report of the Federal Council of Christ in America for the year 1919," 14 (PHS NCC RG 18 79/10).

59. Keller, "Aus meinem Leben," 98.

state. In its wake followed the Conference of Swiss Churches in 1858, which had no office and resulted in no more than weak relations between the Swiss churches. The situation was unsatisfactory. Meanwhile, the blending of denominations within the cantons began.

The establishment of the Federation of Swiss Protestant Churches originated in Adolf Keller's decisive impulse. While visiting the United States, he had observed the broad impact of the Federal Council of the Churches of Christ in America. He realized, moreover, that after the end of the war churches all over the world, including the Protestant churches in Switzerland, faced enormous challenges. While some cantonal churches insisted on their independence, Keller's fiery speeches managed to sway opinion in favor of alliance and cooperation. Thus, the Federation of Swiss Protestant Churches was founded on September 7, 1920. "After four hundred years, organic unity among Swiss Protestantism has been achieved, and now rests upon a democratic and confederate basis," Keller wrote not without satisfaction a few years later.[60] With immediate effect, all cantonal churches became members of the Federation as well as two diaspora associations, the five French-speaking free churches, the Swiss Methodist Church,[61] and the Swiss overseas parishes.

On paper, the Federation of Swiss Protestant Churches was not granted much power. According to its founding statutes of September 7, 1920, "the independence and specific character of the individual members should not be impaired." Nevertheless, the Federation was assigned four important tasks: "besides the cultivation of community among the Swiss churches, representation in common affairs . . . as well as dealing with state authorities and [fostering] relations with our brethren abroad." Particular weight was soon attached to the latter task.[62] The constitution ratified at the 1924 Assembly of Delegates did not alter the limited jurisdiction of the Federation over its member churches.[63]

Its most important bodies were the assembly of delegates and an executive board comprising seven members. Friedrich Wilhelm Hadorn, a church historian from Bern, was elected first president of the board. After a term of office of one year, Hadorn was replaced by Otto Herold, president of the Church Council of Zurich; Herold was appointed at the age of

60. Keller, *Der Schweizerische Evangelische Kirchenbund*, 6.

61. Bishop Nuelsen was elected member of the board of the Federation of Swiss Protestant Churches; see above, p. 38.

62. Keller, *Der Schweizerische Evangelische Kirchenbund*, 6.

63. French version of the Constitution of the Federation of Swiss Protestant Churches, dated June 17, 1924 (BAR J.2.257 1185/126).

seventy-three. Keller became secretary for German-speaking Switzerland (or general secretary in modern parlance). While he was not a member of the board, he was nevertheless granted a say.[64] In effect, however, it was mostly Keller who not only dictated the—rapid— pace at which the Federation of Swiss Protestant Churches conducted its affairs, but also set its agenda. In doing so, he exhausted the limits of its constitution to the full. Within a brief period, the Federation became an important institution within Swiss society, as well as one of the focal points of international Christianity.

The Federation of Swiss Protestant Churches was committed to strengthening solidarity among Swiss Protestants. Care was taken to convene the regular, two-day assembly of delegates in a different place every year. Permanent committees were established, including a Theological Committee, whose members included Keller. The Federation also submitted petitions to the federal government of Switzerland. In 1932, it demanded a total ban on weapons exports—in accordance with Keller's negative assessment of the disarmament conference convened that year by the League of Nations.[65] The Federation also sought to give fresh impetus to church life.

As early as 1925, Keller encouraged the establishment of a national Protestant women's organization (which was not founded until 1947). Most importantly, moreover, he promoted closer cooperation between the various welfare organizations within the *Innere Mission* (Home Mission). Thus far, its numerous charitable and diaconal associations and institutions had been largely independent.[66] Consequently, on February 14, 1927, approximately one hundred representatives of these diaconal organizations gathered under the auspices of the Federation. Together, they formed the *Schweizerischer Verband für Innere Mission und evangelisches Liebeswerk* (Swiss Assocation for the Home Mission and Protestant Welfare). At Keller's request, Alphons Koechlin, a pastor from Basel, was appointed president of the new organization. While independent, it nevertheless maintained contact with the Federation.[67]

64. Ibid., Article 8.

65. Minutes of the Assembly of Delegates of the Federation of Swiss Protestant Churches, dated June 6 and 7, 1932 (BAR J.2.257 285, 2 vols.). See above, p. 37.

66. Minutes of the Assembly of Delegates of the Federation of Swiss Protestant Churches of 1926, 30, and Minutes of the Assembly of Delegates of 1927, 32 (Ibid., vol 1.).

67. Koechlin later followed in Keller's footsteps in both the Federation of Swiss Protestant Churches and in the ecumenical movement.

Following Keller's suggestion, furthermore, the *Schweizerische Missionsausschuss* (Swiss Mission Committee) was established in 1926, and the inaugural *Konferenz Schweizerischer Hilfsvereine* (Conference of Swiss Aid Associations) convened in 1934.[68] The purpose of both organizations was to provide aid overseas. Meanwhile, Keller had been appointed director of the Central Bureau, an international and interdenominational relief organization. From personal experience, he therefore knew about the detrimental effects of a lack of coordination and cooperation among relief organizations. Invitations to the inaugural Conference of Swiss Aid Associations were sent out by the Central Bureau, which in turn stood under the supervision of the Federation.[69] The invitation was accepted by nearly all of the relief organizations contacted. Fortunately, the Conference became an established institution.

Social issues carried particular weight within the Federation. Only the rudiments of a welfare state existed in Switzerland at the time, notwithstanding the precarious economic situation prevailing during the postwar years. In 1925, Keller issued his first call for the establishment of a *Soziale Kommission* (Social Affairs Committee). After years of prodding, the board and the assembly of delegates of the Federation of Swiss Protestant Churches finally carried Keller's motion, two years after the onset of the Great Depression and subsequent mass unemployment. Keller and his old friend Eugène Choisy, who became president of the Federation in 1930, became brothers in arms and championed this important cause. Keller was elected president of the Social Affairs Committee.

Written in 1931, Keller's brochure "Das Christentum und der heutige Wirtschaftsmensch" (Christianity and the Modern Homo Oeconomicus) offers an insight into his economics ethics:[70] while two areas of life were concerned, their link should not be severed. The human being is a single, unified entity, he argued.[71] At the heart of the problem lay the autonomy of economic activity, in the guise of business and industry; such activity, he observed, was governed by the machine, by profit-mindedness, and by international economic interdependence, that is, by inexorable objectivity.

68. Minutes of the Conference of Swiss Aid Associations of May 3, 1934 (BAR J.2.257 1245/133).

69. The Central Bureau (1922–1945) was at the same time an international relief agency and the aid organization of Protestant Switzerland, and as such the precursor of the Swiss Interchurch Aid HEKS (founded in 1946).

70. Keller, *Das Christentum und der heutige Wirtschaftsmensch*.

71. Ibid., 3ff.

Where did this leave both humanity and the individual, Keller asked. In reply, he asserted that Christianity had a say in the matter:

> Christianity places the *human subject*, not the material object or cause, at the center of the economic process. It opposes the autonomy of the economy to the autonomy of the *soul* and its eternal needs, which can be satisfied neither by the mechanization of life, nor by the machine, nor indeed by capital . . . Today's homo oeconomicus *suffers damage* to his soul. [Christianity raises] the question about the meaning of the economic process, and demands *social justice*. Already the prophets demanded this. From this vantage point, Christianity criticizes the injustice prevailing in the distribution of industrial goods in our times . . . For the right to life is the least justice that the human being can demand . . . If business and industry today cannot ensure that human beings will not starve to death, then it has not understood its task . . . Today's economic system has created classes, but not community. Business and industry form . . . an ever greater proletariat and ever smaller "profitariat" . . . Today's society cannot be nothing but cruel toward its members. The idea of the Christian community is necessarily associated with that of *service*. Business and industry should assume the function of a service within the community . . . Intimately intertwined with the notion of service is the notion of *solidarity*.[72]

The message of Christianity thus concerns both capitalism and socialism. While it must be critical—in cultural, social, and economic terms—of both economic and social systems, Christianity must also awaken the readiness to make sacrifices, as well as arouse faith and hope, by virtue of its creative forces, spirituality, and disposition toward love.[73] In short, Keller was among the first to postulate a "social market economy" on a Christian basis.

He succeeded in recruiting competent members for his Social Affairs Committee: besides theologians, these included employers and gainfully employed persons, economists (such as Walther Hug, a lecturer at Harvard, who from 1931 also taught in St Gallen), farmers, politicians, and two university-educated women. The Committee became one of the key pieces of the puzzle of Keller's life and work.

One of the first outcomes of its work was the publication of a leaflet on unemployment in late 1931. It was addressed to all Protestants and

72. Ibid., 10ff.
73. Ibid., 16ff.

appealed to them for help.[74] Following several meetings, a brochure entitled "Die Kirche und die Arbeitslosigkeit" (The Church and Unemployment) was published at the end of 1931;[75] it was hailed as the "first declaration of Swiss Protestantism on the social question."[76] Within a few weeks, the first edition of two thousand copies was out of print, and a reedited version was subsequently prepared for publication. The second edition was broader and more popular in scope, to ensure that society became "more strongly aware of its greater responsibility."[77] Ten thousand copies of the reedited brochure were published, in German and in French. Like the first, the second edition also sold like hotcakes. "If we do not attend to the thousands of unemployed and simply leave them to their own fates," the brochure remarks, "then this is equal to running over someone in the street, and driving on without stopping to attend to them." Furthermore:

> It is the duty of the Christian community to realize what unemployment means today, not only for countless individuals, but also for thousands of families, for our entire economy . . . Not only does redundancy spell dire need, hunger, and worry, but it also means loneliness. Many will withdraw from society, like a wounded deer . . . Life loses its meaning, and existence its value . . . The message of the Gospel about the love of God begins to become meaningless . . . We must not allow God's message to us . . . to become a quiet and hidden property of our soul . . . In teaching us the Lord's prayer, our Lord Jesus Christ has taught us, emphatically, not to pray for "myself" but for "us" . . . *Church is community* . . . Jesus has . . . imprinted the meaning of Christian life on us. *It is to serve* . . . The Gospel does not contain an economic program . . . But it affords us this powerful and truly enlightening indication that all life comes from God.[78]

Along with providing spiritual guidance, the booklet also proposed practical measures. According to the research undertaken by the Social Affairs

74. "An die Glaubensgenossen," *Flugblatt*, November 11, 1931 (BAR J.2.257 1441/156).

75. Schweizerischer Evangelischer Kirchenbund, *Die Kirche und die Arbeitslosigkeit* (text written by Adolf Keller).

76. Board of the Federation of Swiss Protestant Churches to its members, November 11, 1931 (BAR J.1.157 1735/189).

77. Schweizerischer Evangelischer Kirchenbund (ed.), *Kirche und Arbeitslosigkeit*; see also Choisy, Keller, and Lequin to the members of the Federation of Swiss Protestant Churches, October 11, 1932 (BAR J.2.257 1441/156).

78. Schweizerischer Evangelischer Kirchenbund ed., *Kirche und Arbeitslosigkeit*, 6–12.

Committee, young adults and youths under the age of twenty were particularly affected by unemployment.[79] Thus, the Committee was strongly committed to aiding these particular members of society. The major concern was to remove them from the pernicious influence of unemployment, for instance, by having them build or refurbish youth camps or homes, doing housework, carrying out charitable work, or attending further training or reskilling courses. It was essential to encourage them to undergo professional training, to which end scholarships should be provided. For unemployed adults, the Committee suggested that they help plant gardens and build workshops. Proposed work schemes included the construction of youth hostels, swimming pools, playgrounds, paths, and the cleaning up of forests and Alpine areas—that is, kinds of work that would not threaten existing employment. Shelters and "warming-up parlors" should be established for the homeless. "It is most important that all of these facilities leave intact the sense of dignity of those lacking gainful employment."[80] So much for the text of the Social Affairs Committee.

The core mission of the Federation of the Swiss Protestant Churches was to reach out into the world. Its endeavor to provide assistance abroad gathered rapid momentum. Only two examples of these efforts are mentioned here (others are cited below). First, in 1920, Keller, who already maintained many contacts beyond Switzerland, prepared a report dealing with the emergency situation prevailing in France, Germany, and Austria in the aftermath of World War I. From 1920 to 1922, the appeals of the Federation for donations among Swiss Protestants raised almost 400,000 Swiss francs,[81] a considerable sum given the difficult economic situation facing postwar Switzerland. A major share of these funds was transmitted to pastors and church charities in defeated Germany, which almost no one wanted to assist. Keller sent the donations for onward distribution to Professor Friedrich Sigmund-Schultze in Berlin, who had sought to prevent the war with the help of several friends. A substantial sum was sent to churches in the Soviet Union, some in part directly to the Protestant parishes in St Petersburg, Moscow, and Odessa. Secondly, following protracted discussions, Keller succeeding in persuading the Federation already in 1922 to join the World Alliance of Reformed Churches, which had been established in 1877. The stumbling block for accession was that

79. Ibid., 25ff.

80. Ibid., 38.

81. Today this sum would correspond to well over four million Swiss francs. By comparison, a Swiss rural pastor earned between three and four hundred francs per month in those days (exclusive of free housing).

the members of the Alliance were required to make a solemn vow of faith. But under the influence of liberalism during the nineteenth century, most cantonal churches in Switzerland had declared such an avowal voluntary. To Keller's delight, the eastern, that is, European section of the Alliance held its meeting of 1923 in Zurich. From then on, Protestant Switzerland played a pivotal role in the ecumenical movement emerging in those days.

BUILDING BRIDGES: KELLER'S DYNAMIS AND PROTESTANT EUROPE

We can now return to Keller's endeavor to bridge the Atlantic. Published in 1922, his book *Dynamis* sought to "convey a better knowledge of religious life in America."[82] Unusually, it focused not on church history, but instead on the lived present. Its most important sources were conversations with influential persons, official statistics and figures, and the most recent American publications. *Dynamis* shows that while Keller sympathized with America, he did not shy away from expressing criticism.[83] It was important to be mindful of sweeping statements and wholesale judgments, he observed, since 70 million Protestant Christians (out of an overall population of 102 million) were divided among themselves. Whether liberal or fundamentalist, however, they all shared a "forward-surging energy."[84]

Unlike Europe, only free churches existed in America, where particular importance was attached to the freedom of conscience and to religious freedom. But the churches were not always a haven for freedom: "Within its closed circles, coercion savors its opportunities just as much as freedom, notably in the guise of the coercion to profess one's faith, the coercive force of money, and that of influential, powerful figures."[85] Positively, the Americans chose not to conceal their religious persuasion behind the slogan "religion is a private matter." Widespread "lay activity" and "a forceful commitment to social work" also deserved praise. While the free churches had to resist the temptations of money and power, their schooling of Christian character and religious persuasion was exemplary.

The Puritan spirit had left its mark on American sentiment:

82. Keller, *Dynamis*, v.
83. Ibid., vii.
84. Keller, Introduction to *Dynamis*, 1–2.
85. Keller, *Dynamis*, 6ff.

Some of the rigorous strictness of the Puritan ethic remains as yet in public opinion in America . . . America likes to refer to itself as the land of freedom. But public opinion . . . consists perhaps in no other country so easily as in the ban on something. The good consists merely in avoiding and combating of evil [and not in something positive] . . . Hence the prohibition movements . . . : a ban on drinking, smoking, gambling, dancing . . . Whoever possesses any understanding of human psychology knows that the suppression of such activities easily leads to a venting of the suppressed drives by other means. And precisely where the church is the guardian of such a rigorous ethic . . . , it will . . . not always be able to keep away the danger of all imperious custom, namely, hypocrisy.[86]

Religious pragmatism, claims Keller, runs in the blood of Americans. In their eyes, faith had to bear fruit, boast success, and stir the world. This was a dynamic Christianity, or as he phrased it, "*The essence* [of the churches] *was dynamis*."[87] These dynamics bore the danger of external commotion and display, which could entail a "fatal link" between "religion" and "business," which measured religious life in terms of tangible success, the number of newly conquered souls, or the sum of donations and contributions.

American Protestantism carried denominationalism to extremes, and this development had resulted in a countermovement: "America has thus become the country of *unification movements*."[88] Lay organizations like the Young Men's Christian Association (YMCA), the World Student Christian Federation (under John R. Mott), the Bible Society, and the National Missionary Convention had overcome the divide.[89] American Protestantism was inconceivable without the Federal Council, which had become "a paradigm of cooperation among the free churches."[90] During the war, it was responsible for providing a major share of social welfare and for overseeing ministry to the armed forces; other responsibilities included the boosting of public morale and readying the population for the postwar period.[91] The Council dispensed with a dogmatic formulation of its statutory foundation, and thus defined itself as non-Evangelical.[92]

86. Ibid., 11.
87. Ibid., 13–14.; further citations are from page 16.
88. Ibid, 19 (italics original).
89. Ibid., 8–9 and 94.
90. Ibid., 24. In 1922, the Council comprised fifty million Protestant Christians.
91. Ibid., 25.
92. Ibid., 26.

The influence of Christianity in America was more far-reaching than in Western Europe. American churches claimed to be the conscience of the nation. In the hands of its shining examples, such as Henry Sloane Coffin, the American sermon expressed greater interest in life than in theology: "The Gospel is placed within the stream of immediate historical events, the great national and international questions, social distress, psychological problems, and everyday experience . . . The Gospel as the immediate message to the struggling, searching, sinning, suffering human being takes center stage in this sermon."[93]

But many preachers lacked mental depth, and instead sought to build audience response. The academic level at the theological seminaries differed greatly. Harvard, UTS, and Chicago had opened their doors to critical theology, which was also gaining ground in some denominational seminaries. American theology achieved its greatest "originality," Keller asserted, where it had sprung from the psychology of religion and real life.[94] By contrast, he dismissed mass meetings:

> Today's Evangelization on a grand scale . . . adds to the emotional peculiarity of the early proclamation the element of enhanced organization and advertising, an incredible machinery, which governs the psychology of the masses to the finest degree. In doing so, however, it strives for effects, . . . that have little to do with the force of the spirit and Evangelical earnestness. The excitement to which the masses are stirred is no longer the spiritual "power" of the earlier revivals, but rather an electrical charge, which certainly does not deepen religious life.[95]

Affluent America was fraught with tremendous social problems. Poverty was widespread. In 1908, the Federal Council had elaborated a "Social Creed" on the basis of the "Social Gospel."[96] At the time, the American population consisted of ninety-five million whites and ten and a half million blacks. While the education of the black population had somewhat improved, little progress had been achieved in other areas, such as health, housing, and the judicial and corrections system. "An old debt" was taking

93. Ibid., 88.

94. In 1919, Keller visited Elwood Worcester, a pastor and psychologist in Boston. Worcester attended to mentally ill patients in cooperation with psychotherapists. See Keller, *Dynamis*, 92.

95. Ibid., 90.

96. Ibid., 119ff. The Social Gospel corresponds to religious socialism in Continental Europe. On the Social Credo, see above, p. 22.

Adolf Keller

its "bitter" vengeance."[97] The Federal Council had recently issued a call for the introduction of full equal rights of the black population. It had also created a "Research Department," dedicated to investigating social conditions. While some entrepreneurs and industrialists criticized this venture, others, including John D. Rockefeller Jr., came out in support.[98] American society, Keller observed, was deeply divided.

In conclusion, Keller remarks that Europe had fallen behind the United States after World War I. Americans should assume tasks of global significance.[99] None the less, the United States should beware of turning churchly Europe, so often considered old and tired, into a "missionary field."[100] On the other hand, it was extremely positive that $200 million had been raised to alleviate suffering in Europe, which lay in ruins. However, most church welfare organizations in America were organized along denominational lines, a circumstance that scarcely helped do proper justice to the distress prevailing in Europe.[101]

Keller's *Dynamis* earned him great acclaim across the Atlantic. In its annual report for the year 1923, the Federal Council of the Churches of Christ in America commented: "his book *Dynamis* . . . is noteworthy for its discerning and vital interpretation of Protestant life in this country. He is . . . a man of such fairness of mind and breath of sympathy."[102] Another commentator observed: "A book of unusual interest is *Dynamis* . . . It is a careful and able study of the ecclesiastical and religious situation in America."[103] Adolf von Harnack read the book with "vivid interest," and remarked that "it is truly enlightening in the best sense of the word."[104] Albert Schweitzer wrote: "A thousand thanks for *Dynamis* . . . I am learning a great deal. It is wonderfully written!"[105]

97. Keller, *Dynamis*, 102.

98. Ibid., 123–24.

99. Ibid., 128.

100. Ibid., 140–41.

101. Ibid., 139–40. On Keller's relief agency, see below, pp. 68–81.

102. "Annual Report of the Federal Council for the Year 1923," 88 (PHS NCC RG 18 79/1).

103. Ainslie, Review of Keller, *Dynamis*, 318. Ainslie was one of the foremost American ecumenists.

104. Harnack to Keller, June 13, 1922 (WS Ms Sch 152/122).

105. Schweitzer to Keller, Günsbach, June 7, 1922 (WS Ms Sch 153/48).

52

Keller received a request from Charles Macfarland to write *Protestant Europe*.[106] "We need it badly," he added.[107] Until then, no comprehensive discussion of European Protestantism had been available in the English language.[108] Keller worked on the book for several years: "It is very difficult to write a book between America and Europe."[109] While George Stewart, an American theologian, served Keller as a diligent coauthor and translator, he nevertheless shouldered most of the burden. On its publication, *Protestant Europe* was favorably received. Reviewers remarked that it drew "an admirable picture" of Protestant Europe.[110] The annual report of the Federal Council for the year 1927 listed it among twelve books worth reading. *Protestant Europe* was pioneering in three respects: first, it marked Keller's first publication in English; secondly, it was the result of a collaborative undertaking; and thirdly, it was "the first of what may prove to be an ecumenical literature, giving a vision of the whole of European Protestant Christianity to the Christian population of the West."[111]

Following a survey of European church history since the Reformation and of the political, social, and cultural development of Europe during the nineteenth and early twentieth centuries, Keller and Stewart turn to the present day. To gauge European sentiment, they cite from the works of Henrik Ibsen, Leo Tolstoy, Romain Rolland, Bernhard Shaw, Friedrich Nietzsche, and Oswald Spengler. They bemoan "Europe's cultural maelstrom," and deplore the fact that the Four Horsemen of the Apocalypse had ravaged Europe: "war, revolution, famine and disease."[112] In the wake of the war, furthermore, the class struggle and nationalism had grown stronger: "As one looked upon a world of defeated victors and despairing victims and saw the war wounded—the yellow, emaciated widows, the rickety children, and the mad Saturnalia of the dance halls and cafés—he [Keller] could not wonder that one of the most widely read books in Central Europe was Oswald Spengler's *Der Untergang des Abendlandes* (*The Decline of the West*)."[113]

106. Keller and Stewart, *Protestant Europe*. The preface was written by Charles Macfarland. Stewart had studied theology in Germany.

107. Macfarland to Keller, February 11, 1926 (PHS NCC RG 18 73/10).

108. Keller, "Die Europäische Zentralstelle für kirchliche Hilfsaktionen," 7, n. 1.

109. Keller to Archbishop Nathan Söderblom, May 13, 1927 (NLAK C 32).

110. Keller, *Karl Barth and Christian Unity*, xiii (preface). This was the English translation of Keller's *Der Weg der dialektischen Theologie durch die kirchliche Welt*.

111. Charles Macfarland, preface to Keller's *Protestant Europe*, ix.

112. Keller and Stewart, *Protestant Europe*, 20.

113. Ibid.

Keller's description of the ecclesiastical circumstances prevailing across Europe draws on a wide range of sources, including Bishop Ammundsen of Denmark, Bishop Ravasz of Budapest, Archbishop Söderblom of Uppsala, Professor Zilka from Prague, Professor Jan Cramer from Utrecht, Professor Wilfred Monod from Paris, Reverend Theodor Fliedner from Madrid, and Professor Adolf Deissmann from Berlin. Keller had become acquainted with these spiritual leaders through his involvement in the ecumenical movement. Europe, which he also deemed at risk in ecclesiastical terms, desperately needed these churchmen: "If the Reformation is to be saved, it must be by the foresight and statesmanship of Protestant leaders who can persuade separate and independent units to do freely that which is accomplished through the iron discipline and centralized authority of the Roman Church."[114]

While political internationalism had brought forth a new ideal after the war, "The churches, although representing in their message a supranational ideal, have failed to share in any large way in this growing hope."[115] Keller's criticism was leveled chiefly at Europe. While the ecumenical movement had meanwhile got underway, Macfarland and he had harbored much greater hopes, namely, for a loose coalition of the Protestant churches in Europe. *Protestant Europe* does not offer an exhaustive treatment of this idea.[116] Keller did, however, discuss it with various European churchmen and ecclesiastical bodies.[117] For over three decades, the idea came to nothing.[118]

There was also reason for hope: "If the present chaos is thus understood not only as an end but as a new possibility of life, it looks hopeful. Indeed, there are signs of an inner rebirth, a new orientation in the best

114. Ibid., 28.

115. Ibid., 45–46 and 54.

116. Macfarland to Keller, October 1, 1926: "I believe we ought to go ahead with that plan for a meeting next summer of representatives of all the National Church Federations [of Europe]" (PHS NCC RG 18 73/10).

117. At the conference of the British National and Free Church Council of 1926, Keller suggested three possibilities: first, a "Federation of the existing Church federations"; second, a "European organisation including all the Protestant Churches of Europe"; and third, an "Alliance composed of the Reformed Churches of Europe." See Keller to Macfarland, January 18, 1926 and March 17, 1926 (PHS NCC RG 18 73/10). At the conference, various reservations about Keller's proposals were voiced by Söderblom and others. See Keller to Söderblom, January 7, 1927 (NLAK C 32).

118. The Conference of European Churches, which included the Orthodox Churches, was not founded until 1959.

of European leaders."[119] Intellectuals and artists were once again engaged in debate, and religious life was reawakening: "This development of a European consciousness and intellectual collaboration greatly strengthens efforts made by European churches to enter into friendly relations with one another."[120]

While churchliness was self-evident in the United States, albeit often determined by superficial optimism, a great problem in Europe resided "in the fact that many Christians are in doubt as to the usefulness of the church . . . A large number of Christian people are antagonistic to organized religion. The church is criticised . . . for its lack of influence upon the people, the predominance of priestly and ministerial influence, the absence of spirituality and for its pretension to represent the body of Christ in a visible and organized form."[121] Regrettably, as Keller observed, Karl Barth had also contributed to this criticism of the church: "The newest theological movement of the school around Karl Barth instils a measure of scepticism into all constructive efforts of the church and urges believers to build a new organization similar to congregationalism, beginning with the parish. The church is accused of being more interested in social activity than in the preaching of the Gospel . . . The church has become a problem in herself and the major social and evangelistic impulses of recent years have been paralyzed by this deep ecclesiastical pessimism."[122] Nevertheless, *Protestant Europe* discusses Barth's theology at length, as will become apparent below.

One fundamental difference existed between the American free churches and the various forms taken by state churches in Europe: there was a great Lutheran influence, which had an inhibiting effect. Thus: "Lutheranism has never considered it the task of the church to take the lead in social reform. Its conservatism and its attachment to the monarchy have prevented a thoroughgoing social movement." One remark in this respect attracts particular attention: "European Protestantism is aware of the grave social dangers lurking in the present order of dictatorships, materialistic communism, nationalism and fascism." Stalin seized absolute rule in the late 1920s, and Mussolini was already firmly holding the reins in Italy. Given this fatal development, Keller pins his hopes upon assistance from

119. Keller and Stewart, *Protestant Europe*, 54.

120. Ibid., 56.

121. Ibid., 74–75.

122. Ibid., 75. Keller mentions Ernst Troeltsch, who had predicted the demise of the church.

the United States, since, as he explains, "In the inevitable decision between Caesar and Christ, Caesar continues to win the victory . . . The Christian conscience of Europe is threatened with an unbearable dualism. On the one hand it accepts the claims of Christ for a peaceful world, and on the other it feels compelled to obey the commands of Caesar in the midst of a dangerous and warlike world."[123] It is worth remembering that Keller wrote these lines in early 1927!

Keller and Stewart also discuss the subject of theology in Protestant Europe, and thus also the opposition between its orthodox and liberal strands: "There is no doubt that Continental orthodoxy has shown more elasticity in the interpretation of the old doctrines and in the assimilation of critical methods than American orthodoxy."[124] Unlike in the United States, in Europe only some few small groups adhered to the verbal inspiration of the Bible. The historical and linguistic work undertaken by European theologians over the past century should be assessed in positive terms: "[It] has rendered an inestimable service to European Christianity."[125] America should benefit from this scholarship. If the vibrant life of faith and social commitment prevalent in America served Europe as a role model, then in turn the Reformation (particularly in its Swiss guise) and present-day European theology served the same function for America. Keller devoted several pages to "dialectical theology," that is, the "Theology of Crisis." With that, the keyword is minted. Presumably, Keller was the first to make dialectical theology known in the English- and French-speaking worlds.

KARL BARTH AND THE THEOLOGY OF CRISIS

Karl Barth's epochal *Epistle to the Romans* appeared in 1919. In a letter to Barth, Keller wrote: "I hear you; I am reading your epistle to the Romans to great benefit."[126] Twenty years later, he recalled his experience of reading this work:

> I studied it intensely, in its first and second editions, not without struggling against many sides and conclusions of this theology, particularly what at the time was the improperly exaggerated transcendence of this theology, its rejection of experience and

123. Ibid., 125ff.
124. Ibid., 141.
125. Ibid., 156.
126. Keller to Barth, February 6, 1920 (KBA 9320.40).

ethical indifference, which was clearly noticeable in the initial period. Nevertheless, I am deeply indebted to this theology. It once and for all wrenched me away from blending theology with other elements, and opened me up to the meaning of the transcendence in the message of Jesus and his appearance. Whatever subjectivism I had entertained now dropped to the floor, and a great freedom became effective within me, which . . . guided me to the center of all Gospel proclamation, to the fact that Jesus, in the name of God, forgives the sinner and sets him free.[127]

Keller read the writings of Barth and those of the like-minded Emil Brunner from cover to cover without exception. At first, not many theologians followed Keller's example.[128] Others like Paul Wernle, his old friend and now famous professor in Basel, and Leonhard Ragaz opposed so-called dialectical theology. But Keller benefited greatly from the new school of thought. His sermons became more biblical, and referred more closely to God as a transcendental reality: "I look back upon this time of inner growth with joy. Enraptured, I sometimes stood before a congregation that filled the large church and possessed a palpable attunement to the religious change underway at the time, which I was involved in myself and stood for."[129] Nevertheless, he remained critical: "The dialectics that Barth and his friends stand for seems little harmonious with the simple Gospel of Jesus. In particular, it lacks love in my eyes. Also, the notion of creation seems to fall unduly behind that of salvation. Further, I do not believe that in a world so fraught with distress and need that we have the right to simply wait, where God in fact is pointing out such clear ways to us through this adversity. But I nevertheless sense a deep earnestness, and I also believe that the implacability with which he . . . confronts us with the transcendental God signifies a religious strengthening and a catharsis."[130]

Of all times, Keller and Barth fell out precisely when the *Epistle of the Romans* was published. Barth accused Keller of continued adherence to psychoanalysis, an accusation that Keller refuted. Another bone of contention was the League of Nations. Keller told Barth that he was nevertheless "warmly disposed toward" him, even if he could not "storm ahead" in equal manner. Regarding the *Epistle to the Romans*, Keller acknowledged

127. Keller, "Aus meinem Leben," 57–58.

128. In a letter to Brunner of May 27, 1924, Keller noted that he failed to recognize much "knowledge" and insight among theologians (StAZ W I 55, 25).

129. Keller, "Aus meinem Leben," 63.

130. Keller to Ragaz, May 1, 1924 (StAZ W I 67 103.2).

that he felt "infinitely closer" to Barth than the latter assumed. [131] As late as 1939, Barth still reproached Keller for being a liberal theologian, a reproach that the latter energetically disputed:

> The spiritual place where you see me is not my place. I myself was never considered a student of Troeltsch's. Theologically, and as far as the historical method is concerned, I associated myself with Harnack; as far as the transcendental message is concerned . . . with Schlatter . . . That you . . . should speak of unchanged prerequisites makes me sad . . . Basically, it is less your theology, which I have followed a lot further than you assume, than its human manifestation that sometimes disconcerts me . . . Why does a theology that speaks of an unknown God and even of an unknown Christ and unknown Christians know so precisely what the other Christians are? [132]

In a letter to Brunner of May 1924, Keller wrote: "My criticism of you reflects my strong interest." [133] And to Barth, he observed: "In my frequent discussions of your theology with friends, I have never strayed from the line that mine is a serious . . . engagement with your proclamation; of all people, you will no doubt expect that such an engagement be critical and not simply amount to parrot-fashion acceptance." [134] Many of Barth's supporters resented Keller, who was over half a generation their senior, for not joining their camp with flying colors. Possibly Keller played down the liberal part of his theology somewhat. Nevertheless, he became a "Barthian"—even if an unconventional and critically minded one.

In 1924, Keller gave lectures on dialetical theology in various places in the United States and Great Britain, altogether before 6,000 people. [135] In the spring of 1925, he contributed an exhaustive article, entitled "A Theology of Crisis," to *The Expositor*, a scholarly Presbyterian British journal. [136] In a letter dated May 5, 1925, he wrote to Barth: "Since this is the first article to present your work in English, to my best knowledge, I endeavored to cite your own words as often as possible." [137] Keller summarized

131. Keller to Barth, February 6, 1920 (KBA 9320.40).

132. Keller to Barth, October 21, 1939 (WS Ms Sch 152/2).

133. Keller to Brunner, May 27, 1924 (StAZ W I 55, 25).

134. Keller to Barth, Zurich, May 1, 1925 (KBA 9325.173).

135. Keller to Barth, May 8, 1924 (KBA 9324.134); see also Keller, "Eine britische religiös-soziale Konferenz," 197ff.

136. Keller, "A Theology of Crisis," 164–75 and 245–60.

137. Keller to Barth, Zurich, May 5, 1925 (KBA 9325.180). See also H. R. Mackintosh, "The Swiss Group," 73–75; and Jehle, *Emil Brunner*, 241.

the principal theses of dialetical theology, and cited the writings of Barth, Brunner, and Gogarten: the new movement, he concluded, adopted a critical stance toward every theology. It was the expression of a profound crisis if Christians actually saw themselves confronted with the living God: "Crisis is the only word which depicts adequately this situation."[138] For, "what we call God, is not the living God but a humanized image we made of Him. Barth directs, from this point of view, his specific and furious attacks against modern historicism and psychologism." The "Deus absconditus (hidden God)" could not be turned into the object of human experience. "However, if there is no way from men to the transcendent God, there is a way from God to men: Jesus Christ. He is the only revelation of God." Dialectical theology eluded all judgment, and demanded "a decision, a crisis." Further, "It is refreshing to see how this theology goes straight forward into this Holy of holies of the Reformers without looking to the right or the left." Keller translates Barth's "Der ganz Andere" as "God is the totally Different." But to his overall positive appraisal, Keller adds: "Indeed the ethical problem is the weak point of the whole position."

He received many inquiries from Scotland about his article on Barth.[139] Keller assumed a pioneering role in conveying the new theology to the English-speaking world. Presumably, "Theology of Crisis," the English term for Barth's "dialektische Theologie," is indebted to him.[140] Published in early 1927, Keller's *Protestant Europe* also introduced the new theology to a wider audience in the United States, indeed before the first English translation of one of Barth's books was published in 1928.[141] Emil Brunner's *Theology of Crisis* was published in 1929.[142]

We may thus return to *Protestant Europe*. Keller observed that the social problems had sent out a signal

138. Keller, "A Theology of Crisis," 166; for the further citations, see 167, 169, 171, 255, and 256–57.

139. Keller to Barth, Cardiff, June 26, 1925 (KBA 9325.260).

140. Drewes, *Bibliographie Karl Barth*, 779. See also Chauncy W. Goodrich to Keller, New York, May 5, 1925: "Perhaps that which has most impressed me, because it was entirely new, was the first article on 'The Theology of Crisis'" (PHS NCC RG 18 73/9). Presumably, Goodrich had read Keller's article in *The Expositor*.

141. Keller and Stewart, *Protestant Europe*, 146ff. See also Keller, "The Dialectic Theology." In his first letter to Barth, dated March 27, 1930, Visser't Hooft emphasized that he had recently propagated Barth's theology in England—five years after Keller's article had appeared in *The Expositor*; see Herwig and Visser't Hooft, eds., *Karl Barth–W.A. Visser't Hooft*, 3–4.

142. Brunner, *Theology of Crisis*. See also Adam, "Die Theologie der Krisis," 271ff.

for a crisis in Christianity and world culture. It was the revelation of the absolute helplessness of man, even the Christian church, to find a way out from the present chaos by its own means . . . After the first disappointing experiences with social christianity in practical work, a small group of Swiss theologians held that the difficulty of finding an understanding between socialism and Christianity was more than a merely practical social problem . . . Social christianity in their eyes had betrayed God to the world, the revealed God to wordly necessities, to have lost in adaption to a scientific naturalism the sense of the absolute God, and the Christian insight into the eternal tension between sin and grace.

This new theological movement, often called a theology of crisis, should not be considered as a new school, but as a criticism of every theology. It is a protest against the *Zeitgeist* of a whole century of theological thinking as expressed since Schleiermacher in a theology of immanence, a protest against the identification of God's aims and nature with the best in our ethics and religion,—in one word, against "humanism" and its expression in what is called *Kulturprotestantismus*. It constitutes a revolt against religion submerged in culture. Not synthesis but crisis is the slogan of the new movement . . . The theology of crisis directs its attacts equally against the relativism of liberal theology and the tradionalism of orthodoxy . . . Pietism is likewise rejected as being based on a similar subjective element . . . God is a hidden, an unknown God, and it does not behoove men to approach him with human formulae in an undue intimacy.

We touch here the center of this theology, the transcendency of God. He cannot be found in nature or in human experience. God is "the totally Different," unattainable even to the highest moral or religious efforts of men . . . In one place only this hidden God became manifest: in Christ. But even in this sole revelation he remains the transcendent God . . . In Christ's death and resurrection we have not so much historical facts as a mysterous paradoxical irruption of divine forces, the apparition of a new eon.[143]

What was paramount was that "the theology of crisis seeks to build, in place of the ethics of the human will, an ethics of grace stressing forgiveness as the source of the Christian life."[144] The "Theology of Crisis," Keller added, was "of immense importance because of the power and influence

143. Keller and Stewart, *Protestant Europe*, 146–49.
144. Ibid., 151.

it is having especially over large sections of idealistic youth . . . It would be too early to assign a definite place to this new movement in the history of modern theology." [145] None the less, it marked a forceful reaction against the synthesis of religion and culture. While it was a theocentric theology, it granted freedom to critical thinking. "This position may yet reveal a way of escape from the present tension between orthodox and liberal theology."[146]

Written out of personal concern, and yet from a certain distance, Keller's *Protestant Europe* managed to draw an appropriate picture of dialectical theology. Enriched by the new school of thought, he now sought to further advance his ecumencial work.

145. Ibid., 147.
146. Ibid., 150.

3

The Ecumenical Movement

Life and Work and the Central Bureau for Relief

NATHAN SÖDERBLOM AND THE FOUNDING
OF LIFE AND WORK (1920)

WITHIN THE ECUMENICAL MOVEMENT, Keller's first major task, as discussed, was the building of bridges across the Atlantic. Upon the initiative of Eugène Choisy, who had meanwhile been appointed professor of church history, Keller was awarded an honorary doctorate by the University of Geneva for his "eminent services" to establishing relations between the churches in Switzerland and the United States, and between German- and French-speaking Switzerland.[1] In 1923, Keller was appointed European secretary of the Federal Council of the Churches of Christ in America. In a letter dated October 24, 1923, Macfarland thus wrote: "Personally, I regard your appointment as epoch-making in this whole work."[2] From his "watchtower" in Switzerland, Keller's task was to observe church matters

---

1. Eugène Choisy, dean of the Faculty of Theology, to "Monsieur le Doyen et Messieurs les Professeurs de la Faculté de Théologie de l'Université de Zurich," May 31, 1922 (StAZ Z 70.2860, folio 159). In 1922, Keller was also awarded an "honorary degree LL.D." by Heidelberg University in Tiffin, Ohio.

2. Macfarland to Keller, October 24, 1923 (NLAK C 23).

in Europe and to report back to the Americans.[3] Upon mature consideration, he accepted the appointment.[4]

The fact that Keller became *the* communicator between the American
and European churches, among other things, by means of his books *Dynamis* and *Protestant Europe*, was only one of the reasons for Macfarland
to propose to Yale University in 1927 that an honorary doctorate be conferred upon Keller.[5] The laudatory document in honor of Keller includes
the following passage: "In recognition of your success in promoting the
Christian doctrine of good will among men, Yale confers upon you the degree of doctor of Divinity and admits you to all its rights and privileges."[6]

The Yale laudation reflected Keller's meanwhile vastly expanded
ecumenical and humanitarian commitment. Along with cultivating transatlantic dialogue, he had become the driving force behind the ecumenical
orientation of the Federation of Swiss Protestant Churches. From 1920,
moreover, he became closely involved in Life and Work, the large ecumenical movement. Upon his incentive, the Central Bureau for Relief of
the Protestant Churches of Europe, an interdominational relief organization, was established in 1922. Keller became its director, and the Bureau
became his favorite field of activity. These new commitments meant that
he was no longer able to officiate as minister at St Peter's in Zurich. He
retired from office in 1923. Keller was among the first clergymen to commit themselves full-time to the ecumenical movement. His salary was paid
by the Federal Council.[7] These new duties and responsibilities ushered in
the most intense and greatest period in Keller's life and work. In 1920, at
the age of forty-eight, he was highly experienced, a true and honest professional, a man in good health, and brimming with enthusiasm and a zest
for action. Owing to Karl Barth, moreover, he stood on firm theological
ground. Tina Keller realized that from this point in their lives she would
often need to make do without her husband. But she took a positive view
of his professional development. For the time being, the Keller family continued to make their home in Zurich.

3. "Annual Report of the Federal Council of the Churches of Christ in America for
the Year 1923," 28–29.

4. Keller to "Verehrte Herren!" (the Board of the Federation of Swiss Protestant
Churches), November 7, 1923 (BAR J.2.257 1439/156).

5. Macfarland to Keller, May 24, 1926 (PHS NCC RG 18 73/10).

6. For the corresponding passage from President Agnell's laudatory document,
see *The Yale Alumni Weekly*, July 8, 1927 (transmitted to the author by Linda Koch
Lorimer, Vice President and Secretary of Yale University).

7. The annual salary of $4,000 (approximately 24,000 Swiss francs) was generous.
See further Keller to Macfarland, April 12, 1925 (PHS NCC RG 18 73/9).

Let's go a step backwards! Charles Macfarland had taken charge of sending out the invitations to the founding meeting of Life and Work, which was held in Geneva in 1920. The meeting was attended by Protestant delegates from fourteen countries. Attendees included Nathan Söderblom, the archbishop of Uppsala and head of Sweden's Lutheran Church, as well as other Swedish theologians. Adolf Keller and Eugène Choisy represented Protestant Switzerland. Great Britain and Germany were not represented, but Professor Friedrich Siegmund-Schultze traveled from Berlin to attend the meeting at his own expense and responsibility.[8] Evidently, Charles Macfarland was present, as were other American church representatives. The list of participants demonstrates that the Federal Council of the United States, Lutheran Sweden, and Reformed Switzerland were the founding fathers of the movement.

Various circumstances and events led to the establishment of Life and Work. In view of increasing tensions between Germany and Great Britain, theologians from both countries had gathered as early as 1908. In 1911, Macfarland held talks with the leading figures of the British-German Committee, which had resulted from the initial meeting. Its secretary was Friedrich Siegmund-Schultze, professor for social ethics in Berlin. A peace conference involving theologians from several countries took place in the town of Constance on August 2, 1914. No sooner had it begun than the outbreak of World War I forced its abandonment.

A year after war had erupted, Eugène Choisy, among others, called a peace conference in Bern. The name chosen for the emerging movement was the World Alliance for Promoting Friendship through the Churches. In the autumn of 1919, the Alliance held its first postwar conference in the town of Oud Wassenaar in The Netherlands. Participants included both Söderblom and Macfarland, as well as Otto Herold, president of the Church Council of Zurich.[9] Since the Alliance was a movement of individual theologians, an international organization of official churches was established a year later alongside it. This organization was named Life and Work (The Ecumenical Movement for Practical Christianity).

Thus, a so-called "preliminary meeting" of the Universal Conference of the Church of Christ on Life and Work was held in Geneva from August 9 to 12, 1920. Keller met Archbishop Söderblom for the first time on the eve of the meeting; he described their encounter as follows:

8. On Friedrich Siegmund-Schultze, see below, p. 95.
9. On Otto Herold, see above, pp. 38 and 43.

We met for the the first time beneath the shady chestnut trees of the Beau-Séjour Hotel in Geneva. It was the eve of the preliminary conference that was . . . supposed to establish a foundation for the World Church Conference in Stockholm. He was sitting at a table . . . with a group from Sweden. They were reading the New Testament—not the meeting programme—in preparation for the conference the following day. He began the conference with the Bible. For only there could the spirit be found with which he hoped to conquer the ethnic hatred that also threatened a Christian conference in those days . . . One had to hear Söderblom speak to understand the nature of his mind. Despite all his erudition, his temperament was not that of a scholar who withdraws from the world to immerse himself in his subject. He needed people to bring himself fully to bear. Once they were before him, willing, eager, his mind effervesced and effortlessly emitted ideas, suggestions, distant visions, practical suggestions close-by, and witty interjections in inexhaustible abundance. His effervescence did not make holding a debate with him, for example, in committees, easy: he talked, the others listened. If resistance arose, he did not use his power as chairman to defeat it, but humor. Therein, he was irresistible.[10]

Already at the first meeting, the French delegate, Pasteur Frédéric Dumas from Paris, read out a declaration of the Conseil de la Fédération Protestante de France that deplored the largely missing admission of guilt on the part of the German church. The cooperation of the French churches seemed endangered. Keller realized that "the key problem in the mind of Europe is the German-French tension. As long as this deep-seated animosity persits, peace is unattainable for Europe."[11] Between sessions the delegates would take leisurely strolls in the hotel park. On one occasion, Söderblom took Keller by the arm and led him, almost at a run, to the shady trees, where he explained that Sweden and Switzerland, which were both neutral and represented Protestant denominations, should act as intermediaries.[12] He was pushing against open doors.

In Geneva, a resolution was passed to launch Life and Work with a flourish, namely, a world conference. This was to be held in Stockholm, and its stated aim was "to invite all Christian Communions to participate in the proposed conference."[13] After the metropolitan Germanos

10. Keller, *Von Geist und Liebe*, 200–201.
11. Keller and Stewart, *Protestant Europe*, 43.
12. Keller, *Von Geist und Liebe*, 53–54.
13. Records of the Preliminary Meeting to consider a Universal Conference of

Strenopoulos, a representative of the patriarch of Constantinople, had attended the Geneva meeting, the Greek Orthodox Church was almost certain to participate at the Stockholm conference.[14] A spirit of optimism prevailed in Geneva: Macfarland experienced the founding meeting in various respects as "the most crucial of all—both those previously and those subsequently."[15] Similarly, Söderblom asserted that "I was never present at any international conference that meant spiritual action so much as this one."[16]

An international executive committee was formed. Its members included Keller and Choisy. Its initial task was to establish which churches existed in Europe. Further, it sought to win the support of the Anglican and German churches, which it succeeded in doing after some perseverance. Quaker Lucy Gardner, from Great Britian, who was a firm believer in the cause, and Adolf Deissmann, professor of theology in Berlin, who shared her conviction, joined the committee.[17] Keller was sent to Paris to conduct the delicate negotiations with the Federation of French Churches. Wilfred Monod, president of the Union des Eglises réformées de France, and Keller hit it off straightaway. They established a cordial friendship, which pertained to much more than the involvement of the French Protestant churches in Life and Work. By contrast, all efforts to secure the support of Rome failed, despite Söderblom's personal commitment.

At the conference of Life and Work of August 1922, held in the town of Helsingborg in southern Sweden, the following slogan was coined: "Doctrine divides, service unites."[18] It formed part of the vision of the corporate social responsibility of the churches. There was a widespread belief that cooperating on resolving the world's problems would bring the churches closer more swiftly than any theological advances. With a view to the Stockholm conference, the following list of themes was compiled:

---

the Church of Christ on Life and Work (recording clerk unmentioned), Geneva, 17 (WCC).

14. In 1925 Keller traveled to Egypt to present the Coptic and Orthodox Churches with an invitation to the Stockholm conference.

15. Macfarland, *Steps toward the World Council*, 59.

16. Ibid., 99.

17. On Deissmann, see above, pp. viii, 30, and 54. On Quaker Lucy Gardner, see below, pp. viii, p. 30 n. 3 and p. 54. .

18. "Verhandlungen der Allgemeinen Konferenz der Kirche Christi für Praktisches Christentum" (i.e., Minutes of the Hälsingborg Meeting of 1922) (1923), 43. On Faith and Order, the ecumenical movement founded in 1910, see below, pp. 104–5.

1. The Task of the Church in terms of God's Plan for the World.

2. The Church and Economic and Industrial Problems.

3. The Position of the Church on Social and Moral Questions.

4. The Church and International Relations.

5. The Church and Christian Education.

6. Methods of Cooperation, Rapprochement, and the Free Union of Christian Communities.

The archbishops of Uppsala and Canterbury, Arthur J. Brown (president of the Federal Council), and the Patriarch of Constantinople were appointed presidents of the four regional subgroups of Life and Work: Continental Europe, Great Britain, America, and the orthodox world. The American Henry A. Atkinson was appointed general secretary; Choisy, Keller, and the Englishman Thomas Nightingale were appointed associate secretaries. As a team of four, they were responsible for making the practical arrangements for the Stockholm world conference.[19]

With regard to Life and Work, Keller thus became the right hand of Archbishop Söderholm. From 1923 to 1925, Zurich became the capital city of ecumenism. Besides holding several conferences of the interdenominational relief organization under Keller's direction, Zurich also hosted the meeting of the Executive Committee of Life and Work in 1923. Two years later, in April 1925, the European group of Life and Work convened in Zurich to make the final preparations for the forthcoming world conference. This time, at a public church service at St Peter's, Archbishop Söderblom, Bishop Ammundsen of Denmark, Pasteur Jézéquel from Paris, General Superintendent Blau of Poznań, and Bishop Ravasz of Hungary set out the goals and tasks of the conference.[20] For the first time in its history, Lutheran bishops ascended the pulpit of St Peter's to address the Reformed people of Zurich.[21] In a letter to Keller, Söderblom hailed the meeting in Zurich as "magnificent."[22] Conference sessions were held in the new parish hall located in the vicarage of St Peter's while the "friends" of the parish opened their doors to host receptions held in honor of the guests.

19. Ibid., 32.

20. "Annual Report of the Board of the Federation of Swiss Protestant Churches for 1924/25," 10–11.

21. Keller, *Der Schweizerische Evangelische Kirchenbund*, 11.

22. Söderblom to Keller, May 23, 1925 (NLAK C 32).

"A NEW BROTHERLY COMMUNITY OF HELPING LOVE": KELLER'S CENTRAL BUREAU FOR RELIEF

> After the last world war, many of the continental evangelical churches had to face tremendous problems of relief and reconstruction. Destruction of churches, shortage of ministers, ruined institutions of church welfare works, famine and a general impoverishment followed the four years of war like a terrible shadow, and hampered life in many respects.[23]

Given the disastrous situation of many European churches, Keller believed that fundamental change was needed. While he admired the tremendous helpfulness of the American churches, he was critical of the fact that they mostly supported members of their own denomination. One exception was the Federal Council, which had lent cooperative assistance to France and Belgium already during the war. But Keller's ideas ventured further: he envisioned a relief organization, funded jointly by the still intact churches of Europe and America, that would help suffering Protestant Christians in Europe irrespective of nation and denomination. His vision rested upon his observation that the united churches in Prussia and in Poland, consisting of Lutheran and Reformed groupings, and the Protestant minorities in Eastern Europe, had mostly been left empty-handed after the war. And the whole of Germany, too, had missed out almost entirely, since it was allegedly solely responsible for the war. The British provided the small Protestant churches in France with three and a half times as many resources as the German Protestant Church and its forty million members. Moreover, support lacked effective coordination.

None other than Keller had this vision, although an interdenominational relief organization basically aligned with the mission statement of Life and Work. He undertook every possible effort to realize his vision. Aware that nothing could be done without American assistance, Keller had written thus to the Federal Council at the end of 1919: "Only America can bring efficient help and prevent millions of children and old people from starving. . . . It could be the beginning of a practical rapprochement by real help, not only by conventions and delegations. It would be the practical exponent of a new brotherly community of helping love."[24] Macfarland allowed himself to be convinced, but he needed time to win the support of

23. Keller, "Twenty years of the Central Bureau for Relief of the Evangelical Churches of Europe. A Preliminary Survey" (1942), 1 (NLAK C 2,2).

24. Keller to Macfarland, December 5, 1919 (PHS NCC RG 18 10/6).

the churches affiliated with the Federal Council. Söderblom also realized that there were shortcomings in postwar aid. A proven Lutheran welfare organization, the Gustav Adolf Verein, already existed in Sweden, which relied on this agency in particular.[25] However, Keller's enthusiasm soon spread through the Federation of Swiss Protestant Churches.

Conference of representatives of American churches on the situation in Europe, New York (ca. 1925), Adolf Keller standing at the left, before him (sitting) Charles Macfarland (archive Dr. Pierre Keller)

In February 1922, Macfarland wrote to Keller:

> All I can do here is to state that I am willing to do all I can to carry out the proposals of our conference here [in New York, November 2, 1921], which were, that we should participate in a conference, and assist in organizing it if the European brethren desired it. Undoubtedly it could best be summoned by the Swiss Churches. If you decide to summon such a conference, I shall be glad to give any personal help I can to assist in organizing it ... My own judgement is that a real vital interdenominationalism in Europe would just now greatly help an interdenominational approach on the part of the American churches to the European churches.[26]

25. Keller, *Von Geist und Liebe*, 55.
26. Macfarland to Keller, February 16, 1922 (NLAK C 35).

This meant that Keller's suggested project could proceed. In a subsequent memorandum, Keller modestly observed: "The foundation of the Central Bureau was initiated by the representatives of the American and the Swiss Church Federation."[27]

Keller and Otto Herold, the latter having meanwhile been appointed president of the Federation of Swiss Protestant Churches, immediately contacted the European churches.[28] They requested those churches either not or not strongly affected by the war to report on their previous welfare activities. Those destroyed during the war were asked to describe their situation and to compile a list of their most pressing needs. Keller collected and abbreviated the incoming reports, and collated them in a book titled *Zur Lage des Europäischen Protestantismus* (On the Situation of European Protestantism).[29] Presumably, this was the first joint document of European Protestantism.[30]

Its key contents may be summarized as follows: the French, whose church was impoverished in any event and who had suffered greatly during the war, prefaced their report with the following motto: "The Church has ample means for glorifying the great mercies of God."[31] While the French Church had received cooperative assistance via the Federal Council, it required further support.

The German report bore Luther's "Ein' feste Burg ist unser Gott" ("A Mighty Fortress Is Our God") as its guiding motto. Other than the defeat and the humiliation suffered by Germany, it was difficult for the German Church to absorb the disappearence of the territorial princes as its external supporting pillars. Inflation, too, added to its plight, which, in 1922, was becoming even more severe: the social and charitable work of the church was under threat. The Protestant press and Bible societies lacked the funds to purchase paper—whose price had increased by 11,800 percent. In 1922, the financial shortfall of the social institutions of the deaconesses (Protestant nursing sisters) of Kaiserswerth amounted

27. Keller, "Memorandum 8. Present activity of the European Central Bureau for Relief to Suffering Churches" (presumably written in 1942), 1 (NLAK C 2,2).

28. Federation of Swiss Protestant Churches (Herold and Keller) to the European churches, May 26, 1922 (BAR J.2.257 1462160).

29. Keller, *Zur Lage des Europäischen Protestantismus.*

30. Keller, "Minutes on the Negotiations of the Emergency Conference of Copenhagen, August 10–12, 1922," 2 (NLAK C 34). *Protestant Europe* was not published until 1927.

31. For André Monod's report on the situation in France, see *Zur Lage des Europäischen Protestantismus*, 36.

to twenty-four million marks. Keller praised the report's appeal to the German people to critically examine itself: "The path to reconstruction necessitates dutifulness and work, order and discipline, and never again hatred and murder."[32] In the first instance, one hoped not for material aid from foreign churches, but rather for "an affectionate understanding of the spiritual condition of the [German] people and the churches."[33] For Keller, the founding of the Deutscher Evangelischer Kirchenbund (Federation of German Protestant Churches) in May 1922 was also an encouraging sign. Hermann Kapler, a lawyer, was appointed chairman of the board.

In Austria, which had been thrown back upon itself following the downfall of the Habsburg Empire, the diaspora was found to be in a miserable state—only four percent of Austrians were Protestants. Public schools were de facto Catholic. Hence, one was fighting to secure the survival of the remaining Protestant schools.[34] In Hungary, which had gained independence from Vienna, the loss of two of the originally four million Protestants was deplored, since two thirds of the country had been awarded to Romania and other neighboring countries. This had brought Hungarian Protestantism into a difficult situation. The report noted that the country was now dominated by a biased Roman Catholic local administration.[35]

Poland, one of the major theaters of war, had suffered in particular. At the beginning of the war, over 100,000 Lutherans had been banished to the Russian interior. In 1918 and 1919, they returned to their war-ravaged country and torched villages and farms without any financial means. They felt doomed.[36] The American Lutheran Council had transmitted $200,000 for the purchasing of cattle and agricultural machinery, but this sum was not enough. By contrast, the United Protestant Church, whose center was in Poznań, had not been considered at all: the situation of its hospitals, nursery schools, orphanages, and homes for the disabled and elderly was precarious.[37]

32. For August Wilhelm Schreiber's report on Germany, see ibid., 15.

33. Ibid., 18.

34. See the report submittted by the president of the Chief Evangelical Church Council of Vienna on the situation in Austria, ibid., 69.

35. Ibid., 117.

36. See the report submitted by General Superintendent Julius Bursche of the Lutheran Church of Poland in Warsaw, ibid., 75.

37. See the report submitted by General Superintendent Paul Blau from Poznań, ibid., 75 ff.

Adolf Keller

The situation in St Petersburg and its environs, which now belonged to Soviet Russia, was catastrophic.[38] The same was true of the three Baltic states—Estonia, Latvia, and Lithuania—which had recently separated from Russia. Most church buildings had been destroyed during the war, and many clergymen and entire segments of the population had been displaced. The ruble had been devalued. The churches had partly lost their estates, and thus also their income. The Latvians, however, established a laudable principle, namely, that only those communities should receive foreign aid that had already made sacrifices to restore their churches in proportion to their resources.[39] Keller adopted this principle for his relief organization.

According to Keller's summary, European Protestantism was struggling for survival in fourteen countries.[40] The principal causes of this struggle were war-induced poverty, the division of integral church bodies as a result of newly established demarcation lines, and the state policies of some countries. Eluding control, existing aid dissipated the overall capacity of a country or church to lend support, and frequently directed it into accidental channels. Existing relief operations benefited those denominational churches most closely related to themselves.[41] From this, Keller drew the following conclusion:

> Supporting those parts of European Protestantism in need will remain one of the most essential tasks of the Protestant world for many years to come. The Continental European churches lending support . . . are unable to effectively combat the distress: its total number of 15 million souls in five countries faces around 50 million Protestants in 16 countries requiring help . . . Denominational support remains indispensable in future . . . The shared concern for the fate and the protection of European Protestantism as a whole is leading increasingly to associating the national-church or purely denominational perspective with an overall Protestant one, and to subordinating the former to the latter: for . . . a one-sided privileging of some churches creates bitterness and renders apparent the limits of Protestant love; failing such cooperation, energies will become dissipated . . . Such an overarching Protestant relief organization renders

38. See above, p. 48 and below, pp. 139–44.

39. See the report submitted by Bishop Karlis Irbe on the situation in Latvia, ibid., 60f.

40. Keller, *Zur Lage des Europäischen Protestantismus*, 156.

41. Ibid., 158.

indispensable a sense of togetherness among the European churches and enduring cooperation with American Protestantism . . . The solidarity shown amid this distress is the strongest means of promoting Protestant unification endeavors.[42]

The last sentence is especially noteworthy. From August 10 to 12, 1922, the envisaged "emergency conference" was held at Bethesda House in Copenhagen. Keller remarks that for the first time in the history of European Protestantism an official assembly of representatives of the European Protestant churches had gathered to discuss a shared European concern. In addition, a number of American Protestants, including representatives of the Federal Council and its committee for the cultivation of relations with the European churches, were in attendance at Bethesda.[43] The point in time for the conference was cleverly chosen, since most of the participants at the Bethesda conference would be traveling onward to the important Life and Work meeting, which was scheduled to take place in Helsingborg immediately afterwards.[44] While most participants at the Bethesda conference had a copy of *Zur Lage des Europäischen Protestantismus* (On the Situation of European Protestantism) in front of them during the sessions, the oral accounts of those representing the churches seeking assistance were so dramatic that they got under everyone's skin. The need for an interdenominational relief organization was undisputed.

However, no consensus was reached on the tasks of such an organization, since the future development of Europe was not foreseeable.[45] The organization was called the European Central Bureau for Relief (Europäische Zentralstelle für kirchliche Hilfsaktionen); it later became known as Inter-Church Aid. One conference participant suggested affiliating it with Life and Work.[46] Keller shared this view. Others hesitated, because it was unclear whether Life and Work would prove successful. Possible affiliation at a later date was thus envisaged. The conference participants unanimously voted in favor of the following resolution:

> This conference, consisting of 72 representatives of 37 European churches and church alliances in 20 countries, considers it desirable that in the face of the distress suffered by many European

42. Ibid., 160–61.

43. Keller, *Evangelisches Zusammenwirken*, 29–30. The World Mission Conference of 1910 at Edinburgh had not been organized directly by the churches themselves.

44. See above, pp. 66–67.

45. Keller, "Minutes of the Copenhagen Conference of 1922," 3ff. (NLAK C 34).

46. August Wilhelm Schreiber, "Minutes of the Copenhagen Conference," 4.

Protestant churches and their charities a general Protestant relief operation shall be organized and undertaken in a unified fashion. For this purpose, this conference hereby merges to become the representative of European Protestantism. For this purpose, it elects an executive committee, consisting of representatives of those churches that have issued invitations to this conference, and authorizes it to secure further members. This committee shall transfer the undertaking of such a relief operation to a central European office, which shall, however, not replace the relief organizations already existing in individual countries or churches. The Federation of Swiss Protestant Churches is hereby requested to assume responsibility for the organization of this central office with the support of the other churches.[47]

The latter request was Macfarland's. For the Swiss Federation Board, it was a matter of honor not to disappoint this trust.[48] Thus, it was given special responsibility and so to speak the supervision of the relief organization. The posts were filled in personal union: Otto Herold, president of the Federation, became president of the Central Bureau, and Keller, secretary of the Federation, was appointed director of the Central Bureau.[49] Consequently, the Federation and the relief agency were closely intertwined. Since the agency received half of its funding from Protestant Switzerland, it considered it to be its own.

Alfred Jörgensen, a Danish theologian, was appointed vice-president of the Central Bureau. He remained in office until its closure in 1945. The international Executive Committee met once a year to take basic decisions and to advise Keller. Important committee members, along with Herold and Jörgensen, included the Briton Thomas Nightingale, the Scotsmen John Robert Fleming and James Macdonald Webster, the Dutch professors of theology Jan A. Cramer and Franz M. Böhl, John Nuelsen, the Methodist bishop responsible for Europe, and Charles Macfarland. Committee members thus represented the donor churches, and they were all Protestants. Membership soon expanded to Finland, Iceland, the Waldensian Church of Uruguay, and the two Protestant communities of Egypt. On their accession, the latter donated the handsome sum of 9,000 Swiss francs. Keller established the office of the Central Bureau in Zurich. In Jacques Straub he found a trustworthy and longstanding treasurer—he

47. Keller, "Minutes of the Copenhagen Conference," 6 (NLAK C 34).

48. Board of the Federation of Swiss Protestant Churches to its members, September 30, 1922 (BAR J.2.257 1449/157).

49. Keller, *Evangelisches Zusammenwirken*, 33.

remained in office until 1945. Oskar Bauhofer, a young theologian who had recently returned from a year of study at UTS, became Keller's assistant. Tina Keller lent her husband full support in his new role, to which he was ideally suited. No sooner had it started operations than the Central Bureau resembled a beehive.

"EVIDENCE OF AN ECUMENICAL ETHOS": EMERGENCY AID IN EUROPE

Since the duties and responsibilities of the Bureau had remained unclarified, Keller established his own guidelines: the allocation of financial assistance depended upon the efforts undertaken by applicants. Contacts with local churches were meant to safeguard the equal distribution of monies. Other than funding requests from members of the clergy, applications from charitable organizations, schools, and future theologians were considered. Beneficiaries were required to account for the use of donations, and donor churches were kept informed about how their monies were used.[50]

Keller immediately traveled to Germany, Austria, Czechoslovakia, and France to assess the destruction wreaked in these countries. He also spoke to those directly affected.[51] He made at least written contact with other regions in distress, and also maintained extensive correspondence with donors. Other duties and responsibilities included educational work and propaganda. He published articles and distributed pamphlets. He soon realized how forgetful people were: "It is quite simply necessary to incite interest time and again."[52] One example in this respect was a study on the appalling situation of children in the former warring countries.[53] Propaganda work and fundraising became enduring tasks.

Raising funds for Germany proved difficult. Keller pointed out that the war had also caused great suffering to Germany. In a paper written in English, and thus aimed at an American readership, he drew attention to the difficult situation of German professors of theology, among other reasons, as a result of inflation. He referred to the accounts of Adolf

50. Keller, Memorandum titled "Die Schaffung einer Zentralstelle für kirchliche Hilfswerke" (NLAK C 2,3).

51. Keller, *Die europäische Zentralstelle 1922–1932*, 5.

52. Keller, *Von protestantischer Not und Hilfe*, 28–29.

53. "Annual Report of the Federation of Swiss Protestant Churches for 1926/27," 15.

Deissmann and Martin Rade, two professors of theology who were above suspicion:[54] there was a desperate shortage of food, clothing, and coal. Family members or professors themselves were often sick. Many had taken their impoverished parents into their homes. Purchasing books and inviting students to "open evenings" were no longer possible. Most professors were receiving only one third of their prewar salary.

Until the summer of 1924, the Central Bureau raised 1.7 million Swiss francs, a staggering amount at the time.[55] 660,000 Swiss francs came from Protestant Switzerland.[56] This sum was even more astonishing given that it was raised immediately after the fundraising campaign organized by the Federation of Swiss Protestant Churches from 1920 to 1922.[57] Evidently, the new relief organization earned immediate trust in Switzerland. Only in the United States were more funds raised, where 800,000 Swiss francs were collected during the same period, the majority by the Presbyterian and Reformed churches.

Donations from the non-Anglican churches in Great Britain totaled 25,000 Swiss francs, those from the Netherlands amounted to 8,000 Swiss francs, and only minor sums arrived from the other European donor countries.[58] While they were prepared to lend moral support to the Central Bureau, they granted no more than symbolic financial assistance. In the wake of the war, some were either in a state of ruin themselves or they favored their existing denominational relief agencies. However, the Central Bureau was often used as a fund management agency by these organizations, since Keller maintained a wide range of excellent contacts.[59] The Swiss and American churches were—and remained—by far the most important donors of the Central Bureau. The major share of the funds were tied, that is, designated for a specific purpose. Keller fought to attain some latitude in this respect, since he was forever discovering people in

54. Keller, "Statement Concerning the Condition of The Theological and Assistant Professors in Central Europe" (probably written in 1923) (NLAK C 22).

55. This would exceed the tenfold monetary value today.

56. "Annual Report of the Federation of Swiss Protestant Churches for 1922/23," 6; see also Keller, *Von protestantischer Not und Hilfe*, 38.

57. See above, p. 48.

58. For a statement of accounts and a general overview, see Keller, *Von protestantischer Not und Hilfe*, 33–40. In 1926/27, donations totaling 53,000 Swiss francs were received from Great Britain. For the figures for Switzerland, see the "Annual Report of the Federation of Swiss Protestant Churches for the Year 1923/24," 12.

59. For instance, Keller forwarded the sum of $195.50, received from the Huguenot Society in Richmond (USA), to Pastor Merle d'Aubigné in Neuilly-sur-Seine. See Macfarland to Keller, May 29, 1925 (PHS NCC RG 18 73/9).

need who had been overlooked. Immediate action was often called for. Incidentally, the administrative expenses and salaries of the Central Bureau amounted to only three percent of its total expenditure; in this respect, it is worth remembering that Keller's salary was paid by the Federal Council.[60]

Protestants in sixteen countries benefited from the distribution of the aforementioned 1.7 million Swiss francs in the years 1923 and 1924. France headed the list of recipient countries with 600,000 Swiss francs. Upon Keller's recommendation, the Federation of French Churches established a branch office for the distribution of funds. Similar offices were set up in Germany, Austria, and Hungary. The second largest sum—423,000 Swiss francs—was allocated to Germany, partly to the local "central agency," partly to specific communities, facilities, and individuals. Austria and Hungary each received 60,000 Swiss francs. Czechoslovakia and Poland received 55,000 and 44,000 Swiss francs respectively. These countries were followed by Romania, Yugoslavia, Belgium, and Italy. Russia, Lithuania, Greece, Latvia, and Spain were granted sums ranging only between 6,000 and 2,500 Swiss francs. Estonia had to make do with merely 250 Swiss francs. Due to currency differences, "the miracle" of little turning into very much also occurred.[61] The Assyrian Christians received 50 Swiss francs.[62] In their case, Keller for the first time violated the requirement that the recipients of financial aid had to belong to the Protestant faith. Providing emergency relief took priority, as discussed below.

Owing to the generous assistance of the American Quakers, who considered not only their own denomination worthy of support, Keller was able to raise 175,000 Swiss francs for the benefit of Protestant children's relief agencies in Germany. This sum was significantly greater than a drop in the ocean.[63] The cooperation between the Central Bureau and the Deutsche Pfarrhaushilfe (German Protestant Ministers Fund) was also greatly appreciated: the latter organization, to which the Central Bureau allocated considerable sums, had been established to support Protestant clergymen and auxiliary preachers in need. A member of the Bureau's committee was appointed as a fully entitled member to the board of the Pfarrhaushilfe.[64] For Adolf Deissmann, the activities of the Central Bureau

60. See above, p. 63 and n. 7.

61. Keller, *Die europäische Zentralstelle 1922–1932*, 8.

62. Keller, *Von protestantischer Not und Hilfe*, 34–35. On the Assyrians, see below, pp. 136–38.

63. Ibid., 16.

64. "Annual Report of the Federation of Swiss Protestant Churches for 1923/24," 11.

in Germany were among the little lights amid the darkness of the postwar years.[65]

After receiving immediate substantial assistance from the Central Bureau, the heavily destroyed French Protestant churches soon required further urgent assistance. Floods in the Cévennes mountains, the center of Protestantism in southern France, had caused severe damage. The Central Bureau took immediate action. In 1927, Keller collected donations among Swiss clerymen for their impoverished French colleagues. Donations amounted "only" to 18,500 Swiss francs—the remuneration of Swiss pastors at the time was also modest. Nevertheless, Emil Morel, president of the Federation of French Churches, sent an exuberant letter of gratitude: "The gesture which our colleagues from throughout Switzerland have made with such readiness and discretion, has surprised and touched us more than we can say . . . We are therefore profoundly aware of your demonstration of brotherly sympathy, which will strongly bolster our pastors and lend many of them very timely support. This act will remain inscribed in the already long and beautiful history of Swiss protestant goodwill toward Huguenot France."[66]

The existence of small Protestant churches in predominantly Catholic Eastern Europe was under severe threat from state policies directed chiefly at foreign ethnic groups and languages, and thus also affected Protestantism. No other problem, Keller observed, more strongly emphasized the need for Protestant cooperation. The protests of single churches would bear no fruit, he realized. Only a response from Protestantism as a whole possessed such moral weight that it could not be ignored by governments.[67] In conjunction with other organizations, Keller managed to somewhat improve the legal status of Protestants in Poland. In one case, the closure of a church hospice was prevented by adopting a "policy of commotion against Poland's regrettable transgressions."[68] Obviously, material assistance was also provided: "The outstanding piece of relief work in 1928 was our emergency campaign for 'Ebenezer,' the orphanage of the Polish evangelical church, at Cieszyn. In less than a month, $7,000 was raised to meet a sudden payment on the property demanded by the Polish

65. Keller, *Von protestantischer Not und Hilfe*, 24.

66. Emil Morel to Keller, July 22, 1927 (NLAK C 23).

67. "Annual Report of the Federation of Swiss Protestant Churches for 1924/25," 13.

68. Keller to Söderblom, February 13, 1931 (NLAK C 32).

Government and to complete the half-finished orphanage building."[69] Keller attended to the needs of theology students in Warsaw, who, as the responsible dean of faculty confirmed, often subsisted only on bread and tea for weeks.[70] One Bible seminary reported that it could continue to exist only with the help of the Central Bureau, and to retain at least some of its staff.[71]

Czechoslovakia had been largely spared during the war. Protestants were a minority; moreover, they were split into several churches. But within four years, the "Czech brothers" grew by sixty percent to a sizeable 250,000 members. New churches had to be built and additional clergymen recruited. The Central Bureau contributed not only to bearing these costs, but also to those needed by the Protestant Faculty in Prague, whose student enrollment exceeded that of the country's nine Catholic seminaries.[72] Keller attached great significance to the training of young theologians, chiefly in Catholic-dominated countries, particularly in Poland, where Catholicism was the state religion.

In staunchly Catholic Spain, there was a minute and constantly threatened Protestant minority. From 1870 on, Fritz Fliedner, a German pastor, had established a church, youth center, orphanage, bookshop, school, and the El Porvenir Grammar School in Madrid. His son Theodor—one of Keller's friends from his student days in Berlin—had continued his father's work from 1901 on. In late 1924, on a visit to America, Keller heard that the school was in desperate financial need owing to the foreclosure of a mortgage. Keller's American friends knocked on several doors that were reserved for particularly urgent cases like this. But, as Keller reports, he left New York without hearing whether these efforts had borne fruit. On Christmas Eve, Keller was assured the sum of $10,000.[73] The telegram was forwarded to Pastor Fliedner, who was preaching in a rural community on Christmas Day. He discovered it on reaching the pulpit to begin his sermon. Tears rolled down his face; aghast, the congregation believed a great misfortune had occurred.[74] The school had been saved.

69. Cavert, *Twenty Years of the Church Federation*, 127.

70. Keller, "Aus meinem Leben," 121.

71. The passages are taken from letters of thanks. See Keller, *Von protestantischer Not und Hilfe*, 24ff.

72. "Report on the meeting of the Executive Committee, July 20 to 25, 1934 in Edinburgh," 10 (BAR J.2.257 1245/133).

73. Keller, "Aus meinem Leben," 116; the donation was made by Arthur James Curtis, an American railroad entrepreneur.

74. Keller, *Die europäische Zentralstelle 1922–1932*, 8–9.

One of Keller's interventions in Italy enjoyed only limited success: northeastern Friuli had been awarded to Italy at the end of the war. The "Treffener institutions" in the village of Russiz, situated near the town of Gorizia—a retirement home, a school, two children's homes, and a home for alcoholics together with a large estate—had been confiscated. The institutions had been founded by Countess Elvine de La Tour, a prominent Protestant. The Protestant children were driven away, whereupon Catholic ones moved into the dormitories. Subsequently, the Executive Committee of the Central Bureau dispatched Keller to Mussolini to bring to his attention the stir that the dispossession had caused in the large Protestant countries. Following the meeting, the Italian government offered compensation, but only by way of a paltry sum.[75] Keller described his audience with Mussolini at the Palazzo Chigi thus: "It was a memorable occasion when I entered the large hall, at whose end Mussolini was seated at his desk. Obviously, the occasion was arranged such that the visitor would be greeted by his steady and fiery gaze. We spoke French, although I could have held the conversation in Italian. I preferred this powerful man to have to speak to me in a foreign language."[76]

By the end of 1924, the most severe distress in Protestant Europe had been alleviated. But Keller made it clear that the Central Bureau needed to continue operating for a few more years.[77] Three tendencies emerged during its continued existence: first, the focus on specific church-related tasks. These included supporting pastors' families and deacons (social workers of the church), preserving threatened church welfare institutions, assisting individual communities and schools, and fostering young theologians. Providing general emergency aid had to be left to other organizations.[78] Second, the Central Bureau devoted itself increasingly to development aid.[79] For example, there were 220,000 Protestants in newly established Yugoslavia, where Hans Oskar Rihner, a Swiss minister, had founded various social institutions now requiring urgent assistance. On his visit to Yugoslavia, Keller gained firsthand evidence about how well Rihner worked.[80] In Novi Vrbas, for instance, Rihner had established the

75. Ibid., 9. The remuneration corresponded to only one tenth of the value.

76. Keller, "Aus meinem Leben," 118.

77. Keller, *Von protestantischer Not und Hilfe*, 27.

78. "Annual Report of the Federation of Swiss Protestant Churches for 1924/25," 13.

79. "Minutes of the Assembly of Delegates of the Federation of Swiss Protestant Churches," 1926, 25 (BAR J.2.257, 285 Volume 1, 1921–1930).

80. Keller to Alphons Koechlin, January 8, 1926 (BAR J.2.257 1437/155).

first church welfare institutions in Yugoslavia. Keller arranged for eighteen Swiss deaconesses (Protestant nursing sisters) to work under Rihner's supervision, partly in nursing homes, partly in retirement and children's homes of the church. Within his "leadership programme,"[81] he introduced training scholarships for Yugoslav church social workers, as discussed below. Further, hospital amenities and equipment were shipped in support of developing infrastructure. Placing great emphasis on sustainable assistance, Keller supported Rihner for many years.

Keller also considered the development of a Protestant press indispensable. With reference to the excellent Catholic press, he once asked: "How long have we still to wait, until the necessity of a general protestant Press Service is seen?"[82] He envisaged a joint Life and Work magazine.

Thirdly, the Central Bureau provided networking services: "The central office is constantly in contact with numerous churches, and exchanging ideas with them; it has become an information hub for every kind of research and activity in the inter-church domain." Occasionally, Keller also served as an intermediary between churches, relief agencies, and government bodies, for instance, in the case of a German youth worker who had been expelled from Algeria for no reason.[83]

Keller repeatedly emphasized that the alleviation of material need was in itself insufficient. Lending spiritual support was just as important. Further, the relief organization had to be seen as evidence of an ecumenical ethos and of an emerging spiritual cohesion within Protestantism. Thus, he wrote: "The association of outer and inner need, as well as general cooperativeness, can lead to a community of new tasks. This is possible only if we believe in the cause and in the kingdom of our Lord Jesus Christ as the children of the same Father in Heaven, as brothers beyond the confines of nation, race, creed, church, national differences, and denominational peculiarity."[84] Thus, Keller saw the Central Bureau increasingly as a collaborative and mutual venture rather than as an exclusively Protestant one.—The three tendencies, Keller thus described by the end of 1924, are showing that there was a lot more to do. And he did the entire work with only one assistant.

81. See below, pp. 82–88.

82. Keller, "From the Roman Catholic Field," 80.

83. Keller to Friedrich von Bodelschwingh Jr., April 14, 1928 (BAR J.2.257 1447/156). Keller also turned to the Foreign Office of the Swiss Confederation and the Association of French Churches in this matter. Keller knew Bodelschwingh since he had been a student.

84. Keller, *Von protestantischer Not und Hilfe*, 23–24.

"LEADERSHIP PROGRAMME"—
WITH THE ASSISTANCE OF THE UNITED STATES

The two mainstays of the European Central Bureau for Relief were the Federation of Swiss Protestant Churches and the Federal Council of the Churches of Christ in America. Its founding conference, held in Copenhagen in 1922, was attended by important American churchmen, including William A. Brown and Charles Macfarland. They were impressed: "It was the first time, in modern history, that the church bodies of Europe have ever met in an officially representative gathering. The conference had been carefully prepared by Dr. Adolf Keller . . . , and its success was largely due to his unselfish voluntary service . . . It was an impressive gathering, prayerful, mutually sympathetic, brotherly. It showed how close we may be brought together by mutual suffering and need."[85] Further, the Central Bureau would make it possible "primarily to afford a center from which the American Churches can unitedly approach the Churches of Europe in matters of relief. Its significance for the future ought to extend far beyond its present purpose."[86] The Americans were convinced of the ecumenical significance of the Central Bureau.

Besides the Federation of Swiss Protestant Churches, the Americans assumed particular responsibility for the relief organization. They opened a branch office in New York, and established an American Committee to support it. The branch office was affiliated with rather than incorporated into the Federal Council. Its main tasks were propaganda and fundraising. The theologian Chauncy W. Goodrich was appointed director, and he oversaw the work of three members of staff, including the industrious Antonia Froendt. She was responsible for written correspondence with Keller. A few years later, she was appointed managing director of the branch office. Although the Federal Council heralded Keller in 1922 as "one of the outstanding figures in European Protestantism," he was not given carte blanche.[87] On his visit to Zurich in 1923, Macfarland closely examined the accounts and Keller's work. He credited Keller with utmost efficiency, as recorded in the annual report of the Federal Council for the year 1923: "Dr. Keller's qualifications for such a work are quite unusual. Owing to his prominence in church affairs he was at the close of the war the one naturally appointed to successive conferences of representatives

85. Macfarland in Cavert, *United in Service*, 149–50.

86. "Annual Report of the Federal Council for the Year 1922," 14 (PHS NCC RG 18, Folder 12).

87. Ibid., 13–14.

of churches and gained at once the esteem and respect of those associated with him for his personal qualities and his abilities as a leader."[88]

In early 1923, the Federal Council of the Churches of Christ in America requested Keller to embark on a lecture tour of the United States, since it had been unable to win the support of many of its members for its involvement in the Central Bureau. Hopes were pinned on Keller's powers of persuasion. His principal task would be to provide information. Keller hesitated about accepting the invitation, since he was reluctant to leave his family for three months. Moreover, he was still serving at St Peter's at the time. Eventually, however, he undertook the tour, traveling from city to city from April through July 1923, addressing church committees, clergy, missionary and women's associations, theological faculties, business-men's clubs, youth groups, labor unions, and speaking on numerous radio stations. He wrote articles for daily newspapers and church magazines, including *Christian Work, The Congregationalist, Presbyterian Magazine, The Observer, The Reformed Church Messenger*, and the Federal Council's *Bulletin*.[89]

On his tour, Keller was forced to recognize that there were "thousands of ministers who know better what is going on in a Mission station in China than what is the condition in the mother-countries of the Reformation."[90] Some churches reacted negatively to Keller's speeches, either because they favored denominationalist assistance or because they were suffering financial difficulties owing to the postwar recession. The newly awakened political isolationism also took its effect. Considering these factors, then, it was a success that between 1923 and 1927 the following churches joined the New York branch office: "The Presbyterian Church (U.S.A.), Presbyterian Church U.S., Reformed Church in America, Reformed Church in the U.S., United Presbyterian Church, United Church of Canada, Presbyterian Church in Canada, Congregational Church, Protestant Episcopal Church, Methodist Church, Methodist Church South, Church of the Moravian Brethren and the Evangelical Synod."[91] Among the missing churches were the Lutheran Church, part of the Anglican Church, and the more funda-mentalist denominations.

88. Goodrich in the "Annual Report of the Federal Council for the Year 1923," 87 (PHS NCC RG 18).

89. Keller, *Hands across the Sea*, 8.

90. Ibid., 74.

91. "Annual Report of the Federal Council for the Year 1927," 74 (PHS NCC RG 18).

On his return journey from the United States, Keller met the British members of the Executive Committee of the Central Bureau in London. He also paid a courtesy visit to the Anglican Church, which thus far had remained uninvolved. In his meeting with George Bell, Dean of Canterbury and an ecumenist, Keller made a clever move in pointing out that relief efforts focused not on the Protestant churches themselves but rather on their threatened social welfare institutions and organizations. Nevertheless, quite some time lapsed before his intervention bore fruit.[92]

No sooner had he returned to Switzerland than Keller was summoned by the Federal Council of the Churches of Christ in America to return to the United States. His presence during the envisaged fundraising campaign of the American churches in the autumn was indispensable: "To both Dr. Macfarland and myself [Chauncy W. Goodrich] it seems of the highest importance that you should reach New York at the earliest date for which you planned . . . Letters to nearly 70,000 ministers are now going out and articles are appearing in the press preparing the public mind so that when you reach the United States and begin to meet audiences face to face you will find yourself here at the very 'nick of time' for crystalizing a general interest into helpful action. It is particularly at this moment that you can give the push that will count the most."[93]

Reluctantly—his fourth child, Esther, had just been born[94]—Keller complied with the Council's request. What complicated matters was that accepting this invitation would effectively terminate his office as a parish minister. In a moving service at St Peter's, the congregation and Keller took leave of each other. 150 young members of the parish came to bid him farewell.

The fundraising campaign in the United States in late 1923 was followed by another in late 1924. The campaign "itinerary"[95] reads as follows: November 25: "With Dr. Macfarland to the dinner of the Council of Foreign Relations at Sherry's"; November 26: "Conference with Mr. Williams and Dr. Goodrich"; November 27 (Thanksgiving): "Opportunity to write the article requested by Dr. Speer.[96] Latter part of the day at Dr.

92. Three years later, Keller wrote to Macfarland before traveling to England to lecture there: "We should use this opportunity to raise greater interest in the British public," Zurich, January 18, 1926 (PHS NCC RG 18 73/10).

93. Goodrich to Keller, November 30, 1923 (NLAK C 23).

94. Keller to the Board of the Federation of Swiss Protestant Churches, November 7, 1923 (BAR J.2.257 1439/156).

95. Keller's itinerary is reproduced here in abbreviated form (NLAK C 22).

96. Robert F. Speer, a distinguished Presbyterian, was president of the Federal Council of the Churches of Christ in America.

Goodrich's home for dinner and the night"; November 28: "Conference with Dr. Beach, Dr. Goodrich and probably Dr. Chapman on Ukraine";[97] November 29: "To Buffalo by train"; Sunday, November 30: "Speak in the morning at the Central Presbyt. Church. In the afternoon give the Sunday wireless service conducted by the Buffalo Council of churches. Evening service before a group of Lutheran churches"; December 1: "Speak at the lunch of the Presbyt. Fellowship Club, preceding mass meeting in the afternoon of Presbytery of Buffalo where the topic 'War and Peace' will be discussed. Evening train back to New York"; December 2: "Leave for Atlanta after ten o'clock."

In financial terms, Keller's fundraising in the United States proved successful: in the fiscal year of 1925/26, two thirds of the total revenue of the Central Bureau (634,000 Swiss francs) came from the United States.[98] From 1922 to 1927, the American branch office received donations over $742,000, which amounted to approximately five million Swiss francs at the time: "America has been generous to Europe; but in proportion to their resources the American Churches have not done as much for their sister Churches in Europe as have the Churches of Switzerland, for instance," the report of the American Committee remarks self-critically.[99] Keller approached his propaganda campaigns with psychological acumen, thus, for instance, opening a radio speech in Buffalo as follows: "Do you know how happy this country is? You live in comfortable homes, you can give a good education to your children, you are well fed and clothed. Many of your churches are gorgeous and wonderful buildings and God's word is accessible to all who wish to hear it . . . And then the children [in Europe]! This present young generation has really to pay the cost of the war. A great menace of tuberculosis is hanging over a whole generation of young people. You should have seen these children."[100]

In *Hands across the Sea*, a bulletin specifically addressed to an American audience, Keller describes the predicament of a Protestant welfare institution in Poland struggling to meet the needs of one hundred and fifty

97. On the situation in the Ukraine, see below, pp. 88–92.

98. "Accounts of the European Central Bureau for Church Relief Work for the Year beginning April 10, 1925 and ending May 20, 1926" (PHS NCC RG 18 73/10). The sum of 53,000 Swiss francs came from Egypt!

99. "Report of the American Committee of the Central Bureau for the Relief of the Churches of Europe," in the "Annual Report of the Federal Council for the Year 1927," 74.

100. Keller, radio speech delivered in Buffalo on November 30, 1924, ms., 3 and 8b (NLAK C 22).

orphans, and blind and disabled persons that lacked food supplies.[101] His bulletins also included photographs—whose effect he was well aware of. In his speech before the Fifth General Assembly of the Federal Council in Atlanta in December 1924, which he delivered without notes, as became speakers in America, Keller emphasized the ecumenical significance of the relief organization:

> It is very regrettable that not all American Protestant Churches see the great opportunities which our cause presents to them. The question is not only whether European Churches can get relief for their suffering pastors, theological students and evangelical institutions. This whole relief work has a spiritual aspect exceeding by far the special interests of American Churches in their own denominational sister churches in Europe. The question is whether there exists an American Protestantism strong and united enough to take the lead in a statesmanlike Protestant policy of construction and whether a deeper and larger feeling of Protestant responsibility is in formation.[102]

He also spoke of the shortage of spiritual leaders in Eastern Europe, particularly of professors of theology. The scattered congregations had to be visited, encouraged, and spiritually strengthened. In Germany, eighty-eight Protestant welfare institutions had been forced to close since the end of the war, while the Catholics had established over seven hundred such facilities: "Against this Roman Catholic advance we do not wish to struggle with political or wordly means. The only thing which we can do and are allowed to do is to strengthen our churches, to unite forces, to deepen our religious life."[103] And finally: "We do not care for denominational interests in a moment when the whole house is burning."[104] The Atlanta General Assembly subsequently sent a "Message to the European Churches," formulated in German, in which it expressed its sympathy for the suffering churches and its willingness to cooperate with the Central Bureau.[105]

101. Keller, "Poland," 31–32.

102. Keller, "A Visit to America," 21.

103. Ibid., 23. See further "Report of the Federal Council for 1920–1924," 53–54.

104. Keller, "The Crisis of European Protestantism," 24–25.

105. "Message to the European Churches of the 5th General Assembly of the Federal Council, Atlanta, December 3 to 9, 1924" (BAR J.2.257 1438/157).

One of Keller's most original ventures was the "leadership pro-gramme." Its principal aim was to promote the training of church leaders in Eastern Europe:[106]

> Aid to theological students, who are mostly poor. Aid to dor-mitories, students' homes. Scholarships for enabling students to study in foreign countries.—Aid to professors and assistant professors, especially in view of helping them to come in con-tact with foreign movements, to give their whole time to the education and studies, to buy the books necessary for their work.—Aid to faculties, preachers seminaries, especially in view of completing their libraries and the subscription of theological periodicals . . . Travelling Fellowships for ministers, professors and assistant professors, who profit more from such journeys than young students.—Education of social workers, deacon-esses, evangelists, "levites," education of deaconesses and par-ish sisters for such countries as Yugoslavia, where such work is nearly unknown or just beginning.[107]

The program enjoyed an enthusiastic response in New York: "One of the most important tasks of the Bureau is to help our sister Churches overseas to develop the Christian leadership of the future."[108] In 1926, its budget ran to $90,000.[109] Until early 1927, the Central Bureau awarded over a hundred traveling bursaries to students from Eastern Europe.[110] Keller attended personally to those scholarship holders who came to Switzerland.

He approached the Rockefeller Foundation about the "leadership programme." His application for support was reviewed by several commit-tees.[111] Impatiently, he wrote to Macfarland: "Your silence about the Rock-efeller people is mortifying. Please tell them that we have here some 150 demands for help from all sides and that my heart is bleeding sometimes when I have to say No."[112] Then, he received welcome news: "Mr. Rock-

---

106. Keller, *Die Europäische Zentralstelle*, 12 and 17; see also Keller to Van Du-sen, presumably autumn 1955 (UTS Presidential papers, 25/3, corr. Henry P. Van Dusen–Keller).

107. Keller, "Our New Programme," 79–80.

108. Cavert, *Twenty Years of the Church Federation*, 124.

109. The sum corresponded to 540,000 Swiss francs, approximately about 6 mil-lion Swiss francs today; see Kenneth Miller, "Annual Report of the Federal Council for the Year 1926," 80 (PHS NCC RG 18 79/15).

110. Keller to George Bell, May 3, 1927 (LPL Bell 18 Part 1 f. 50).

111. Macfarland to Keller, January 2, 1925 (PHS NCC RG 18 73/9).

112. Keller to Macfarland, January 17, 1925 (ibid.).

efeller himself is warmly interested." Rockefeller was prepared to donate $50,000.[113] Only after Keller had submitted a detailed list of his projects did a liberating and at the same time somewhat disappointing telegram arrive in June 1925: "Rockefeller has given twenty-five thousand."[114] The donation went toward funding the "leadership programme" and the development of Protestant welfare institutions in Eastern Europe.[115] In 1926, Rockefeller sent Keller, whom he knew personally, $15,000 for scholarships, presumably from his private coffers.[116] In 1927, the Central Bureau was able to award a hundred scholarships, thanks to a new legacy from the Rockefeller Foundation. In 1928, funds enabled many young people to embark on studies in their own country; other received scholarships for further training in Switzerland, France, Germany, and Austria.[117]

One good example of the successful cooperation between America and the Central Bureau is the assistance lent to Galicia. Located in present-day northwestern Ukraine and Ukrainian-speaking, this region was awarded to Poland at the end of the war, after the downfall of the Habsburg Empire. Warfare raged here for another three years, now between the Ukrainian and Polish armies. Numerous German Protestant parishes, many Protestant schools, and two grammar schools, one in Lemberg,[118] the other in Stanislau,[119] had existed in Volhynia and Galicia since the eighteenth century. Moreover, Theodor Zöckler, the German Lutheran Bishop of the United Protestant Church, had founded Protestant welfare institutions, an apprentice workshop, and even a factory for agricultural machinery in Stanislau, his place of residence.[120] During the war, he was forced to flee the area with his 350 charges—among them elderly, sick, and disabled persons, as well as war orphans.[121] On his return to Stanislau, he discovered that the facilities had suffered severe damage. Already in 1920, he sent a first appeal for help to Keller, whereupon the Federation of Swiss

113. Goodrich to Keller, February 17, 1925 (ibid.).

114. Antonia Froendt to Keller, June 13, 1925 (ibid.). See also Goodrich to Keller, June 18, August 7, and October 6, 1925 (ibid.).

115. "Annual Report of the Federation of Swiss Protestant Churches for 1925/26," 16.

116. Keller to Miller, July 27, 1926 (PHS NCC RG 18 73/10).

117. Keller, *Die Europäische Zentralstelle für kirchliche Hilfsaktionen*, 12.

118. Lemberg today = L'viv.

119. Stanislau today = Ivano Frankivs'k.

120. Wagner, *Ukrainische Evangelische Kirchen*, 34. See also Zöckler, *Ein Leben für die Kinder*.

121. For Theodor Zöckler's report on Galicia, see Keller, *Zur Lage des Europäischen Protestantismus*, 81.

Protestant Churches transmitted funds.[122] Following the establishment of the Central Bureau, Zöckler received regular donations.

Parish council of an Ukrainian Protestant congregation
(from Adolf Keller, *Von Geist und Liebe*, fig. 24)

In 1926, Keller visited Galicia for the first time, accompanied by the American theologian David Nelson Beach and by Basil Kusiv, the minister at the Ukrainian-Presbyterian Church in Newark, New Jersey. The group visited Zöckler, and particularly the Ukrainian Protestant parishes that had been established after the war and whose membership already totaled approximately 30,000. The parishes had sprung from the missionary work of American Ukrainians and of Ukrainians who had become acquainted with the Bible as prisoners of war in Germany. What Keller witnessed in the Ukrainian Protestant congregations in Galicia reminded him of early Christianity:

> An old couple gave their house for holding the service in their single room while they slept in a barn beside the house. I attended a service in that room. It was filled with strange people . . . : the women barefooted in their sheepskins, beautifully embroidered, the men, with full, sympathetic faces, in ancient costumes, all singing their Ukrainian hymns with an indescribable fervour and enthusiasm. The room was crowded, and, through the windows, more people from the outside of the house tried

122. Keller, *Die Europäische Zentralstelle für kirchliche Hilfsaktionen*, 6.

to catch the preacher's words. In another village I heard Mr. and Mrs. Buczak [Lev Bychak] preach. A large congregation came together; whole families arrived on their waggons with wife and children, and brought their food to spend the day at the place of their common service, because they lived so far away. In a village near Stanislau the congregation and the pastor built their church with their own hands, and the chapel was just ready for the inauguration, when I arrived.[123]

The Polish government declared the Ukrainian Protestant parishes unlawful. Further pressure on the parishes was mounted by the Greek-Catholic Church, which was united with Rome and to which the majority of the Galician population belonged. In Keller's view, an independent Protestant Ukrainian Church could not exist, "not only because of the just mentioned legal difficulties, but also because the young Movement lacked the leaders and the experience necessary to build up a Church of its own."[124] Zöckler's long-established Church was discriminated, but in principle recognized by the state. He agreed to take the Protestant Ukrainians under his wing, and was assured international support: "The European Central Bureau has formed an Interdenominational Ukrainian Council, consisting of one representative from Lutheranism, a representative from the Presbyterian Alliance, one from the Central Bureau [Keller], Dr. Zöckler and a Ukrainian."[125]

The "leadership programme" was now afforded an opportunity to prove its merits: whatever the circumstances, Keller was determined to prevent the movement from sliding into sectarianism. Besides promoting the training of ministers and parish elders, his other projects included a translation of the Bible into the Ukrainian language and the publication of a multilingual songbook. A new form of Protestant churchdom emerged: Protestant in its faith, it was Orthodox in its liturgy, cult, and customs.[126] On the Ukrainian Council, Keller enjoyed an exceptionally cordial working relationship with the theologian Robert E. Speer, one of the most important American churchmen.[127]

123. Keller, *Religious Revival*, 6.

124. Ibid., 4.

125. Macfarland to Keller, May 6, 1926 (PHS NCC RG 18 73/10).

126. Wagner, *Ukrainische Evangelische Kirchen*, 54.

127. Keller to Speer, August 31, 1931 (PHS 68–0221 BFM/COEMAR 1 of 5 1790 1936–1939). Speer was responsible for "The Board of Foreign Missions of the Presbyterian Church in the U.S.A." The Speer-Library at Princeton Theological Seminary is named in honor of Robert E. Speer.

The new church in Kolomyja
(photograph by Marianne Jehle-Wildberger, 2007)

But difficulties arose: there were dissenters. The Protestant movement split—against Keller's will—into Lutheran and Reformed (that is,
Presbyterian) wings. Further, the Catholic Church in Poland sought to
obstruct the dissemination of the Bible among the population. Protestant
preachers were attacked; Keller was extremely concerned. In 1933, he
visited Galicia again. Keller and Speer agreed to dispatch Basil Kusiv to
Galicia to serve as Reformed Superintendent. To Keller's relief, the situation gradually became more stable. In 1935, a divine service was held in

the Galician provincial town of Kolomyja, the center of the movement, to consecrate a large, new church, which had been built to replace the small church originally erected for the Protestant congregation.[128]

Then, World War II erupted. German and thereafter Russian troops invaded Galicia. The invasions spelled the end of the German and Ukrainian Evangelical churches. Kusiv returned to the United States, Zöckler to his native Germany. Keller wrote: "The situation of the 50 evangelical Ukrainian congregations . . . remains entirely in the darkness behind the iron curtain of the Russian occupation."[129] It was one of the saddest moments of his life, not least since he had committed such great effort to this cause. Gradually, reports seeped through that "thousands . . . were sent away to Turkistan or God knows where."[130] Some Ukrainian preachers were imprisoned, others deported, one was shot, and others were reported missing.[131] But then news arrived that a Protestant church elder had remained at his post and was serving his congregation under extremely perilous conditions.[132] In 1942, the Central Bureau sent food parcels to the Ukrainian preachers Bychak, Zurylo, Huculjak, and Maksumujk.[133] Thereafter a deafening silence ensued. Some of the Reformed Ukrainian congregations survived underground. Up to the age of ninety-nine, Fylymon Semeniuk, who was serving as a minister in Galicia when war broke out and later spent eleven years imprisoned in the Gulag Archipelago, was working on rebuilding the congregations—he died in 2011.[134] Supported by the Presbyterian Alliance, young Protestant pastors are once again working in the region today.

128. Today, the church is used by the Greek-Catholic Church.

129. Keller, "The Conditions of Evangelical Churches in Poland," December 15, 1939 (PHS 68–221 BFM/COEMAR 2 of 5 1790 1936–1939).

130. Keller, *Christian Europe Today*, 55.

131. Keller, "Memorandum IV: Über die Lage der ukrainischen Bewegung," August 14, 1940, 3 (BAR 1243/132).

132. "Minutes of the Conference of Swiss Relief Organizations, March 11, 1942," 2 (BAR J.2.257 1243/132). In a personal conversation with the author on April 3, 2007, Pastor Markus Wyss, commissioner of the Reformed Alliance for Galicia, mentioned that the congregation was called Murza Nikon.

133. Central Bureau headquarters in Geneva to the New York office, presumably July 1942 (NLAK C 2,2).

134. Personal message to the author from Pfarrer Markus Wyss, Spiegel bei Bern, fall 2011.

1925: STOCKHOLM, KELLER, AND THE GREAT MOMENT OF ECUMENISM

> Let us never forget that Bethesda was before Stockholm, and that Stockholm would not be what it is without Bethesda. Stockholm is like a great trumpet; before that, however, from the house of mercy in Copenhagen the fine sounds of a harp resounded over Europe, still bleeding from a thousand wounds and devastated by a gruesome human earthquake. We traveled to Helsingborg bearing these Bethesda sounds in our souls, and the first "official" meeting of the delegates of the four large areas of the Church [America, Great Britain, Continental Europe, the Orthodox World], which today form our world conference, reached beyond ecclesiastical officialdom and—by transcending this officialdom—soon entered a basic Christian atmosphere, the first beginnings of a brotherly mutual trust of those who knew . . . they were united in service.[135]

This praise of Keller's Central Bureau is from Adolf Deissmann's address delivered at the 1925 World Conference of Life and Work in Stockholm.

Together with Henry A. Atkinson, general secretary of Life and Work, Eugène Choisy, and Thomas Nightingale, Keller was among those responsible for preparing the conference.[136] Archbishop Nathan Söderblom remarked: "Perhaps one ought to say that the Swiss were those who have done most for our Meeting."[137] Elsewhere, he refers to "Evangelical Christianity in Switzerland as a leader and collaborator in our movement."[138] George Bell, Dean of Canterbury and an ecumenist of the first hour, praised the "invaluable assistance" that Atkinson and Keller had lent Stockholm.[139]

With thirteen delegates, the two and a half million Swiss Protestants enjoyed above-average representation at the Stockholm conference. Over 610 church delegates from thirty-seven nations representing three hundred million Christians were in attendance. These figures in themselves illustrate the substantial weight that Protestant Switzerland carried in the early years of Life and Work. Owing to his superior network of contacts

135. Deissmann, *Die Stockholmer Bewegung,* 117–18. See also the Conference of Life and Work at Helsingborg in 1922.

136. See above, p. 67.

137. Sundkler, *Nathan Söderblom,* 365.

138. Söderblom to Friedrich Wilhelm Hadorn, January 13, 1926 (NLAK C 32).

139. Bell, *Die Königsherrschaft Jesu Christi,* 28.

and knowledge of ecumenism, Keller was a highly coveted source of information at the conference. During the plenary sessions, he was seated on the platform beside Söderblom. In his role as host, the latter dominated the conference. However, Charles Macfarland, general secretary of the Federal Council, also deserves great credit for the first non-catholic world conference becoming a reality. Stockholm was a milestone within the history of Christianity.

The conference began with a divine service at the Stockholm Store Kirk:

> The *Te Deum* or the great chorale of the Reformation resounded mightily through the church. The German sang "Ein feste Burg," the Frenchman beside me "C'est un rempart que notre Dieu," the Englishman behind me "A Mighty Fortress Is Our God," the Waldensian "Rocca forte è il nostro Dio," and from somewhere I even heard the Greek "Theos to phrourion imon aspis en tis kindynis." Different words were uttered, but in the same spirit; different languages, but *one* melody; different temperaments, but *one* will, to praise the eternal God with the human word and common prayer . . . When the great congregation, consisting of all churches, prayed the Our Father, each in his own language, everyone knew that in this submission to God . . . , we belonged closer together in spirit and in our love of Christ than in any dogmatic deliberations and practical ventures.[140]

There would be much to report about the conference. But suffice it to say that Macfarland set everyone at ease by delivering his speech in both German and French, thereby contributing to unpoisoning the atmosphere between the former war enemies.[141]

As Keller had anticipated, however, there were problems. In his eyes, Leonhard Ragaz, the most consequential representative of the religious social movement in Switzerland, should have been at the conference. Keller sought to obtain a personal invitation, but Söderblom declined his request.[142] Vice versa, Keller observed that pietist circles and friends of Karl Barth in Germany raised theological reservations.[143] He advised Söderblom to consider this, "if there is still time." Otherwise, he felt, their efforts would be in vain: "I hear already at the door the feet of those that

140. Keller, *Von Geist und Liebe*, 210.

141. Deissmann, *Die Stockholmer Bewegung*, 37.

142. Ragaz had turned his back on what he considered to be a too-indecisive official church.

143. Keller to Söderblom, June 2 1924 (NLAK C 32).

would like to carry this [Conference] to the cemetery."[144] But theological debate could not be settled by any last minute administrative device, and this unresolved problem resulted in continual misunderstanding at Stockholm, as well as at later conferences."[145] Moreover, Keller feared that Stockholm would displease Barth himself.[146] Barth criticized Life and Work as a movement that failed both to attend to the most pressing concerns and to address the Church's theological distress.[147]

One theological issue at the forefront of the conference was the "Kingdom of God." Can and should the Church be involved in building this kingdom? The American Charles F. Wishart, a staunch supporter of the Social Gospel, proposed that the earthly realm be shaped as a suitable threshold to heaven.[148] By contrast, Ludwig Ihmels, the bishop of Saxony, invoked Luther's doctrine of the two kingdoms to argue that nothing could be more mistaken and fatal than the notion that human beings should erect the kingdom of God in the world.[149] When Friedrich Siegmund-Schultze, a fellow German and a member of the religious social movement, wanted to raise the Church's commitment to peace and justice for discussion, conservative Lutherans threatened to leave the conference. Whereupon Siegmund-Schultze withdrew his speech. "Söderblom embraced him, saying: 'You have saved the Conference.'"[150]

This episode illustrates how difficult finding a basic consensus proved to be. As early as 1915, Keller had come between the theological fronts to serve as an intermediary.[151] Now, in Stockholm, he presented a well devised set of theses on the Kingdom of God:

144. Keller to Söderblom. June 4 1925 (NLAK C 32). This is an allusion to Acta 5,9.

145. Sundkler, *Nathan Söderblom*, 375.

146. Keller to Barth, Cardiff, June 26, 1925 (KBA 9325.260). The theologian Eduard Thurneysen, who was close to Barth, observed: "America also seems to want to appear as the great wholesale purchaser on the religious market; its capitalism amonts to such an incredibly godless . . . soulcatcher Christianity, which will probably be propagated both vociferously and violently at the world conferences praised by Adolf Keller." See Thurneysen to Barth, July 21, 1925, in Thurneysen, *Karl Barth–Eduard Thurneysen*, 354. See above, p. 94.

147. Keller, "Denkschrift über den gegenwärtigen Stand der ökumenischen Bewegung" (1932), 3 (NLAK C 30).

148. Charles F. Wishart, cited in Weisse, *Praktisches Christentum und Reich Gottes*, 289.

149. Ibid., 286. It is worth noting that this interpretation of Luther was one-sided.

150. Sundkler, *Nathan Söderblom*, 373. On Siegmund-Schultze, see above, p. 48 and p. 64.

151. See above, p. 23.

1. The Christian peoples draw their ideal of community from the Gospel. Not only does this emphasize the infinite value of the human soul, but also gives us an indication of the final and highest form of community, the Kingdom of God. This is both God's gift and effect. But the Christians nevertheless attain from the proclamation of the Kingdom of God an intuition and an ideal of the highest and most valuable form of community possible among human beings. Amid a torn and hostile world fighting itself, they gain a hope for the realization of a community of individuals and peoples under the leadership and rule of God's spirit. Thus, they attain an aim, toward which their efforts may strive, even if they are aware that it is not these efforts but God's will that drives and guides them toward this aim. 2. From our immersion in the proclamation of the Gospel, we obtain the general outline of this highest form of community, by which all communities created by man are measured and by which they are directed." These main features include "Awe of the Creator," "Justice that takes neither any personal or national advantages from the disadvantaging of the weak," "Love as a Will to Community," and "Purity of the Will."[152]

Keller's theses, among other things, helped paper over the cracks in Stockholm. The closing statement of the conference seems reasonably balanced. Barth, however, remarked that the German delegation of forty people had included eight German nationalists: "Dear me, and World-Adolf [*Weltadolf*] as a counterpart . . . and in a Christian church, of all places— one does feel like beating one's fist on the table . . . I fear that [if I had been present] I would have given once more a 'bloody shave' [to the whole assembly], but not only in view of the Westerners [but to the Lutherans as well!]."[153] Presumably, Barth had coined the nickname "World-Adolf." Irony became tainted both with envy and probably also with admiration. Everything was driving "toward the sea, toward the ocean, upon which we actually have more to seek than Adolf Keller," Barth noted already in 1922.[154] Keller found the criticism voiced by the dialectic theologians most

152. Keller, "Die Kirche und die internationalen Beziehungen. Thesen zum 4. Thema des Programms für die Allgemeine Konferenz für praktisches Christentum in Stockholm" (1925), 1–2. The title of the fourth theme was "Die Kirche und die internationalen Beziehungen" (WCC Br 280.241).

153. Barth to Georg Merz and Eduard Thurneysen, October 4, 1925, in Thurneysen, *Karl Barth–Eduard Thurneysen*, 371. On Keller's nickname "Weltadolf," see also Thurneysen to Barth, May 31, 1933, in Algner, *Karl Barth–Eduard Thurneysen*, 412 (see main text and n. 5).

154. Barth to "Liebe Freunde [Dear Friends]," October 16, 1922, in Thurneysen, *Karl Barth–Eduard Thurneysen*, 113.

hurtful. He did, however, acknowledge Emil Brunner's reservations as no less than justified.[155] In 1927, he approached Brunner with the desire to discuss the subject of ecumenism. Keller maintained that today one knew that sheer industriousness was just as unhelpful as sheer theology.[156] Keller also remained in contact with Barth: "I shall gladly wait until a certain color blindness recedes from you."[157] Neither nationalist tendencies nor excessive optimism appealed to Keller.[158] In this respect he agreed with Barth.

After the Stockholm conference, German cooperation in the ecumenical movement was called into question.[159] Conversely, Macfarland was consternated by the accusation that American religious feeling was purely a matter of activism.[160] Keller sought to calm the waters: theological divides, he argued, also ran through single countries. However, the spirit of Stockholm afforded a positive outlook. While the differences and tensions had been palpable, great self-discipline had been exercised, with some few exceptions. Among the differences, sadly nationalism was the most poignant.[161] A synthesis of enthusiasm with caution would strike the proper balance.[162]

The Stockholm conference also considered the future of Life and Work. Keller sat on a committee especially appointed to discuss this matter.[163] He observed:

> Immediately after the conference, the first committee meeting was held while we were still in Stockholm. I moved into the front line, since I was appointed associate general secretary alongside Atkinson, the American. Later, I heard that my former teacher Harnack had pointed me out to the conference leaders. Professor Deissmann and the Germans in general strongly supported this candidacy, besides which, as far as I knew, there was none other from Europe . . . My actual duties and responsibilities were to be outlined in closer detail only at the next committee

155. Keller to Brunner, January 10, 1927 (StAZ W I 55,25).

156. Keller to Brunner, January 24, 1927 (ibid.).

157. Keller to Barth, September 21, 1927 (KBA 9327.401).

158. Keller, "Der amerikanische Protestantismus," 206ff.

159. Kerner, *Luthertum und Ökumene*, 293.

160. Keller to Macfarland, November 14, 1925 (PHS NCC RG 18 73/9).

161. Keller, "Das Ergebnis von Stockholm."

162. Keller, "Die Weltkirchenkonferenz von Stockholm (Papier 2)," 3–4. (NLAK C 29).

163. "Commissions on Life and Work" (NLAK C 31).

> meeting, but my later appointment as general secretary of the proposed International Social Science Institute seemed to be in the air already at the time.[164]

Keller now belonged to the innermost executive circle of Life and Work. Atkinson, who had acted as the sole general secretary up until Stockholm, opposed the election of an associate general secretary; the division of duties and responsibilities was also unclear.[165] The reasons for appointing a second general secretary were related to the different theological outlooks existing between conservative German Lutheranism and the Social Gospel Movement prevalent in America and Great Britain. The ecumenist Nils Ehrenström assessed matters as follows: "The appointments of Dr. Atkinson and Dr. Keller in a way expressed a dialectical, and at times admittedly tiring tension between standpoints that could, albeit not quite appropriately, be called American, on the one hand, and European, on the other; this tension beleagured future collaboration for years."[166] For Keller, the situation was even more unpleasant as it entailed a personal altercation between Söderblom and Macfarland. Immediately before the Stockholm conference, Keller had accompanied Macfarland on his visit to church leaders and statesmen in Eastern Europe. At the conference itself, Söderblom was seated on the platform, with Keller beside him. Macfarland felt overlooked and thereafter withdrew into ill humor. "Just . . . let the genial Archbishop of Uppsala and the other episcopal dignitaries carry the golden sceptres,"[167] he wrote to Keller a few months later. Keller, a "servant of two masters," acknowledged both Söderblom and Macfarland not only as his sponsors but also as his friends. He was careful not to fan the flames any further.

In early 1926, Söderblom commissioned Keller to oversee preparations for the continuation committee of Life and Work, which was to convene in Bern, the capital of Switzerland.[168] Program topics included the responsibility for the war and the founding of the International Social Science Institute. With reference to the attendance of the King of Sweden and the entire Ministery of State at the opening of the Stockholm conference,

164. Keller, "Aus meinem Leben," 157.

165. Macfarland to Keller, November 27, 1925, and Keller to Macfarland, January 18, February 16, March 15, 1926 (for all letters, see PHS NCC RG 18 73/9).

166. Ehrenström, "Die Bewegungen für internationale Freundschaftsarbeit und für Praktisches Christentum, 1925–1948," 195.

167. Macfarland to Keller, December 3, 1925 (PHS NCC RG 18 73/9).

168. Söderblom to Keller, February 6, 1926 (NLAK C 8).

Keller and Friedrich W. Hadorn, the Bernese church historian, were given official assurances that Heinrich Häberlin, president of the Swiss Government, would host a reception to mark the conference opening.[169] Following the conflicts that had become evident in Stockholm and thereafter, there was some anxiety whether the conference would be attended at all. To great relief, the conference was inaugurated on August 26, 1926 in the principal hall of the Swiss Senate; in attendance were numerous church representatives and distinguished magistrates.[170] Presumably by design, Macfarland did not attend the Bern conference. Once again, Söderblom occupied center stage: "the whole Conference of some eigthy delegates were all his closest friends and co-workers, and he was happy to work with them again."[171] Keller was satisified: "We enjoyed some magnificent weather, with a rare view of the snow-clad peaks of the Bernese Alps."[172] The church services were held in Bern Minster. The atmosphere during the sessions was conciliatory.

Discussing responsibility for the war, the Frenchman Wilfred Monod remarked: "Dear Colleagues from Germany, brothers of Jesus Christ, and sons of our Father in Heaven, without imposing any obligation on your part, we would very much like you to leave Bern both with fresh inspiration and with fresh vigor so as to partake in the communal work of Christianity."[173] Hermann Kapler, president of the German Church Board, cited Colossians 3:13–14: "Forbearing one another, and forgiving one another, if any man have a quarrel against any: even as Christ forgave you, so also *do ye* / And above all these things *put on* charity, which is the bond of perfectness" (KJV). Deeply moved, Keller translated both statements.[174]

The idea for an International Christian Social Institute had already been proposed in Stockholm. Envisaged as a visible expression of Life and Work, the Institute would need to adhere to strict academic principles, in

169. Hadorn and Keller (on behalf of the Federation of Swiss Protestant Churches) to Häberlin, March 6, 1926, and Häberlin to the Federation of Swiss Protestant Churches, March 9, 1926 (BAR J.2.257 1437/155).

170. "Minutes of the German Delegation of the Conference of the Continuation Committee, Bern, August 26-30, 1926" (EZA 51 / O III c2).

171. Sundkler, *Nathan Söderblom*, 393. The conference was held at the Villa Favorite, a guesthouse ran by deaconesses in Bern.

172. Keller, "Aus meinem Leben," 158. The seating arrangement at the banquet has survived (EZA 51 / O III c1).

173. Speech delivered by Monod (WCC 241.002 Doc. Choisy).

174. "Minutes of the Conference of the Continuation Committee" (1926) (EZA 51 / O III c2); original emphases.

order to avoid accusations of partiality. Its academic character should not exclude those representing practical life, both employers and employees. Further, it would have to maintain permanent contact with the International Labor Office (ILO) and the churches.[175] According to Keller, the proposed remit was not without "a certain difference of opinion."[176] An institute committee was founded, and Arthur Titius, Keller's former teacher in Berlin, appointed president. Further members included the Englishman Alfred E. Garvie, the Frenchman Elie Gounelle, a member of the religious social movement, the Americans Worth M. Tippy and Charles Macfarland, Alfred Jörgensen, Bishop Einar Billing from Sweden, and Keller.[177]

The Swedes favored the Swiss theologian Alphons Koechlin, who in 1925 had made a positive impression as a translator in Stockholm, as head of institute. Koechlin, however, declined the appointment.[178] Macfarland, Harnack, and the French preferred Keller. "I am rather frightened by this proposal, being already overburdened."[179] Macfarland advised him to "accept the Institute for general direction with *assistance*."[180] Söderblom, too, requested Keller to accept the proposal.[181] The committee suggested associating the Institute with the Central Bureau, and to appoint Keller as director, at least for a term of one year.[182] It pledged to recruit professional staff and secure funding. It was obviously an advantage that the Federal Council would continue to pay Keller's salary.

Eventually, after some hesitation, Keller accepted the post.[183] This was courageous, since the opposing expectations would require him to square the circle. Other factors also remained subject to negotiation, including organizational matters, work schedules, funding, the actual location, and staffing. In prospect, however, the appointment excited Keller: "In fact, the task is very beautiful to build up something quite new."[184] What influenced his decision was the meanwhile clarified definition of the duties

175. Deissmann, *Die Stockholmer Weltkirchenkonferenz 1925*, 674.

176. Keller to Macfarland, May 11, 1926 (PHS NCC RG 18 73/10).

177. Deissmann, *Die Stockholmer Weltkirchenkonferenz*, 746f.

178. Koechlin to Keller, May 21, 1926 (BAR J.2.257 1437/155).

179. Keller to Macfarland, July 6 1926, and September 9, 1926 (PHS NCC RG 18 73/10).

180. Macfarland to Keller, July 19, 1926 (ibid.); original emphasis.

181. Keller, "Aus meinem Leben," 159.

182. Keller: "Das Christliche Sozialinstitut. Zusammenfassung der Diskussion," August 23, 1926 (NLAK C 8).

183. "Minutes of the Continuation Committee, Bern 1926," 12 (EZA 51 / O III c2).

184. Keller to Macfarland, September 9, 1926 (PHS NCC RG 18 73/10).

and responsibilities of the two general secretaries: Atkinson was responsible for the administration of Life and Work, Keller for its Institute.[185] On October 6, 1926, Keller wrote to Macfarland: "In remembering how you steered me on this way, I have often thought these last months what an influence one man can have in another man's life and destiny. I take it as God's guidance."[186]

KELLER AND THE ECUMENICAL MOVEMENT FAITH AND ORDER

Before discussing Keller's new assignment, let us turn briefly to the first World Conference of Faith and Order. This was held in the summer of 1927 in Lausanne, Switzerland. As an ecumenical movement, Faith and Order focused on questions of faith, theology, and those concerning the church constitution. It had been founded in 1910 by the American Charles H. Brent, who served as bishop of the Episcopal Church, first in the Philippines and subsequently in New York. Keller was convinced that Stockholm and Lausanne were inseparable and were possible only as works of faith.[187] Brent approached Keller personally to secure the participation of the Swiss churches in Lausanne.[188] Thereupon, the Federation of Swiss Protestant Churches delegated Keller, Choisy, and Hadorn to the conference, which was attended largely by the same figures as those present in Stockholm two years earlier.

Keller was asked to introduce the plenary discussion on the second conference topic, "The Gospel as the Message of the Church to the World." In his introduction, he advanced eight theses:

> 1. The message of the Church to the world is the Gospel of Jesus Christ . . . – 2. The Gospel is for us the revelation of the living God. . . . Man is dependent upon God both in his creation and in his salvation, and honors God in this knowledge. – 3. God's gift of mercy, which we possess in the form of the Gospel, is constituted for our faith by what Jesus Christ brings us and does for us . . . – 4. In that God affords man knowledge and forgiveness

185. Keller, "Denkschrift über den gegenwärtigen Stand der ökumenischen Bewegung" (private, secret, and confidential), written after August 1, 1931, 13 (NLAK C 30).

186. Keller to Macfarland, October 6, 1926 (PHS NCC RG 18 73/10).

187. Keller, "Vorbemerkungen zur Lausanner Konferenz," 122.

188. Brent to Keller, June 2, 1926 (PHS NCC RG 18 73/10).

of his sins through the Gospel of Jesus Christ, he reestablishes the community with him, through which man also gains new community with his brothers . . . – 5. With the salvation that God proclaims and proffers to man in the Gospel, God not only seeks to liberate the individual but also to redeem humanity. . . . – 6. We are afforded this proclamation of the Gospel, whose scope is all-inclusive, especially by Jesus's message of the Kingdom of God . . . – 7. We have the heavenly treasure of the evangelical proclamation in the earthly vessels of human tradition and church organization. . . . – 8. But the appropriation of the Gospel can occur solely through the faith that the Holy Spirit awakens in our hearts. Gospel and faith are correlates. . . . But the promise of the Holy Spirit as the presence and living effect of God's mercy also forms part of the Gospel.[189]

Whereas the conference participants reached a broad consensus on the basis of these claims, opinions differed on "The Nature of the Church": on the one hand stood the notion of the Church as a divine salvation institute in the catholic sense—according to the Anglican and Orthodox churches; on the other was the conception of the Church as the invisible community of believers.[190] Opinions also diverged on another conference topic, "The Spiritual Office of the Church."[191] The close relationship between Anglicans, Orthodoxy, and Old Catholics became clearly evident, just as that prevaling among the actual churches of the Reformation.[192] Notwithstanding these difficulties, Bishop Brent and other Anglican exponents nevertheless sought to develop an ecumenical theology.[193] Reflecting on the Lausanne conference, Keller wrote that it was "much better than we dared to hope."[194] He was elected to the Continuation Committee of Faith and Order.

---

189. Keller, "Die Schweiz an der Weltkirchenkonferenz in Lausanne, Teil 2," 139–40.

190. Keller, "Die Weltkirchenkonferenz in Lausanne I," 127.

191. Keller, "Die Weltkirchenkonferenz in Lausanne II," 143.

192. Keller, "Die Weltkirchenkonferenz in Lausanne I," 128.

193. Keller, "Die Weltkirchenkonferenz in Lausanne," *Basler Nachrichten*.

194. Keller to Bishop Woods of Winchester, September 13, 1927 (*NLAK C* 23).

THE INTERNATIONAL CHRISTIAN SOCIAL INSTITUTE IN GENEVA

With his appointment as associate general secretary of Life and Work, Keller reached the zenith of his career. He was the acting secretary of the Federation of Swiss Protestant Churches, and serving as bridge-builder between the European and American churches. He was director of the Central Bureau and actively involved in Faith and Order. And now he assumed responsibility for the International Christian Social Institute of Life and Work. His schedule for January 1927 looked as follows: [195]

> Conference with Sir Henry Lunn[196] concerning the publications of the Review of the Institute. The manuscript of my book "The Churches and Peace" has been finished . . . Organization of a conference for Inner Mission, Evangelization and Social work of the Swiss Churches with a view of forming a Swiss Home Missions Council . . . Have written a number of articles in Swiss, German, English Reviews. Conference with Mr. Kelatia, a wealthy representative of the Assyrian people . . . Conference with Rev. Rihner from Jugoslavia who wishes to extend his work to the Orthodox Church there. Conference with the Committee of the Swiss Society for the Evangelicals in Austria [concerning cooperation in the Balkan countries. Organization of a lecture for Prof. D. Arseniew on the situation of the Orthodox Church, especially in Russia] Public lectures in Neuchâtel, Lausanne and Geneva on Protestant unitiy on the basis of federation . . . Conference with Mr. Thélin "Officier de liaison" between the [International] Labor Office [ILO] and the Institute . . . Conference with the leaders of the Italian Church in Geneva concerning relief . . . Conference with Professor Raoul Allier of Paris concerning the creation of a Protestant centre in the Cité Universitaire of Paris. A new report on the evangelical movement in the Ukraine . . . Draft of a programme for the Social Institute and a circular letter to the correspondents, and a questionnaire. Visit from the director of an evangelical work in Russia, "Licht dem Osten (Light for the East)" . . . Preparation of a new course at the University [Zurich] on "Present federative and cooperative Christian movements."

195. Keller, "Report of the Activities in January and February 1927" (PHS NCC RG 18 73/11).

196. Henry Lunn was a medical doctor, hotel proprietor, and patron of the ecumenical movement.

The British Lady Lucy Gardner (in the easy chair at the left) visits the team of the International Christian Social Institute, besides her from left to right the translator Mme. Béguin (presumably), Dr. Georges Thélin from the ILO, Adolf Keller, and his secretary Oskar Bauhofer (archive Dr. Pierre Keller)

Even this list is not exhaustive. How did Keller cope with this wide range of duties and responsibilities? Had he not overreached himself by accepting the post of Institute Director? Numerous tasks at the Central Bureau had meanwhile become routine. In a letter to Söderblom, Keller mentioned that he had reduced his other activities to devote his energies to undertaking the preparations for succesfully establishing the Institute.[197] He often worked into the late hours: "I can only say that very often at 1 or 2 in the night my wife stood up to get me to bed."[198] But he remarked reassuringly: "I praise God for the health he gave me, but the work on my shoulders is really at the limits of my capacities."[199] Söderblom made it plain to Keller that he could not possibly bear "such an enormous workload and responsibility" single-handedly in the long term. It was "a miracle and by the grace of God" that Keller had shouldered such an enormous task.

197. Keller to Söderblom, October 2, 1926 (NLAK C 23).

198. Keller to George Stewart, November 1, 1926 (PHS NCC RG 18 73/10).

199. Keller to Macfarland, September 9, 1926 (ibid.).

While the running of the Institute had been placed "in the most capable hands," Keller needed an assistant with a training in social ethics, since it was necessary for the entire ecumenical cause that he continued to head the relief organization.[200] He had, for the Central Bureau and the Institute together, the help of only one assistant and two part time secretaries.

Scant funds were received for the Institute, and no professional staff were in sight. But Keller had competent advisors, including the American William A. Brown, Elie Gounelle, a member of the religious-social movement in France, the German Arthur Titius, and Lucy Gardner, a British Quaker schooled in social ethics. Keller was in permanent contact with Georges Thélin, a lawyer at the International Labor Organization (ILO) of the League of Nations. Fortunately, he had dealt with social issues during his student days. He began immersing himself in current academic literature, since the Institute was expected to undertake research. Basically, he held the view that the Christian proclamation included a social message, and thus conceived not only solace and salvation for the individual soul, but also the social renewal of humanity as a whole.[201]

In May 1927, Keller published the first issue of the trilingual *Bulletin Life and Work*. Its purpose was to provide information on developments within Life and Work. With a view to the continuation conference of Life and Work in the summer of 1927, Keller contributed a report on the social activities of the churches. In effect, this task alone would have provided work for several years. At Söderblom's instigation, Keller received assistance from two young Swedish theologians—at least for a few weeks. Together, the team of three managed to survey the current situation.[202] Rather than painstakingly enumerating the social activities of the individual churches, Keller attempted to spotlight the driving forces: the parable of the good Samaritan was the spiritual foundation for the work of the "Home Mission" in all countries. Particularly in Europe, such work was undertaken by independent Christian organizations. However, these bodies were becoming increasingly aware of the fact that such work belonged to the essence of the church. The significance of the Home Mission and of social welfare work for church life and public welfare could not be esteemed highly enough.[203] The church became socially engaged in a

200. Söderblom to Keller, February 8, 1927 (NLAK C 23).

201. Keller, "Die soziale Erneuerung der Menschheit durch das Christentum," 266–85.

202. Keller, *Die Kirche und die soziale Arbeit*.

203. Ibid., 19.

strict sense, he noted, "when the powerlessness of merely occasional welfare and charity is clearly recognized, when doubt arises that such partial
work creates true and lasting public welfare, when one turns from individual suffering and that of particular groups to distress and misery at large
. . . , when the need for justice comes to stand imperatively alongside the
need for love, when true altruism takes the place of heavenly egotism . . .
When this happens, then a new social responsibility is born."[204]

Keller's report was received favorably at the continuation conference
of Life and Work, held at Farnham Castle in Winchester in July 1927: "'A
Dieu Foi, aux Amis Foyer! (For God, faith; for friends, hospitality!)' this
inscription stands written above the fireplace in the great hall of Farnham Castle. Nothing could better express the spirit and atmosphere of
that wonderful episcopal see."[205] He offered a delightful description of the
atmosphere prevailing in the imposing Norman castle:

> Many a conference participant would lose his way in the angular
> passages before he found the enormous hall, . . . Here, we would
> convene after the day's work . . . Here, Archbishop Söderblom's
> fiery mind would emit its irresistible plans. His laughter would
> boom like a bronze bell, when he suddenly broke from deepest
> earnestness into his golden humor. Here, the solemn dignity
> and quiet denominational resistance of Ihmels, the bishop of
> Saxony, would thaw . . . Not only does Farnham Castle possess a
> large hall for social occasions but also a chapel for prayer. When
> the day's work was completed, we gathered in the candlelit cha-
> pel. The guests knelt in the ancient carved chairs, behind us the
> servants. Mrs. Woods played the organ. Quietly, the bishop read
> the evening prayer from the *Prayer Book*.[206]

On Sunday, July 17, 1927, the continuation conference celebrated a
joint communion service in the chapel—a bold step.[207] The lord of the
castle, Bishop Frank Woods, the most prominent English ecumenist at
the time, recounted the castle legend and gave it a new twist: "We have
here in Winchester, in the famous Castle, an ancient table. Round this
table, according to the legend, King Arthur and his Knights used to gather,
and there pledged themselves in Christ's Name to war against all injustice
and wrong, and to uphold the standard of truth, right, purity, and fellow-

204. Ibid., 20.
205. Keller in *Bulletin Life and Work* 2 (November 1927), 45ff. (WCC Archive)
206. Keller, *Von Geist und Liebe*, 110ff.
207. "Minutes of the Executive Committee of the Conference on Life and Work,
July 16–19, 1927" (WCC 24.001).

ship. To that crusade, on a far greater scale, and in a far more complicated world, we are here to dedicate ourselves. As representing many nations and many Churches, we gather at this Round Table of Life and Work."[208]

The continuation conference at Farnham Castle in Winchester, 1927; second row from right to left: Eugène Choisy [second], Adolf Keller, Wilfred Monod, Bishop Frank Woods, Archbishop Nathan Söderblom
(archive Dr. Pierre Keller)

The Farnham conference was devoted to the Institute. According to Söderblom, it was meant to be a "workshop" for the "forging of a shared Christian thought amid today's great ethical and social problems."[209] Those present concurred "that the valuable services of Dr. Keller should be gratefully recognised and that he be requested to continue the work as General Secretary for the Social Institute for the next two years."[210] The main points of the Institute Statute, as elaborated by Keller and now ratified by the conference, were:

208. Keller, "Winchester 1927," *Bulletin Life and Work* 2 (November 1927), 53 (WCC 24.001).

209. Ibid., 56 (WCC 24.001).

210. "Minutes of the Executive Committee" (Continuation Committee), July 27, 1927, 4 (WCC 24.001).

1. It shall become a center for the mutual understanding, association, and cooperation of all socially active Christian organizations in the various churches, communities, and countries ... 2. It shall dedicate itself to studying the social and economic facts and problems in the widest sense in the light of Christian ethics according to strict academic methods in order to attain greater clarity about Christian social principles, and to assist the churches in adopting practical action. 3. It shall be a center of information, through which knowledge, experience, and methods can be fostered that can assist the churches in fulfilling their socio-ethical tasks.—Its work shall therefore combine scholarly research methods with practical purpose.[211]

The Statute largely clarified the differences concerning the aims of the Institute. Owing to its affinity with the Council of the League of Nations and the International Committee of the Red Cross, the Institute was headquartered in Geneva. Hence, the Keller family and the Central Bureau both moved from Zurich to Geneva in the spring of 1928. Although Tina Keller's sister Alice was married in Geneva, neither she nor her children, some of whom were already adolescent, found adjusting to the French-speaking environment easy. Tina completed her medical studies in Geneva, and subsequently opened a private practice as a psychiatrist—as one of the first women to do so in Switzerland. Keller knew Geneva quite well from his earlier term of office as a parish minister.

The headquarters of the YMCA, YWCA, and the World Student Christian Federation were also moved to Geneva. Keller found a large house to accommodate the various Christian organizations. The advantages of this arrangement were self-evident: shared reception and meeting rooms, a joint library, as well as joint translation, telephone, janitorial services, and so forth. In 1937, the organizations relocated to the representative and spacious Palais Wilson, the former seat of the Council of the League of Nations, which had been purchased thanks to the generosity of the Swiss churches.[212] Geneva now definitely became the center of the ecumenical movement.

In June 1928, the Federal Council of the Churches of Christ in America sent the experienced Worth M. Tippy to Geneva for several weeks to assist Keller with his various tasks.[213] Owing to a shortage of staff

211. Keller, *Die Fortsetzungsarbeit*, 15. See below, p. 109.

212. Leiper, "For Such a Time as This," March 1944 (PHS 97–1027 Henry S. Leiper Papers 3/4).

213. Worth M. Tippy was a member of the Federal Council's research department.

and funds, conducting intensive social research remained inconceivable. Nevertheless, Keller published two highly respected brochures, "Die Fortsetzungsarbeit der Stockholmer Kirchenkonferenz" (Continuing the Work of the Stockholm Church Conference)[214] and "Die Sozialen Programme der Kirchen" (The Social Programs of the Churches).[215] Given the limited resources, Keller's research effort until the end of the 1929 was most impressive: it comprised four brochures, the *Bulletin*, exhaustive annual reports, and the first two volumes of the academic journal *Stockholm* (the latter will be discussed below).

Chiefly, however, his work focused on providing information and establishing a network. Keller visited the Social Department of the Council of the League of Nations, and contacted the "League for the Protection of Natives" and the "Peace Office."[216] From the International Labor Organization he procured information and material. At the University of Zurich (where he held a lectureship from 1926 on), he lectured on "Die soziale Tätigkeit der Kirchen" (The Social Activity of the Churches).[217] In 1928, he visited the church authorities in Vienna, Budapest, Prague, Berlin, Frankfurt, and Heidelberg to sensitize them to social issues. In London, he conferred with labor leaders and industrialists.[218] He visited the Krupp iron rolling mills in the Ruhr area.[219] In Nuremberg, he gave a talk on "International Socialism and Ecumenism."[220]

Presumably, Keller's greatest achievement at the Institute was the publication of the ambitious journal *Stockholm*, on behalf of the Institute Committee. Arthur Titius, professor of theology in Berlin, had suggested its establishment. Envisaged as a quarterly, its purpose was "the academic and socio-ethical inquiry into social questions." Its editors were Alfred E. Garvie (who was responsible for the British edition), Arthur Titius (German), Elie Gounelle (French), and Worth M. Tippy (American). The first—thick—issue appeared at the beginning of 1928.[221] Keller noted that

214. See p. 108, n. 211.

215. Keller, *Die Sozialen Programme der Kirchen und freier religiöser Organisationen.*

216. Keller, "Bericht über die Tätigkeit des Internationalen sozialwissenschaftlichen Instituts pro 1927/28," 10.

217. Keller, *Das Internationale Sozialwissenschaftliche Institut in Genf, 1928–29,* 13.

218. Keller, "Notes," 1.

219. Ibid., 10–11.

220. Keller delivered the talk at the interdisciplinary Sozialer Lehrgang (social training course) in Nuremberg (NLAK C 5).

221. Keller, ed., *Stockholm* (WCC Archive).

it "was a huge effort all these last weeks to bring it out."[222] But he enjoyed the work.[223] The first issue framed the concept of the journal as follows:

> It shall serve no single church or churchly direction . . . , but only bring to bear the *general Christian principles* . . . It seeks to serve neither workers' nor employers' interests, but *the community of life that encompasses both in equal measure* . . . It hopes to bring together *economic experts of all persuasions*, theorists and practitioners, with the *men of the Church* and *socio-ethical thinkers*, in a *fruitful exchange* on the difficult present-day problems of labor and its connection with the economy; it wants to help consider these questions in a purely objective light and thus to prepare for their nonpartisan treatment and reading.[224]

Almost all prominent ecumenists, even the aged Adolf von Harnack, contributed prefatory remarks to the first issue. Their tone was consistently optimistic; only Söderblom warned: "The application of the Evangelical principle to the new circumstances of our epoch is a difficult problem . . . , which can be resolved only by joining forces, with the best possible knowledge, and by sharp and clear minds."[225] Leonhard Ragaz contributed the first article to appear in the first issue; it was titled "Die Kirchen und der Klassenkampf" (The Churches and the Class Struggle). Keller himself noted that ways toward establishing a "sense of the social responsibility of the Church" had to be found, "when the need for justice [stands] imperatively alongside the need for love," and when "true altruism takes the place of heavenly egotism."[226]

Reactions to the first issue were mixed. "You are an admirable servus servorum oecumenicus," Söderblom wrote to Keller, and added: "*Stockholm* is admirable and has of course aroused very much interest in our country."[227] Conversely, Miss Gardner and Henry Atkinson were not satisfied, observing that the journal looked too German.[228] The divide that had opened in Stockholm once more became apparent. The lack of funds was a source of grievance. Originally, all contributions were to be published in separate German, French, and English issues. This approach proved to be

222. Keller to Macfarland, Zurich, January 11, 1928 (PHS NCC RG 18 73/11).
223. Keller, "Aus meinem Leben," 163.
224. Keller and Schriftleiter, *Stockholm* 1 (1928), 28.
225. Ibid., 5.
226. Keller, "Der kirchliche Ausdruck einer neuen sozialen Gesinnung," 85ff.
227. Söderblom to Keller, February 3, 1928 (NLAK C 32).
228. Keller to Söderblom, Zurich, February 14, 1928 (ibid.).

unrealistic. Instead, summaries were provided in the other languages. No one, including Keller, found this arrangement satisfying.

Cover of the journal *Stockholm* (1931, no. 2)

It was promising that Keller had managed to secure contributions from business leaders, economists, jurists, sociologists, and theologians from different denominations and nations. In 1929, however, he received an array of articles on a wide range of subjects, including "Arbeitszeit, Arbeitslohn und Arbeitsleistung" (Working Hours, Pay, and Performance), "Die deutsche Arbeiterdichtung" (German Working Class Poetry), "Eingeborenenarbeit" (The Work of Indigenous Peoples), "Das Verhältnis von Kirche und Staat" (The Relationship between Church and State), "The Relation of Theology to Social Service," and "Ame étrangère et langue étrangère" (Foreign Spirit and Foreign Language). Keller attempted to establish some makeshift order among this sprawling collection by dividing the subjects into seven sections: Editorial Affairs, Fundamental Issues, Individual Social Questions, Church Welfare and Social Work, Social Movements and Conferences, Bibliography, Summaries. Evidently, establishing more than rudimentary order was at first barely possible. As Keller noticed, a common mode of thought as regards social ethics was only just emerging within the Church.[229] In particular, discussion between the disciplines was still in its infancy.

Increasingly, however, Keller managed to attract the interest of experts from different countries, denominations, and disciplines in the same topic, and thus to interrelate the various approaches. In 1929, six articles were published on "The Just Price" from the perspectives of theology, history, and economics. In 1930, Keller succeeded in initiating a debate between two eminent economists, one French, the other German, on the controversial issue of "War Debts": "The discussion on war debts, which began with the contributions from [Professor] Charles Gide and Professor [Hermann] Schumacher in the last issue, is supplemented in the present issue with the simultaneous printing of both authors' answers to the previously published articles. Aside from its purely economic significance, the problem reaches deep into the entirety of social conditions currently prevailing in Europe."[230].

In the last issue published in 1930, selected papers given at the Conference of the Ecumenical Council of Life and Work (as it was called from 1930 on) were published. They focused on the reception of the Stockholm movement in various countries. In 1931, the focal topic was "Unemployment," which was becoming more increasingly acute; among other subjects, contributions to this issue considered "Rationalisierung und

229. Keller, *Die Sozialen Programme der Kirchen*, Preface, 3.
230. Keller, "Notizen," 109.

Arbeitslosigkeit" (Rationalization and Unemployment), "Arbeitslosigkeit der Jugend" (Youth Unemployment), "Permanent Preventives of Unemployment," and "Kartelle, Konzerne, Trusts und Arbeitslosenproblem" (Cartels, Corporations, Trusts, and the Problem of Unemployment).[231]

No sooner had this interdisciplinary socio-ethical debate begun properly than the journal came under pressure.[232] The world economic crisis had erupted. The churches lacked money. In 1931, only 536 copies were sold, compared to nearly 1,000 in 1929.[233] By this time, Macfarland had retired and Söderblom had died: the old stalwarts were no longer able to salvage matters. In late 1931, both *Stockholm* and the *Bulletin Life and Work* were suspended. In Keller's eyes, the decision had been taken in a state of panic.[234] He was bitterly disappointed. At least he was able to render fruitful the experiences that he had gained as head of the Institute for his involvement in the Social Affairs Committee of the Federation of Swiss Protestant Churches.[235]

There was a ray of hope: in 1930, Karl Barth was awarded an honorary doctorate by the University of Glasgow, for his epochal theology; practically at the same time, the same award was conferred upon Keller by the University of Edinburgh, for his pioneering role within the ecumenical movement.[236] It was apparent that Keller's commitment to reconciliation and to human welfare had made a profound impression in Scotland.

231. See the Table of Contents for the year 1931.

232. Letter from the administrative department of the Ecumenical Council to the Stockholm Conference, end of 1931 (WCC 24.064 Life and Work Study Dep. 1929-1939); Garvie to Keller, October 27, 1927, observing that funds were lacking in England (ibid.).

233. Hans Schönfeld to the Stockholm Committee, Geneva, November 11, 1931 (WCC 24.064 "Stockholm-Journal").

234. Keller, "Aus meinem Leben," 164.

235. See above, pp. 45–48.

236. Keller to Barth, July 21, 1930 (KBA 9330.426).

4

Crisis and a New Beginning at Life and Work, and from the Central Bureau to Inter-Church Aid

THE CRISIS AT LIFE AND WORK AND KELLER'S RESCUE PLAN

IN THE SECOND HALF of the 1920s, Europe appeared to recover from the effects of World War I. French and German political leaders began to resume dialogue. The Weimar Republic became more firmly established. Ostracized for several years, Germany now entered the Council of the League of Nations and thus regained its place in the world community. Several democracies became established in Eastern Europe. The world economy was in a much healthier condition. Hope budded.

The International Christian Social Institute also took a positive outlook on the future when finally, in the spring of 1929, an economics specialist, the young German theologian Hans Schönfeld, who held a doctorate in economics, arrived in Geneva to take up his post at the Institute.[1] He was dispatched by the Federation of German Churches, who also covered the costs of his remuneration. "The effects of Dr. Schönfeld's appointment, a proven expert, became immediately evident," Keller wrote.[2]

---

1. In 1930, the Swedish theologian Nils Ehrenström joined the Institute as a second permanent member of staff, along with two secretaries, thus establishing the conditions for undertaking intensive research.

2. Keller, *Das Internationale Sozialwissenschaftliche Institut in Genf,* 16.

However, their characters and working methods differed considerably.[3] Like all the ecumenists of his generation, Keller was an "all-rounder," who now faced an assiduous young man trained according to "modern" German academic principles. He was utterly unaware that in 1931 Schönfeld wrote to Hermann Kapler behind his back, observing that Keller's "work for the journal [*Stockholm*] is satisfactory neither in organizational nor in conceptual terms." Keller, continued Schönfeld, was damaging international church welfare work.[4]

The approaching demise of both journals—*Stockholm* and the *Bulletin Life and Work*—was symptomatic of the crisis unfolding within Life and Work. In September 1929, the Wall Street Crash occurred, throwing the whole world into a maelstrom of severe depression. Particularly in Germany, mass unemployment ensued. The ecumenical movement suffered financial losses. In Germany and elsewhere, the Great Depression boosted nationalism. Notwithstanding this shift, the ecumenical movement remained international.

Besides the consequences of the world economic crisis and of nationalism, Life and Work was afflicted by another problem: the impetus of the first years had lapsed. In 1929, Macfarland said: "Stockholm is dead and forgotten as far as the American Churches are concerned," and remarked that Atkinson had failed in this respect.[5] Both the Americans and the British gave Keller reason for concern: particularly the latter were often insular-minded, he observed.[6] Regretfully, he realized that also in France the interest in ecumenism had not grown far beyond the circle of the church leaders. The movement indisputably had its most profound impact in Germany, Sweden, and Switzerland. While the Orthodox Churches were interested in the ecumenical idea, they shunned social work. The missionary churches were taking a much greater active interest in ecumenism than various Western churches. Many non-theologians were disappointed that thus far no tangible results had been achieved in promoting international reconciliation, world peace, and surmounting social and denominational differences. Siegmund-Schultze, Keller asserted,

3. The different temperaments are reflected in their written styles: while Keller's texts are easily accessible and vivid, Schönfeld's are dry and concise.

4. Schönfeld to Kapler, June 6, 1931, cited in Weisse, *Praktisches Christentum*, 418–19.

5. Macfarland to Keller, October 28, 1929 (PHS NCC RG 18 73/12).

6. Keller to Brunner, February 3, 1931 (StAZ W I 55,25); see also Keller, "Die Lambeth-Konferenz."

had indicated the inefficacy of the work undertaken in the wake of the Stockholm conference.[7] Söderblom was concerned, but believed that every movement suffered a crisis after about five years. Possibly, a merger between the Central Bureau and Life and Work would have been able to give fresh impetus to the movement. But its Executive Committee lacked the will to do so.

Along with the Great Depression, nationalism, and lacking motivation, what shook the foundations of Life and Work was the loss of most of its early protagonists. Keller was personally affected by the latter development. He lost several of his key allies, starting with the death of Friedrich Wilhelm Hadorn, the first president of the Federation of Swiss Protestant Churches, in 1929. Otto Herold, who had sent Keller on his first visit to the United States at the time, retired as president of the Central Bureau in 1928, and as president of the Federation in 1930. In 1929, Bishop Charles H. Brent, the founder of Faith and Order, died, leaving behind a tremendous gap. In 1930, the enterprising Charles Macfarland retired. In France, the sagacious Wilfred Monod reached retirement age. In 1931, Nathan Söderblom died, which came as a shock for the entire ecumenical movement. In 1932 followed the death of Bishop Woods of Winchester, thus far the most important British representative of Life and Work. Following Hitler's rise to power in early 1933, Siegmund-Schultze emigrated, while Deissmann and Kapler were silenced.

No one had promoted Keller more than Charles Macfarland, who placed complete trust in Keller and had always stood by him. Both Macfarland's retirement and Söderblom's death spelled tremendous losses for Keller, although he was sometimes under the impression that Söderblom, head of the Lutheran Church of Sweden, whose succession was unbrokenly apostolic, failed to consider the Reformed (that is, Presbyterian and Congregational) churches as equals. Notwithstanding his doubts, Keller instigated the awarding of the 1930 Nobel Peace Prize to Söderblom.[8] Immediately upon receiving the award, Söderblom wrote to Keller: "The Nobel Peace Prize is for our joint ecumenical work. It could equally have been awarded to either of us. I extend my sincere gratitude to you for your essential contribution, to which the fact bears witness that our collaborative effort has been afforded such recognition as is apparent to the whole world. I remain, my dear and loyal friend, your most grateful

7. Keller, "Denkschrift," 6, 9–10, and 1 (NLAK C 30).

8. Keller to Söderblom, December 17, 1929 (NLAK C 32). The international law expert Max Huber supported Keller's proposal within the Nobel Peace Prize Committee.

and humble Nathan Söderblom. PS: I know that this would barely have happened without you. Yours, N. S."[9] Keller dedicated *Von Geist und Liebe* (On Spirit and Love), a book commemorating the ecumenical movement, to the memory of Söderblom.

Nathan Söderblom (archive Dr. Pierre Keller)

Thus, an almost complete change of generations occurred between 1929 and 1932. The remaining important ecumenists of the first hour were the American William A. Brown, the orthodox archbishop Germanos, George Bell, meanwhile elected bishop of Chichester, Eugène Choisy, and Keller. Both knowledge and experience were under threat of being lost. In his quest to safeguard continuity, Keller demanded that a "History of Ecumenism" be written. (It didn't happen!) Macfarland remained on the Executive Committee of the Central Bureau. At Life and Work, however, Henry Smith Leiper now became the leading American figure. Leiper and

9. Söderblom to Keller, December 2, 1930 (NLAK C 23). Söderblom wrote the postscriptum by hand.

Keller were compatible and struck up an excellent working relationship. In France, Marc Boegner received promotion within Life and Work and also to the Executive Committee of the Central Bureau. In Great Britain, Bishop George Bell became the leading figure of the ecumenical movement. The church historian Eugène Choisy, Keller's trusted old friend, became president of the Central Bureau in 1928 and soon afterwards, in 1930, of the Federation of Swiss Protestant Churches. They both lived in Geneva and were cooperating closely, albeit Keller was more active.

In 1929, the Continuation Committee of Life and Work convened in Eisenach, which marked its first-ever meeting in Germany. This gave Keller hope. But representatives of newly awakened nationalism in Germany, including the well known theologians Paul Althaus and Emanuel Hirsch, leveled fierce criticism at ecumenism. When delivering lectures at German universities, Keller realized that the nationalist disposition was rampant within large sections of both the academic world and the clergy. The Social Gospel, one of the driving forces behind Life and Work, began to lose impetus; on a positive note, this meant that the dispute on the Kingdom of God subsided. Karl Barth, however, continued to regard Life and Work as a "Tower of Babel." In response, Keller insisted that the theological questions were being tackled by Faith and Order. However, "this was in vain," since "ecumenism must burn."[10] Notably, Keller himself deplored, and emphatically so, the lack of serious theology at Life and Work.[11]

Theology was among various reasons for the frosty climate prevailing between the two general secretaries, Keller and Atkinson: shortly before the Eisenach meeting, Atkinson had heavily criticized Keller.[12] Conversely, Keller accused Atkinson of jingling coins in his trouser pocket in demanding that Life and Work be placed on a sound theological basis.[13] Macfarland took sides with Keller: "I regret to say that he [Atkinson] has almost entirely lost the confidence of the responsible members of the Federal Council . . . So, my dear fellow, . . . don't get too much annoyed by the critics . . . Well—just keep at the job—play with your children—talk it over

10. Keller, "Aus meinem Leben," 167–68. The phrase alludes to the statement made by the Patriarch of Jerusalem in Gotthold E. Lessing's drama *Nathan der Weise*, Act IV: "That's nothing! Still the Jew is to be burnt."

11. Keller, for instance, in "Denkschrift," 2.

12. Weisse, *Praktisches Christentum*, 434, n. 235.

13. Keller, "Aus meinem Leben," 165.

with your wife when you need to relieve your feelings—and above all, keep your sense of humor and don't get too self-conscious and subjective."[14]

And this was Keller's rescue plan: published in 1931, Keller's *Der Weg der dialektischen Theologie durch die kirchliche Welt* (The Path of Dialectical Theology through the World of the Church) boldly demanded that dialectical theology become the binding agency of the ecumenical movement.[15] Thus far, this was both Keller's most theological book and also one of his most important. He ushers in his main point at the very beginning:

> Dialectical theology provides us with a standpoint that lies either beyond or above that of any single church. It faces the same difficulties as the ecumenical movement in its attempt to observe the human being not from this or that subjective psychological or theological angle, but rather from God's . . . Because from that perspective, it is not the penultimate questions that are addressed to man, namely, about his affiliation to this or that Church, or about the intellectual formulation of his faith, but instead the ultimate question, that concerning his affiliation with God.[16]

Dialectical theology, so Keller argued, did not make its assertions with cool academic serenity, but instead spoke out in the passionate debate with contemporary man. It existed in an antithetical relationship not only with culture but also with theology and the Church. It was a combative theology, he observed emphatically, and a necessary reaction against the relativism of the entire modern disposition, whether in the guise of idealism, humanism, individualism, subjectivism, or critical philosophy.[17] It fought against a so-called "theology of experience," and quite rightly swept out Pelagianism—though it sometimes neglected the fact that theology must always be "theologia ad hominem (a theology which considers man)."[18] And yet, as Keller affirmed, it rightly demanded that the Church become "essential."[19] Man's relationship with God, in line with Barth, should be characterized as an "existential encounter."[20] This theology, Keller believed, would strengthen Life and Work.

14. Macfarland to Keller, October 28, 1929 (PHS NCC RG 18 73/12).

15. Keller, *Der Weg der dialektischen Theologie.* See below p. 122, n. 31.

16. Ibid., 7–8.

17. Ibid., 13 and 15.

18. Ibid., 16–17, and 62.

19. Ibid., 29.

20. Ibid., 31 and 33.

Adolf Keller

After considering how various churches had adapted Barth's theology in various different countries, Keller's final chapter, "Ökumenische Bewegung und dialektische Theologie" (The Ecumenical Movement and Dialectical Theology), returns to his reflections at the outset of the book. The ecumenical movement had emerged from "essential distress," and constituted "a movement of faith."[21] For the sake of truth, however, a normative dogmatic theology was needed. However: "An ecumenical theology equipped with understanding is humble enough not to impose its own understanding upon others in the first instance, based on the traditional certainty of faith, but instead it listens to what God wants to say to the world through the other Church."[22]

Under no circumstances did Keller want ecumenical, "understanding" theology to be conceived as a form of theological syncretism. But the ecumenical movement asked the Church whether it believed in its own avowal of faith, particularly that article of faith that reads "I believe in the One, Holy, and Universal Church." It was precisely the weakness of the Church that revealed that God, who had entered lowliness, was present on earth, where He should be proclaimed and heard.[23] What ecumenism displayed was "in effect weakness": "No one knows this better than those who stand in this movement . . . Karl Barth will be able to accept this on condition that the first, the essential distress of the Protestant Church, namely, the agony suffered on the cross, be properly understood and felt. I dare not . . . claim that this [distress] is ubiquitous. But it is precisely in this respect that I believe that the question raised by dialectical theology can also serve the ecumenical movement."[24]

The ecumenical movement sought to answer the question of what the Gospel meant in our time.[25] It took seriously the prayer, "Thy will be done in earth, as it is in heaven."[26] Ecumenism and dialectical theology were mutually dependent in Keller's eyes:

> Dialectical theology can evade the ecumenical movement just
> as little as vice versa. Insofar as it does not assume a certain

21. Ibid., 168–69.

22. Ibid., 180.

23. Ibid., 189–90. Keller is referring to Karl Barth's article "Die Not der evangelischen Kirche," 89–117; see further ibid., 117–23, and also Barth, *Der Götze wackelt*, 33–62.

24. Ibid., 191–92.

25. Ibid., 193–94.

26. Ibid., 197 and 200.

theology of time, but instead an interchurch, interdenominational, supranational, and supratheological standpoint, and
wants to be a crisis of every historical churchliness and theology, it becomes, whether it wants to or not, a kind of parallel
movement of ecumenism . . . It is of utmost importance that the
ecumenical movement take seriously the dialectical question.
But it is to be hoped just as much that dialectical theology also
treat ecumenical questions in earnest.[27]

Keller lent his thesis even more explosive force by adding:

The ecumenical movement is facing criticism from newly awakened national thinking . . . Ecumenism strives not to weaken a
justified national sentiment, but . . . to sharpen its responsibility, to be . . . mindful of the limitations and weaknesses of one's
nation, of the contribution that it is supposed to make to the
human community, of the great shared tasks that no nation can
accomplish alone . . . The ecumenical movement is therefore a
question addressed to the Church, whether it really wants peace
between nations, whether it places the community of blood or
the community of the spirit first, whether it truly believes . . . in
the power of the Gospel to bring nations together.[28]

Here, dialectical theology could carry particular weight, so that God's
cause remained central. It could become a "bridging theology" because it
started from the very concern that God brings before man:

Both the ecumenical movement and dialectical theology . . .
lead the churches to knowledge of the harrowing dimension of
the world's problems, which exceed all human measure, and to
the conviction that in this situation no other help exists but that
man turn to God.[29]

In a letter to Henry Sloane Coffin, Macfarland expressed his appreciation for the book: "It is, in my thought, so unusually good as an
interpretation of the so called Barthian theology that I have arranged
with Macmillan to publish a translation . . . In addition . . . his [Keller's]
volume has unusual practical value on the life of the churches and especially on the movement for Christian Unity and Social Christianity. He
[Keller] is better than any Barthian disciple would be."[30] The English edi-

27. Ibid., 188–89.

28. Ibid., 179ff.

29. Ibid., 202ff.

30. Macfarland to Coffin, May 14, 1932 (UTS Presidential Papers, 25/3, Keller,
Prof. Adolph II).

tion appeared in 1933.[31] However, only very few ecumenists switched to dialectical theology.

How did the dialecticians respond to Keller's work? Thurneysen no more than sneered at it.[32] Barth, however, gave it his serious attention. According to Charlotte von Kirschbaum, Barth's close associate, he devoted an entire day to it.[33] In a four-page letter to Keller, Barth commented on the book as follows:

> It was very moving to be taken around the entire globe, and to be afforded the opportunity to be my own curious and surprised spectator. I am grateful for what you have shown me . . . It will amaze you, but that is how it is: while I was reading your book, I actually tried for the first time to realize that the ecumenical movement and dialectical theology have something to do with one another, and could probably even go hand in hand. Now is it merely my own stupidity that accounts for this? Or is this perhaps, irrespective of me, not actually related to matters that exist on different levels? . . . I am seeking the ecumenical as it were in situ . . . And could or should I even take matters in hand even better by attending conferences to listen to talks on the ecumenical, or even give such talks myself.

In his view, Barth continued,

> the ecumenicity of the Church, in the serious theological sense of the term, can only be given to us and rendered visible in this manner: that it reveals itself, precisely, when it can be and should be thus, and that thereupon we do not place our hands in our laps, nor should we run after ecumenism across countries and oceans . . . With this, I by no means intend to refute or overturn as undone what you . . . desire and are doing. I see a practical task—to which I by no means object, but with which I sympathize—in the different churches helping one another, and that they therefore need to know and understand one another. . . . But what I do not quite understand is . . . that ecumenism itself literally becomes the goal.[34]

31. Keller, *Karl Barth and Christian Unity*; see also Keller, "Le rapprochement des Eglises et la théologie dialectique de Karl Barth."

32. Thurneysen to Barth, November 28, 1930, in Algner, *Karl Barth–Eduard Thurneysen*, 63–64.

33. Kirschbaum to Thurneysen, December 2, 1931, in ibid., 192.

34. Barth to Keller, December 1, 1931 (KBA 9231.381).

Although Barth acknowledged the work of the Central Bureau, for instance, he found Keller's theses unconvincing. He left unmentioned Keller's appeal to close ranks against burgeoning nationalism. On this subject, Keller's view was more far-reaching than Barth's. Two years later, Keller observed that he had benefited greatly from his close reading of the first volume of Barth's *Kirchliche Dogmatik* (Church Dogmatics, the new edition of volume one of *Christliche Dogmatik im Entwurf*—Church Dogmatics in Outline).[35] He stood before this theological accomplishment with nothing less than great admiration. He merely regretted not having a copy of Barth's work at hand when he wrote *Der Weg der dialektischen Theologie durch die kirchliche Welt* (The Path of Dialectical Theology through the World of the Church). Barth had thought beyond, and thus answered and rendered obsolete, much of his work, Keller admitted.[36] Barth, meanwhile, had developed his doctrine of Christ as the mediator between God and man, and thereby softened his strict theological position. In early 1934, Barth assured Keller that "I have no particular feeling of anger against the ecumenical church [*sic*] and movement."[37] They seemed to be moving toward a consensus. In England and America, Keller was often criticized as Barth's "defender" by theologians and professional journals, among others *The Christian Century*.[38]

In his review of *Der Weg*, Brunner hailed Keller's manifold interests, his intellectual agility, and his ability to understand the particular nature of others. Notwithstanding all reservations, Keller's attempt could be considered successful, although his knowledge lacked precision on occasion. In reading the book, one noticed

> that behind it . . . stands a man in whose heart the distress of the Church burns, and who desires to pave the way for the truth of the Gospel in his own way . . . One may grant him, without further ado, that the *una sancta* must necessarily be the aiming point of the theological endeavors of the Church, and that this idea reveals the reality of the Church in its pitifulness. Keller distinguishes too little between this question and the practical question whether the existing unification endeavors provide means properly suited to their realization. Keller can account for the fact that dialectical theology . . . answers this question

35. Karl Barth, *Die Kirchliche Dogmatik*.

36. Keller to Barth, October 23, 1933 (KBA 9333.799).

37. Barth to Keller, January 12, 1934 (KBA 9234.9).

38. Keller to Barth, October 21, 1939 (WS Ms Sch 152/2). *The Christian Century* was an important, progressive, ecumenical magazine.

> in the negative only because he lacks knowledge of the facts
> ... This reveals, however, that he has not fathomed the thought
> central to dialectical theology ..., namely, that the unity of the
> Church can stem only from the truth, not from goodwill or
> from compromises. It is precisely the passion for the truth that
> both the Stockholm and Lausanne movements lacked to such a
> deplorable extent.[39]

While Brunner's attitude was without doubt dismissive, a thawing occurred in early 1934: "Your altered stance toward Stockholm pleases me," Keller observed.[40]

THE DEPARTMENT FOR EDUCATION
AND EXTENSION, AND NEW CRISES

In 1929, the working methods of the two general secretaries of Life and Work began to attract criticism. Atkinson was accused of a neglectful and autocratic approach to his office.[41] In a letter to Söderblom, Bishop Bell offered the following remarks on Keller: "We ought to be able to get a stronger man and a man with more grip."[42] By contrast, Macfarland wrote to Keller: "There is, I judge, a rather general feeling that you ought to be identified with the general work of federation and cooperation rather than with social research as one department of work."[43] Söderblom and Macfarland, who were both still fully involved in Life and Work at this stage, wanted to retain Keller, albeit not as head of the Institute, but in a role better suited to him.[44] Keller, presumably rather unsettled, considered resigning from Life and Work to devote himself entirely to the Central Bureau, which he regarded as his "actual work."[45]

At the annual meeting of the Continuation Committee in 1930, held in the French-speaking Swiss village of Chexbres, the reorganization of Life and Work was the principal item on the agenda. Atkinson and Keller therefore tendered their resignations. The Continuation Committee

39. Brunner, "Adolf Keller," 183–84.

40. Keller to Brunner, January 19, 1934 (StAZ W I 55,25).

41. Weisse, *Praktisches Christentum*, 434.

42. Bell to Söderblom, August 28, 1930, cited in ibid., 434 and n. 234. Possibly, Bell was influenced by Schönfeld; see above, p. 115 and n. 4.

43. Macfarland to Keller, June 17, 1929 (PHS NCC RG 18 73/12).

44. Söderblom to Keller, February 27, 1929 (WS Ms Sch 153/53).

45. Keller, "Aus meinem Leben," 169.

was renamed as the *(Provisorischer) Ökumenischer Rat für Praktisches Christentum* (Provisional Ecumenical Council of Life and Work). It was decided to establish three instead of two departments: one for administration; one for outbound work (titled Education and Extension); and one for social research. Since no suitable candidates were found, Atkinson was appointed head of the first department—albeit reluctantly and only on a temporary basis. Söderblom confided in Keller: "I do not exaggerate if I say that I have been thinking about the succession of Dr. Atkinson nearly every day."[46] After months of wavering, the third department was entrusted to Hans Schönfeld, whose work did not meet with undivided praise: "I confess to very serious questions concerning the justification of doing the type of research study that . . . dealt almost entirely in academic and theoretical matters . . .The theological section of the paper is simply ghastly," remarked Henry S. Leiper, for instance, in 1933.[47]

In Chexbres, only Keller was appointed. He was now the regular general secretary of the second department. Its tasks were "Education and Extension," to which he was predestined and which mattered greatly to him. Moreover, this department was bitterly needed, since the ecumenical movement was, as Keller put it, "an army of officers without soldiers."[48]

He set to work immediately. In the autumn of 1930, he gave talks on ecumenism in Paris, Montpellier, Heidelberg, Tübingen, Darmstadt, Frankfurt, and Stuttgart. At Berlin University, instead of delivering single lectures, he gave "a series of lectures to students, which kindled new sympathy."[49] The radio church service broadcast in November 1930 was an avant-gardist event: "It was a truly continental and ecumenical service, in spirit as well as organization. The pipe organs originated in Hamburg, the hymns were performed in Leipzig by the famous choir of St Thomas, the liturgy was celebrated in Frankfurt . . . , and the sermon delivered at Geneva by Dr. Keller. The service embraced, and was transmitted to, the whole of Europe by Radio Frankfurt."[50] Keller's presence was ubiquitous. "He said that there is only one way by which any movement can be made effective, and that is by some individual embodying that movement in

46. Söderblom to Keller, Uppsala, February 10, 1931 (NLAK C 32).

47. Leiper to Cavert, April 18, 1933 (PHS NCC RG 18 12/18). Cavert served as general secretary of the Federal Council from 1930.

48. Keller, "Aus meinem Leben," 170.

49. Conseil Oecuménique Du Christianisme Pratique (ed., respectively Atkinson), *Lettre d'Information* no. 1 (Geneva, January 8, 193), 5 (BAR J.2.257 1114/114). The *Lettre* succeeded the *Bulletin Life and Work*.

50. Ibid., 5.

themselves. He emphasized the importance of personal contacts."[51] He also sought to arrange meetings with Orthodox Christians.

Upon the initiative of the Rockefeller Foundation, Keller had traveled to the Balkan region for the first time as early as 1925. While his mission was to survey the situation among the Protestant faculties of theology, he also made contact with the Greek Orthodox Church. In Greece, he held meetings with the leaders of the Protestant synod. He visited the Archbishop of Athens and the Patriarch of Constantinople in Saloniki, who was one of the four designated presidents of the Stockholm conference. He summarized his impressions thus: "The whole Orthodox Church which is passing a still more terrible crisis than European Protestantism, has come closer to the Western evangelical churches during these last years. The Western churches feel a new sympathy for this old Christian church and are highly interested without proselytising, in awakening a new religious life in this old venerable church."[52]

Since Life and Work generally considered contact with the Orthodox Church to be insufficient, a special committee for fostering better relations was established under the direction of Bishop Bell in 1929.[53] On its behalf, Keller gave talks at the theological faculties of Budapest, Sopron, Papa, Cluj, Sibiu, Debreczen, Novi Sad, and Athens in May 1931.[54] He met the Patriarch of the Serbian Orthodox Church in Belgrade; he visited the Monastery of St Kyrill in Stanimaka in Bulgaria, and conferred with Professor Stefan Zankow, an ecumenist, in Sofia.[55] Keller's tour marked the first systematic advertising campaign for the ecumenical movement at Orthodox faculties in the Balkans. Unfortunately, Keller observed, the nationalist wave was also sweeping across the Eastern countries: "Our educational task is, therefore, to show the difference between a vague internationalism, polluted by all kinds of political interests, and true oecumenism which has its roots in a deeper understanding of the Gospel."[56]

51. "Minutes of the Executive Committee of Life and Work, Cambridge, August 25–28, 1931" (WCC 24.001).

52. Keller, "A Journey to the East," 76ff.

53. Keller, "Eisenach 1929," Bulletin Life and Work, 5ff.

54. Keller, "Bericht über die Aussenarbeit," Geneva, August 22, 1931, 3–5 (WCC 24.064). Keller was awarded an honorary professorship by the theological academy of Papa (Hungary); see letter dated January 11, 1933 (NLAK A Prof. Dr. Adolf Keller, Persönliches).

55. For details of the itinerary of Keller's journey to the Balkans in 1931 and for the correspondence maintained in this connection, see his private papers (NLAK C 20).

56. Keller, "Bericht über die Aussenarbeit," 1 (WCC 24.064).

Archbishop Germanos appreciated Keller's commitment: "With regard to the progress of the movement among the Eastern Churches, I should like to call the attention of this Council to the visit of Dr. Keller last year in the East . . . Every such visit does contribute very much to the progress of our work."[57]

In Romania, Keller noticed that agricultural reform (the allocation of land from large estates to smallholders) had deteriorated both the quality and quantity of production. He concluded that social reforms without social education were a double-edged sword.[58] In general, the Orthodox Churches lacked social awareness, he noted. Two years later, in 1933, the first conference of the Orthodox Churches on social questions was held in Bucharest under the auspices of Life and Work; Keller was made conference president.[59] Among the conference participants were twelve official delegates from Bulgaria, Greece, Romania, and Yugoslavia, as well as a number of Orthodox professors and students of theology. Among the guests was the leading American Methodist John Mott. "Professor Keller points out that the mission of this initial Orthodox conference for the study of social questions consists above all in clearly returning to essential common tasks, which forces the Orthodox churches to consider the prevailing social problems."[60] Delivered by exclusively Orthodox theologians, the talks at the Bucharest conference focused on land reform and peace-keeping. Following the conference, committees dealing with social questions were established in each Balkan country; they worked in cooperation with their "Holy Synod," the Orthodox Churches of other countries, and the International Christian Social Institute in Geneva. Incidentally, until 1937, the Central Bureau transmitted 400,000 Swiss francs to Orthodox churches and institutions on the Balkans and in the Near East.[61]

Keller's commitment to Education and Extension began to bear fruit.[62] His approach of direct engagement—speaking to people, eating with them, and holding church services—was proving effective.

---

57. "Report of the Sub-Committee appointed to consider the Future of the review 'Stockholm,'" Cambridge, August 24, 1931 (WCC 24.001).

58. Keller, "Soziale Probleme im Balkan."

59. "Minutes of the Administration Committee of Life and Work, Berlin, February 3 and 4, 1933" (WCC 24.001).

60. "Rapport de la Conférence régionale balkanique tenue à Bucarest du 14 au 19 mai 1933," 7 (WCC 24.043 Orthodox Conferences).

61. Keller to Henriod and Schönfeld, June 13, 1937 (WCC 42.0042, file 1).

62. Keller, "Denkschrift," 15.

Adolf Keller

Following Söderblom's death in 1931, profound commotion seized Life and Work. Once again, reform plans were considered. Keller entered the debate on the future of ecumenism.[63] He warned against defeatism: "The belief in the necessity of the cause, in God's leadership, and remembering our original inspiration should save us [from such thoughts]. Nor should the movement be judged only in terms of its tangible results, but instead one should distinguish between growth and action. Growth, however, needs time."[64]

He thus also referred to his previous work. Nor did he deny that the responsible leaders and officials, including himself, had been overwhelmed by too many substantial duties and responsibilities and had been unable to draw upon previous experience. New forces, like that brought by Alphons Koechlin, were needed.[65] He hoped that Bishop Bell's appointment as one of four joint presidents of Life and Work in the spring of 1932 would help ecumenism gain a new foothold. In a letter to Bell, Keller wrote: "It is a matter of real joy for me to hear that you have been nominated as Joint President of Life and Work."[66]

Before the second conference of the Ecumenical Council in Chexbres in 1932, Keller once again tendered his resignation: "As the Council will again have to face a reorganization of our movement, it seems appropriate that I should do it independently from any personal consideration."[67] Macfarland advised him that he should "not, under any conditions, allow that body [Life and Work] to be divided by any dispute of which you are the subject or object, even in the face of injustice: . . . This is the time to keep your feet warm and your head cool und your temper sweet."[68] Keller's resignation was accepted. Following the dissolution of all three departments, Atkinson vanished from the scene and Schönfeld retained his research assignment. Reverend Henry-Louis Henriod, from Neuchâtel, Switzerland, who had for some time been engaged in ecumenical organizations, was appointed as the only general secretary of Life and Work

63. Keller, "Memorandum IV (confidential). Zur Lage und zukünftigen Gestaltung der Ökumenischen Bewegung," 1 and 5 (EZA 51/0 III 1 @m).

64. "Minutes of the Executive Committee of Life and Work, Cambridge, August 25–28, 1931" (WCC 24.001).

65. Keller to Henriod, October 23, 1933 (ibid.).

66. Keller to Bell, April 5, 1932 (LPL Bell 18 f. 291 Correspondence Bell-Keller). There were now four "Joint Presidents": Bell, Germanos, Cadman (president of the Federal Council), and Bishop Ammundsen.

67. Keller to Bell, July 8, 1932 (WCC 42.0042 1,1).

68. Macfarland to Keller, August 2, 1932 (NLAK C 23).

in 1933, in fact in the hope that this would end the longstanding discord between the so-called American and European positions, and help resolve the dispute between the various departments and their directors. But was not Henriod perhaps overwhelmed by this difficult function?[69]

However, one did not want to dispense with Keller's expertise and services. He was appointed "Honorary Lecturer." When he asked what this meant in practical terms, Bishop Bell said vaguely: "I think that it is the general view that the post should be the post of a collaborator."[70] When clarification was still unforthcoming after several months, Adolf Deissmann reminded his fellow executives what Keller, "and only he can and must achieve for this movement also in the future . . . Under all circumstances . . . the contents of this position must be clear, so as to enable Professor Keller to fully exploit his great experience, knowledge, and unique personal contacts for our work."[71] Deissmann's letter dates from February 1, 1933, two days after Hitler's feared rise to power.[72] The letter had the desired effect, and thus the administrative committee took the following decision: "(1) The General Secretary is instructed to keep in close touch with Dr. Keller, and to see that he is fully informed of the work of the Council on all its sides. (2) With a view to securing full access to the work of the Committee and Commissions of the Council, the administrative Committee nominates Dr. Keller (who is already a member of the Executive Committee) as member of the following Committees and Commissions: Advisory Committee on Research; Committee on Cooperation with the Orthodox Church; International Social Commission; Press Commission; Theologians and Youth Commission."[73]

Keller's position within Life and Work thus seemed secure. He was satisfied,[74] and even appreciated "[having] the freedom for academic and

69. Henriod and Keller were on good terms. A few years later, however, Keller reached the following conclusion: "Henriod did his very best and his affable nature disarmed quite a lot of resistance. But what was needed was a different theological equipment and a stronger dynamics than he possessed to steer the ecumenical movement through those critical years"; see Keller, "Aus meinem Leben," 174.

70. Bell to Keller, August 22, 1932 (LPL Bell 18 Part 2 ff. 408–9).

71. Deissmann to the Administrative Committee of the Ecumenical Council, February 1, 1933 (WCC 42.0042 1,1).

72. In his capacity as president of Berlin University, Deissmann had sought to tame National Socialist students prior to the Nazi takeover in 1933. After 1933, he was temporarily placed under house arrest; see Frischmuth, "Adolf Deissmann," 290 and 280.

73. Paper of the Administrative Committee of Life and Work (presumably February 1933; WCC 24.001).

74. Keller to Bell, March 25, 1933 (LPL Bell 18 Part 2 ff. 548–50).

literary activity, and most of all the scope for organizing an ecumenical seminar."[75]

Tina Keller spent the two-month summer holidays together with their five children in a chalet in the mountains, and "[Keller] would join us for about 3 weeks and these times were delightful."[76] Occasionally, they found time to play music. In a letter to her eldest daughter, Tina Keller wrote that "we are all very content, and father and I have just played Brahms."[77] But Keller reached the limits of his strengths: "This month is truly terrible!," he wrote in June 1930.[78] The years of toil and the often unfair criticism eventually took their toll in 1933. Keller came down with a high fever: "I developed bronchitis, which lasted a bit too long, and I am tired to death."[79] Presumably, he was suffering from pneumonia. He rested for a few days, before traveling to the ecumenical conference in Copenhagen. Leiper was concerned: "Keller is not at all well and I feel worried about him. He ought not to be on this trip to Denmark. But he drives himself on because he feels that he must. His rest in Switzerland did him a lot of good but he needs more."[80] On his return from Copenhagen, Keller spent several weeks in a sanatorium in Switzerland. Only half recovered, he traveled to the United States to lecture at Princeton.[81]

In honor of Keller's sixtieth birthday in 1932, Koechlin wrote: "Upon him and upon very few others lies the heavy burden to strive after an understanding and credit for the work of the ecumenical movement amid the spiritual and economic confusion of our day and age, and amid nationalist and denominational reactions. Despite his activity across the world, we should not forget what Keller's tireless work has done for our Swiss Church."[82] Keller promoted Koechlin and purposefully groomed him as

75. Keller to Henriod, August 15, 1932 (WCC 42.0042 1,1). On the Ecumenical Seminar, see below, pp. 146–57.

76. Tina Keller, "In Memoriam."

77. Tina Keller (who played the violin) to Doris Sträuli-Keller, April 8, 1937 (NLDSK).

78. Keller to Gounelle, June 3, 1930 (WCC 42.0042 1).

79. Keller to Henriod, July 22, 1933 (ibid.).

80. Leiper (and Worth Tippy) to McCrea Cavert, September 2, 1933 (PHS NCC RG 18 12/18).

81. Keller to Henriod, September 28, 1933 (WCC 42.0042 1,1). On Princeton, see below, pp. 161–67.

82. Koechlin, "Professor D. Adolf Keller zum 60. Geburtstag," *Basler Nachrichten*, February 7, 1932 (WCC 301.43 25,8).

his successor within Life and Work and the Federation of Swiss Protestant Churches.

FROM THE CENTRAL BUREAU
TO INTER-CHURCH AID

The European Central Bureau for Relief underwent a positive development, and Keller looked ahead optimistically. At the 1925 conference of Life and Work in Stockholm, his talk culminated in the following bold vision: "that a permanent organization for Christian aid be affiliated to the subsequent work of this conference [Life and Work]. Like the Red Cross, such a central organization for emergency assistance and brotherly love must be prepared at all times to provide urgent help, and moreover strive to serve the weaker churches in their work by means of resources, experience, and the methods of the stronger [brother]."[83]

While such affiliation did not materialize in the near future, the relief organization received undivided recognition, also from Karl Barth, who was otherwise so critical of ecumenism.[84] The New York office emphasized the agency's strategic importance, and that Keller's "scholarly attainments, his linguistic ability and, above all, his commanding personality have won for him the respect and confidence of churchmen of all nations and denominations."[85] There were new donor churches: the American Lutherans, the Irish Presbyterians, the Australian Church Federation, and the Dutch Reformed Church in South Africa.[86] In 1931, all Protestant church federations, and most recently also the Lutheran Church of Sweden, were represented on the Executive Committee of the Central Bureau.[87]

While remaining aid recipients, several churches, including those of France, Poland, Hungary, Germany, Austria, Bulgaria, and Czechoslovakia, also made donations, albeit on a modest scale.[88] Consequently, their representatives were appointed to the Executive Committee in 1928, including Hermann Kapler (Berlin), Emil Morel (Paris), and Julius

83. Deissmann, *Die Stockholmer Weltkirchenkonferenz*, 615.

84. See above, pp. 96–97 and 122–23; see Barth to Keller, December 1, 1931 (KBA 9231.381).

85. Kenneth D. Miller (Goodrich's successor) in the "Annual Report of the Federal Council for the Year 1926," 78.

86. Keller, "Kurzer Bericht," 8, 11 (BAR J.2.257 1245/133).

87. Keller to Söderblom, February 13, 1931 (NLAK C 32).

88. Keller, *Die Europäische Zentralstelle für kirchliche Hilfsaktionen*, 21.

Bursche (Warsaw). Within the Central Bureau, the giving and accepting of assistance became established as reciprocal principles. Such a view was completely forward-looking; as a result, and still in the year 1928, the Executive Committee decided to ratify a change of name: the relief agency was now called the European Central Bureau for Inter-Church Aid (*Bureau Central Européen pour l'entre'aide des Eglises*). It was customarily referred to as Inter-Church Aid. Only in the German-speaking world was its former name, *Europäische Zentralstelle für kirchliche Hilfsaktionen*, more common.

However, the turbulences affecting Life and Work and financial problems did not fail to leave their mark on Inter-Church Aid. Various problems had become evident already before the outbreak of the world economic crisis: thus, from 1926, donations declined.[89] Moreover, there were doubts about whether assistance in Continental Europe was still needed. Macfarland and his associates did not share this view: "We are all behind you [Keller] and have a growing faith in you and your work."[90] Nevertheless, Keller was concerned. To his dismay, in 1928 the New York office made inquiries in Geneva about whether the relief organization was still required. The reason for this inquiry was that the Federal Council had budgeted a financial shortfall of $425,000 for 1929. Keller replied with immediate effect: "There can be no doubt as to that the crying distress and misery of the first post-war years has in a large measure disappeared in most continental countries and churches. This however should not be taken to mean that the grave consequences of the war, the extensive pauperization of entire classes of people, the breakdown of the economic basis of numerous congregations and institutions will not be felt very heavily for a long time to come."[91] For instance, Inter-Church Aid regularly sent medicines, medical equipment, and bed linen to Eastern Europe, where supplies were urgently required.[92]

To ensure the continued, broad-based existence of Inter-Church Aid, Keller sent out invitations for a new "Bethesda" conference. Held in Basel on August 23 and 24, 1929, it was attended by eighty-five delegates representing forty-seven churches in twenty-five countries in Europe and

89. "Annual Report of the Federation of Swiss Protestant Churches for the Year 1927/28," 21.

90. Macfarland to Keller, presumably early 1926 and January 12, 1926 (PHS NCC RG 18 73/10).

91. Keller, "Report on the Activity of the European Central Bureau 1927 to 1928," 1 (PHS NCC RG 18 73/11).

92. Ibid., 2–3.

America. Delegates decided to continue the relief organization for another five years, and agreed upon the following core working areas:

> A. *Relief Work*—Stabilization of the welfare institutions of the churches . . . B. *Constructive Work*—Encouragement and support of the established missionary and evangelization work as well as assistance on behalf of new Protestant movements in various countries.—The 'leadership programme' scholarship to students and young ministers; exchange professorships and fellowships.—Building up the social welfare program of the churches.—Training of deaconesses and other women workers.[93]

Keller attached particular importance to the continuation of the "leadership programme." Cooperation between the "leadership programme" and the Life and Work committee of professors of theology had existed already since 1927. As Keller wrote in a letter to Macfarland, "I was also coopted as a member of the Commission of theological Professors (Chairman: Deissmann) . . . , which contemplates in connection with the European Central Bureau the exchange of students, theological professors, furtherance of libraries and international scientific cooperation."[94] Deissmann considered the "leadership programme" to be "extremely valuable and needed. It is very important that young students, especially from Middle and Eastern Europe, are getting the opportunity to continue their studies at prominent Divinity schools abroad. These young theologians, picked from the best of their Churches, represent for the future life of their Churches an elite which will inspire the young generation. It is also important that not only students, but Professors and Assistant Professors have been enabled by subsidies . . . to get a personal knowledge of other Churches . . . There is no doubt that a new spirit of Christian energy and fellowship is inspiring the young leaders in different centres."[95]

Following the outbreak of the world economic crisis, donations from the American Churches plummeted. Macfarland unabashedly remarked: "The Swiss . . . contributed to the Central Bureau in 1930 more than three times as much as our American Committee."[96] In 1935, America raised

93. "Agenda for the Conference for Inter-Church Aid, August 1929" (PHS NCC RG 18 73/12).

94. Keller to Macfarland, September 9, 1926 (PHS NCC RG 18 73/10); see also *Bulletin Life and Work* 2 (November 22, 1927), 51–52.

95. *Bulletin Life and Work* 2, 51-52.

96. Macfarland to Speer, July 10, 1931 (PHS 68–0221 BFM/COEMAR Records, 1 of 5 1790–2 Board on Foreign Missions 1920–1944).

73,000 Swiss francs, compared to 313,500 Swiss francs in Switzerland.[97] In the 1930s, over half the entire revenue of the relief organization came from Switzerland. In New York, one even feared the closure of the branch office. That said, the Federal Council was aware that "In Europe it comes on top of fifteen years of warfare, political and social upheaval, famine, revolution and the world-wide economic breakdown as a finishing touch."[98] Leiper lamented the fundamental resistance in the United States to Inter-Church Aid, which had originally been established as an "emergency relief agency." Moreover, "a pale imitation of European nationalism" was also spreading.[99]

However, the Federal Council accepted Keller's vision of a permanent relief organization as an integral part of Life and Work: "It is proposed that the Central Bureau shall become a permanent body for mutual interchange of help and sustentation [sustenance], as well as a sort of Church Red Cross to meet emergencies as they arise."[100] The New York office, which continued to exist, was also integrated into the American Life and Work movement, and thus into the Federal Council. By contrast, developments in Europe had not yet advanced that far.[101]

Keller's management of incoming donations had always been circumspect. Already in 1925, Macfarland had remarked, "Economy and wisdom have been exercised by the Central Bureau in the distribution of funds. There is a notable absence of complaint and a general warm appreciation everywhere of the work of the bureau. Its expense has been almost negligible in proportion to the funds handled."[102] Given the world economic crisis, Keller placed his meeting, speaking, and publication fees at the disposal of the agency's administration.[103] Nevertheless, Inter-

97. "1935 Financial Report, Central Bureau" (PHS 68–0221 BFM/COEMAR 1 of 5 1790–2).

98. "Annual Report of the Federal Council for the Year 1931," 60.

99. Keller, "Kurzer Bericht über die Tagung des Internationalen Komitees des Central Bureau," August 28–September 1, 1936, 9f. (BAR J.2.257 1245/133).

100. Cavert, Twenty Years of the Church Federation, 128.

101. For the organizational chart and corresponding text, see "Annual Report of the Federal Council for the Year 1932," 142–43.

102. Macfarland, "Report of the Federal Council Commissioner to Europe," in "Annual Report of the Federal Council for the Year 1925," 115–16.

103. In 1939 the total expenditure on administration, including salaries paid to clerical staff, ran to 18,032.34 Swiss francs, as against revenue of 563,655.79 Swiss francs, that is, 3%; for further financial details, see "Einnahmen/Rechnungen der Zentralstelle 1933–1948" (BAR J.2.257 1248/133). See above, p. 77.

Church Aid was forced to curtail its material assistance. In Transylvania, for instance, for which considerable sums had been raised, only some few scholarships for students of theology could be awarded. The agency had always sought to provide information, establish contacts, and coordinate aid efforts. Such work could be undertaken at no expense, and was thus continued. For instance, it served as a switchpoint between Lutheran welfare institutions in Poland and the Baltic States on the one hand, and Scandinavian and American Lutherans on the other.[104]

Notwithstanding such difficulties, Keller managed to extend relief efforts beyond Europe—not to Africa, where responsibility rested with the missionary societies, but instead to the ancient Christian populations of Armenians and Assyrians in the Near and Middle East, and to China.

During World War I, the Turkish government had driven the Armenians out of their ancestral lands. On hunger marches toward the South, hundreds of thousands lost their lives. Others survived, emaciated, deprived of their homes and possessions, and often sick. Keller contacted Jakob Künzler, a Swiss citizen who had worked as a male nurse and self-taught doctor administering pastoral care in a hospital in Turkey during World War I, where he had witnessed the persecution of the Armenians and their subsequent expulsion. He had managed to rescue hundreds from deportation. After the war, and based in Beirut, he selflessly attended to Armenians stranded in Lebanon or Syria, initially in cooperation with the Near East Relief, an American relief agency.[105] In cooperation with the *Bund Schweizerischer Armenierfreunde* (Union of Swiss Friends of Armenians), Keller raised 150,000 Swiss francs in 1929, which he transmitted to Künzler in Beirut.[106] In 1938, Keller invited Künzler to submit a report to the Executive Committee of Inter-Church Aid on the renewed Turkish oppression of the Armenian people and on the resulting refugee movements: "40,000 are already living in the Lebanon and along the railway, and refuse to live scattered in the villages because a village can offer no shelter in the case of a massacre. They remain attached to their Church. They need

---

104. "Minutes of the Conference of Swiss Aid Organizations 1934," 9 (BAR J.2.257 1245/133).

105. Künzler later became director of a home for the blind, an orphanage, and a hospice for widows in Ghazir, near Beirut.

106. Financial Reports of the Central Bureau for 1930 and 1935 (PHS 68–0221 BFM/COEMAR 1790–1)

priests and schools."[107] Letters between Künzler and Keller reveal a very profound bond between the two men.[108]

Early on, Keller also became aware of the equally tragic fate of the Christian (Nestorian) Assyrians in the border region between Turkey, Syria, and Iraq. Tens of thousands of Nestorians were murdered before and during World War I. Scattered groups managed to flee either to Aleppo, or into the Iraqi heartland, or to Europe.[109] Initially, Keller met the needs of Assyrian refugees in Marseille. Later, he established a Subkomitee für Assyrerhilfe (Subcommittee for Assyrian Aid) which looked after refugees in Syria and Iraq.[110] In Iraq, the Assyrians usually found no employment, not even with Western petroleum companies.[111] Keller was present when the twenty-five-year-old Assyrian patriarch Mar (Lord) Shimun XXIII (he had "inherited" his high office in 1920 from one of his uncles as a boy of twelve years) addressed the Council of the League of Nations in Geneva: "When the war erupted [World War I], we feared that we could face the same fate at the hands of the Turks as the Armenians. We fled and left our villages and children in the hands of the Turks, who had unleashed the Kurds on us. We descended to the plains of Iraq and hoped that war would bring us freedom. Our men joined the allied army. We have been bitterly disappointed. The allied forces defeated the Turks, but they left land and power to Turkey . . . Today, we are a poor, oppressed people."[112]

---

107. Keller, "Report of the Meeting of the Executive-Committee of the European Central Office for Inter-Church Aid, August 18–21, 1938," 7–8 (BAR J.2.257 1247/133).

108. Correspondence between Keller and Künzler (NLAK C 35).

109. Keller to Koechlin, December 21, 1925 (BAR J.2.257 1437/155).

110. Keller, "Minutes of the Conference of Swiss Relief Organizations, 1934," 4 (BAR J.2.257 1245/133).

111. Keller, Vom Unbekannten Gott, 63.

112. Keller, Von Geist und Liebe, 180–81.

The Assyrian Patriarch Mar (Lord) Shimun XXIII
(from Adolf Keller, *Von Geist und Liebe*, fig. 23)

In 1934, Keller submitted the following report: "Since Great Britain gave up her Mandate in Iraq, these Nestorians have been left more or less at the mercy of the Iraqi Government. More than a thousand were massacred a year ago. Their widows and children were taken care of in a concentration camp . . . The Office [Inter-Church Aid] approached the Council of the League on their behalf already last year."[113]

In London, Keller discussed the situation with the Archbishop of Canterbury, who was in contact with the "American Mission in Iraq" and

113. Keller, "Report on the meeting of the Executive Committee (Central Bureau), July 20–25, 1934," 22 (BAR J.2.257 1245/133).

the French authorities in Syria.[114] In 1935, accompanied by Eugène Choisy and General Secretary Henriod, Keller paid a visit to Salvador de Madariaga, a member of the Assyrian Committee of the Council of the League of Nations.[115] Inter-Church Aid supported Assyrian refugees in France, the Lebanon, and the Baltic states. Moreover, Keller channeled funds to the Assyrians in Iraq through Künzler.[116] There were plans to allow the Assyrians to emigrate to Abyssinia, but these were obliterated by Italy's attack on the country. Attempted resettlement in Syria also failed: "After the break down of the League's plan to procure a national home to 35,000 Assyrians in the region of the Ghab on the Orontes in the mandate of Syria, the situation of this remnant of an old Christian people is becoming catastrophic . . . The help which could be granted hitherto by the international Nansen Office for Refugees and by the European Central Bureau is not sufficient for protecting the people from hardness [hardship] and real distress and it is to be feared that the process of extermination will rapidly continue."[117]

In 1937, Keller and a delegate of the Archbishop of Canterbury approached the Council of the League of Nations in an attempt to prevent the fate of the Assyrians from being disregarded.[118] He also discussed the issue with Guiseppe Motta, the Swiss Foreign Minister. He did everything in his power to assist the Assyrians. It was a bitter episode. To be sure, only very few people other than Keller were as acutely aware of the plight of the refugees in the Near and Middle East. His awareness and insight mattered greatly, since the refugee problem reached a new dimension with the rise of Stalin and Hitler to power. In 1940 Mar Shimun XXIII was forced to emigrate to the United States.

A brief word on China, where a famine broke out in 1929: Leonhard Ragaz requested Keller to launch a fundraising campaign in support of the suffering Chinese population. Donations totaled 93,000 Swiss francs. Once again, Keller also sought to achieve coordination with the Council of

---

114. Keller, "Bericht über die Reise nach England, 1.–21. März 1934" (BAR 1245/133).

115. Keller, Paper on "Nestorians, Assyrians," January 15, 1935 (WCC 42.0042 3).

116. "Report of the meeting of the Executive Committee (Central Bureau)," Edinburgh, July 20-25, 1934, 21–22 (BAR J.2.257 1245/133).

117. Keller, "Statement concerning the situation of the Nestorian Assyrians submitted to the Universal Christian Council for Life and Work," June 15, 1937 (WCC 42.0042 3,1).

118. Keller (on behalf of the Subcommittee for Assyrian Aid), September 27, 1937 (BAR J.2.257 1247/133).

the League of Nations and the Red Cross.[119] Keller's famine relief in China also benefited non-Christians. This was a novelty. Thus, Inter-Church Aid sought to assist those in need, irrespective of their origin and outlook. This open-mindedness also became apparent with the aid granted in the Soviet Union.

COMBATTING HUNGER IN THE SOVIET UNION

Keller considered Bolshevism a perversion of high-minded "true socialism." In the Soviet Union, it had assumed dangerous and evil forms.[120] Capable of seducing the masses, Bolshevism must be seen as a "national religion," which possessed both creed and a messiah—the latter in the guise of Stalin: "Bolshevism and Nationalism are new national religions hidden in political and social programs."[121] Keller observed parallels between Bolshevism and National Socialism. Both ideologies were totalitarian, as he recognized early on. Attending to their victims struck him in both cases as a self-explanatory humanitarian duty.

After the Russian Revolution of 1917, several million Russian emigrants fled to Western Europe, including several hundred thousand to the city of Paris alone. There were plans to establish a Russian Orthodox Academy in Paris (it was to be named St Serge) as a spiritual and theological center for Russian refugees. Keller attached great importance to the project. In late 1925, he wrote to Macfarland about the "Orthodox Academy which is to be organised by the Metropolitan Eulogios in Paris. This institution deserves your attention, and I hope for help of the Protestant Episcopal Church."[122] Some weeks later, he added: "I may say that I consider the whole thing of very great importance. It seems to be clearly along the lines of the Conference of Stockholm when we help this institution in its first year of struggle."[123] Some outstanding professors were already working at the Academy, he noted, and no less than thirty-two students had embarked on their studies.

In March 1926, Keller presented his relief organization to the Archbishop of Canterbury: "I tried especially to interest [him] in the Russian

119. Keller to Ragaz, November 19, 1929 (BAR J.2.257 1446/156), and July 21 and 27, 1930 (StAZ W I 67 103.2).

120. Keller, *Das Christentum und der heutige Wirtschaftsmensch*, 17 and 19.

121. Keller, *Religion and Revolution*, 13–14; see also below, pp. 162–63.

122. Keller to Macfarland, November 14, 1925 (PHS NCC RG 18, 73/9).

123. Keller to Macfarland, March 11, 1926 (PHS NCC RG 18 73/10).

Orthodox Academy in Paris."[124] He knew that the Anglicans greatly sympathized with the Orthodox Church; consequently, it came to a sporadic cooperation between the relief agency and the Anglicans on behalf of the academy. In 1930, Keller founded the Russian Subcommittee of the Inter-Church Aid, in connection with the intensifying persecutions of Christians in the Soviet Union. He handed over the presidency of this committee to Alphons Koechlin, who organized concert tours through Western Europe for a Russian choir. The proceeds benefited the Russian academy in Paris.[125] In connection with his Ecumenical Seminar, which will be discussed later, Keller cooperated with the Academy.[126]

The many Germans whose ancestors had emigrated to Russia several generations earlier could often not return home after 1917. Owing to a combination of factors—World War I, the Russian Revolution, civil war, and starvation—these emigrants came under massive pressure.[127] Thousands lost their lives during the "Great Terror." About one million Protestants lived in and around the city of St Petersburg; two thirds were Lutherans, the rest either Reformed or Baptists. Along with German- and Russian-speaking congregations, there were also Latvian, Estonian, and Finnish communities. The National Lutheran Council in New York and the Swedish Gustav-Adolf-Verein sent the Lutherans large sums. The young Federation of Swiss Protestant Churches sent the Reformed congregations around 200,000 Swiss francs.[128]

The situation worsened as Stalin's dictatorship intensified. The International Home Missions Conference of 1926 in Amsterdam requested Keller to attend to the needs of the approximately eighty Reformed ministers and congregations in the region of Leningrad (the former St Petersburg).[129] The Lutheran World Council was already administering to the needs of the stricken Lutherans.[130] In late 1926, Keller organized the shipping of 15,000 Bibles and songbooks to Leningrad.[131] Moreover,

124. Keller to Macfarland, April 1, 1926 (ibid.).

125. Keller, "Bericht der Europäischen Zentralstelle für kirchliche Hilfsaktionen 1937," 10, and "Minutes of the Federation of Swiss Protestant Churches, 1934," 3 (BAR J.2.257 1247/133 u. 1245/133).

126. See below, p. 150 and 153.

127. Keller, Zur Lage des Europäischen Protestantismus, 97.

128. See above, p. 48.

129. Keller to Macfarland, September 9, 1926 (PHS NCC RG 18 73/10).

130. Keller, Die Europäische Zentralstelle für kirchliche Hilfsaktionen, 9.

131. "News Sheet," issued by the European Central Bureau, October 1, 1926, 3 (PHS NCC RG 18 73/10).

money transfers (which were soon prohibited, however) and food packages were sent to Leningrad, particularly to intellectuals, the families of Protestant pastors, and Orthodox priests. Shipments continued under the most difficult circumstances via the Baltic states until the outbreak of the Second World War. Since organized aid was forbidden, Keller had fictitious uncles, aunts, sisters, and cousins in Switzerland send parcels to their alleged relatives in the Soviet Union.[132] Receipts and letters sent to him prove that the consignments reached their intended recipients.[133] From 1933 to 1936, Inter-Church Aid raised 500,000 Swiss francs for Protestant and Orthodox Christians in Russia.[134] Evidently, Keller succeeded in tapping new sources of funding for this purpose.

From 1929 on, the persecution of Christians intensified. Numerous Protestant ministers and parishioners were arrested. Many perished in death camps. Without being officially prohibited, the Protestant churches were virtually exterminated until 1938. Keller supported a number of Protestant ministers detained in Soviet prisons, "notably Rev. David Schaible, the former pastor of the Reformed Church in Odessa," who had been detained as early as 1930.[135] Schaible, from Württemberg, was among the few survivors of decade-long imprisonment, during which he nevertheless conducted clandestine baptisms, weddings, and funerals.[136] In 1937, all Lutheran pastors in Odessa—which had once been a cosmopolitan metropole—were shot. From 1937 on, while the Orthodox congregations in the Ukraine were no longer functioning,[137] some remained active in other parts of the Soviet Union.

132. Keller, "Aus meinem Leben," 127.

133. Keller, "Berichte Zentralstelle 1937," 5–6; see also the report for 1938/9, 8 (BAR J.2.257 1247/133).

134. Keller to Joseph Oldham, June 29, 1936 (WCC 42.0042 1). Today this sum would amount to more than five million Swiss francs.

135. "Annual Report of the Federal Council for the Year 1931," 59; see above, p. 92.

136. The Reformed church in Odessa was transformed into a puppet theater. Schaible did not return to Germany until 1974. A few years ago, the fundamentalist American Presbyterians took over the church.

137. To the famine in the Ukraine see below pp. 143–44.

Adolf Keller

WE'RE NOT THROUGH YET!

with the Russian Evangelical Refugees in Manchukuo, because we've got
to find a way of sending this man and 164 of his fellow exiles to South
America, where a hard job of pioneering is waiting for him.

*An evangelical refugee from Russia arriving in Harbin, with the temperature
16 degrees below zero. Emaciated—almost a hunger grin on his face—worn out,
but undaunted after a seven-months' trek. His worldly goods are reduced to
the package he has in his hand, but he brings with him faith, courage, stead-
fastness, energy, thrift, intelligence, honesty, and a capacity for hard work which
will make him an asset and not a liability to the country which gives him a home.*

Bulletin of the Central Bureau of Relief
of the Evangelical Churches of Europe
(archive Dr. Pierre Keller)

142

In late 1929, there were reports that the "Volga Germans," who were partly Mennonites, partly Lutherans or Reformed, had been driven out of their farming villages for their continued adherence to the Christian faith. Thousands were deported to the White Sea or Siberia, while hundreds died of starvation and sickness. Keller telegraphed the American office of Inter-Church Aid, which sent him $2,000 by return post.[138] In 1930, he convened an "International Russian Aid Conference" in Basel, which was attended by Protestant and Orthodox relief organizations to discuss aid coordination.[139] One outcome of the conference was the aforementioned Russian Subcommittee of the Central Bureau.[140] Within half a year, Inter-Church Aid managed to raise 72,000 Swiss francs for the Volga refugees and for those who had remained in Russia.[141] Several thousand refugees were able to flee to China. Keller published a photograph of one of these refugees, beneath which he wrote: "An evangelical refugee from Russia arriving in Harbin, with the temperature 16 below zero. Emaciated—almost a hunger grin on his face—worn out, but undaunted after a seven-month's trek. His wordly goods are reduced to the package he has in his hand."[142] Inter-Church Aid provided aid for the 1,200 Evangelical-Russian refugees in Harbin. In cooperation with the Nansen Office,[143] the agency managed to secure their passage to Brazil and Paraguay, where their settlement was reasonably successful.[144]

Between 1931 and 1933, Stalinist collectivization resulted in severe famines in the Ukraine, which was then part of the Soviet Union. Current research estimates that seven million people starved to death. In mounting a coordinated aid operation, Keller secured cooperation with Germany, Switzerland, Great Britain, America, France, Italy, Czechoslovakia, and even with the Christian churches and with individual groups in India and

138. "Quadrennial Report of the Federal Council, 1932," p. 147ff. (PHS NCC RG 18 79/20).

139. Keller, *Der Schweizerische evangelische Kirchenbund*, 130; see also "Minutes of the Conference of Swiss Aid Organizations, 1934," 3 (BAR J.2.257 1245/133).

140. See above, p. 140.

141. "Minutes of the Assembly of Delegates of the Federation of Swiss Protestant Churches, June 16 and 17, 1930," 23.

142. See the illustration and corresponding caption, "Over there with the Churches of Christ," *Bulletin No. 14 of the American Office of the Central Bureau* (New York, presumably 1933), 3 (NLAK C 35).

143. The Nansen Office was a refugee organization.

144. Keller, "Report on the meeting of the Executive Committee, July 20–25, 1934), 14 (BAR J.2.257 1245/133); see also Keller, "Russische Flüchtlinge in China," *Basler Nachrichten*, March 1, 1932, newspaper cutting (WCC 301.43.26).

Eastern Asia, for instance, in Taiwan.[145] In 1932 and 1933 alone, Inter-Church Aid raised 350,000 Swiss francs.[146] How much actually reached the starving is uncertain, since the Soviets sought to prevent relief supplies from reaching their destinations. Owing to droughts and the requisitioning of harvests for the army and the cities, the rural population was once again hit by a famine in the years 1933 and 1934. "During a certain period the Bureau [Inter-Church Aid] received between 70 and 90 letters per day asking for help."[147] In late 1933, Keller, the Cardinal of Vienna (Theodor Innitzer), president of a relief agency providing aid in the Soviet Union, and the Chief Rabbi of Vienna (David Feuchtwang), head of the Jewish aid fund for Russia, issued a joint call for donations.[148] Such a coordinated venture was quite extraordinary at the time. In a letter to Bell, Keller considered it "a duty borne of the most fundamental humanity and pure charity to raise the voice of conscience for the benefit of the starving and dying."[149]

APIDEP: AFFORDABLE LOANS, NOT HUMBLE DONATIONS

As early as 1924, Keller contemplated the idea of providing financially weak churches with inexpensive loans: "it would be desirable to consider another form of assistance besides the voluntary gifts made hitherto: the establishing of a Protestant bank, which would grant emerging Protestant churches and welfare institutions secured long-term loans, which could benefit other institutions following repayment."[150]

He felt vindicated when he heard that Caritas, the Catholic relief agency, was granting inexpensive loans in Germany: "If the Catholics can do this, why not we?"[151] His survey of European churches in 1926 revealed that the "Churches of Europe have long been asking for loans, prefer-

145. Keller, "Minutes of the Conference of Swiss Aid Organizations 1934," 9 (BAR J.2.257 1245/133).
146. Keller, "Report on the meeting of the Executive Committee of Inter-Church Aid, 1934," 15 (BAR J.2.257 1245/133).
147. Ibid.
148. Keller et al., "Eine interkonfessionelle Hilfskonferenz für die Hungernden in Russland," *Evangelischer Pressedienst* 1 (January 3, 1934) 197.
149. Keller to Bell, January 14, 1935 (LPL Bell 19 f. 430).
150. Keller, *Von protestantischer Not und Hilfe*, 21.
151. Keller to Miller, June 21, 1926 (PHS NCC RG 18 73/10).

ring them to gifts."[152] Once again, Keller approached the Americans. In response, they were concerned about securitization of such loans. Instead, various respected Swiss bankers considered Keller's proposal. They drew up statutes for the envisaged Association Protestante Internationale de Prêts (International Protestant Association for Loans; hereafter APIDEP), so that in 1929 Keller could confidently observe:

> The guiding idea of this association is to support, on a commer-
> cial basis, donations towards protestant projects and institutions
> in need of funding . . . It should rest on a commercial rather
> than philanthropic foundation, since its chief purpose will be
> to furnish adequate means to protestant efforts at a moderate
> rate of interest. Just now this is imperative, as one will readily
> understand when noting that these days, for example in Austria
> or Yugoslavia, a rate of 10 to 15% is considered normal. Some
> time ago, a protestant organization has had to borrow at the rate
> of 26%. Numerous such groups must be able to obtain a nor-
> mal rate of interest in order to get their projects going. Several
> prominent Swiss bankers, who have withheld neither their time
> nor effort in launching a new form of mutual assistance, are of-
> fering every guarantee for the soundness of the enterprise.[153]

At the Inter-Church Aid conference of 1929 in Basel, there was unanimous agreement on the proposed project. The next step involved raising the initial capital. Due to the outbreak of the world economic crisis, however, the majority of churches considered the purchasing of share certificates impossible. Instead of the targeted 3.5 million Swiss francs, only 400,000 were raised, of which ninety percent came from Switzerland. Nevertheless, the cooperative association was established in 1932. F. Marc Sauter was appointed director, and the governing board included the bankers Alfred Sarasin and Gustave Hentsch, as well as Adolf Keller. While APIDEP and Inter-Church Aid were separate institutions, in practice they cooperated very closely.

Notwithstanding limited funds, which accrued only slowly, until the outbreak of the war around ten loans could be granted every year, to church welfare organizations in Austria, Bishop Zöckler's welfare facilities in Galicia, Protestant Women's Aid in Germany, and to a congregation in Czechoslovakia, among other institutions. Loans were returned promptly,

152. Kenneth Miller in the "Annual Report of the Federal Council for the Year 1926," 80.

153. "Annual Report of the Federation of Swiss Protestant Churches for 1928–1929," 14.

whereupon they were made available to other borrowers, true to the principle of solidarity. Moreover, APIDEP became a kind of management consultancy for church institutions.

Keller remained on the APIDEP board until 1948. Under the auspices of the Provisional Ecumenical Council, the Ecumenical Church Loan Fund (ECLOF) was placed alongside APIDEP in 1946. Owing to increased cash flow after the war, ECLOF developed swiftly.[154] In contrast to APIDEP, funds for loan aid were made available to ECLOF with no hope of a return on investment, and were hence exempt from taxation. ECLOF was (and remains) a non-profit organization.[155] While the organizations had varying legal structures, their purpose was the same.[156]

The APIDEP annual report for 1963 contains a valedictory address dedicated to the memories of Adolf Keller, an honorary member who had previously died, and of Gustave Hentsch, the deceased Geneva banker and member of the board, who served as president of ECLOF from 1946 until his death: "It is thanks to the energetic drive of Professor Keller that our Association has seen the light of day, and it is with profound feeling that our Council salutes, in the persons of the honorable Adolphe (sic) Keller and Gustave Hentsch, two of the most faithful fashioners of its effort."[157] Besides empowering organizations and institutions to engage in self-help, which marked a highly progressive approach at the time, the purpose of APIDEP and Inter-Church Aid was to strengthen solidarity among the churches.

ANTICIPATING BOSSEY: KELLER'S ECUMENICAL SEMINAR

The Ecumenical Seminar arose from one of Keller's visions. It originated in his lectures on comparative ecclesiology (Kirchenkunde), a new discipline that he established and began teaching at the University of Zurich in 1926. In 1929, Keller was appointed honorary professor by the government of Zurich. Following his relocation to Geneva in 1928, he also began

154. Personal conversation between the author and Muhungi F. Kanyoro, President of ECLOF, WCC, January 26, 2005.

155. Messenger and Lee, *The Story of the Ecumenical Church Loan Fund*, 14.

156. Sauter, "Report of APIDEP for the 1963 financial year," 1 (WCC). Because various churches still owned shares, APIDEP continued to exist alongside ECLOF until 1973.

157. Ibid., 7.

lecturing at the University of Geneva, which also appointed him honorary professor after nine years of service, "in recognition of the eminent services which he has rendered to the cause of international protestantism, the importance of his writings, and his participation in the Faculty of Theology, where he has taught for many years."[158]

Comparative ecclesiology focuses on learning about and comparing present-day churches. Keller had already explored comparative ecclesiology in his books *Dynamis* (1922) and *Protestant Europe* (1927). His lectures discussed the religious practices of the various churches, their welfare work, their spiritual wealth, their theology, their structure, and the shared convictions of the churches. He identified three distinctive features of all the churches: first, they originated in Pentecost, secondly, there was only *one* Church; and thirdly, the Church was characterized by its *universality*, that is, its catholicity. The theological significance of the unification movements among the churches was that they placed the notion of the essence of the Church, which included unity, universality, a common spirit, and a community of love, alongside the innumerable, coincidental forms of churches.[159] It was impossible to undertake comparative ecclesiology without approaching as closely as possible the real life of the other churches. How can one become acquainted with Anglicanism, he inquired, if one has never knelt down to pray in its chapels and cathedrals, or never sung and prayed from its prayer book? Following such close, firsthand experience, however, there was a need to stand back for reflection; such distance, he maintained, taught one to see.[160]

The principal aim of the Ecumenical Seminar, founded by Keller, was to train the future bearers of the ecumenical movement. And thus its story began. In 1928, Ralph W. Brown, general secretary of Faith and Order, sought Keller's advice on determining priority tasks. In response, Keller sent the following words of counsel:

> To follow up the work of the Conference [of Lausanne 1927], it is necessary to continue to spread mutual information on the nature and life of the different churches. We have made just a beginning at Lausanne and a large part of Protestants have there, for instance, faced the Anglican position for the first time in their life, and vice versa . . . This should be done [by] proposing to the

158. Paul Lachenal (on behalf of the Council) to Prof. W. Rappard (president of the University of Geneva), July 6, 1937 (archive of the University of Geneva 1984/35/6/D85).

159. Keller, "Wesen und Form der kirchlichen Gemeinschaft," 11ff.

160. Keller, *Der Weg der dialektischen Theologie durch die kirchliche Welt*, 7.

theological Faculties to introduce courses on Kirchenkunde i.e.,
information on present day Church problems in the different
countries . . . I have been giving such a course at the University
of Zurich and I hear that other Faculties in Germany are also introducing their students into these problems . . . Beside studying
dogmatical differences and the way to overcome them, the piety
of the different Churches should be studied, the simple religious
life and the significance of the cult . . . It should be considered
whether the churches should not found an ecumenical Institute
with the tasks prescribed above.[161]

Keller proposed "a permanent teaching centre," that is, "a graduate
school of ecumenical studies."[162] However, the Continuation Committee
of Faith and Order failed to show an interest in Keller's suggestions. In
1929, Bishop Brent, the founder of the movement, died. Subsequent discussions reached "something of a deadlock."[163] Owing to a lack of funds,
the office of Faith and Order was closed and Brown dismissed from his
post. Nor were any regular meetings of the Continuation Committee held
from that period onward.

Keller now took the initiative himself. To begin with, however, the
Executive Committee of the Ecumenical Council of Life and Work was
not the least interested in an "Ecumenical Institute." But Keller persevered
in his quest to establish such a venture on various occasions, including at
a meeting convened Paris in 1931: "Dr. Keller presented a report on the
establishment of a Christian study Centre in Geneva, where lectures are
given, and there is founded a common library and provision made for
common research, and study groups to be accommodated."[164] He envisaged a course of study lasting one to two semesters. Courses should be
run in conjunction with the international Christian organizations based
in Geneva and with the University of Geneva.[165] They were aimed at
young theologians. A breakthrough was achieved at the conference of the
Ecumenical Council of 1932 in Chexbres. Keller, who had recently been

161. Keller to Ralph W. Brown, June 2, 1928 (WCC 23.4.003 corr. Ralph W. Brown).

162. Weber, *A Laboratory for Ecumenical Life*, 14.

163. Keller, "The Position of Protestantism in Relation to Faith and Order," 11–12.

164. Executive Committee of Life and Work, Paris, February 18–22, 1931 (WCC 24.001).

165. Keller, "Memorandum on the organisation of ecumenical courses in Geneva," February 13, 1931 (WCC 24.002 Life and Work).

appointed honorary lecturer, was given a free hand to pursue his proj-ect.[166] However, no financial support was pledged to the undertaking.[167]

In late 1932, Keller promoted his plan at twenty-two theological faculties and seminaries in the United States, including Andover Newton Theological School near Boston,[168] McCormick Presbyterian Seminary in Chicago, Yale, Princeton Theological Seminary, Columbia University, and Union Theological Seminary in New York.[169] His idea met with approval and sympathy. At its meeting of August 1933, the Administration Com-mittee of the Ecumenical Council decided to appoint a tenured professor for the envisaged institute, and was already seeking a suitable candidate for the post.[170] However, Keller's canvassing for funds from America re-mained unsuccessful. In Rockefeller's case, he advanced only as far as his private secretary.[171] Doors also remained closed at the Carnegie Founda-tion. Thus, the idea of a permanent ecumenical institute foundered.

In their endeavor to salvage the project, Keller and Auguste Gampert, dean of the Faculty of Theology at the University of Geneva, agreed upon a scaled-down version, namely, a three-week course, an Ecumenical Semi-nar, to be convened in the summer of 1934.[172] Its provisional Executive Committee was composed of Gampert, Keller, and Visser't Hooft, who later became general secretary of the Ecumenical Council.[173] Its stated aims were as follows: "1. Study of contemporary tendencies of theological thought in the Churches of various nations; 2. Study of the principles and problems of the 'Ecumenical' Movements." Keller was appointed director.

166. Keller, "Aus meinem Leben," 183; see above, pp. 128–30.

167. "Arbeitspläne der Kommissionen und Anträge an das Budget des Ökumen-ischen Rates für das Rechnungsjahr 1932/33" (WCC 24.001).

168. Dean V. Darbney of Andover Newton about Keller to Macfarland, September 9, 1932: "We feel we are very fortunate to have so distinguished a person." (NLAK C 23).

169. Keller, "Bericht über die Vortragsreise in Amerika, 10. Okt.–22. Dez. 1932" (WCC 24.067 1 Life and Work Ökumenisches Seminar).

170. "Minutes of the Administration Committee, Paris, August 4–5, 1933" (WCC 24.001).

171. Keller, "Bericht über die Vortragsreise in Amerika, 1932," 2 (WCC 24.067 1).

172. Prospectus entitled "International Theological Seminar under the auspices of the Autonomous Faculty of Theology of the University of Geneva," July 30 to August 18, 1934 (NLAK C 3).

173. Visser't Hooft represented the YMCA and the World Student Christian Fed-eration. Although he was involved in the Seminar, he mentions neither it nor Keller as its initiator in his autobiography *Die Welt war meine Gemeinde*. See below, pp. 236 and n. 177.

The minimum admissions requirement was a Bachelor of Divinity. Tuition fees amounted to twenty-five Swiss francs, and six francs were charged per day for board and lodging. Thirty-three young theologians enrolled—from Holland, Russia, Romania, Poland, Czechoslovakia, Great Britain, Canada, the United States, Switzerland, and Germany, and included Protestants, Anglicans, Orthodox, and Old Catholics. Some students were awarded an Inter-Church Aid scholarship. Keller managed to recruit Emil Brunner as a lecturer. From this period on, Brunner became actively involved in Life and Work. Brunner and the other lecturers, who were all highly qualified, waived their fees. The Société Jean Calvin and various friends of Keller's from Zurich, including Max Huber, covered the arising travel and accommodation expenses. Keller paid for the costs of operating the course office out of his own pocket.

The inaugural Ecumenical Seminar opened on July 29, 1934, with an ecumenical service held in St Pierre Cathedral in Geneva. The University of Geneva provided teaching rooms for the duration of the course. Classes were taught in German, English, and French. Brunner spoke about "The Theology of Revelation," Choisy about "Calvin and the Modern World," Martin Dibelius, the German New Testament scholar, about "The Kingdom of God," Elmer G. Homrighausen, an American theologian, about "Main Trends in American Theological Thinking," and Fritz Lieb, a Swiss theologian, about "The Life of the Russian Orthodox Church in its Relationship with Western Christianity." Other speakers included Arvid Runestam, from Sweden, S. B. Cassian, a lecturer at the Académie St Serge in Paris, as well as Visser't Hooft, Schönfeld, and Keller.[174] Besides the lectures, the program also featured small group discussions.

The theological level of the majority of participants was extraordinarily advanced. Notwithstanding the cross-section of participants, a fraternal atmosphere prevailed during sessions, according to Keller's final report. However, it had become apparent that a systematic discussion of the key issues and of far-reaching questions would require more time.[175] While reiterating the idea of a "permanent Ecumenical Seminar," he advocated the continuation of the summer course for the time being.[176] *The Churches in Action*, the newsletter published by the Ecumenical Council,

174. Keller, "Die heutige Mission der Ökumenischen Bewegung" (Report on the Seminar of 1934), 12 (WCC).

175. Ibid., 13–14.

176. Ibid., 14.

assessed the inaugural seminar "as a very successful experiment."[177] Bishop Bell welcomed both Keller's final report and his proposals.[178] The Ecumenical Council approved the convening of courses in the summer of 1935.[179] Along with Geneva's Faculty of Theology, it now stood patron for the Ecumenical Seminar and funded it with 1,000 Swiss francs. For the remaining 3,000 Swiss francs, Keller once again turned to his friends in Zurich. Outstanding American professors of theology, including W. A. Brown, Walter Horton, Reinhold Niebuhr, and Paul Tillich, were involved in the 1935 Seminar and those thereafter.

In the autumn of 1934, it became apparent that Karl Barth would be forced to terminate his professional activities in Germany. Keller hoped to recruit him as a tenured professor for the Seminar, an appointment that would have helped place the course on a permanent institutional basis.[180] When Keller heard that the University of Basel had offered Barth a chair, he requested him to at least participate in the summer course of 1935.[181] Barth hesitated: "While an ever so small rumor of an international, League-of-Nations-type hyperactivity (Adolf Keller's) makes me shy away from Geneva, once again Visser't Hooft has sent word from there, in such a fine and distinguished manner, that I cannot possibly assume that matters there are nothing but seriously minded."[182] In late December 1934, Keller informed Bishop Bell about his efforts to secure Barth's services:

> Recent developments in Germany, and especially the deposition of Karl Barth, gave a new stimulus to the project . . . It would be superfluous to point out the importance for the seminar, the ecumenical movement and Geneva, if Karl Barth would accept at least for the summer semester . . . In this case also, a friend of Barth's would guarantee his salary . . . We talked the matter over yesterday with Dr. Sloane Coffin, President of the Union

177. *The Churches in Action* 6 (November, 1934), 5.

178. "Minutes of the Administrative Committee, Chichester, October 25–26, 1934" (WCC 24.001).

179. "Universal Christian Council for Life and Work. Minutes of the Meeting on May 16, 1935 in Paris" (ibid.).

180. Keller, "Zweites Ökumenisches Seminar in Genf, 22. Juli bis 10. August 1935," printed cover, typescript, 1 (WCC).

181. Keller to Barth, December 15, 1934 (KBA 9334.1286).

182. Barth to Thurneysen, December 24 [–26], 1934, in Algner, ed., *Karl Barth–Eduard Thurneysen. Briefwechsel*, vol. 3, 808–9; see also ibid., 809, n. 43.

[Theological] Seminary at New York, who was my guest last
night, and he was keenly interested in the proposal.[183]

Not only was Bell interested in the proposal but he also offered to
help secure the services of a qualified English-speaking lecturer for the
Seminar.[184] In February 1935, Barth accepted Keller's invitation to lecture
on the summer course.[185] "We are looking forward to having you with us,"
Keller reassured him.[186] The prospect of meeting Karl Barth had a mag-
netic effect. Eighty-five students enrolled for the 1935 Seminar, including
sixteen Germans, one participant each from Japan and South Africa, and
Theodor Zöckler's son Martin from Stanislau (Ivano-Frankivsk), as well
as forty to fifty members of the general public, who were often non-theologians.[187] Women were relatively well represented, with their enrollments
numbering seventeen, including at least eight qualified female theologians. However, no member of the Church of England attended.

Besides delivering four lectures on "The Church and the Churches,"
Barth held a six-hour seminar on the beginning of Calvin's Catechism. Eberhard Busch, Barth's biographer, cites Barth's impressions of the Seminar,
and then comments on these:

> "It was an extremely exhausting business, because I just had
> to be available to discuss things with every conceivable person
> from early in the morning until late at night." In his lectures
> Barth showed a critical yet expectant interest in the ecumenical
> movement, which was slowly beginning to take shape, though
> "All in all . . . for the moment this ecumenical business hasn't
> made much of an impression on me." He used the occasion to
> formulate his view of the ecumenical problem, developing the
> thesis: "The question of the unity of the church must be identical
> with the question of Jesus Christ as the specific head and Lord of
> the church . . . Jesus Christ, as one mediator between God and
> man, *is* himself church unity."[188]

183. Keller to Bell, December 28, 1934 (LPL Bell 6 f. 520).

184. Bell to Keller, January 9, 1935 (LPL Bell 7 f. 32).

185. Executive Committee of the Seminar to Barth, Geneva, February 8, 1935; see
also Keller to Barth, February 11, 1935 (KBA 9335.170 and 9335.181).

186. Keller to Barth, (May or June) 16, 1935 (KBA 9335.547).

187. List of participants at the 1935 Ecumenical Seminar (NLAK C 3). On Theodor Zöckler, see above, pp. 88–92.

188. Quoted from *Karl Barth, His Life from Letters*, 263–64 (italics original).

One participant observed that Barth had emphasized the impossibility of basing ecumenism on humanitarian, idealist, and political unification endeavors. According to Barth, the manifold number of churches only served to make every church aware of both its shortcomings and its guilt before God, so that it could do precious little other than strive after the unity that already existed in Jesus Christ. Keller had also raised the question about the proper kind of theology. Both in his lecture on the "Ökumenische Bewegung als theologisches Problem" (The Ecumenical Movement as a Theological Problem) and in the subsequent discussion, he had repeatedly highlighted the need for recourse to stringent fundamentals and for a continuous struggle for the Word of God that is Jesus Christ; in doing so, he refuted the arrogance of man's attempt to build church unity."[189] As this account suggests yet again, the positions held by Barth and Keller positions were not that far removed! Eduard Schweizer, who was influenced by Barth's theology and later became professor of New Testament in Zurich, offered the following assessment:

> The fact that Karl Barth was invited shows that the unification of all churches is neither embraced with a grand hallelujah nor approached by brushing aside all truly serious questions in this respect. The Seminar seeks to undertake clear theological work . . . This is probably the most pleasing and at the same time the most important impression gained in Geneva . . . The second most important one was the attention devoted to Church Studies . . . And the third . . . were the strolls taken together, the brief morning services . . . , but particularly the casual discussions during the day.—There were various shortcomings, of course. For instance, there were too many lectures . . . more profound discussions barely occurred, since too little time was reserved for debate. But these are all shortcomings that . . . we made known to Professor Keller, and which he gladly welcomed . . . In any event, the Seminar has made us raise *questions*, questions that lead further in fact.[190]

Barth wrote to Keller: "I think back fondly to those days in Geneva, even though they were somewhat strenuous. In any event, I am pleased to have become more closely acquainted with ecumenism, not least as represented by yourself."[191] However, he had not "converted" to ecumenism.

189. Feldges, "Ökumenisches Seminar in Genf," col. 229–30.

190. Eduard Schweizer, "Bericht über das zweite ökumenische Seminar" (NLAK C 3).

191. Barth to Keller, August 2, 1935 (KBA 9235.218).

Far from it, since he described the 1936 conference of Life and Work in Chamby as "a Punch and Judy show."[192]

The third Ecumenical Seminar of 1936 was devoted to the themes to be discussed at the forthcoming conference of Life and Work in Oxford. Once again, Keller managed to secure the services of three leading theologians: Paul Tillich, Reinhold Niebuhr, and Toyohiko Kagawa, the acclaimed Japanese theologian. From Germany, the young Hanns Lilje attended along with Martin Dibelius. Just as in 1935, Boris Vycheslavtseff represented the Russian-Orthodox Academy of Paris. Even Eduard Thurneysen,[193] Barth's closest associate, participated. There were ninety-nine enrollments, including some young professors of theology. Keller observed that the Seminar "may really be described as a postgraduate institute."[194] Moreover, "the center of the theological work of the Seminar was occupied by a study of the message of the Gospel. It is a matter of gratification to see how the young theological generation of the Continent is going back to the sources of evangelical life in the Holy Scriptures."[195] The following remark is revealing: "Here the question of the religious meaning of history comes in. Prof. Tillich gave a comprehensive survey on this problem, including America as well as Europe, and showed how the Church created what is called historical consciousness. His philosophical survey led to a lively discussion on the relation between natural and revealed theology. A controversy which is parallel to the actual discussion between Protestantism on one side and Anglicanism as well as Orthodoxy on the other."[196]

After the course, Keller expressed a bold wish: "It seems desirable that the members of the Seminar should live together in the same house during the whole time of the Seminar, in spite of advantages that a town like Geneva offers. It is therefore contemplated . . . to convene the future Seminars to places outside of the town."[197] With the acquisition of Bossey Castle in 1946, Keller's dream became a reality thanks to a generous donation from John D. Rockefeller Jr., who had already funded the "leadership programme."

192. Keller to Barth, Chamby, August 23, 1936 (KBA 9336.674).

193. For Thurneysens's mocking of Stockholm 1925, see pp. 95–96 and n. 146.

194. Keller, "The Third International Theological Seminar in Geneva, July 28 to August 14, 1936," 3 (NLAK C 3).

195. Ibid., 4.

196. Ibid., 4.

197. Ibid., 6.

Adolf Keller

154

Instead of the Geneva Seminar, a special program for young people accompanied the Oxford conference of Life and Work, 1937. Another Seminar was convened in Geneva in 1938. Martin Dibelius, Hanns Lilje, and Hans Sommerlath all promised to attend, but pressure from the German government forced them to withdraw:[198] "The German government now appears to consider the Seminar as the actual whipping boy of the ecumenical movement."[199] On this occasion, a Benedictine monk attended. In the summer of 1939, the impending war made holding the Seminar inconceivable. From 1940 to 1942, however, Keller convened several Seminars for theologians and non-theologians in the United States.[200]

The Ecumenical Seminar in Geneva, presumably 1938 (Keller sitting in the middle; the first one at the left in the front row is Willem A. Visser 't Hooft) (archive Dr. Pierre Keller)

Keller received positive appraisals of the Geneva Seminar from the participating lecturers. For instance, William A. Brown wrote: "I congratulate you on the fine work you are doing."[201] "Prof. Tillich said that this

198. Keller to Bell, Geneva, March 22, 1938 and June 21, 1938 (LPL Bell 9 ff. 204–5 u. Bell 20 f. 485).

199. Keller to Barth, Geneva, June 30, 1938 (KBA 9338.481).

200. See below, pp. 228–30.

201. W. A. Brown to Keller, August 21, 1935 (WS Ms Sch 152/83).

collaboration meant for him one of the happiest souvenirs and that the theological level of the students was unusually high."[202] Martin Dibelius commented:

> Adolf Keller not only employed his unique organizational talent to ensure that a small, youthful ecumenical movement convened, but he had also recognized with theological insight that the members of this movement did not always have to discuss inter-church dialogue, but that everyone, teachers and students alike, should bring to bear their theologies or those of their churches . . . I shall never forget the beginning of the Seminar year of 1934 . . . The atrocities of June 30 [the Röhm-Putsch] were still fresh and gruesomely present in my mind. . . . Now I was welcomed as a lecturer at the Ecumenical Seminar, and I hear Fritz Lieb . . . quickly whisper to me: "you may speak your mind here" . . . I vividly recall teaching a seminar on "The Church and Churches," in scorchingly hot weather, in the wonderfully shaded old park of a villa in the environs of Geneva,[203] and how various colleagues, Orthodox, Lutherans, and members of the English and American "free churches" had the courtesy to sit among my students.[204]

In early 1934, a year after Hitler's accession to power, Keller alerted Bishop Bell to the following problem: "One of the greatest problems in *Germany* is whether the Evangelical Church, mostly represented in the opposition, can have in the future an *evangelical ministry*, which is not trained by the official State theology and the Hitler party . . . It is easy to see the danger to influence a whole generation in the well-known nationalistic spirit . . . Our Leadership Programme could, of course, easily include . . . students . . . , if our programme could be maintained in the old form."[205] Notwithstanding these efforts, only scarce funds were raised for the program. Nevertheless, these were sufficient to award three scholarships to students from the resistance within the German Church to study in Basel, where Karl Barth had begun teaching in 1935.[206]

202. "Minutes of the Meeting of the Theological Commission at St Peter's Hall, 1936" (WCC 42.004 3,1).

203. In 1935, 1936, and 1938, the seminar participants were received by Mr. and Mrs. Edmond Fatio at their country estate on Lake Geneva; see Keller, "Zweites Ökumenisches Seminar in Genf, 22. Juli bis 19. August 1935," 4 (NLAK C 3).

204. Martin Dibelius, "Erinnerung an das Ökumenische Seminar" (NLAK C 3).

205. Keller to Bell, February 22, 1934 (LPL Bell 5 f. 211).

206. Barth to Keller, February 26, 1936, and June 24, 1936 (KBA 0236.72 and 9236.158).

No explicit politicizing occurred in the Ecumenical Seminar, but Nazi Germany was obviously omnipresent. The Seminar was always attended by some German students who belonged to the oppositional Bekennende Kirche ("Confessing Church"). In 1938, four young Germans were able to attend owing to Barth's efforts on their behalf. Keller would have liked to have invited them in greater numbers, but he lacked the necessary funds. Barth, however, asserted that the young Germans in effect needed "more solid fare."[207] In 1938, Barth informed Keller that he could not commit himself to the Seminar, since "just as with the entire ecumenical movement, the matter, if it is to afford me pleasure, needs to have a more unequivocal face."[208] Keller was "the best example of a noble disposition . . . , but who nevertheless seems to have the popular image of a wholly-other fanatic ineradicably fixed in his mind."[209] Keller, a longstanding adherent to Barth's theology, replied that perhaps he served Barth and his cause more than his "blind followers."[210]

Other than encouraging ecumenical exchange, the Ecumenical Seminar thus also promoted theological debate on the malevolent spirit of National Socialism. It may be considered one of the most creative and longstanding ventures in the life and work of Adolf Keller.

207. Barth to Keller, Basel, June 1, 1938, and Basel, July 5, 1938 (KBA 9238.78 and 9238.89).

208. Barth to Keller, Basel, July 5, 1938 (KBA 9238.89).

209. Barth to Keller, Basel, October 5, 1939 (KBA 9239.166)

210. Keller to Barth, Zurich, October 8, 1939; see also August, 1936 (KBA 9339.535 and 9336.666).

5

Opposing National Socialism, Supporting German Refugees

"OBEDIENCE TO THE GOSPEL, NOT TO BLOOD, THE RACE, THE PEOPLE, THE IDEA"

ON JANUARY 30, 1933, Adolf Hitler became chancellor of the German Reich. Upon his appointment by the president of the Reich, he immediately began dismantling constitutional democracy. Germany became a totalitarian state, with the "Führer" as its unchallenged leader. Already in the years before Hitler's rise to power, Keller had closely monitored ill-fated political developments in the Soviet Union, Italy, and Austria. Events in Germany, however, utterly captivated him, leaving him breathless. His honorary lectureship now meant enlightening the ecumenical churches about Germany. Such enlightenment was much-needed in the United States and Great Britain, but also in Switzerland, since there was a widespread lack of knowledge. Keller remained active in Germany, albeit no longer as a lecturer or public speaker as political upheaval brought to an end "at once every educational activity of the honorary lecturer."[1] Nor could his books and articles appear any longer in Germany, with some few exceptions. Since he had opposed nationalism and racism since World War I, he saw through National Socialism much earlier than most of his contemporaries.

---

1. Keller, "Report of the Honorary Lecturer," August 17, 1934 (WCC 42.0042 3,1).

Multiethnic Switzerland had summoned what was a unique strength in Europe to "escape the dull, oppressive forces of blood and race." Significantly, Keller made this remark not in 1933, but as early as the outbreak of World War I.[2] Following the end of the war, he became an unwavering advocate of the League of Nations. Thus, on principle, he still backed it when its weaknesses, such as its failure to halt rearmament and its silence on Italy's attack against Abyssinia, had become obvious. His commitment to the international ecumenical movement resulted as a matter of course from his conviction that reconciliation must begin among the churches and that their common voice could and must promote peace and justice in the world.

Following a period of relative political stability and economic recovery, Keller, as discussed, observed the resurgence of nationalism around the year 1930.[3] He considered ecumenism a means of stemming the nationalist wave. In early 1931, he wrote to Henry S. Leiper:

> A new wave of nationalism is sweeping over Germany in a new form of that well known Hitlerism . . . But the whole movement has got such an influence on the academic world and many pastors that one has to count with also from an international point of view. Hitlerism is not very favorable to the ecumenical movement because Ecumenical and International are nearly synonyms for them. From this point of view it is very important that one can show the opposition coming from this side that the ecumenical movement stands also for international justice.[4]

In *Der Weg der dialektischen Theologie*, published in 1931, he argued that ecumenism would "be critical of rampant nationalism, which idolizes the people. For the central belief of the ecumenical movement is its . . . obedience to the Gospel, and not to blood, race, the people, and the idea. Ecumenism will therefore exercise a resolute critical effect on the nationalist constriction of the Evangelical idea."[5]

But it was precisely during that period that the ecumenical movement was at an ebb. To revitalize it, Keller believed that more—and better—theology was needed. He therefore sought to make dialectical theology the backbone of the ecumenical movement, and thus to strengthen it at the same time in its struggle against nationalism. This idea came as

2. See above, p. 33.

3. See above, pp. 115–16 and 118.

4. Keller to Leiper, January 22, 1931 (NLAK C 26).

5. Keller, *Der Weg der dialektischen Theologie*, 179–80; see above, p. 121.

a surprise to Barth.[6] Keller visited Germany shortly before Hitler's rise to power. In the face of mass unemployment, he feared that German society would descend into profound despair and widespread pessimism that knows no values that make life worth living. A subterranean mole was at work, agitating not only in meetings and stirring emotions with provocative articles, but also burrowing its way into human consciousness.[7] Clearsighted, he anticipated the dangers emanating from Hitler, the rat catcher.

Protestant Switzerland adopted an inconsistent stance on the transition of power in Germany. While some ministers welcomed it, others, including Leonhard Ragaz, expected this "blasphemous regime" to entail a catastrophe.[8] Ragaz trenchantly referred to Hitler's promises, also those made to the churches, as "lies."[9] Presumably, the majority of Protestant ministers shared the ambivalent view expressed by one professor of theology in April 1933: "Who dares to reach a definite verdict on current events in Germany? There can be no doubt that what has value and is healthy, as well as that which leads out of the mire, blends with what arises from the depths, and is characterized by exaggeration, a spirit of violence, the idolization of folklore and race . . . However, we may judge others and offer them good counsel only with the greatest restraint."[10] In a letter to his mother written in late February 1933, Karl Barth, who was serving as a professor in Bonn at the time, wrote: "Don't worry about Hitler etc.! . . . I am convinced that things will not turn out as bad as they seem."[11] Only a few days later, however, after the *Reichstag* fire on February 27, 1933, he changed his opinion radically. He became the spiritual leader of the struggle of the Protestant minority in Germany against National Socialism.

6. See above, pp. 122–23.

7. Keller, *Vom Unbekannten Gott*, 61.

8. Ragaz, *Neue Wege* (April 5, 1933), 189.

9. Ragaz, *Neue Wege* (March 14, 1933), 124 and April 5, 1933, 175.

10. Ernst Staehelin, *Kirchenblatt für die reformierte Schweiz* (April 6, 1933), 97.

11. Karl Barth to Anna Barth, February 25, 1933, in Busch et al., *Karl Barth: Briefe*, 73.

The L. P. Stone Lectures, Princeton Theological Seminary, 1933

RELIGION
AND
REVOLUTION

*Problems of Contemporary Christianity
on the European Scene*

By
ADOLF KELLER, D.D., LL. D.,
(*Univ. Yale, Zürich and Geneva*)
*Honorary Lecturer, Universal Christian Council for
Life and Work*

NEW YORK
Fleming H. Revell Company
LONDON   AND   EDINBURGH

Front page of "Religion and Revolution" (cf. p. 162)

Keller endeavored to promote compassion for the victims of the revolution.[12] As regards Hitler, however, he all of a sudden wavered. This is surprising. Presumably, this was related to his participation in the conference of the Provisional Ecumenical Council from March 8 to 15, 1933, in Rengsdorf near Koblenz. The German conference participants praised both Hitler's attitude toward the Church and his alleged intention to found the new state on proven moral values. Hermann Kapler, president of the board of the German Federation of Protestant Churches, asked Bishop Bell to exercise patience with the Germans, who were a bulwark against

12. Keller, "Protestantismus und deutsche Revolution," 131; see also Kaiser, *Deutscher Kirchenkampf und Schweizer Öffentlichkeit*, 181, n. 23.

Bolshevism.[13] In effect, the political opposition was subject to merciless persecution in the Soviet Union at the time, and the Ukraine was in the throes of the famine caused by Stalin. Keller believed that it was important to take into account the opinion of those German ecumenists who were not Nazis.[14] What was positive about Hitler, he said, was his endeavor to unite the nation and to link valuable elements of the conservative tradition with new social ideas.[15] In July 1933, he still gave Hitler a certain amount of credit.[16] Then, however, he changed his mind.

In the summer of 1933, Keller worked on the Stone Lectures, which he would be delivering in Princeton in the late autumn. His subject was the unfolding of events in Germany. On his transatlantic passage, he wrote to Barth, remarking that he would have liked to have spoken to him before his departure, even more so because he was likely to receive inquiries about Barth from the faculties he addressed. In Keller's eyes, Barth's *Theologische Existenz Heute* (Theological Existence Today) commented unequivocally on the current situation; he added that he would draw upon the pamphlet in his lectures.[17] Keller's lectures at Princeton were published as a spectacular book, titled *Religion and Revolution*.[18] Two important American professors of theology took it under their wings: "I have to thank my friends, Dr. Douglas Horton and Dr. Wilhelm Pauck, for the revision of these lectures and for help in preparing them for publication."[19] Published in May 1934, the principal thesis of *Religion and Revolution* was the following:

> The revolutions of the twentieth century have emerged, consciously or unconsciously, from a religious background; they can hardly escape being considered religious problems.— They have developed creeds for which millions are willing to suffer and to die. They have their Messiahs, apostles and martyrs who

13. Lindt, ed., *George Bell–Alphons Koechlin*, introduction, 23.

14. Keller, "Denkschrift zur Lage in Deutschland, 25. März 1933," quoted in Kaiser, *Deutscher Kirchenkampf*, 191ff.

15. Ibid., 183–84.

16. Keller to Pastor Gasser, July 13, 1933 (BAR J.2.257 1447/156).

17. Keller to Barth, October 23, 1933 (KBA 9333.799). In the first issue of *Theologische Existenz heute*, published in June 1933, Barth suggested that in the face of the prevailing situation in Germany nothing other than "theology and only theology should be practiced."

18. Keller, *Religion and Revolution*. This was the American edition; the British edition was titled *Religion and the European Mind*.

19. Keller, *Religion and Revolution*, 9.

inspire the masses with a feeling of adoration and with the hope of salvation and victory. They have adopted symbols which have exercised a profound influence upon the collective imagination, and they are teaching an eschatology which anticipates a day of Judgement and a Kingdom to come. Bolshevism and Nationalism are new national religions hidden in political and social programs. Christianity is here confronted again with that natural religious force immanent in the human soul.[20]

Keller perceived Bolshevism and National Socialism as "national religions," and thus bracketed them as parallel phenomena.[21] Ultimately, both were secular movements:

Continental Protestantism is engaged not only in theological controversy, but in a decisive battle between genuine Christianitiy and a religion of secularism in various forms. "Religion versus religion," or rather, "the Gospel versus religion"—such a description best expresses the true character of the present spiritual struggle . . . Nationalism and Communism could not exercise such fascination on large masses of people on the Continent, if they were not *religions*. Indeed . . . they are man-made religions set against a Christian faith based on God's revelation. New battlefronts between Christ and the world are being drawn up everywhere. They are, perhaps, nowhere so distinct as in Germany, and nowhere have the issues been worked out more elaborately than in the astounding revolution of ideals which has taken place in the German mind.[22]

National Socialism had given rise to a new myth: "A new myth has been materializing, the myth of race, the mysticism and religion of 'blood' and 'nation.' This mysticism of blood tends to replace the mysticism of the absolute spirit and of universal human society. Humanity, an international peaceful organization of the whole world, a world Church, an idealized scientific conception of the universe—these appear to the present generation mere abstractions."[23]

According to Keller, the bible of the new cult was Alfred Rosenberg's *Der Mythos des zwanzigsten Jahrhunderts* (The Myth of the Twentieth Century) (1930).[24] "Rosenberg, himself, told me a short while ago, that

20. Ibid., 13–14.; see above, p. 33.

21. See above, p. 159 and p. 162.

22. Keller, *Religion and Revolution*, 107–8.

23. Ibid., 109–10.

24. Rosenberg, *Der Mythos des Zwanzigsten Jahrhunderts*.

Christian love and the protection of the weak and the sick are bad selective principles. The Christian doctrine of love, he said, is a way to slavery rather than to liberty."[25] Seen thus, the Jews were

> not only a foreign element—an inferior race—but a "dangerous poison" menacing the purity of the German blood . . . Suffice [it to] say here that Jewish blood is made responsible not only for the parasitism of the Jewish people, the acquisitiveness of Jewish nature, and the consequent exploitation and unemployment of the German people, but also for the disintegrating and analytical tendency in modern art and literature, and the negative and destructive qualities embodied in Bolshevism and Atheism. The present harshness in the application of the Aryan paragraph is, therefore, "the legitimate defense of the German genius against the Jewish demon" . . . The State of Adolf Hitler is doing away with this Semitic "nuisance" by establishing a nation of pure Aryan blood. The State is . . . the nation, the whole nation itself, and the "totalitarian" expression of all its functions . . . The era of liberalism, with the ideals of personal liberty, freedom of teaching, liberty of migration and commerce, its parliamentarianism and socialism, equality of the sexes, emancipation of women and equality of men, has gone . . . The Revolution means the end of such "humanistic hallucinations."[26]

This leads us to the so-called "German Christians," who had already formed before Hitler's accession to power. In *Religion and Revolution*, Keller refers to them as the "key group" between anti-Christian German paganism and traditional Christianity. In his eyes, they represented a natural theology taken to extremes. German Christian theology described the state, people, and race as orders of creation. Thus, it pointed in a dangerous direction. The true inheritance of Evangelical freedom was at stake.[27] The German Christians claimed that the swastika and the Christian cross formed an inseparable unity, a notion that Keller categorically rejected. The boundaries between nationalism and Christianity were being blurred, he argued, by the nation and state being elevated to ultimate and absolute facts. The German Christians, who became very popular after the Nazi takeover, saw themselves as a "movement of faith . . . because they believe in the religious significance of the race as God-given, and in the Gospel

25. Keller, *Religion and Revolution*, 111. Keller met Rosenberg in early September 1933; see below, p. 175.

26. Ibid., 111–13.

27. Keller, "Protestantismus und deutsche Revolution," 131.

as the deepest constructive character-building power in a nation."[28] It was most alarming that they refused to recognize the Jewish provenance of Jesus.[29] Emanuel Hirsch, the prominent German professor of theology emphasized the fact that God had created the state. Whoever opposed the state, opposed God.[30] For Keller, however, the German state was not well disposed to the church, but instead indifferent or hostile.[31] He described the German Christian Bishop Hossenfelder's comment that "by God's grace, a new sun is rising for the German nation in the person of Adolf Hitler" as utterly whimsical.[32] Furthermore, "The German people are not simply indulging in hero-worship: they have clad their leader in the religious glory of a Messiah sent by God Himself to deliver His people from dishonor, slavery and misery. They hail him as their mystically appointed Fuehrer even though he rules them with a rod of iron. The new National Socialist state in Germany, therefore, is founded not only on the hero-worship of an enthusiastic nation or on the political will of a party, but on a well-elaborated system of metaphysics and an underlying theology of the state."[33]

Germany had reached an either-or situation: "The question before the German people is whether they will hold to the Church of Christ or create a new church of a Christianized Germanic race."[34] He added, "Christian faith and national idealism must be kept apart . . . A *Politisierung* [politicization] of the Church would mean nothing less than the death of evangelicalism."[35] Presumably, Keller was familiar with, and adopted, the position that Barth took in "Reformation als Entscheidung" (Reformation as Decision), an address given on October 30, 1933: one could not once again take a middle position between deciding and not deciding. Sitting in the middle could only mean defecting to the enemy.[36]

The world, as Keller concluded in *Religion and Revolution*, was "under the power of Satanic influences."[37] He was pessimistic about further developments: "the world is doomed. God's judgement is hanging over

28. Keller, *Religion and Revolution*, 121.

29. Ibid., 125.

30. Ibid., 122–23.

31. Ibid., 159.

32. Ibid., 125.

33. Ibid., 163.

34. Ibid., 126.

35. Ibid., 140–41.

36. Karl Barth, "Reformation als Entscheidung," 55.

37. Keller, *Religion and Revolution*, 174.

it—but also God's grace."[38] He demanded observance of the biblical commandment of love and a return "to the sources of evangelical life, and to an enthusiasm for religious liberty, a willingness to suffer for Christ's sake."[39]

Keller's verdict on National Socialism in *Religion and Revolution* has remained valid until the present day. He was among the first to perceive developments at the time with such clarity. The general secretariat of Life and Work acknowledged "the author's wide knowledge and balanced, objective critical powers . . . The two last chapters, on the fundamental causes of the conflict of Protestantism in Germany, . . . are of particular present-day interest, and raise questions on which the action of the Church is urgently required . . . This book is warmly to be recommended. From the first page to the last, it cannot fail to interest those who, whether theologians or not, are in search of a survey of the current trends and problems in Protestant Europe."[40]

Among his more than twenty books, *Religion and Revolution* is without doubt one of Keller's most important works. For obvious reasons, it was not translated into German.[41] Owing to a lack of knowledge of the English language, it was scarcely noticed in Continental Europe.[42] However, enlightenment was bitterly needed in the English-speaking world, where Hitler's dictatorship was frequently not seen through for a long time. Henry S. Leiper, who spoke to various church leaders in early September 1933, that is, before Keller lectured in Princeton and before Ludwig Müller became *Reichsbischof* (bishop of the German Evangelical Church, subsequently called the Reich Church), was among those duped: "Müller [is] anxious for the closest relations with us and with the Ecumenical Movement . . . Some very basic mis[interpre]tations of the German situation are still being made in other lands. Gleichschaltung apparently does not mean in the minds of such men a weak uniformity. It does mean trying to tune together . . . von Bodelschwingh . . . is not desired as leader by the majority in the churches . . . [T]he general feeling is that Germany

38. Ibid., 170–71.

39. Ibid., 178 and 183.

40. *Churches in Action: Newsletter* 7 (February 1935), 10; the reviewer's name is not mentioned.

41. The outstanding German publishing houses (Eugen Diederichs Jena, Furche-Verlag Berlin, Kaiser-Verlag Munich, Klotz-Verlag Gotha), which had published Keller's previous books, could not risk publishing this highly political book.

42. Keller published a German summary, "Schicksalsfragen des Europäischen Protestantismus"; see also Keller, "L'influence des Révolutions continentales sur le Protestantisme."

still hangs in the balance . . . the eventual success of Hitler is not assured . . . The curious thing about him is that he seems to inspire hope and new idealism."[43]

Another example is Charles Macfarland, who actually knew Germany very well. After Hitler had granted him a meeting in late 1933, Macfarland argued the case for giving the new Germany a chance.[44] It was not until 1937 that he accused Hitler, albeit emphatically, for having "wrecked Christian ideals."[45]

Years later, Visser't Hooft remarked that the correspondence between Koechlin and Bishop Bell illustrated "how extraordinarily difficult it was in those days to understand the sign of the times."[46] 1933 had been a "time of illusions."[47] Evidently, Keller was an exception.

On the occasion of the twenty-fifth anniversary of the Federal Council, which was celebrated in Washington in early December 1933, Keller also addressed the issue of Germany. The churches needed to close ranks against the evil spirit and conduct themselves like mountaineers in the Swiss Alps: "when a party is crossing a dangerous glacier, with hidden . . . crevasses, all the climbers are linked together with a strong rope. If someone falls into a crevasse he is held by the others . . . : We have something to say and we try to say it in common, to voice the Christian conscience the world over, together with our Catholic brethren."[48]

THE "CHURCH STRUGGLE": KARL BARTH AND ADOLF KELLER IN UNISON

The German Christians sought to establish a hierarchical German Reich Church under their dominance. To begin with, the Reverend Ludwig Müller, Hitler's advisor on the Protestant Church, was nominated *Reichsbischof* (bishop of the Reich Church) on May 23, 1933. No such office had existed until then. Two days later, in a move designed to forestall the German

43. Leiper to McCrea Cavert, September 2, 1933 (PHS NCC RG 18 12/18). On von Bodelschwingh, see below, p. 6 and p. 81.

44. Macfarland, *The New Church and the New Germany*.

45. "Text of the Macfarland Letter Denouncing Hitler," *The New York Times*, Wednesday, June 9, 1937. On Müller, see below pp. 176–78.

46. Visser't Hooft in Lindt, ed., *George Bell-Alphons Koechlin*, 6.

47. The first volume of Klaus Scholder's *Die Kirchen und das Dritte Reich* is subtitled *Vorgeschichte und Zeit der Illusionen 1918–1934*.

48. Keller, "Address delivered at the anniversary of the Federal Council of Churches at Washington," December 6, 1933, 4 and 6 (NLAK C 6).

Christians, the board of the Federation of German Evangelical Churches, under Hermann Kapler, appointed Friedrich von Bodelschwingh Jr, director of Bethel hospices, as *Reichsbischof*. Von Bodelschwingh's appointment received the retrospective approval of the regional church bodies.[49] Kapler resigned as president, but von Bodelschwingh was unable to assert himself. On September 27, 1933, Ludwig Müller was formally ordained as *Reichsbischof*. Described as a devout old hand, he commanded both a pious idiom and the brisk tone of the Reichswehr casino. Basically, however, he was a rather weak figure.[50]

The ecumenical movement faced a dilemma over the Church in the new Germany, as Keller explained at the conference of the World Alliance of Reformed Churches in Belfast in the summer of 1933: "Today, every church community committed to the German Church faces the difficult question whether it should simply and blithely protest against the disenfranchisement of the Jewish and other minorities, as well as against the violation of the Church, or whether it is more advisable, with a view to the possible effects [of such protests], to wait for the revolution to take its turbulent course, to hope for a return to normal conditions, and to leave it to the powers within Germany to grapple with the revolution."[51]

At stake were the right tactics. Since it had absolutely no wish to fan the flames, the World Alliance refrained from protesting, and so did Bishop Bell.[52] Alphons Koechlin was reserved: "We must exercise patience, we must be cautious with our judgments. We must not abandon the spiritual community with our German brothers."[53] Even Friedrich Siegmund-Schultze, a professed enemy of National Socialism, at first disapproved of the protests abroad.[54] It was feared that these would cause further harm.

The board of the Federation of Swiss Protestant Churches seemed to shirk responsibility somewhat, as the following statement suggests: "It is Keller who bears responsibility for relations with churches in other countries."[55] On the board, it was Keller who had the strongest backbone to

49. Friedrich von Bodelschwingh Jr. was a fellow student of Keller's during his university days in Berlin.

50. Scholder, *Die Kirchen und das Dritte Reich*, 1:391–92, 588, 734.

51. Keller discussed the "difficult existential battle of our brethren"; see his "Der reformierte Weltbund in Belfast," 232–33.

52. *EPD (Bulletin of the Evangelical Press Service)* 49 (November 14, 1933).

53. Koechlin, "Bericht über eine Reise in Deutschland 12.–20. Okt. 1933," in Lindt, ed., *George Bell-Alphons Koechlin*, 70.

54. Bell to Koechlin, July 4, 1933, in Ibid., 43.

55.. "Meeting of the Board of the Federation of Swiss Protestant Churches, February declare resistance against Germany whereas the Federation could be seen to be whitewashing matters in the early months. At its meeting of April 26, 1933, the board decided to refrain from lodging an official protest owing to the complexity of the situation in Germany. However, Keller's request for a public—albeit cautious— announcement was granted:[56]

> The board . . . was under the impression, however, that it is not allowed to interfere in the political rebuilding of another country. On the other hand, the course of the German revolution as regards the fate of the German Church is still very uncertain, and the German churches are themselves engaged in the necessary struggle for their spiritual freedom with such endeavor that at the present time, and given their endangered freedom, they can be hardly expected to voice their opinions on the political actions of the state. Notwithstanding its sympathy for the victims of racial difference[,] . . . the Federation sees no reason to comment on a revolution whose situation is changing on a daily basis.[57]

In a letter of congratulations to Friedrich von Bodelschwingh, however, the Federation expressed its "delight" at his election as *Reichsbischof*.[58] To bolster its significance, the letter was published in the *Neue Zürcher Zeitung*, the major broadsheet in Switzerland, particularly because the German Christians were pursuing the *Gleichschaltung* (forced alignment) of the Protestant churches with ever-increasing insolence.[59] A few months later, the newly appointed *Reichsbischof*, Ludwig Müller, was warded off with a dryly worded letter of admonishment.[60] Keller had meanwhile become very firm, not only in his stance but also in his tactics.

In the autumn of 1933, Reverend Martin Niemöller established the Pastors' Emergency League (Pfarrernotbund), an alliance of ministers which opposed the tendency in parts of the German church to accept Nazi

---

17, 1933," quoted from Kaiser, *Deutscher Kirchenkampf und Schweizer Öffentlichkeit*, 176.

56. "Meeting of the Board of the Federation of Swiss Protestant Churches, April 26, 1933," quoted from Kaiser, *Deutscher Kirchenkampf*, 193.

57. "Aus dem schweizerischen evangelischen Kirchenbund," *EPD* (May 9, 1933; Archiv Reformierte Medien).

58. Board of the Federation of Swiss Protestant Churches to Reichsbischof von Bodelschwingh, June 3, 1933, published in *EPD* B/12 (June 7, 1933).

59. Wildberger, "Die schweizerischen evangelischen Kirchen," 22

60. Board of the Federation of Swiss Protestant Churches to *Reichsbischof* Müller, November 6, 1933, reprinted in ibid., 23, n. 2.

values. The Pastors' Emergency League dismissed certain aberrations of the German Christians and opposed their continued transgression, but it submitted a pledge of loyalty to Hitler on behalf of its 2,500 members. Only the so-called "Sports Palace (Sportpalast) rally" of the German Christians, held on November 13, 1933, where there was mention of the "scapegoat theology" of "Rabbi Paul" and of a "heroic Jesus,"[61] opened the eyes of many members of the Pastor's Emergency League. While a vast majority of them still shied away from criticizing the Nazi state, and focused on defending the freedom of the Church, the seed for the "Confessing Church" (the followers of the Barmen Declaration, discussed below) had been planted. The "Church Struggle" (Kirchenkampf) ensued, in which the German Christians and the Confessing Church now faced one another. Between these opposing forces stood a group of conservative Lutherans, known as the "Lutheran Council."

Behind the church struggle, which both parties initially depicted as a purely inner-church dispute, Keller identified a fundamental theological problem. In *Religion and Revolution*, he wrote that over the course of the nineteenth century Christian *piety* (and not God or Jesus Christ!) had become the essence of Christianity.[62] So-called Cultural Protestantism had developed, and associated therewith the erosion of the theology of revelation of the Reformation and the rise of the old *theologia naturalis* (natural theology). No one took a more uncompromising stance against the synthesis of the divine and human spirit than Karl Barth: "Barth stands somewhat alone in his attempt to safeguard the exclusive dynamic sovereignty of God."[63] The German Christians had declared war on Barth's theology because for them God was the God of history:[64] they believed that God spoke to them under the prevailing historical circumstances. However, representatives of the Pastors' Emergency League also opposed Barth.[65] Many Lutherans praised Luther "as a hero of the German nation," and considered the Lutheran Reformation to be "God's call to the German nation."[66] The Lutheran majority in Germany faced a Reformed minority

---

61. Busch, *Reformationstag* 27 and 24; see also the introduction.

62. Keller, *Religion and Revolution*, 33. (Piety printed in italics by Keller.)

63. Ibid., 70, 96, 100.

64. Ibid., 85ff.

65. Ibid., 96 and 100.

66. Ibid., 97–98.

that believed less in the state and adhered to a democractic structure of the Church.[67] But the fronts between them were not rigidly entrenched.

On March 21, 1934, the board of the Federation of Swiss Protestant Churches convened in Bern.[68] The purpose of the meeting was to discuss events in Germany, following the recent appointment of the youthful Theodor Heckel as director, that is, bishop of the newly established Kirchliches Aussenamt (Foreign Office of the Church) in Berlin. The Office was responsible for ecumenical affairs. Heckel was the subordinate of Reichsbischof Müller; he was not a German Christian but a conservative Lutheran. Heckel talked up cooperation with the Swiss churches. The Federation now had to respond to his initiative. Keller managed to push through the not predominantly Barthian-minded board a "declaration" he had prepared on Germany and addressed to Heckel.[69] The members of the board seemed oblivious to the fact that particularly the second thesis, which heralded Christ as the only Lord, was very Barthian. Keller landed this coup with the support of Eugène Choisy, the Federation president, who combined a liberal theology with an ecumenical attitude.

Keller's so-called Bern Declaration was modeled on the "Erklärung über das rechte Verständnis der reformatorischen Bekenntnisse in der Deutschen Evangelischen Kirche der Gegenwart" (Declaration on the Proper Understanding of the Confessions of the Reformation Era within the Contemporary German Evangelical Church). The latter had been ratified at the Free Reformed Synod, held in the German town of Barmen-Gemarke on January 3 and 4, 1934, which was attended by several hundred Reformed (not Lutheran!) ministers and elders. Both the Synod and the Declaration contributed greatly to the emergence of the "Confessing Church."[70] This (first) Barmen Declaration had been written by Karl Barth.[71] Inspired by this document, Keller formulated five concise theses:

> 1. For a Church founded on the Reformation, the Bible of the Old and New Testaments, irrespective of historical-critical research, is the only source and norm of its proclamation.

---

67. Ibid., 99.

68. Keller to Barth, March 12, 1934 (KBA 9334.346).

69. Maiwald, *Ökumenischer Kirchenkampf.*

70. Held on January 3–4, 1934, the Synod preceded the so-called Evangelical Confessing Synod of the German Evangelical Church, also held in Barmen, May 29–31, 1934.

71. Scholder, *Die Kirchen und das Dritte Reich,* 1:740–41.

2. According to general evangelical understanding, the character of a church founded on the Reformation rests particularly upon its recognition of Jesus Christ as its only Lord and upon justifying itself by its faith in Him, but not upon any kind of natural virtues or accomplishments as a precondition for salvation.

3. The church of the Reformation has fought for the freedom of Christians. Even today, spiritual freedom is indispensable to a Protestant Church for the proclamation of its message.

4. In broad agreement with the faith of the Protestant Christianity, an evangelical church, irrespective of national peculiarity, has a supranational character, which is based on the calling by God. His children belong to every blood, every race, and every people, and with the church he has given us a community of spirit and faith, but not one of blood or race, or indeed of state allegiance.

5. The current distress and confusion of the church in many countries drives us to serious penance, as well as to a new, joint deliberation on the true essence of the church of Jesus Christ and its proclamation, as it was newly awakened by the Reformation and needs to be attained time and again.[72]

Keller pursued two objectives with the Bern Declaration: first, to set out in plain terms the theological preconditions for the struggle of the church opposition in Germany, and thus to strengthen it, and to remind the newly formed German Evangelical Church of its duties and responsibilities;[73] and secondly, to initiate theological reflection within the ecumenical churches, and thereby to foster "actual ecumenical participation" in the Church Struggle, and, by further implication, to launch an "ecumenical church struggle."[74] He realized that not only the German Christians embraced natural theology.[75] Natural theology, or so-called Semipelagianism, also enjoyed recognition, albeit not particularly overtly, in Anglicanism, Orthodoxy, Catholicism, American pragmatism, and liberal theology. Keller's Bern Declaration reiterated the demand made in *Der Weg der Dialektischen Theologie*, namely, that dialectical theology

72. Keller, "Thesen vom 22. März 1934" (BAR J.2.257 1288/137).

73. Letter dated March 22, 1934, accompanying the Bern Declaration; see also the Federation of Swiss Protestant Churches to its members, March 28, 1934 (BAR J.2.257 1288/137 u. 1287/137); see Maiwald, *Ökumenischer Kirchenkampf*, 29.

74. Maiwald, *Ökumenischer Kirchenkampf*, 29–32.

75. Keller to Koechlin, March 3, 1934, quoted from Maiwald, 30.

become the backbone and binding agency of ecumenism.[76] Only in this way would it carry the necessary weight to effectively counter German Christian theology. As regards the Church Struggle, Keller thus completely espoused Barth's line.

On the surface, the Bern Declaration was a failure. It is hardly surprising that it peeved the German Christians.[77] After a lengthy delay, Heckel's non-committal response arrived. In Germany, Keller wrote to Barth, only the "friendly statements" of the Bern Declaration were repeated while everything else was omitted.[78] He tried to kindle Bishop Bell's interest in the Declaration: "I am strongly in favour . . . after having discussed the situation in detail with my friend Karl Barth and many others, also in Germany—to build up around Germany a wall of simple statements declaring . . . what are the essentials for a church."[79] While Bell expressed his gratitude, Keller's intervention came to nothing.[80] Equally, none of the other ecumenical churches adopted any of Keller's theological "bulwark conception."[81] Eberhard Busch, Barth's biographer, has observed that Keller independently took up the insights that Barth had gained from the Church Struggle to launch what presumably marked the first attempt by a non-German church "to perceive the ecumenical significance of the German church struggle."[82]

Barth, however, was pleased about the Bern Declaration: "Yesterday I spoke to World-Adolf. Also, it seems as if the Federation of Swiss Protestant Churches is finally becoming seriously involved."[83] A few weeks later, Keller met Barth in Paris. He enjoyed the meeting and their evening walk along the Champs-Elysées: "Not until that evening had I understood how necessary you are amid the prevailing theological situation. I feel the benefit of your kindness, despite all the criticism."[84] Keller had repeatedly served as a projection screen for Barth's criticism of ecumenism, although he probably deserved this least of all its protagonists. Now, however, in the

---

76. See above, pp. 119–21.

77. Kaiser, *Deutscher Kirchenkampf und Schweizer Öffentlichkeit*, 308.

78. Keller to Barth, April 29, 1934 (KBA 9334.471).

79. Keller to Bell, April 1, 1934 (LPL Bell 5ff. 335–37); see also Keller to Koechlin, March 31, 1934, quoted from Maiwald, 72–73 and 119.

80. Bell to Keller, April 25, 1934 (LPL Bell 5 f. 381).

81. Maiwald, *Ökumenischer Kirchenkampf*, 34.

82. Eberhard Busch, Preface to ibid., 10, 12, 13.

83. Karl Barth to Peter Barth, March 27, 1934, quoted in ibid., 72.

84. Keller to Barth, April 29, 1934 (KBA 9334.471).

critical phase of the Church Struggle, Barth and Keller were closer than ever.

From May 29 to 31, the "Bekenntnissynode der Deutschen Evangelischen Kirche" (Confessional Synod of the German Evangelical Church) was held in Barmen. It was attended by Reformed and Lutheran theologians. The Synod passed the famous "Theologische Erklärung zur gegenwärtigen Lage der Deutschen Evangelischen Kirche" (Theological Declaration Concerning the Present Situation of the German Evangelical Church). The Declaration is based on Barth's thinking and was in its essence drafted by him. Its contents align with the aforementioned first Barmen Declaration of January 1934, and its form with the Bern Declaration of March. It became the spiritual foundation of the "Confessing Church." In 1934, Barth prompted the ecumenical churches to welcome the "Barmen Declaration" and thus its theology—so now after all![85] On behalf of Henry S. Leiper, Keller asked Bishop Bell, in his capacity as the chairman of Life and Work, "whether an unofficial recognition of the Barmen Synod would be advisable."[86] Such recognition failed to materialize.[87] Switzerland remained alone with its Bern Declaration.

Given Keller's endeavors to establish a common ecumenical front against German Christian ideology, it is hardly surprising that he was most alarmed when the long-smouldering dispute between Karl Barth and Emil Brunner over natural theology escalated in the summer of 1934: notwithstanding his allegiance with the "Confessing Church," Brunner published a brochure titled "Natur und Gnade" (Nature and Grace). Barth's response was an abrupt "No!"[88] Basically, Keller felt sympathetic toward Brunner, who argued for the priority and exclusiveness of mercy, but for which he saw a "starting point" in individual personality and responsibility.[89] But the timing of the publication of Brunner's brochure struck him as completely mistaken. In turn, Barth's reaction also startled him. In view of the Church Struggle, he considered such discord a catastrophe.

85. Boyens, "Ökumenische Bewegung und Bekennende Kirche," 208; see also Maiwald, *Ökumenischer Kirchenkampf*, 17–18. See above Keller's initiative, pp. 171–73. In advance of the conferences at Oxford and Edinburgh, Barth reiterated his demand—but in vain.

86. Keller to Bell, June 8, 1934 (LPL Bell 6 f. 30).

87. Boyens, "Ökumenische Bewegung und Bekennende Kirche," 208ff.

88. Barth, "Nein! Antwort an Emil Brunner."

89. (Xenos=Keller), "Streitgespräch zwischen Emil Brunner und Karl Barth," 1–2.

CHURCH DIPLOMAT AND CHURCH FIGHTER

In September 1933, Keller received instructions from the Executive Committee of Life and Work to hold discussions with Ludwig Müller, the nominated Reichsbischof;[90] with the Nazi ministers Frick, Neurath, and Goebbels; and with Alfred Rosenberg, one of the chief ideologues of National Socialism. It was an extremely delicate mission. At this meeting, which was held in Berlin, Keller made it perfectly clear that ecumenical sympathies for Germany were at stake should the Church be deprived of its freedom by the State. He also expressed reservations about the "Arierparagraph" (Aryan Paragraph), according to which Protestant clergy with Jewish ancestors were removed from their posts.[91]

After the meeting, Barth inquired whether Keller's visit meant that the German Christian church regime was now recognized by the ecumenical movement.[92] Keller denied this, and replied that it would remain to be seen whether the movement could grasp hold of the steering wheel, "since the driver was drunk."[93] The French churchman Wilfred Monod wrote to Keller:

> I understand your anguish . . . You went to Berlin? Alas! At present, you will be better informed about racist antisemitism . . . Besides, the findings that you have reported from Berlin darken the case of German protestantism . . . No, I don't want to believe that certain of our German friends, our beloved brethren in Christ Jesus, maintain their silence before the "Apocalyptic Beast!"—My dear friend, already I hope for the occasion of meeting you here [in Paris]. What a heavy business! Lord have mercy on us! . . . I am rather uneasy about the future of the ecumenical movement, since Hitler's government officially condemns anything smacking of pacifism, internationalism, universalism . . . But we shall talk over all these things peaceably, loyally, eye to eye and heart to heart.[94]

90. Ludwig Müller, a confidant of Hitler's, had already been appointed Bishop of the Old Prussian Church on July 6, 1933.

91. Keller to Barth, September 15, 1933 (KBA 9333.677). The Old Prussian Union, which was dominated by German Christians, had introduced the "Aryan Paragraph," pursuant to which pastors "of non-Aryan descent" were dismissed from their posts.

92. Barth to Keller, September 21, 1933 (KBA 9233.248).

93. Keller to Barth, late September 1933 (KBA 9333.683).

94. Monod to Keller, April 21, 1933 and July 22, 1933 (WS Ms Sch 153/26).

Half a year later, the Federal Council (Henry S. Leiper and President Samuel P. Cadman) dispatched Keller as an envoy to Berlin to enter a formal protest with Reichsbischof Müller, Theodor Heckel, and "Rechtswalter" (state commissar) August Jäger, their juridical advisor, who had become the driving force of the Reich Church. These had begun to oppress the recently formed church opposition, to suspend unpopular pastors, and to force the state churches into line. The assignment weighed heavily on Keller's mind.[95] On his journey to Berlin, he spoke to Karl Barth, member of the "Confessing Church." The meeting in Berlin on May 11, 1934, lasted two hours.[96] In his opening statement, Keller expressed the concern of the churches abroad about preserving the character of the oldest Reformation church. He presented three grievances on behalf of the Federal Council:

> First. The departure from the legal basis of the constitution of the German Church and the violent measures associated therewith . . . I refer to the statements issued by the Confessing Synods in the Rhineland and in Westphalia, . . . the 190 Silesian pastors, 230 Baden pastors, the dissolved presbyteries . . . Taken together, this affords foreign countries the impression of the greatest legal uncertainty . . . For these reasons, we cannot approve of the departure from the legal basis and the introduction of an autocratic church regime. A second point concerns the application of the Aryan Paragraph to the Church . . . One must seriously question whether the internal political benefit attributed to this new order is not profusely abrogated by the damage to foreign policy . . . and by Germany's increasing isolation. The enforcement of the Aryan Paragraph also directly affects foreign countries by the necessity to attend to German refugees. In this respect, I would like to mention that I alone have received 42 such inquiries from Germany . . . A third point concerns the measures that could be regarded as an attack on the substance of the Church itself. While we can understand the efforts to establish a single German Evangelical Church, the methods employed to achieve this objective . . . have profoundly shaken the trust in the present church government.[97]

Müller hastened to reply: the disciplinary measures implemented against some pastors had been partly revoked. Jäger categorically denied their practical significance. On this subject, Müller asserted that the bringing into line of the state churches was legal, whereupon Jäger claimed that

95. Keller to Barth, April 29, 1934 (KBA 9334.471).
96. Keller, "Eine Demarche des Federal Council," May 14, 1934 (WCC 301.43.19/5).
97. Ibid., 3–4.

these measures concerned only the external order of the Church and that the profession of faith remained unaffected. Müller spoke of his "mission" to lead the people "back to our Lord Jesus Christ." While he conceived of that objective in terms of National Socialism, it amounted to nothing else than Prussian Protestantism. In reply, Keller pointed out that particularly for the Reformed adherents the question of faith was also at stake. Müller attempted to divert attention from the subject: millions of Germans supported the church regime. Keller countered this view with reference to the fact that minorities felt violated by the new order. Jäger promised that the legitimate wishes of Reformed adherents would receive "the most sympathetic" consideration. As regards the Aryan Paragraph, Müller played his trump card: if the state sought to introduce purity of blood, the church could not obstruct this endeavor. Would a white American congregation appoint a black pastor? Jäger accused the Jews outright and unguardedly of moral poisoning. Müller spoke of the reeducation of the victims of the Aryan Paragraph. Heckel remained virtually silent. In conclusion, Keller demanded that changes be introduced to German church policy, whereupon Müller reassured him that "if the churches abroad are justifiably remonstrating with us, then we shall be the first to accept such criticism."[98] The next day, Keller had a private meeting with Heckel, who made an ambivalent impression on him.

Keller gleaned three vague promises from the Berlin meeting: the acknowledgment of responsibility for the victims of the Aryan Paragraph, the prospect of revoking certain disciplinary measures, and the making of concessions to the Reformed wing. The following day, he wrote to Müller, informing him that he took him at his word, in response to which Müller sent instant confirmation.[99] Bishop Bell said: "Your extractic [sic] of the promise from Jäger and the statement by Müller, seems a happy result."[100] But Keller was wary: "The near future will show what the . . . promise is worth." Further: "My personal impression of Heckel . . . was that [he] at least understand[s] the difficulties, the theological background and the international tension. Bishop Müller and especially Dr. Jäger evidently not."[101] Keller's assessment proved correct: a few weeks later, the Synod

98. Ibid., 4ff.

99. Müller to Keller, May 17, 1934 (WCC 301.43.19); see also Keller, "Eine Demarche," 8. (WCC 301.43.19/5).

100. Bell to Keller, May 16, 1934; see also Keller to Bell, May 17, 1934 (LPL Bell 5 f. 470 u. f. 173).

101. Keller to Bell, May 25, 1934 and May 30, 1934: (LPL Bell 5 f. 495 u. f. 501).

of the Reich Church, which was dominated by the German Christians, legalized Müller's and Jäger's unlawful actions.[102]

Letter by Adolf Keller to Bishop George Bell (April 14th, 1934)
(Lambeth Palace Library)

102. Keller to Bell, August 12, 1934 (LPL Bell 6 ff. 113–14).

How uncertain many ecumenists remained about the Church Struggle as late as the summer of 1934 is reflected by the discussion following Keller's lecture on "The Three-fold Struggle of European Protestantism," which he delivered to the Executive Committee of Inter-Church Aid in Edinburgh in July of the same year. In response to his comment that in the totalitatarian states the church was fighting for its very existence, for the freedom and truth of the Gospel, Professor Zilka from Prague remarked that this picture was too bleak. Henry S. Leiper, moreover, warned "against all kinds of defeatism." Only Alfred Jörgensen, vice-president of Inter-Church Aid, agreed with Keller unreservedly.[103]

Despite much wavering within Life and Work, the Church Struggle—paradoxically—gave the organization fresh impetus. This became apparent at the conference of the Ecumenical Council, which was held on the Danish island of Fanø from August 24 to 30, 1934. The conference theme was "The Church and the Problem of the State Today." When the World Council of Churches was definitely founded in 1948, Bishop Bell referred to the Fanø conference as the "decisive meeting" for the future of ecumenism.[104] Keller played a role of utmost importance at the conference.

Bell invited Bishop Heckel, who was responsible for ecumenical relations, to Fanø. Keller warned Bell that Heckel might obstruct honest debate.[105] Hans Schönfeld, now responsible for social research at Life and Work in Geneva, advised his friend Heckel to "emphasize the fundamental issues and avoid the 'concrete' ones."[106] An invitation was also sent to the "Confessing Church." Moreover, Keller sought to persuade Adolf Deissmann to attend the conference. Deissmann, however, feared confrontation. In a letter to Bell, Keller remarked that "I tried to dissuade him"—albeit unsuccessfully.[107] Pressed to do so, other opponents of the Reich Church also cancelled their participation. When Dietrich Bonhoeffer, a member of the "Confessing Church" and close to Karl Barth, demanded that one take sides with the "Confessing Church" already before the Fanø conference, Keller reminded him that while the ecumenical movement unanimously rejected the politics of violence of the Reich Church, unfortunately

103. "Report on the Meeting of the Executive Committee, July 20–25, 1934, Edinburgh," 5 (BAR J.2.257 1245/133).

104. Bell, "Praktisches Christentum—Entwicklung der Bewegung" (1948), 3 (NLAK C 24 Amsterdam 1948).

105. Keller to Bell, August 8, 1934, (LPL Bell 1 ff. 159–60).

106. Bethge, *Dietrich Bonhoeffer*, 406–7. and 403; for the English edition, see Bethge, *Dietrich Bonhoeffer*. On Schönfeld, see above pp. 114–15 and 125.

107. Keller to Bell, August 8, 1934 (LPL Bell 1 ff. 159–60).

in terms of faith it partly shared the views of official German theology.[108] He therefore repeated his demand "to build a wall of such [theological] declarations around the opposition," but once again his motion fell on deaf ears.[109]

In his subsequent reflections on Fanø, Marc Boegner, president of the Protestant Council of Churches of France, observed: "Heckel repeatedly told us that we were unable to understand the German situation and took refuge in religious and political philosophizing . . . Keller promptly and forcefully controverted him."[110] In the face of Heckel's flight into theological abstractions, Keller was the very first to draw attention to specific complaints: the Aryan Paragraph, the forsaking of the law, the establishment of an autocratic regime, the blending of religious and political motives.[111] Notwithstanding Heckel's resistance, a resolution was passed to issue a public statement on the situation of the church in Germany. The document was drafted by Bishop Bell, Bishop Ammundsen of Denmark, Marc Boegner, Henry S. Leiper, and Adolf Keller—"who were all very familiar with circumstances in Germany and manifest friends of the Confessing Church."[112] The resolution was passed against the votes of Germany and Austria, which had already come under the influence of National Socialism. The statement objected to the autocratic government, the use of violence, the oath of service, and the banning of free speech.[113] It did not deal with theological questions. The "Confessing Synod" was assured prayers and affectionate solidarity, but the document also expressed solidarity with the entire Christian brethren in Germany.[114] Passionate polemics were avoided, as Keller observed after Fanø. The resolution, however, had lent support to the "Confessing Church."[115] Bonhoeffer's appointment as advisor to the Ecumenical Council underlines Keller's verdict.

Hans Schönfeld and Joseph H. Oldham, his Scottish counterpart, were entrusted with preparing the 1937 World Church Conference, to be

108. Scholder, *Die Kirchen und das Dritte Reich*, 2:297–98.

109. Keller to Bell, August 12, 1934 (LPL Bell 6 ff. 113–14); see above, pp. 171–73.

110. Boegner, *L'Exigence Œcuménique*, 61.

111. Keller to Ragaz, October 7, 1934 (StAZ W I 67 103.2).

112. Scholder, *Die Kirchen und das Dritte Reich*, 2:300.

113. Bethge, *Dietrich Bonhoeffer*, 443.

114. "Text der Resolution," Annual Report of the Federation of Swiss Protestant Churches for 1934/35, 13–14.

115. Keller, "Der ökumenische Rat und der deutsche Kirchenkonflikt."

hosted by Life and Work in Oxford.[116] Schönfeld endeavored to be loyal both to the ecumenical movement and to the Reich Church in Berlin.[117] Purportedly, Heckel also continued to support ecumenism, but in reality he stood more and more for the policies of Berlin.[118] While contact between Schönfeld and Henriod, general secretary of Life and Work, and Heckel's office was close, that with the "Confessing Church" was low-key.[119] Henriod appears to have followed in Schönfeld's steps, even though he had spoken out against Hitler's "barbarity" and the persecution of the Jews already in early 1933.[120] Keller was forced to maintain contact with Heckel, since the latter represented Germany both on the Executive Committee of Inter-Church Aid and in the Ecumenical Seminar. Bell also invited both parties, as well as the Lutheran Council, to the 1936 conference of Life and Work in the village of Chamby, above the Lake of Geneva, since certain leaders of Faith and Order, above all Bishop Headlam of Gloucester, supported the Reich Church and opposed the "Confessing Church." Since plans for a merger between Life and Work and Faith and Order already existed at the time, Bell was keen to prevent the two movements from drifting further apart.[121]

"CHURCH AND STATE": BISHOP GEORGE BELL AND ADOLF KELLER

Bishop Bell, the leading figure of Life and Work since 1932, initially appears to have underestimated Keller.[122] From 1933 on, however, his stance changed abruptly. Bell spoke only little German, and therefore had only scant knowledge of events in Germany. In June 1933, Alphons Koechlin, who had been loosely associated with Life and Work since 1925, traveled to Chichester on his own initiative. He became one of Bell's most

---

116. Bonhoeffer, Oldham, and Keller's relationship with Schönfeld was strained; see Bethge, *Dietrich Bonhoeffer*, 619ff.

117. Bell, *Die Königsherrschaft Jesu Christi*, 150 and 38–39.

118. Boyens, *Ökumenische Bewegung und Bekennende Kirche*, 138, 169, 259–60.

119. Bethge, *Dietrich Bonhoeffer*, 546, 540, 552.

120. Henriod to W. A. Brown, March 31, 1933 (WCC 301.43.17). Bell and Koechlin were also concerned about Schönfeld; see Lindt, ed., *George Bell–Alphons Koechlin*, 294ff. and 326–27.

121. Boyens, *Ökumenische Bewegung und Bekennende Kirche*, 117ff.

122. Possibly, this occurred due to misinformation. See above, p. 124, n. 42.

important advisors on Germany.[123] Koechlin recommended Bell to read *Religion and the European Mind* (as the British version of Keller's *Religion and Revolution* was entitled), which he did.

In March 1934, Bell organized a lecture tour of Great Britain for Keller.[124] On his tour, Keller addressed theology students in Lichfield, Oxford, Cambridge, Liverpool, and at the University of London. In a letter to Barth, he mentions that his lectures addressed the theological background of the Church Struggle: "This is of particular interest because this mostly clarifies our reason for action, since the natural theology of the German Christians has another name and obviously another form in Great Britain, namely, Semipelagianist Anglicanism. But this dents neither the sympathy for you nor for your cause."[125] On May 29, 1935, Keller gave a radio broadcast on the BBC titled "The German Church Today."[126] "My Broadcasting talk . . . was, of course, taken notice of in Germany . . . A 'German Christian' paper had attacked me."[127] Keller was continually publishing articles on Germany in English, Scottish, American, and Canadian journals. Sometimes, they even appeared in South Africa, Australia, New Zealand, and Japan.[128] In early 1938, he informed Barth that German newspapers had received instructions "not to publish any of your, Brunner's, or my writings. If anything, this can be no more than to our credit."[129]

Keller's most valuable contribution to the Oxford conference is his book *Church and State on the European Continent*.[130] Amid the flood of publications on this subject, he adopted a completely independent stance by interpreting events in Germany, Italy, and the Soviet Union from a perspective of analytical psychology. Keller's book seamlessly follows on from his earlier *Religion and Revolution*, but offers a far more exhaustive treatment of its subject. It originated in his Beckly Lectures, which he gave

123. Lindt, ed., *George Bell–Alphons Koechlin*.

124. Keller to Bell, March 3, 1934 (LPL Bell 5 f. 234).

125. Keller to Barth, March 12, 1934 (KBA 9334.346).

126. Keller to the Church of England Council for Foreign Relations, June 12, 1935 (BAR J.2.257 1288/137).

127. Keller, "Report on a journey to Berlin, June 28th–30th 1935" (NLAK C 28).

128. Keller to Barth, January 19, 1937 and May 18, 1937 (KBA 9337.40 u. 9337.247). Among other newspapers and journals, from 1935 to 1940 Keller regularly contributed articles on the situation in Germany to *The British Weekly*.

129. Keller to Barth, March 1, 1938 (KBA 9338.159).

130. Keller, *Church and State on the European Continent*.

at the 1936 annual meeting of the Methodist Church of Great Britain, notably as the first Continental European ever granted this privilege.[131]

Continental Christianity, Keller wrote in his preface, was "nothing less than the battle-field where a decisive battle for or against Christ is being fought."[132] "The present book is an attempt to supply the practical illustration necessary to give realism to the theoretical study which is in process as a preparation for the World Conference at Oxford . . . I have confined myself to the central problem of Church and State in their present concrete empirical relationship. But one cannot speak of the modern State without studying its ideology."[133] According to Keller, a sense of uncertainty prevailed in the totalitarian states: "Germany and other dictator-States seek shelter behind a strong man—they all feel insecure, and compensate for this sentiment of fear by a sham firmness, by a hero-worship, behind which hearts tremble in uncertainty about the future." God, moreover, was for mankind no longer the Father in heaven who tended to his children.[134] "They have fear in their hearts, and fear is hatred, fear is defiance, fear is superstition, fear is the ghastly flight of men running for their lives."[135] There existed, he maintained,

> a terrible liberty for the newly-discovered and frightening possibilities of free motion . . . , the liberty of man to destroy and to create, to create his own heaven and his own hell, the liberty of the soul to play with happiness and terror, with angels and demons, with good and evil, with the destiny of individuals and peoples, as if they were the toys of a giant. This new liberty of motion is exerting a magic spell on the creative imagination of leaders and masses. Even if it be an illusion, at least we are moving. We are going somewhere—maybe to paradise, maybe to hell—anything is better than to stay where we are.[136]

Keller cites Georges Sorel's *Réflexions sur la Violence*, which had influenced Mussolini in particular. The unconscious was manifesting itself: "All these revolutions are explosions of irrational, subconscious tensions,

---

131. John Henry Beckly endowed the Beckly Lecture in 1926.

132. Keller, *Church and State on the European Continent*, 10.

133. Ibid., 12–13; see also Schönfeld, ed., *Die Kirche und das Staatsproblem*, and Brunner, Huber, Oldham, Paton et al., *Totaler Staat und christliche Freiheit*.

134. Keller, *Church and State on the European Continent*, 21.

135. Ibid., 23.

136. Ibid., 23–24.

suppressed desires, religious or anti-religious passions."[137] Lenin, Mussolini, and Hitler had instrumentalized these passions, and thus incarnated a profound mystical power:

> With the renunciation of self-reflexion which characterizes the initiators of the present revolutions, the human mind enters into the sphere of a mystical or religious consciousness. A man announcing a superhuman message of the perfect society, of a totalitarian State, of a reborn nation must become a superman, a hero with a religious halo, a savior. The faith and life he calls forth, as by a magic wand, from the souls of millions, spring from the deepest aspirations of which man is capable . . . A new life-sentiment is born, filling body and soul with an immense enthusiasm . . . of a chiliastic or eschatological character. The surface transformations which are taking place to-day in political and social events are evidently a repercussion of deeper changes in the collective subconsciousness, which is the fertile hot-bed for revolutionary dreams of a new man and a new society.

Furthermore, he observed, "The present revolutions are building up a new world from below, from the soil, the blood, the race, from the instincts of man, from the imaginative passions of the subconsciousness.—The role of the spirit, of reason and mind becomes suspect, because they are critical, controlling, sifting and hampering powers."[138]

Notwithstanding certain theoretical writings, social transformation had ensued not from reflection, but instead from sheer violence.[139] Out of violent upheaval arose a state that pretended to be a secure stronghold. This state dominated the entire life of the people, economy, culture, education, and sciences. It possessed a worldview and a creed.[140] Conflicts between church and state were thus bound to occur.[141] "The present struggle between State and Church . . . is therefore a struggle between two philosophies of life, two metaphysics, between the *Logos* and the *Mythos*." The myth, a product of the collective unconscious, possessed three characteristic elements: the collective, power, and language:

137. Ibid., 25.
138. Ibid., 28, 37, 39.
139. Ibid., 30.
140. Ibid., 31–32.
141. Ibid., 34.

Its language is not that of ideas, but that of symbols. Both the Bolshevists and the leaders of the Fascist and National Socialist revolutions are . . . masters in the art of inventing and using glittering symbols. They have the power of expressing deep collective and unconscious desires of the masses . . . , tokens and mystical emblems, which marshal together large and disparate groups into a kind of mystical communion. The very fact that these movements have discovered the tremendous value of symbols, and have invented, not in the first instance the dogma, but the liturgy of a revolution which binds together millions in a common act of voluntary or forced worship of collective ideals, shows their obvious affinity with religion and its forms of expression.[142]

It is the strong collective life of the whole nation which is passing over the individual, like the ocean wave which carries away the little man standing in its way. This overwhelming experience is felt to be the *unio mystica* of the individual with the group, the redemptive act which breaks the fetters of the ego and unites it with the nation, that mysterious, supraindividual personality, the myth of a sacred collectivity . . . They are themselves the Church, including and holding their members in the holy grip of one mighty divine will which is incarnate in the leader.

It is a power with a religious halo, power interpreted as a kind of manifestation of the divine . . . The *State* itself has become a myth . . ., a mythical divinity which, like God, has the right and might to lay a totalitarian claim on its subjects; to impose upon them a new philosophy, a new faith; to organize the thinking and conscience of its children.

The Bolshevist, Fascist, and National Socialist surrogate religions had prophets and martyrs, soteriology and eschatology.[143] What was specific about the Soviet Union were the "gospel of class war and hatred" and the "myth of the *proletariat*," "a magic mirror transforming the ugly face of poverty, the wrinkles of sorrow and scars of a hard life, into the beauty and strength of a young conquering hero." The class struggle became the "jihad against the infidels." The classless society was "the satirical answer of these proletarians to the Christian message of brotherhood." The Child of God in Christianity faced the "engineer of his own life" in Bolshevist anthropology, who, however, dissolved helplessly in a "grey . . . anonymous collective happiness." Furthermore, "Bolshevism is today the declared enemy

142. Ibid., 39–40; for the further citations, see 43–44, 46, 57.
143. Ibid., 40; for the further citations, see 36, 55, 56–57, 74, 79, 62, 81, 76.

of Christianity," which goes back less to early Marxism than to Russian nihilism. Consequently, where the state or the classless society were God, God had to leave.

What typified Fascist Italy was according to Keller the education of man to violence, to battle, to self-sacrifice. "Fascism is therefore opposed to pacifism." Moreover, "only in fighting is man lifted up to that ideal of santità e eroismo in which Fascism believes."[144] Mussolini's state had come to an arrangement with the Catholic Church; but since the state was omnipotent, it could not enter into harmony with the sovereign God.[145]

Three aspects were particularly significant in the case of Germany: "The first is the conception of the biological *Wesenseinheit* (consubstantiality) . . . The people, the 'nation itself,' is, according to Hitler's own words, the 'source of all strength.'"[146] Second, anti-Semitism was the core of the National Socialist creed. While anti-Semitism pretended to be real, it was in effect unreal.[147] "The racial ideology of national socialism . . . is the real hotbed in which the most dangerous germs of conflict between State and Church are growing."[148] Third, state and party were identical. Ultimately, the "Führer" is the state. "In the writings of Adolf Hitler, one breathes the air of Nietzsche's philosophy of power."[149]

In *Church and State*, Keller's preoccupation with analytical psychology bore fruit: the book provides an exciting and stimulating account of its subject. Keller's reflections are somewhat apocalyptic; in the face of the great dangers, he argued, there was no place for half-truths: "Christianity knows that only God can stand up to the demons, not the human being. It therefore sees only in faith the power to surmount the world and its demons, and neither in the will to power nor in moral benevolence."[150] In a letter to Keller, Robert E. Speer praised the book as follows: "It is one of the best books that I have read."[151] Bishop Bell, too, was enthusiastic: "I am deep in its pages at this very moment. I think it [is] a wonderful book and am much thrilled as well as much instructed by the picture you paint. Not

144. Ibid., 107 and 101–2.

145. This is a reference to the Lateran Treaty of 1929; see ibid., 105.

146. Keller, *Church and State on the European Continent*, 114.

147. Ibid., 113 and 116; Keller anticipated current interpretations of anti-Semitism.

148. Ibid., 117.

149. Ibid., 41; see also Rauschning, *Die Revolution des Nihilismus*.

150. Keller, "Geist und Dämonie in der Geschichte," 728.

151. Speer to Keller, July 14, 1937 (PHS 68-0221 BFM/COEMAR Records, 2/5, 1790, Central Bureau 1936–1939).

only is it full of information, but full of thought and inspiration. I do think that you have done a very great service to the oecumenical movement by writing such a book. Who else is there amongst us who could have . . . the qualifications required for such a work?"[152] Keller's book featured among those announced as preliminary reading and preparation for the Oxford conference. Like *Religion and Revolution*, it was not translated into German or French, and therefore little noticed on the Continent.[153]

Bishop George Kennedy Allen Bell, 1940
(archive Dr. Pierre Keller)

The preparations for Oxford were now in full swing. "The Lordship of Chichester asked me . . . to come with him to Berlin to study the situation and to find out about the possibilities of a German delegation to

152. Bell to Keller, September 11, 1936 (LPL Bell 2 f. 83).

153. Jakob Baumann, who reviewed Keller's *Church and State*, observed: "Eine deutsche Übersetzung des Werkes wäre sehr zu wünschen! [A German translation of the work would be highly desirable!]"; see *Kirchenblatt für die reformierte Schweiz* (October 1, 1936), 318–19.

Adolf Keller

the Oxford conference. He wished me to prepare this visit and the many contacts for which I had the help of Dr. Lilje."[154] The talks were held from January 28 to February 1, 1937. Among others, Bell met with Theodor Heckel, Hanns Lilje, Otto Dibelius, and Wilhelm Zoellner, now chairman of the Board of the Reich Church (Bishop Müller had been dropped), but less with representatives of the "Confessing Church." Fears ran deep. Keller, who served as interpreter, observed: "A deep pessimistic mood is prevailing in the headquarters of the various groups."[155] Everyone Bell talked to was opposed to participation at the Oxford conference, since the tensions within the Church were too great and since the German government could cause difficulties. Martin Niemöller, the figurehead of the church opposition, was also skeptical. Since his vicarage in Berlin-Dahlem was under surveillance, Keller arranged for a secret meeting between Bell and Niemöller to take place in Dahlem, in Olga Hasselbach's house, a former member of his congregation in Cairo.[156] "Niemöller . . . spoke about the preliminary conditions which must be fulfilled before any agreement could be made with the other groups; the faith of the Church in Jesus Christ must involve a personal responsibility of each group and must precede any other considerations of ecclesiastical policy and any tactics."[157]

Bell expressed his gratitude to Keller for his assistance:

> I do want to say how exceedingly grateful I am to you for all the trouble you took about our visit to Berlin. Nobody could have been more thorough in preparing the way, or more the personification of kindness and ability in securing and assisting the many conversations that we had. I cannot tell you what a difference it made to me to have you, and what great strength it added to one's confidence in the soundness of the visit. I learnt an enormous amount, and I feel very sure that it was abundantly worth while. I think the moment at which we went was a most vital moment, and that the visit in every way was most timely . . . Once more, a thousand thanks, in which my wife wholeheartedly joins. Yours ever, George Chicester.[158]

A few weeks after the meeting in Berlin, Niemöller was arrested. In the late summer of 1937, no delegates from Germany attended the Oxford

154. Keller, "Report on a Journey to Berlin, End of January 1937" (NLAK C 28).
155. Ibid., 7.
156. See above, p. 9.
157. Ibid., 1–2.; see also Keller, "Aus meinem Leben," 187.
158. Bell to Keller, February 3, 1937 (LPL Bell 8 f. 333).

188

conference of Life and Work, with the exception of some pro-Hitlerite free churches. On the other hand, some prominent German emigrants—including Paul Tillich, Friedrich Siegmund-Schultze, and Otto Piper—were present.

Keller attended both the Oxford conference and the subsequent meeting of Faith and Order in Edinburgh. He welcomed the merger of the two ecumenical movements, which had been decided at the Oxford and Edinburgh conferences.[159] But Oxford also gave him reason for irritation. First, Joseph H. Oldham had forgotten to invite both the Swiss Protestant Church, whose membership totaled two and half million and which had played an important role in Life and Work and Inter-Church Aid. After Oxford and Edinburgh, Keller complained that the verdict reached on the totalitarian state at the two conferences, which were both dominated by the Anglican contingency, had been too "mild"—both Karl Barth and Friedrich Siegmund-Schultze fully agreed with his complaint.[160]

Keller also experienced personal disappointments: in the forefront of the Oxford conference, he was not involved in the "Committee of 35," which convened to discuss the future of ecumenism. In a letter to Leiper, he wrote that "It strikes me somehow that the 'Committee of 35' will discuss before Oxford the future of the ecumenical movements without having included a representative of the European Central Bureau and a man who has probably been connected with the past of these movements more than all who discuss now about the future."[161] Leiper was outraged: "It is a shame that you are not on the Committee of thirty-five. I urged that you should be put on it."[162] Bell shared Leiper's view: "Both Visser't Hooft and I spoke about you and the European Central Office."[163] Henry-Louis Henriod, who was responsible for the composition of the "Committee of 35," accounted for Keller's omission under reference to pressure from all quarters:[164] Koechlin had been appointed, as the representative of the Mission, the international Christian Youth Organizations, and Protestant

---

159. Keller, "Europe's Regret at Lack of Virile Leadership."

160. Ibid., September 30, 1937 (WCC 42.0042 3.1).

161. Keller to Leiper, February 26, 1937 (NLAK C 2,3).

162. Leiper to Keller, March 8, 1937 (ibid.). At the time, Leiper was serving as executive secretary of the American section of the Ecumenical Council and was a member of the Executive Committee of Inter-Church Aid.

163. Bell to Keller, July 12, 1937 (LPL Bell 8 f. 518).

164. Henriod to Keller, Geneva, June 22, 1937 (ibid.).

Switzerland. What became evident was that Keller's position as honorary lecturer lacked secure institutional underpinning.[165]

At least the conference documentation mentioned Inter-Church Aid along with Life and Work, Faith and Order, the World Alliance for Promoting International Friendship, the International Missionary Council, and the Christian youth organizations as one of nine existing ecumenical organizations. Moreover, Keller gave the opening lecture in the accompanying program for young people, which replaced the Geneva Ecumenical Seminar. The conference minutes also contain the following remark: "In surveying the program made in the years between Stockholm and Oxford the Chairman [William A. Brown] reminded . . . the fundamental contribution . . . especially through the services of Dr. Keller and of Prof. Choisy throughout those creative years."[166] What is more, the Federal Council of the Churches of Christ in America invited Keller, who was highly esteemed in the United States, to give talks on the two world conferences.

At the May 1938 conference of the Ecumenical Council in Utrecht, a "provisional committee" of 28 persons was appointed. At Boegner's suggestion, Keller became "a regular consultative member."[167] The conference heaped praise on Inter-Church Aid.[168] Henriod was dismissed as general secretary of Life and Work. Willem A. Visser't Hooft was appointed general secretary of the Provisional Committee of the Ecumenical Council, while William Paton and Henry S. Leiper were made adjunct general secretaries. Marc Boegner became president for Continental Europe, Archbishop Temple for Great Britain, and John Mott for America. Following the appointment of the "Barthian" Visser't Hooft, Barth's theology began to shape ecumenism, a development long desired by Keller. Within the ecumenical movement, Keller was presumably the most decided opponent of National Socialism.

165. See above, pp. 129–30.

166. "Minutes of the Executive Committee of Life and Work, Oxford, July 26, 1937" (WCC 24.001).

167. "Minutes of Life and Work, Utrecht, May 13, 1938" (WCC 24.023).

168. Keller, "Bericht der Europäischen Zentralstelle, 1937," 11 (BAR J.2.257 1247/133).

INTER-CHURCH AID AND ITS PIONEERING WORK FOR GERMAN REFUGEES

As early as the spring of 1933, the first victims of Hitler's repressive politics sought Keller's assistance. Inter-Church Aid was well known in Germany. Those affected were often "Jewish Christians," that is, Christians with Jewish ancestry. In effect, they were persecuted like the Jews themselves. In 1933, the Jewish population of Germany approached 600,000. The number of "Jewish Christians" can only be estimated, but also amounted to several hundred thousand. Keller was among the first Christians to speak out in support of the persecuted Jews and "Jewish Christians" worldwide. Besides, he was the first Protestant Swiss churchman to tend to their needs not only in theological but also in practical terms.[169] Not only did he oppose anti-Semitism but he also objected to anti-Judaism, which was widespread in Switzerland and elsewhere among conservative Christians, who defined it not along biological lines but in terms of the history of salvation. He rejected the Christian Mission among the Jews, which hardly anyone questioned at the time.

Keller maintained contacts with Jews already before 1933. In 1926, he helped prepare the Christian conference on the situation of the Jews, which was held in Budapest and Warsaw under the aegis of the International Missionary Council.[170] In the autumn of 1929, he stepped into a synagogue in Warsaw. Many men had gathered for prayers. The eldest asked him to step up onto the "Bima," the elevated place of honor, from which the Torah or Talmud are read aloud. Keller knew the rabbi from earlier times: "He was a great man in the people of Israel, wearing a small black velvet cap, a long beard, his eyes warm and knowing. He accompanied me to a hospital, an orphanage, and we discussed the Chassidim, with which Martin Buber had reacquainted us."[171]

The first wave of Jews and "Jewish Christians" began fleeing Germany immediately after the ordering of the boycott of Jewish shops on April 1, 1933. Three weeks afterwards, Keller wrote to Henry S. Leiper:

> It seems to me that our attitude towards the persecution of the Jews must be threefold: 1. A maximum effort to understand the

169. On his visit to Berlin in May 1934, Keller mentioned that he had received inquiries from forty-two pastors who were victims of the Aryan Paragraph; see above, p. 176.

170. Keller to Macfarland, September 9, 1926 (PHS NCC RG 18 73/10).

171. Keller, "Nordische Reise IV."

facts . . . 2. The raising of the voice of the Christian conscience against the harshness and injustice of which innocent victims are suffering not so much from boycott but from the social and economic ruin to which they are exposed. 3. Practical steps to grant shelter and aid to political refugees from Germany . . . At least for an elite of very high-standing Jews and Christians of Jewish extraction and socialist tendencies who feel compelled to leave the country such as: Prof. Heimann, Prof. Mendelssohn-Bartholdy, Prof. Cassirer, . . . , Prof. Tillich . . . , Prof. Wünsch . . . A cooperative society could be formed including Christians and Jews which could raise the necessary means for offering salaries for new posts . . . In this way a number of refugees could be employed as assistants, research-workers, librarians, teachers, journalists in various organisations in Switzerland, Holland, France, Great Britain and the Northern countries. . . . May I therefore suggest to approach . . . governments and academic societies . . . , [to] show Jewish societies these possibilities and to ask them to collaborate.[172]

Conspicuously, Keller did not distinguish between Social Democrat, Jewish, or "Jewish Christian" refugees. Moreover, he suggested cooperation between Christians and Jews in organizing the relief operation. By no means was a collaborative arrangement self-evident at the time. Keller, however, held back from open protesting against the persecution. On behalf of the Federation of Swiss Protestant Churches, he immediately contacted the appropriate, decision-making church authorities in Berlin. He demanded that they issue a call for justice and love.[173] Just as at the onset of the inner-church disputes in Germany, his concern was to avoid placing anyone in even greater jeopardy. But when he heard that church leaders who did not belong to the German Christians, among others even Otto Dibelius and Adolf Deissmann, played down the repression of the Jews, he wrote to Kapler, stating that in Switzerland the boycott of the Jews was perceived as the outbreak of systematic anti-Semitism.[174]

In May 1933, the first German refugees arrived at the office of Inter-Church Aid in Geneva. Moreover, Keller received numerous written and telephone appeals for assistance.[175] The religious, denominational,

---

172. Keller to Leiper, April 20, 1933 (WCC 301.43.17/2).

173. Kaiser, *Deutscher Kirchenkampf und Schweizer Öffentlichkeit*, 179.

174. Boyens, *Ökumenische Bewegung und Bekennende Kirche*, 39; see also Kaiser, 180–81.

175. "Minutes of the Board Meeting of the Federation of Swiss Protestant Churches," January 3, 1940 (BAR J.2.257 286).

political, professional, and social background of the refugees was not homogeneous. Many were academics, including quite a few theologians. Most were Christians with Jewish ancestors, while others were Jews, non-religious, or oppositional Protestants or Catholics. The Executive Committee of Inter-Church Aid encouraged Keller to take upon himself the "new, difficult task."[176]

The Swiss government accepted "military refugees," including deserters, without fuss or quibble. By contrast, its treatment of "civilian refugees" was very restrictive. Only so-called "political" refugees, that is, members of the opposition, were recognized as "civilian refugees." Swiss law made no provisions for refugees on "racial grounds," and such individuals were not considered "real" refugees. They were not allowed to seek employment, and were obliged to leave Switzerland again within a short period of time. The government offered them no assistance. Private relief organizations as a rule provided assistance only to those with either religious or political affiliations. This approach struck Keller as absurd. The refugees seeking his assistance "do not present themselves under specific categories. Many of these Non-Aryan Christians were baptised, or their parents were, but they do not care about special relations to the Christian church, but present themselves just as persons in need. We therefore do not make any distinction in helping refugees knocking at our door, except in specific cases."[177]

Disappointed by the inactivity of the German church, Keller wrote: "It is a matter of gratification that of late opposition to anti-Semitism has been developing within the Church. Ever since the growing anti-Semitism led to boycotting of the Jews and to undeniable acts of violence and injustice, the evangelical churches in other European countries have been expecting a strong protest to come from the German Evangelical Church. But before the application of the Aryan paragraph to the church went into effect, very few voices were raised against anti-Semitic outbreaks."[178]

Owing to the assistance that he granted to Jews in Berlin, Professor Friedrich Siegmund-Schultze was forced to emigrate already in the summer of 1933. In Zurich, where he became a student pastor, he supported those suffering the fate of forced emigration. Seeking to establish a large ecumenical relief organization with Siegmund-Schultze, Bishop Bell asked

176. Grotefeld, *Friedrich Siegmund-Schultze*, 152.
177. Keller to Bell, January 4, 1935 (LPL Bell 7 f. 8).
178. Keller, *Religion and Revolution*, 144ff. and 149.

Keller whether he would be amenable to such a project.[179] Keller replied as follows:

> What is difficult . . . is not incident help, but permanent help for a long time . . . , partly in opening Palestine . . . , partly in finding out what countries could offer permanent work to emigrating Jews . . . It seems to me that the whole proposition is too big for being handled as a whole by my friend Siegmund-Schultze, who is sick, who has difficulties in Germany and who lives now in Switzerland. The whole proposition is before the League of Nations and should find a solution there . . . Our Bureau is willing to collaborate but the problem is of such magnitude that larger organisations have to deal with it, because not only some ministers and social workers of Jewish extraction are involved. There exists certainly a special responsibility of the Christian church for the Hebrew Christians who are victims of the Aryan paragraph. But we can deal only with emergency cases as no survey exists about the number of the Hebrew Christians in Germany. One speaks of 2–300,000 . . . Increasing demands reach our Central Bureau. . . . The whole problem is surpassing our possibilities.[180]

Keller's reaction makes sense given that his office consisted of no more than a secretary and himself, and that he faced a great many other tasks. Bell's plan was not realized. In the autumn of 1933, however, the Executive Committee of Life and Work appointed Inter-Church Aid as an "agency for the distribution of funds for refugees."[181] That is to say, until further notice.[182] At that time, Keller came to the conclusion that Christians with Jewish ancestors were "in a worse position than Jews," since while they were subject to the same persecution as Jews, they received assistance neither from Christians nor from Jews: Christians considered them Jews,

179. Bell to Keller, October 4, 1933 (LPL Bell 27 f. 29). See also Gerlach, "Zur Entstehung des Internationalen kirchlichen Hilfskomitees für deutsche Flüchtlinge 1933–1936," 35 and 38.

180. Keller to Bell, October 7, 1933 (LPL Bell 27 f. 45–47) and October 14, 1933 (LPL Bell 27 f. 94–95). There were an estimated 600,000 German Jews in 1933, and 160,00 to 500,000 "Jewish Christians"; for a discussion, see Vuletic, *Christen jüdischer Herkunft im Dritten Reich*, 36–43, and Grotefeld, *Friedrich Siegmund-Schultze*, 233 and n. 154.

181. Keller to Henriod, December 26, 1933 (WCC 42.0042 1,1).

182. Universal Christian Council for Life and Work. Administrative Council, Paris, May 30, 1934 (WCC 24.001).

and vice versa Jews considered them Christians.[183] Moreover, there was deep-seated prejudice, also in Switzerland, that they had converted to Christianity out of opportunism.

How should one imagine Keller's refugee aid? First, he listened attentively to those suffering persecution, in order to discuss and find possible alternatives and solutions. Until 1934, for instance, thirty-nine German ministers and church welfare workers sought his assistance in securing posts abroad. Given an abundance of ministers in Switzerland at the time, he was able to find places for only some very few in the country. He therefore also made efforts on their behalf to find positions in Alsace and Great Britain.[184] In November 1934, sixty refugees were in his charge, before their number surged considerably. In early 1935, he wrote: "I see almost every day from seven to eight refugees . . ."[185] By June 1935, 350 refugees were under his supervision.[186] Many refugees paid several visits to Kellers' office. Negotiations with the political authorities were often difficult.

Only rarely does individual plight become tangible among these cases, since Keller had no time for documentation. On one occasion, he gave fifty Swiss francs, received shortly before from a friend, to a penniless German scholar.[187] On another, he put in a good word with Bishop Bell for the theologian Otto F. Piper, who had repeatedly solicited his assistance and whom Keller credited for being "one of the most remarkable theological professors." Thus, he wrote: "I recommend him to you particularly. I am deeply moved by this disaster which has befallen an excellent man."[188] Piper, who was fully committed to pacifism, ecumenism, and constitutional rule, was subsequently able to emigrate first to England and later to America with his wife, who came from a Jewish family, and his children. There were "many cases for which we spent only 10 or 12 francs," for instance, board and lodging for one night.[189] But the means available to Keller were insufficient to provide even such modest assistance, since

183. Keller to Bell, October 7, 1933 (LPL Bell 27 f. 45–47).

184. Keller to Bell, April 2, 1934 (LPL Bell 5 f. 340). Some cantonal churches refused to employ foreigners.

185. Keller to Bell, January 4, 1935 (LPL Bell 7 f. 8).

186. Keller to Bell, November 8, 1934 and June 15, 1935 (LPL Bell 27 f. 367 and 7 f. 261).

187. Albert Oeri (Member of the Swiss House of Representatives in Bern) to Keller, Basel, June 20, 1934, and Keller to Oeri, Geneva, June 25, 1934 (both BAR J.2.257 1447/156).

188. Keller to Bell, October 7, 1933 (LPL Bell 27 f. 45–47).

189. Keller to Bell, November 1, 1935 (LPL Bell 20 f. 129).

most Inter-Church Aid funds were earmarked for specific purposes. Lack of funding was one of the greatest problems.

Much to Henry S. Leiper's regret, no assistance came from the United States. Following his proposal, however, the American Committee for Christian Refugees was founded in 1934. Committee members included Samuel McCrea Cavert and S. Parkes Cadman, general secretary and president of the Federal Council respectively, as well as professors Paul Tillich, Henry Sloane Coffin, Reinhold Niebuhr, and William A. Brown, who were all ecumenists and good friends of Keller's.[190] Already in early 1934, the Committee reached the conclusion that the Nazi regime intended to eliminate the majority of the 600,000 Jews living in Germany.[191] But encouraging American Christians to make donations proved difficult. The first campaign in late 1934 raised only $6,666. By contrast, $1,800,000 had been raised by American Jews.[192] Bishop Bell also sent Keller an apology: "I wish we could do more for the relief of non-Aryan Christians."[193] In late 1935, he sent £55, shortly thereafter £20, amounting to 1,125 Swiss francs—which was no more than a drop in the ocean.[194] Thus, the ecumenical churches failed in their endeavor to provide assistance, even though they had officially assigned Keller to take charge of refugee care. In the summer of 1934, he therefore launched the first-ever fundraising campaign for German refugees among the Swiss Protestant cantonal churches:

> The German revolution and its anti-Semitism has forced not only the Jewish population out of civil service and public life but also many Christians of Jewish descent. The Christian churches have without doubt a particular responsibility to assist their brethren of Jewish descent . . . Families are concerned, families whose children are suddenly boycotted, whose fathers lose their employment because they have either a Jewish father or grandfather . . . [Thirty percent] of refugees have no financial means. They therefore live in constant fear of deportation. Many are already erring backward and forward between the borders, . . . and we cannot leave them to starve in the meantime. Among

190. "Minutes of the American Christian Committee for Refugees 1934–1940" (PHS NCC RG 18 3/12). 1934.

191. Leaflet of the American Committee on Religious Rights and Minorities, January 1934 (BAR J.2.257 1115/115).

192. "Minutes of the Committee for Refugees, November 5, 1934," (written by Leiper) (PHS NCC RG 18 3/12).

193. Bell to Keller, November 2, 1934 (LPL Bell 27 f. 364).

194. Keller to Bell, October 15, 1935 and November 8, 1935 (LPL Bell 27 f. 427 und 28 f. 25).

the refugees there are many women and children who lack basic necessities . . . Each case must be treated on an individual basis . . . In some cases, emigrants must be granted travel assistance . . . Such individuals are also wandering around Switzerland in search of assistance. We must not hustle them from country to country, but instead should help them at least until they are able to secure a new livelihood . . . Those who have found consolation and strength in the psalms and prophets of the Old Testament, those who recall that Jesus, just as the first apostles, was himself a Jew by birth, should open their hands and for the sake of the community created by our Lord, which extends beyond the confines of nations and races, should help those who are now losing their homeland and as yet have no new one.[195]

A paltry 1,000 francs were raised.[196] Matters were thus no better in Switzerland. Keller observed that "a strong wave of intolerance exists in the world, and is by no means limited to one country."[197] In February 1935, he reiterated his appeal to the Protestant churches of Switzerland. On this occasion, his criticism of the official measures adopted against the refugees was more outspoken: "The police authorities of the various nations are playing football with them. No one wants them."[198] This appeal, too, faded away almost unheard. Evidently, it was inconceivable that people were being persecuted simply because their grandmother was Jewish, for instance. Presumably, anti-Semitism also played its part. However, at least 3,000 francs were raised on this occasion.[199] On the National Day of Prayer (the Swiss parallel to Thanksgiving in America) in September 1935, Keller wrote directly to all Protestant congregations in Switzerland—a tremendous undertaking: "We ask those who have a homeland, a roof over the heads, who can sit down at table, to remember those . . . who no longer even resemble the foxes and birds who have lairs and nests in which they can conceal themselves."[200]

In July 1935, Inter-Church Aid, the Verband Schweizerischer Israelitischer Armenpflegen (Association of Swiss Israelite Poor Relief), and

195. Keller, "Die Verantwortung der christlichen Kirchen für judenchristliche Flüchtlinge," June 1, 1934 (BAR J.2.257 1245/133).

196. Kocher, *Rationierte Menschlichkeit*, 64–65.

197. Keller, "Bericht über die Flüchtlingsfrage" (1935), 2–3. (WCC 212.012 1 World Alliance Refugees).

198. Kocher, *Rationierte Menschlichkeit*, 65.

199. Keller to Henriod, May 12, 1935 (LPL Bell 19 ff. 491–92).

200. Marianne Jehle-Wildberger, *Das Gewissen sprechen lassen*, 50.

some other relief agencies submitted a joint motion to the Swiss government. Those lending assistance to refugees, the document stated, faced enormous difficulties: even the most rudimentary financial and structural prerequisites were lacking. The attitude of the federal authorities was too restrictive. The petitioners suggested five amendments to official government policy: first, the issuing of provisional residence and work permits to refugees; second, stateless refugees should be given identity cards valid for a period of one year; third, rejected refugees should not be extradited; fourth, relief agencies should receive state subsidies; and fifth, no bail should be levied when admitting refugees.[201] On August 28, 1935, discussions were held between agency representatives and Federal counsellors Johannes Baumann and Giuseppe Motta as representatives of the Swiss government. Keller was present, and he spoke about the international aspects of the refugee problem. The outcome of the meeting was devastating:[202] "With regard to Switzerland's contribution to the alleviation of suffering . . . no consensus was reached on any of the items on the agenda. The agency delegates had already emphasized in their motion that a country could make its voice heard in the Council of the League of Nations only if it were prepared to actively provide refugee aid itself; this point was reiterated by delegates during the meeting. In Switzerland, however, there was a noticeable tendency to keep away as many refugees as possible."[203]

By the summer of 1935, Keller had personally tended to around six hundred refugees. On September 15, 1935, the Nuremberg Laws were enacted, dividing the population of the German Reich into citizens "of German blood" and those possessing only inferior rights. Marriages between "Jews" and "Aryans" were forbidden. The laws also affected the "Jewish Christians." For instance, a niece of Wilhelm Dilthey, the world-famous philosopher, was denied a place at university.[204] The Nuremberg Laws caused a large stream of refugees. At the end of the year, Keller issued a new call for assistance to Protestant Switzerland, one whose urgency could barely be outdone:

> Pastors who could no longer hold their positions, less due to direct persecution than to hostility among the population; doctors who are forced to hand over their practices to "pure-blooded"

201. Kocher, *Rationierte Menschlichkeit*, 66 and 68.
202. Ibid., 69.
203. Ibid., 67.
204. Keller, "Report on a Journey to Berlin, End of January 1937," 9 (NLAK C 28).

> competitors; . . . Faceless, unnamed misery prevails upon all
> categories and quarters. There is a lack of papers, and without
> papers a human being is no longer a human being these days . . .
> Most refugees are utterly deprived of means, even if they possess
> assets in their homes; many are on the verge of suicide . . . Never
> before have we stared into a similar abyss of human helpless-
> ness and utter desperation. On the streets lies human "garbage,"
> which the German government simply sweeps before the doors
> of other nations. One sees them dying, and many know with
> frightening clarity that they are certain to die if no assistance
> is provided soon . . . The Swiss Aliens Police points to the large
> number of unemployed of Swiss nationality and is seeking to
> sever the inflow . . . Other governments adopt the same stance.
> Such defensive policies paralyze every goodwill to provide assis-
> tance . . . The signatory [Keller] underlined before the Commit-
> tee of the League of Nations [High Commission for Refugees]
> that, unless it deals with this entire question, the whole mass of
> refugees, who have nowhere to go, are doomed to die.[205]

The Nuremberg Laws and the ever more imploring appeals made by Keller and some other prominent individuals ultimately managed to alarm at least part of the Protestant cantonal churches. In the autumn of 1935, a local refugee committee was established in Geneva, followed by one in Zurich and Berne in 1936. In Basel, the Church became active through existing relief agencies.[206]

In 1936, there was still mention of the "prevailing apathy" on the part of the American people regarding the "Jewish-Christian" German refugees.[207] Until 1936 it collected $35,000, which were used largely for the six thousand refugees admitted into the United States until then.[208] In 1936 the Committee transmitted several hundred dollars to Geneva for the first time: "We are not getting any large sums of money for the non-Aryan Christians."[209] So, the refugee aid provided by Inter-Church Aid was funded predominantly by Protestant Switzerland. Keller repeat-edly pointed out that the greatest source of assistance had come from the Jews themselves and that numerous Swiss citizens were working for neu-tral relief organizations. This was the case not without good reason, he

205. Keller, "Die Flüchtlingsfrage," 406ff.

206. Keller to Bell, November 1, 1935 (LPL Bell 20 f. 129).

207. "Minutes of the Committee, January 13, 1936" (written by Leiper) (PHS NCC RG 18 3/12).

208. Leiper to Keller, March 27, 1936 (NLAK C 2,3).

209. Leiper to Keller, February 2, 1937 (NLAK C 2,3).

added, because singling out a particular category amid the uncontrollable mass of refugees, and establishing its affiliation to a church as fact, was far from easy.[210] Thus, he made it clear to Bishop Bell that "individual refugees are the difficult problem. Because the handling of individuals requires so much time and a special staff." If he received no assistance, then he would continue to receive eight to ten refugees everyday, as was his practice. But this would take several hours, "which I can not give."[211] Besides Keller, as observed, the total number of staff at Inter-Church Aid (including his other spheres of work) consisted only of his secretary, Elisa Perini, and a translator, who worked by the hour.[212] Thus, he did his work almost single-handedly.

THE INTERNATIONAL CHRISTIAN COMMITTEE FOR GERMAN REFUGEES (ICC)

Now, however, movement occurred: Bell returned to his plan for an ecumenical relief organization. In August 1935, this idea was discussed in the village of Chamby, on Lake Geneva. Inter-Church Aid had been assigned no more than a standby role in refugee work. Keller recommended cooperation with agencies that were not focused solely on "Jewish Christians" but who also addressed the concerns of Jewish and non-church refugees. Thus, he continued to object to the categorizing of refugees. He agreed to maintain the refugee aid of Inter-Church Aid—on condition that he finally received financial assistance and staff.[213] He failed to assert himself: "To my surprise the Committee passed over this statement."[214] Both Siegmund-Schultze and Bell favored a relief organization dedicated exclusively to assisting "non-Aryan Christians."[215] Keller, Siegmund-Schultze, Henriod, and a representative of the High Commission for Refugees of the League of Nations were tasked with overseeing preparations for the establishment of such an agency. They made contact with the Reverend

210. Keller, "Bericht über die Flüchtlingsfrage" (1935), 2 (WCC 212.012 1 World Alliance Refugees).

211. Keller to Bell, January 11, 1936 (LPL Bell 20 ff. 170–171).

212. Keller, "Bericht der Europäischen Zentralstelle" (1937), 17 (BAR J.2.257 1247/133).

213. "Minutes of the Meeting of the Administrative Committee, Chamby, August 17–23, 1935" (WCC 24.001).

214. Keller to Leiper, March 2, 1937 (WCC 212.012 6).

215. Gerlach, "Zur Entstehung des Internationalen kirchlichen Hilfskomitees für deutsche Flüchtlinge 1933–1936," 35ff.

Hermann Maas, who was attending to Jews and "non-Aryan" Christians in Heidelberg. A few weeks later, they learned that the High Commission for Refugees of the League of Nations, with which Keller had cooperated closely, was on the brink of collapse—which boded ill.[216]

Nevertheless, the relief agency was founded in London on January 31, 1936, as envisaged. It was called the International Christian Committee for German Refugees (ICC).[217] Its designated seat was Geneva, and an office was established in London. Together with Bishop Bell, who was appointed chairman, Keller, Siegmund-Schultze, and Henriod were elected as committee members. Archbishop Eidem of Uppsala, Bishop Bell, and Pastor Marc Boegner offered their services as "Joint Presidents."[218] America remained uninvolved. National branch offices were established in Europe, such as in 1936 the Schweizerisches Hilfskomitee für nicht-arische Flüchtlinge aus Deutschland (Swiss Aid Committee for Non-Aryan Refugees from Germany). The committee consisted only of Keller, Siegmund-Schultze, and Henriod. Their search for further members was in vain.[219] In 1936, Keller and Emil Brunner launched a new fundraising campaign on behalf of refugees.[220] For the first time, their efforts were relatively successful, with Inter-Church Aid receiving donations totaling 12,477.25 Swiss francs. Compared to the many million francs that the agency had distributed to others in need, the sum, however, was diminutive.[221]

The British subcommittee of the International Christian Committee (ICC) urged the settling of "non-Aryan" Christians in Latin America. Siegmund-Schultze and Keller raised serious doubts about this proposal.[222] No less than 65,000 Swiss francs were earmarked for the first trial.[223] In February 1937, sixty "Jewish Christians" and members of the opposition

216. "Minutes of the First Session of the Commission, October 4, 1935" (WCC 212.012 2 u. 3).

217. "Minutes of the ICC Session, London, January 31," 1936, 3 (WCC 212.012 5).

218. "ICC Half Yearly Report, January 31 to July 31, 1936" (WCC 212.012,1).

219. Keller (resp. Branch Committee of the ICC) to the Swiss churches, March 3, 1937 (WCC 212.021 6).

220. "Minutes of the Executive Committee of the ICC, Geneva, March 2, 1936" (WCC 212.012 1).

221. Keller, "Memorandum concerning the oecumenical character and activity of the European Central Office for Inter-Church Aid," June 15, 1937 (WCC 42.0042 3,1).

222. Meeting of the ICC Committee, February 17, 1937; see Grotefeld, *Friedrich Siegmund-Schultze*, 244–45.

223. "Minutes of the ICC Meeting, Chamby, August 19–20, 1936" (WCC 212.012 1).

traveled to Columbia. A year later, the attempted settlement had virtually failed. Many of the emigrants had withdrawn from the scheme.[224]
Moreover, the means of the ICC were exhausted. Another grievance was
that Hermann Maas had not succeeded in establishing an ICC subcommittee in Germany. Even the "Confessing Church" stepped out of line.[225]
From 1938 on, the questions concerning international refugee aid were
discussed informally by Keller, Visser't Hooft, the new general secretary
of the Provisional Committee of the Ecumenical Council, and Henriod,
now general secretary of the World Alliance. Siegmund-Schultze limited
his involvement to the Swiss subcommittee of the ICC.

In late 1938, after the Nazi occupation of Austria had resulted in
another stream of refugees, a government-level refugee conference was
held in the French town of Evian. Keller had submitted a motion to the
conference and took part as an observer. He was deeply disappointed by
its failure.

In September 1938, Keller, Visser't Hooft, and Henriod asked all large
Protestant churches in the world for vacancies for fifty pastors belonging to the "Confessing Church."[226] After the so-called Reichskristallnacht
(Night of the Broken Glass, i.e., the pogroms in the whole Reich) of November 9 and 10, 1938, they addressed an urgent appeal to the churches of
the world to lend support to "non-Aryan" refugees.[227] Since the ICC had
ceased operations, Keller single-handedly took charge of the ecumenical
refugee aid provided by Inter-Church Aid. In April 1940, he referred to
2,200 individuals to whom he had attended personally since 1933.[228]

In early 1939, Bishop Bell relaunched ecumenical refugee aid: he appointed Adolf Freudenberg, a German lawyer and theologian, whose wife
was Jewish, as full-time secretary responsible for international refugee
work.[229] Freudenberg worked closely with Heinrich Grüber, who had been
looking after victims of the persecution in Berlin since the summer of

224. Keller to the Swiss churches, July 15, 1938 (EZA 51 / H II c14).

225. See Grotefeld, *Friedrich Siegmund-Schultze*, 238.

226. "Aide Mémoire on help to 'non-Aryan' Pastors," September 22, 1938 (WCC
301.43.30 1); see also "Minutes of the Swiss Church Aid Committee for Evangelical
Refugees," November 14, 1938 (BAR J.2.257 1264/135).

227. Henriod, Visser't Hooft, Keller to the ecumenical churches, November 16,
1938 (BAR J.2.257 1247/133).

228. Keller, "Kurze Übersicht über die Tätigkeit [. . .] der Zentralstelle," April 2,
1940, 7 (WCC 42.0042 2,2).

229. Freudenberg's wife was a cousin of the three "Jewish Christian" Liefmann
siblings; see below, p. 226.

6

World War II and the Postwar Period

"WE HAVE SOMETHING TO SAY—
TOGETHER WITH OUR CATHOLIC BRETHREN"[1]

ON THE NIGHT OF March 11, 1938, German troops invaded Austria. It
so happened that on the following morning of March 12 Keller arrived
in Vienna to attend a conference. In a letter to Bell, he noted: "Instead of
having this meeting I . . . became witness of a tremendous historic event."[2]
Furthermore:

> In the streets, I saw motorized German troops, and I am sure
> there were five hundred airplanes in the skies above the city.
> Gradually, other branches of the German military entered the
> city. I also saw the German commander, General von Bock, at
> the Grand Hotel, where I was staying . . . On March 14, Hitler
> himself arrived. I saw his procession from not that far off and
> heard him speak several times. The jubilation among the crowds
> was indescribable . . . Half an hour after Hitler had received
> Cardinal-Archbishop Innitzer, I visited the latter at his palace
> . . . He received me quite leisurely and evidently in the hope
> that after his meeting with Hitler a new age had dawned also
> for the Church. When I asked him whether he genuinely meant
> his words "to gladly and willingly obey," uttered in response to

1. Keller, "Address delivered at the anniversary of the Federal Council of Churches
at Washington, December 6, 1933" (NLAK C 6); see above, p. 167 and p. 207.

2. Keller to Bell, March 22, 1938 (LPL Bell 9 ff. 204–5).

Hitler's demand, he replied in his homely dialect, "Well, what can you do?"[3]

Innitzer ordered the church bells to be rung during Hitler's procession through Vienna. Hitler, it is worth remembering, had been brought up as a Catholic and was a native Austrian. Besides, the Concordat of July 20, 1933, between the Vatican and the Hitler regime, had largely protected the German Catholic Church against state intervention until shortly before the German annexation of Austria. Keller, however, did not shy away from asking Innitzer about his stance on Hitler. A few months after the annexation, thuggish Hitler Youth and SA gangs stormed the archbishop's palace in Vienna, slashing a picture of Christ with knives. The cardinal was brought to safety at the last minute.[4] It is worth recalling that earlier in 1933, Keller had joined forces with Innitzer and the Chief Rabbi of Vienna to arrange the transfer of funds to the Ukraine to help feed the country's starving population.[5]

On returning to Switzerland, Keller wrote: "The situation of the Jews and Non-Aryan Christians in Austria is already becoming very serious. I saw it even in the streets. There is an increase of suicide. Non-Aryan pastors have also to go. We [the Swiss subcommittee of the International Christian Committee] approached already the Alsacian churches to the effect that they should try to get from the French Government the permission to open the Church to foreign pastors as they have not enough. The whole refugee problem is becoming again very acute."[6] More circumspect Austrians, he observed,

> were afraid of the sharp-edged methods of National Socialism
> . . . Already during the very first days, their grip was much more
> extensive than even the most German-friendly Austrian had
> dreamed of . . . The Protestant Church of Austria is even more
> firmly in favor of annexation . . . It is evident that it is seek-
> ing a closer community of faith with Protestant Germany. At
> the same time, however, it wishes to keep the German church
> struggle away from the Austrian Church, in order to allow it to
> exist as an intact Church, just as this was possible in southern

3. Keller, "Aus meinem Leben," 197–98.

4. Personal statement made by Cardinal Schönborn in conversation with Adrian Schenker and Frank Jehle on October 31, 2005; see also http://religion.orf.at/projekto2/news/0411/neo41117–samida.htm/.

5. See above, p. 144.

6. Keller to Bell, March 22, 1938 (LPL Bell 9 ff. 204–5); see also Report of the ICC, London, May 19, 1938, 6 (WCC 212.012 1).

> Germany. With integration becoming increasingly imminent,
> this hope appears to be vanishing . . . [The Jews] were relieved of
> their public functions with immediate effect.[7]

Jews were seeking to reach third countries via Switzerland. The Swiss government allowed thousands to enter the country. When persecution was stepped up in July 1938, thereby causing a new wave of refugees, the border was closed. Eugène Choisy and Keller rushed to the Swiss Federal Department of Justice and Police to demand the reopening of the border. And yet: "The Federal Council [of Switzerland] has once again upheld the closure of the border for refugees . . . , notwithstanding our intervention at the Office of the Federal Alien's Police."[8]

Despite the lingering effects of the culture struggle after the First Vatican Council, Keller had adopted an unbiased approach to the Catholics already in the 1920s, at a time when Rome was dismissive of the ecumenical movement.[9] Leiper wrote, "leaders of the ecumenical movement have repeatedly approached the Vatican with requests for cooperation. These approaches have been courteously received, often by the pope in person, but always the suggestion of even informal cooperation has been officially rebuffed as, 'subversive of the foundation of the Catholic faith'. . . . There is but one way in which the unity of Christians may be fostered and that is by furthering the return to the one True Church of Christ."[10]

In his encyclical *Mortalium animos*, decreed in 1928, Pope Pius XI leveled fierce criticism at the ecumenical conferences of Stockholm and Lausanne. Notwithstanding his disappointment, Keller formulated a measured response:

> But it is safe to say that the Vatican, which is otherwise so well-
> informed, has perhaps been seldom quite so mistaken about
> the meaning and spirit of a movement than here . . . This . . .
> unfriendliness . . . , however, is a source of particular embarrass-
> ment for a large part of the Catholic world, for Catholics, who

7. Keller, "Zur Beurteilung der österreichischen Revolution," March 19, 1938 (BAR J.2.257 1247/133).

8. Keller to the members of the Board of the Federation of Swiss Protestant Churches, November 26, 1938 (BAR J.2.257 1189/127).

9. Keller had contacts to Caritas in the late 1920s.

10. Leiper, "Relations beween the Evangelical Movement and the Vatican in the Twentieth Century," 1 and 5, presumably 1949 (PHS 97-1027 Henry S. Leiper Papers 2/4); the citation within the citation is from the papal encyclical *Mortalium Animos* (1928).

are engaged in a practical struggle for a Christian life, also sense
that today contact and cooperation are indispensable . . . The
best answer to the Encyclical . . . is that we must time and again
emphasize the positive, practical aims of the unification movement, in a spirit of brotherliness and love, forsake all unnec-
essary polemics, and forever maintain that we are prepared to
cooperate with a Christian Church on the plight of the world.[11]

He neither denied that there were Protestant agitators, nor that many
Catholic theologians criticized the individualism, subjectivism, and ratio-
nalism of Protestantism. Some scholars, however, such as the Jesuit Max
Pribilla—a friend of Keller's since Stockholm—were seriously attempting
to understand the Reformation.[12] Thus, Keller observed: "One helpful element is that in spite of militant agitators in both camps there is an increasing number of Christian men and women, both Catholic and Protestant,
who deplore all confessional controversy and are striving for a mutual
understanding and tolerance, or at least for an honest presentation of the
spiritual claim of each party."[13]

In the struggle for social justice and peace, Keller saw a possibility for
cooperation with the Catholics. In his capacity as the general secretary of
the International Christian Social Institute of Life and Work in Geneva, he
contacted Caritas and various other Catholic welfare agencies. Ever since
Karl Barth's famous essay on "Der Römische Katholizismus als Frage an
die Protestantische Kirche" (Roman Catholicism as a Question addressed
to the Protestant Church),[14] a theological rapprochement between the
two denominations had occurred, according to Keller, for instance in the
writings of Max Pribilla and Romano Guardini: "In any event, dialectical
theology has attracted new attention on the Catholic side, in a manner not
experienced by Protestant theology for a long time."[15]

Following the Nazi takeover, Keller considered maintaining contact
with the Catholic Church more necessary than ever. Speaking in Washington in late 1933, he declared: "We have something to say—together with
our Catholic brethren."[16] Addressing the Church of England Council for

11. Keller, "Der gegenwärtige Stand der Einigungsbewegung mit besonderer
Berücksichtigung von Stockholm," 17ff. (presumably written in late summer 1928)
(NLAK C 31).

12. Pribilla, *Um kirchliche Einheit.*

13. Keller and Stewart, *Protestant Europe,* 176.

14. Barth, "Der Römische Katholizismus als Frage an die Protestantische Kirche."

15. Keller, *Der Weg der dialektischen Theologie,* 136–37.

16. Keller, "Address delivered at the anniversary of the Federal Council of Churches at Washington," December 6, 1933 (NLAK C 6); see above, p.

Foreign Relations in 1935, he stated, "The relationship between Catholics and Protestants is visibly improving since both groups are undergoing the same persecution in Russia as well as in Germany. Numerous contacts, although unofficial, are formed, and we know today that even in Roman Catholic quarters the conviction exists that the present struggle for religious liberty needs close cooperation and even a common front."[17] After the definite end of the reprieve for the Catholic church in Germany, Keller spoke of "suffering sister churches" and of a "fellowship of suffering between Catholics and Protestants."[18] In late January 1937, he visited the archbishop of Munich, Cardinal Max Faulhaber:

> The fact that the Protestant as well as the Roman Catholic Church feel the oppression and the great menace of a Pagan attack on a common heritage, brings both Churches much nearer to each other although no joint organisation or official contacts is projected as a common defense against a common enemy . . . Cardinal Faulhaber in Munich, to whom I had already last year introduced Dr. Cavert,[19] had answered very kindly an article of mine in the "Living Church" in which I spoke of the common defense of a Christian heritage and approved this thesis . . . On the way back [from Berlin] I saw my old friend Pribilla, editor of a Catholic Magazine[20] and author of a famous book on the Stockholm conference . . . He took me to the Cardinal who received me most kindly and said that since a long time he had wished to see me . . . Pribilla as well as the Cardinal resent likewise as the Confessional Church the attack of the political religion on the Christian religion. The Cardinal explained spontaneously that we should not consider it as an unfriendliness if the Catholic Church could not participate officially in our conferences . . . He would have liked to greet the Bishop of Chichester . . . He said that movements towards more unity could be supported in the present only by an elite which is not always understood by the masses in both Churches.[21]

17. Keller to the Church of England Council for Foreign Relations, June 12, 1935 (BAR J.2.257 1288/137).

18. Keller, *Christian Europe Today*, 108ff.

19. Cavert was the acting general secretary of the Federal Council at the time.

20. The Jesuit magazine edited by Priballa is called *Stimmen der Zeit: Monatsmagazin für das Geistesleben der Gegenwart* (today: *Die Zeitschrift für christliche Kultur*).

21. Keller, "Report on a Journey to Berlin, end of January 1937," 10–11. (NLAK C 28).

In his subsequent report to Leiper, Keller observed: "I was quite struck by the cordiality with which Cardinal Faulhaber in Munich received me. I shall not become a Roman Catholic for that, but it shows that in spite of the controversy going on all the time, an elite can speak together."[22] In response to the National Socialist demand for "a racial church in a racial state," Faulhaber had found the best possible answer on the pulpit: "We have not been redeemed with German blood, but with the precious blood of our Lord Jesus Christ."[23] Further, as Keller noted, "Catholic leaders as Cardinal Faulhaber, [and] Count von Galen, Bishop of Münster, . . . have come out in an open fight, and show in their declarations the seriousness of the situation for the Catholic Church . . . In the last public speeches of Count Galen . . . a remarkable fact took place when the Protestants were called brethren."[24]

Of particular importance in this respect is the correspondence between Keller and Marius Besson, bishop of Lausanne, Geneva, and Fribourg. Besson was a personal advisor to the pope, but positively disposed toward ecumenism. In answer to Keller's question concerning the pope's views on the matter, Besson replied: "It remains the case, however, that the pope, to whom my books are not unknown, has never once intimated that he disapproves of my way of operating . . . Dear Sir, some are more or less understanding than others. But I am certain that those who still wish to see different Christian communities deal with each other in sincere charity are no less 'Catholic' than others."[25] On February 2, 1940, a few months after the outbreak of war, Besson and Keller both spoke about "Vers la paix religieuse" (Toward Religious Peace) at the Auditorium Maximum of the Swiss Federal Institute of Technology in Zurich. They were convinced that Catholics and Protestants shared enough common faith to offer joint testimony to the Christian ideal of love and to stand together against the dark powers. Moreover, they rejected reaching shoddy compromises on the question of truth.[26]

22. Keller to Leiper, February 11, 1937 (NLAK 2,3).

23. Keller, *Christian Europe Today*, 83.

24. Keller, "The Relations of Germany and the Vatican," 2–3 (NLAK C 2,3).

25. Besson to Keller, late 1936 (archive de l'Evéché de Lausanne, Genève et Fribourg, dossier Besson-Keller). See Marianne Jehle-Wildberger "Marius Besson und Adolf Keller. Ein frühes ökumenisches Gespräch."

26. Besson, "Vers la paix religieuse"; see also Keller, "Wege zum religiösen Frieden."

Henry S. Leiper (archive Dr. Pierre Keller)

In the second week of April in 1940, Keller traveled to Rome to discuss the fate of "Jewish Christians" living in mixed Protestant-Catholic marriages.[27] Pursuant to Faulhaber's suggestion, the Vatican was endeavoring to secure Brazilian visas for three thousand "non-Aryan" German Catholics.[28] Keller hoped that the refugees in his charge could be included in this arrangement. His efforts were of no avail.[29] However, Besson arranged a private audience for Keller with Pope Pius XII, who had recently spoken out against war atrocities and an Italian entry into the war. The German attack on France was imminent.

27. "Annual Report of the Central Bureau for 1939/1940," 21 (BAR J.2.257 1257/133).

28. Faulhaber to Pope Pius XII, Munich, March 31, 1939, in Blet et al., *Le Saint Siège et les Victimes de la Guerre*, 62ff.

29. Keller to Bell, January 8, 1954: "We [*Inter-Church Aid*] have tried . . . to seek cooperation with the Catholic Refugee Department in the Vatican—in vain" (LPL Bell 220 ff. 324–29).

Keller wrote two secret reports on his papal audience, one of them to Leiper; unfortunately, they have gone missing. The archives of Pius XII will remain closed until 2028. After the end of the war, Keller described his meeting with the pope as follows in a letter to the Catholic philosopher Jacques Maritain: "During [the meeting] I was deeply impressed by the elevated moral aim of the projects for peace described by the pope, and by his grasp of the religious situation of contemporary Christianity."[30] Lasting twenty-five minutes, the audience appears to have addressed the issues of peace and the situations of the churches in Germany and the Soviet Union; it is uncertain, however, whether the plight of the German refugees was discussed.[31]

NEW REFUGEES: "THEIR ENTIRE EXISTENCE HAS BECOME THAT OF FEAR"[32]

The German invasion of Poland on September 1, 1939, marked the beginning of World War II. Keller was deeply perturbed, but he also sought to provide consolation:

> That Europe that we loved so much had died! No longer is that impressive community of a spirit that united us beyond all confines and tensions! No longer is that sacred responsibility for a shared cultural heritage . . . !
>
> It is dark at the foot of the lighthouse . . . Human distress is bottomless . . . Night has fallen, and for brief moments, when the light high above us revolves, we see a bright light in the distance. This must be enough in the prevailing darkness . . . Then we know that the lighthouse is still standing, and the same light shines across the world.
>
> The joyous message is that God is drawing closer to us. . . . The joyous message is that he has us say: what concerns you, also concerns me . . . At first, it says that God is with us and goes through everything with us . . . If God comes to us and goes through everything with us, then we are consoled and dare to continue doing so.[33]

---

30. Keller to Jacques Maritain, February 2, 1945 (WS Ms Sch 152/37).

31. Keller, "Aus meinem Leben," 208–9.

32. Keller, "Annual Report of the Central Bureau for 1939/40" (BAR J.2.257 1243/132).

33. Keller, *Am Fusse des Leuchtturms*, 145ff., 208ff., 213ff.

In late August 1939, the Executive Committee of Inter-Church Aid held its annual meeting in Geneva. While its German delegates were absent, Choisy, Leiper, Boegner, and Jörgensen, among others, were present.[34] In the event of war, Keller would be responsible for maintaining relations between the churches, emergency assistance, and refugee aid. In mid-session, they received word that the outbreak of war was imminent. Before returning home, delegates celebrated the Last Supper, and Keller managed to secure their approval for a resolution he had drawn up:[35]

> It is the hope of the Executive Committee of the European Central Bureau . . . that peace shall be preserved. Should war, however, once again divide the world into enemies, the Church of Jesus Christ must not be allowed to lose its inner unity, not even in times of such battles. Its duty, whatever may happen, is to support its members with its prayers and to assist them as far as possible. We therefore request the churches to preserve solidarity according to the Gospel . . . and to mutually strengthen trust among Christians, so that love may be stronger than hatred.[36]

During the war, the Executive Committee was unable to meet *in corpore*. For the time being, however, relations with France continued to exist. Also, the New York branch office maintained its operations. After the outbreak of war, Keller alerted the Americans to the new streams of refugees.[37] In late 1939, he issued the following appeal: "For the love of Christian Brethren, help them in the ordeal through which they are passing to-day . . . Swiss protestantism does . . . its utmost for our brethren. But the burden is too heavy, and we need your cooperation and help."[38] He could now count solely on the assistance of the Swedish and Swiss churches. In response, the Americans expressed their understanding for the problem and their endeavor to help as much as possible: "We sympathize with you deeply."[39]

34. "Report of the Meeting of the Executive Committee of the European Central Office for Inter-Church Aid," August 25–27, 1939 (PHS BFM/COEMAR records 1/5 1790–1); see also "Annual Report of the Central Bureau for 1938/39," 21–22. (BAR J.2.257 1247/133).

35. "Report of the Meeting of the Executive Committee" (1939), 12–13.

36. Keller, "Annual Report of the Central Bureau for 1939/1940," 1 (BAR J.2.257 1247/133).

37. Keller, "Memorandum on the Emergency Activity of the European Central Office for Inter-Church Aid," Geneva, September 15, 1939 (PHS 68–0221 BFM/COEMAR 2/5 1790, Central Bureau 1936–1939).

38. Keller to the Presbyterian and Reformed Churches, December 20, 1939 (ibid.).

39. Board of Foreign Missions to Keller, December 19, 1939 (ibid.).

Nevertheless, the United States government erected barriers against assistance for Europe.

Geneva became the center of non-catholic assistance for war victims and refugees. Along with Inter-Church Aid, other international Christian organizations based there as well as the Red Cross, contributed to the relief program, whose core areas were coordinated. Just as after World War I, Inter-Church Aid concentrated its efforts on providing the churches with emergency aid, besides focusing on refugee aid. In many cases, entire population segments besides Jews and "Jewish Christians" were fleeing from the war. The first country to be affected was Poland.

In a letter to Keller, General Superintendent Blau of Poznań deplored the attacks carried out by the local Polish population on the German-speaking members of his congregation—in response to the German invasion of the country.[40] Keller refused Blau's call for assistance—since this would soon be arriving from Germany anyway. However, he spoke out on behalf of Bishop Julius Bursche, the seventy-eight-year-old head of the Lutheran-Polish Church in Warsaw. Strongly rooted in the Polish population, Bursche's church was also loyal to the Polish state. At the beginning of the war, Bursche had been arrested and detained in the concentration camp at Dachau. Keller petitioned Bishop Heckel, of the Foreign Office of the German Evangelical Church, for eased conditions, just as he had done for German pastors imprisoned in England. Besides claiming that Bursche was not at Dachau, Heckel rejected the comparison with German pastors as unacceptable: the latter had done nothing wrong, whereas Bursche had subjected the Germans in Poland to "despicable and unchristian" treatment. Keller refused to be intimidated. He submitted an official application for eased conditions to Otto Köcher, the German ambassador to Switzerland (who approved Keller's plea), requesting him to forward it to the "proper authorities" in Berlin. There, it once again landed on Heckel's desk, who remained impassive. Bursche died in Sachsenhausen concentration camp in 1942; his relatives were told that he had passed away in the state hospital in Berlin.[41]

Many Polish Protestants, including "Jewish Christians," fled to Romania, Hungary, or Lithuania, from where they turned to Inter-Church Aid for assistance.[42] Keller sought to alleviate their plight with clothing consignments. The Soviet occupation of the three Baltic states obstructed

40. Blau to Keller, October 17, 1939, 4ff. (WCC 42.0042 2,2).

41. On Bursche, see Boyens, *Kirchenkampf und Ökumene*, 33ff.

42. Keller assumed that there were 52,000 Polish refugees in Hungary and 32,000 in Romania.

relief work in the region.[43] Following the occupation of Galicia, first by German and thereafter by Russian troops, the fate of Protestant Ukrainians seemed sealed.[44]

In December 1939, the Soviet Union invaded Finland, resulting in mass evacuation and the relocation of villages and congregations. Inter-Church Aid and the Federation of Swiss Protestant Churches issued appeals for assistance to the Finnish Lutheran Church.[45] Keller was able to transmit the sizeable sum of 200,000 Swiss francs to Helsinki.[46] In the Soviet Union, numerous Protestant ministers were either deported to Siberia or murdered, and their families subject to harassment.[47] The existing Reformed congregations were completely "swept away." Nevertheless, the longstanding relief work undertaken by Inter-Church Aid in Russia continued in secret. Many packages reached their addressees through diverse channels. Even after the Soviet occupation of the Baltic states, through which an important transit route had run, relief supplies still entered these countries.[48] However, much of the infrastructure erected or supported by Keller now lay in ruins.

In April 1940, Hitler occupied Denmark and Norway, followed by Holland, Belgium, and northern France in May. Hundreds of thousands of Belgians fled to unoccupied southern France, including many young men keen to avoid conscription into the German army. Keller approached the churches in America and South Africa. Within a few weeks, 10,000 Swiss francs were raised in Switzerland for the Belgian Protestants. Millions of French citizens—Protestants, Catholics, Jews, and "Jewish Christians"—also sought refuge in the south, where the Vichy Republic had meanwhile been established. The Federation of French Protestant Churches relocated from Paris to Nîmes. Many refugees soon returned home: "Thousands endured great hardship and misery on the road . . . Indescribable confusion prevailed in Paris as floods of refugees engulfed the city . . . Refugees

43. Keller, "Annual Report of the Central Bureau for 1939/1940," 6 (BAR J.2.257 1247/133).

44. See above, p. 92.

45. Keller, "Memorandum I über die Lage der europäischen Kirchen," December 31, 1939 (BAR J.2.257 1247/133).

46. "Annual Report of the Central Bureau for 1939/1940," 6; see also Keller, "Memorandum III (*Zentralstelle*)," June 1 to July 8, 1940 (BAR J.2.257 1247/133).

47. "Annual Report of the Central Bureau for 1938/39," 5 and 8ff. (ibid.).

48. Keller to the Executive Committee of the Central Bureau, June 25, 1940 (BAR J.2.257 1246/133).

are suffering great distress both in occupied and in unoccupied France."
[49] Moreover,

> Their entire existence has become that of fear. Hunger, insom-
> nia, freezing . . .—that is nothing, but the anguish: . . . How will
> one bother to ask the five million refugees roaming the streets
> of France in despair, who are either sleeping or are left behind
> in stables, barns, sheds, and ditches, "Who are you?" "Do you
> deserve help?" But we know who they are: *human beings.*[50]

> The Federation of French Protestant Churches contacted
> the European Central Bureau shortly after war broke out . . .
> Ever since September 1939, we have managed to send regular
> sums of money . . . to France . . . To date, an estimated 100,000
> Swiss francs have been transferred from Switzerland . . . But
> this assistance has been no more than a drop in the ocean.
> . . . Together with representatives of the Ecumenical Council
> and the European Central Bureau, joint meetings have already
> been held with the director of the International Red Cross.[51]

According to Keller, the assistance that Inter-Church Aid granted to
refugees in Finland, Lithuania, Spain, Romania, Belgium, and France during the years 1939 and 1940 cast the refugee question in a new light: a
"racial issue" had become "a general problem." It was to be hoped, Keller
observed, that this shift would help "detoxify" the issue, and that Jews and
"Jewish Christians" would receive better treatment.[52] During the first year
of the war, Keller abandoned several projects aimed at evacuees, prisoners
of war, and civilian prisoners to devote himself entirely to saving lives.[53]
Once more, he appealed to churches in the United States, Sweden, Canada,
and South Africa to support their European mother churches.[54] His pleas
became increasingly dramatic:

> The suffering of refugees is our modern-day inferno, a funnel-
> shaped Hell . . . Mankind's greatest culprits were gathered in

49. Keller, "Annual Report of the Central Bureau for 1939/40," 7f. (BAR J.2.257
1247/133).

50. Keller, *Am Fusse des Leuchtturms,* 153; emphasis original.

51. "Annual Report of the Central Bureau for 1939/40," 8–9. (BAR J.2.257
1247/133).

52. Ibid., 9–10.

53. Ibid, 23–24.

54. Ibid, 28. See also Keller to the Executive Committee, June 25, 1940 (BAR
J.2.257 1246/133), and Keller to Siegmund-Schultze, July 30, 1940 (EZA 51 / H II e6).

Dante's Inferno. In today's hell, however, innocent people are subjected to modern torture. What evil have the women done who must flee across the Perthus pass [in the Pyrenees] through rain and snow drifts at the height of winter, sometimes dragging a bag containing their belongings across the snow slopes, . . . their feet sore, with holes in the shoes . . . What about the children? What happens to them, on the myriad of roads on which they wade through dirt, hungry, crying, freezing, holding their mother's hands or in her arms because their feet have frozen— this is a massacre of the innocents, an infanticide at Bethlehem . . . Here great *injustice* is being done.[55]

As mentioned, Adolf Freudenberg, who had served as delegate for refugees of the Provisional Ecumenical Council since early 1939, had been based in Geneva since the beginning of the war, from where he now co-ordinated the refugee aid hitherto provided by Inter-Church Aid. Most of the funds came from Protestant Switzerland. Freudenberg was supervised and advised by the Ecumenical Committee for Refugees (Comité oecuménique pour les Réfugiés) thus chiefly by the experienced Keller, W. A. Visser't Hooft (Ecumenical Council), and Henry L. Henriod (World Alliance).[56] Together, this team of three had overseen international ecumenical refugee aid since 1938, following the collapse of the ICC.[57] Keller, that is, Inter-Church Aid, was responsible for raising funds for Freudenberg's office. Once more, Protestant Switzerland was the principal sponsor. Great Britain and the United States were not able to provide any funding. (Neutral Sweden was an exception.)

The German occupation of northern France resulted in a concentration of Jewish and "Jewish-Christian" refugees in southern France. The majority of funds were therefore transmitted from Geneva to the leadership of the French Protestant Church in Nîmes, which tended to the refugees and their needs in an exemplary fashion. Marc Boegner, member of the Executive Committee of Inter-Church Aid and president of the Ecumenical Council for Continental Europe, frequently traveled to Geneva for meetings with Freudenberg and Keller.[58] 5,000 Protestant refugees of Jewish descent were now interned in camps in the German-friendly Vichy Republic, eight hundred alone in the camp at Gurs:

55. Keller, *Am Fusse des Leuchtturms*, 2–3 (italics original).

56. Freudenberg, "Bericht des Ökumenischen Ausschusses für Flüchtlingshilfe," January 1942, 4 (WCC 425.1.023 B,2, Freudenberg archives refugees).

57. See above, p. 202.

58. Boegner, *L'Exigence Œcuménique*, 138.

In undertaking these relief efforts, which are funded exclusively by the Ecumenical Committee for Refugees, Protestant clergymen have been assigned to the various camps, where congregations have been formed; in Gurs a Protestant barrack [serving as a church] has been established . . . This church work, which has been placed consciously under the responsibility of the French Protestant Church, involves a widely ramified relief organization. Its efforts consist of donations to meet the most pressing needs, in procuring foodstuffs and clothing, and, in cooperation with other organizations, helping to improve conditions in the camps.[59]

Along with the resident pastors, young French Protestants lived with those interned in the camps at Gurs, Rivesaltes, Rébédou, Brens-Gaillac, Marseille, and Toulouse. They established foyers, managed by Madeleine Barot, conducted church services, organized lectures and concerts, and attended to no less than 1,600 children. This relief work also benefited the Jewish refugees, who were by far the largest group. Overall, it helped alleviate the misery in the camps. In July 1940, Henry S. Leiper observed that unfortunately the "transmission of funds" remained difficult.[60] Shortly afterwards, however, he managed to send $1,000 to Freudenberg and $1,400 to the Ecumenical Council, which was also suffering from a shortage of funds.[61] In a letter to Choisy, Keller wrote that in 1940 Inter-Church Aid "could transmit nearly Swiss francs 500,000 to France."[62]

In 1942, Freudenberg observed: "The Provisional Ecumenical Council of Churches could not have established an affiliated Office for Refugee Work without the incentive of the longstanding refugee work within the ecumenical movement. Here, the name of Professor Dr. Adolf Keller must be mentioned, who has fully committed himself for many years to alleviating the distress prevailing among refugees in the European Central Bureau for Relief, in the Swiss Church Aid Committee for Evangelical Refugees, in the International Committee for Christian Refugees, and in many other organizations."[63]

59. Freudenberg (presumably), "Entwurf," written after January 28, 1941 (WCC 425.1.006).

60. Leiper to Keller, July 8, 1940 (NLAK C 2,2).

61. Keller to Visser't Hooft, July 15, 1940 (WCC 42.0042 2,1).

62. Keller to Choisy, May 22, 1941 (NLAK C 2,2).

63. Freudenberg, "Bericht des Ökumenischen Ausschusses für Flüchtlingshilfe," January 1942, p. 3 (WCC 425.1.023 B,2 Freudenberg archives). Freudenberg also mentions Siegmund-Schultze, Maas, and Bell.

Adolf Keller

Particularly owing to the fate of the refugees, the Federal Council invited Keller in the spring of 1940 to go on a lecture tour in the United States. He hesitated. Prior to his departure, he first wanted to meet church representatives in Berlin to discuss continued assistance for the German-occupied territories in Eastern Europe. He also wanted to assess the current situation of the Protestant Church and that of the "Jewish Christians." In September, he traveled to Berlin.

Bishop Heckel invited Keller—much to the latter's discomfort—for a luncheon with members of the Foreign Office and of the Reich Church Ministry. At the subsequent, decisive meeting, which was attended by Heckel, Eugen Gerstenmaier, and Hans Schönfeld, Keller was told that assistance in the occupied territories was possible only with the consent of the German government and the Wehrmacht (German Armed Forces); moreover, the involvement of the Foreign Office of the Church was "indispensable."[64] Besides, Inter-Church Aid would have to consult the German "Protestant Relief Organization for Internees and Prisoners."[65] Keller feared that these terms and conditions could result in "control" or even "absorb" his own agency. When Heckel assured him that German involvement amounted to no more than the "technical enabling of assistance," Keller consented on condition that the Executive Committee of Inter-Church Aid approved the plan with retroactive effect. To be sure, he was performing a genuine balancing act! However, Inter-Church Aid was subsequently able to continue sending food packages to occupied Eastern Europe.[66]

In a report marked as "secret," Keller discussed the situation of the Church in Germany.[67] Representatives of the "Confessing Church" told him that at the beginning of the war, the "church struggle" seemed to be abating. This assessment had proven wrong. At that time, between five and ten pastors were in jail, while another six were in concentration camps. Moreover, numerous measures had been imposed on pastors belonging to the "Confessing Church." Rumor had it that they were conscripted for military service in above-average numbers, in order to silence them. The

64. Keller, "Bericht über meine Reise nach Deutschland, 13. bis 22. September 1940," 4 and 8–9 (BAR J.2.257 1243/132). Gerstenmaier was a member of staff at the Church Foreign Office in 1940.

65. The "Protestant Relief Organization for Internees and Prisoners" had a nationalistic leaning; see Boyens, *Kirchenkampf und Ökumene*, 33ff.

66. Keller, "Überblick und Jahresbericht der europäischen Zentralstelle über die Zeit vom Ausbruch des Krieges bis Mitte August 1941," 8 (NLAK C 2,2).

67. Keller, "Die innere kirchliche Lage," autumn 1940 (BAR J.2.257 1243/132).

"Confessing Church" was prohibited from making public statements on the war. Many pastors were no longer receiving any remuneration. A cause for great concern was "the secret endeavor to employ 'euthanasia' to eradicate individuals unfit for the community." The "Confessing Church" was not praying for a German war victory.

A second secret report concerned ecumenism.[68] The Nazi regime had branded the ecumenical movement, Jews, and the Freemasons as enemies of the Reich. While the sense of spiritual isolation weighed heavily on those Germans who managed to keep their heads, there was widespread embitterment even among them that Germany was "misunderstood" and its "demands misinterpreted." As Keller remarked, he had repeatedly indicated, "even to very qualified authorities," that Germany was feared owing to its racial, church, and expansionist policies, "which operate with such terrible slogans as the 'Lebensraum' or 'master race.'" In a letter to Barth, Keller wrote that Gerstenmaier and Schönfeld, who both began leaning toward resistance at the time, "secretly introduced him to high-ranking army officers" who belonged to the "Confessing Church."[69]

Keller also met Reverend Heinrich Grüber, who was providing assistance to Protestant "non-Aryans." Grüber asked Keller to dispel fears in the United States that they represented a "fifth column."[70] Until his arrest in early 1941, Grüber repeatedly succeeded in assisting "Jewish Christians" to leave Germany, with the help of the New York and Zurich branches of Hapag, the international shipping company. For instance, Grüber, Freudenberg, Keller, and Leiper (who made available $5,000) managed to secure emigration for sixteen persons in early 1940.[71]

68. Keller, "Die Möglichkeit der ökumenischen Bewegung in Europa," September 24, 1940 (BAR J.2.257 1243/132).

69. Keller to Barth, July 3, 1945 (KBA 9345.471). In 1942, Gerstenmaier and Schönfeld joined the oppositional Kreisauer circle. Gerstenmaier was elected president of the Parliament of the Federal Republic of Germany in 1954.

70. Keller, "Die Möglichkeit der ökumenischen Bewegung in Europa," 3 and 11 (BAR J.2.257 1243/132).

71. Grüber to Freudenberg, February 6, 1940; Freudenberg to Leiper, February 14, 1940; Freudenberg to Keller, August 16, 1940 (WCC 425.1.022, corr. Freudenberg – Attenberger, Hapag – Grüber).

ADVOCATING ON BEHALF OF GERMAN REFUGEES IN THE UNITED STATES

"Come this spring," read one telegram from the Federal Council of the Churches of Christ in America in late February 1940.[72] Other summons followed, requesting Keller to report on the political situation in Europe, the plight of the war-ridden churches, and the fate of the refugees; he was also asked to issue a call for donations.[73] Evidently, hopes were pinned on his ardent passion in order to work miracles. But could he leave Europe now, at the height of war?[74] The threat of a German invasion of Switzerland was dispelled after May 1940, at least for the time being. Also, after the first year of the war, many of his duties at Inter-Church Aid had become routine, which his experienced secretary, Elisa Perini, was capable of handling on her own. Moreover, she could count on the combined support of Eugène Choisy (president of Inter-Church Aid), Marc Boegner, and Marc Sauter (director of APIDEP). Keller, however, was mindful of his family, which he was most reluctant to leave alone back in Switzerland.

In October 1940, he nevertheless accepted the offer to fly from Lisbon to the United States on board of an American military aircraft. It was his first transatlantic flight. Originally, his stay was supposed to last a couple of months—which then extended to two years. Shortly before his departure, Keller rushed to dictate his memoirs, which suggested that he doubted an early return, and perhaps even feared much worse.

Upon his arrival in the United States, he joined the National Christian Mission of the Federal Council, together with Leiper and John Mott. Its aim was to gather the Christian forces in America amid difficult times.[75] As observed, Keller's task was to cast light on Europe at war. He gave talks in towns and cities across the country, from New England to Texas, addressing senior executives and audiences in factory halls, hospitals, and, which he loathed, at mass events in sports stadiums. He met Americans who were utterly impassive about the plight of European Christians.[76] Many

72. Telegram, February 27, 1940, signed W. A. Brown, Leiper, and Froendt (NLAK C 2,3).

73. Keller, "Report on my activities in America, October 1940–April 1941," 9 (NLAK C 2,2).

74. "Minutes of the Board of the Federation of Swiss Protestant Churches, June 12, 1940 and July 3, 1940" (BAR J.2.257 1189/127 and 2193/286).

75. *The National Christian Mission Manual* (New York 1940/1941), Foreword (PHS NCC RG 18 62/12).

76. Keller, "Überblick und Jahresbericht der europäischen Zentralstelle für

believed that any assistance granted would not reach the suffering and that there was no resistance in Germany.[77] Others were convinced "that Continental Protestantism cannot survive, that the Ecumenical Movement has to be written off." Keller noted: "I am facing the fatal opinion, that nothing can be done at the present moment for the suffering churches of the Continent, that help would further political aims, that the whole Continent is occupied and helpless . . . The whole interest of the American public goes mostly to the allied cause and Great Britain."[78]

Keller's daily two-hour "seminar," which he held in many places for a week and which provided in-depth information, was a great success. In Washington, he even needed to run two parallel events: "I had to speak for a full week before six hundred participants."[79] In a letter to Choisy, he wrote: "Wherever I speak here, I can awaken interest, as I see from letters and reports; the Seminar in the National Christian Mission was one of the most successful ones and the president of the Federal Council acknowledged it in a letter of unusual warmth."[80] In Washington, Keller met representatives of the Red Cross to discuss humanitarian problems. And: "In the State Department I saw the key men dealing with relief appeals going across this country on the refugee question ."[81]

Keller's "mission" ended in the spring of 1941, but he decided to postpone his return to Switzerland: "The main point, however, was the conviction that my activity in America could be more effective than that in Geneva, at least for the moment, when a new interest in this country had to be stimulated."[82] I have here an educational task which is simply necessary. Here are potentialities for relief and interchurch aid as we do no longer have them in Europe."[83]

---

kirchliche Hilfsaktionen über die Zeit vom Ausbruch des Krieges bis Mitte August 1941," 10 (NLAK C 2,2).

77. Keller to Barth, July 3, 1945 (KBA 9345.471).

78. Keller to Visser't Hooft, April 17, 1941; Keller to Choisy, May 22,1941; Keller to the Central Bureau in Geneva, December 23, 1940 (for all letters, see NLAK C 2,2).

79. Keller, "Memorandum 8. Present activity of the European Central Bureau, Spring–Summer 1942," 3 (NLAK C 2,2).

80. Keller to Choisy, May 22, 1941 (ibid.)

81. Keller, Report on my activities in America, October 1940–April 1941," 3 (NLAK C 2,2).

82. Ibid., 11.

83. Keller to Choisy, May 22, 1941 (NLAK C 2,2).

The more evident the lack of knowledge in America became to him, the more urgent he felt the need to prolong his stay.[84] In a letter to Barth, he explained that he would extend his stay for the sake of the cause, which he could serve better in America than in the besieged (Swiss) fortress. He was also fighting to ensure that the ecumenical movement would not be an "Anglo-American enterprise."[85] "Some . . . advise me directly to stay here . . . or even made me the spontaneous proposal to let my family come over, for a year or two."[86] Koechlin wrote, "I think your attitude is right, though I am deeply aware of the great sacrifice imposed upon you and your family."[87] William Temple, Archbishop of Canterbury, was pleased to learn that Keller would be remaining in America, because he could greatly contribute to preserving unity among Christians.[88] John Mott also asked him to stay.[89] At the time, Keller was the only permanent representative of the European churches in America. He was well looked after by his friends, who hosted a dinner for him on the occasion of his seventieth birthday.

Tina Keller remained in Geneva with their younger children. "My wife is very courageous in this respect and understands fully that I gave my life to a cause and that this means sacrifice."[90] But he received word that she was "most concerned," and found their long separation difficult.[91] On Keller's seventieth birthday, Visser't Hooft wrote to Tina Keller: "From our own experience, we honor the great sacrifices made by the wives of those serving ecumenism on behalf of this common cause . . . In the past one and a half years, we have often felt for you and your children."[92] Keller himself admitted that "It is hard for me to be away so long from my family and not be able to share their life."[93]

84. Keller, "Überblick und Jahresbericht der europäischen Zentralstelle, Kriegsausbruch bis Mitte Aug. 1941," 11 (NLAK C 2,2).

85. Keller to Barth, July 17, 1941 (KBA 9341.416).

86. Keller to Choisy, May 22, 1941 (NLAK C 2,2).

87. Koechlin to Keller, March 21, 1941 (ibid.).

88. Temple to Keller, July 3, 1941, in Keller, ed., *Auswahl einiger Äusserungen*, 21.

89. Keller, "Bericht über meine Tätigkeit in Amerika, 11. Okt. 1940–4. Okt. 1942," 4 (WCC 425.1.006).

90. Keller to Choisy, May 22, 1941 (NLAK C 2,2).

91. Jacques Straub-Bachofner to Keller, June 28 and December 18, 1941 (NLAK C 2,1)

92. Visser't Hooft to Tina Keller, February 6, 1942 (WCC 42.0042 2,1).

93. Keller to James M. Webster, January 4, 1941 (WCC 42. 0042 2,1).

In a report on his activities in America, Keller wrote: "During my whole stay in America I was dealing all the time with the problem of Christian refugees."[94] Further, "There is no doubt that this is now the most important task which I can do here."[95] At Keller's suggestion, there was now closer cooperation between the American Committee for Christian Refugees, the Quaker relief agency, and the American Committee for the Central Bureau.[96] Despite attempts to provide enlightenment, the prevailing opinion was "that little can be done and that this is a task for government."[97]

Keller's American friends were not to be blamed: Already in late 1939, the Federal Council had issued the following message: "He is homeless, penniless, driven from the land . . . This country to which he escapes gives him no welcome. He is prevented from working. What gross crime has he committed to make the world so shun him so? Perhaps it is the crime of being a Jew, or a 'non-Aryan' Christian."[98] 4,000 Christian refugees were completely dependent on the American Committee. Leiper lamented the anti-Semitic tendencies in America.[99] Long after the war, he observed: "I often received letters . . . threatening me for my opposition to Hitler's methods and of course we were charged with being Communists because 'anyone opposed to Hitler must be in favor of Communism since Hitler opposes Communism.'"[100]

Freudenberg in Geneva requested Keller to draw American attention to the appalling conditions at Gurs and the other camps.[101] Visser't Hooft, Koechlin, Barth, and Brunner asked him to exert pressure on the American Committee for Christian Refugees. He replied:

> There is no money here which you can simply take out of a treasury. It must be collected, and public opinion must be roused

94. Keller, "Report on my activities in America, October 1940–April 1941," 14 (NLAK C 2,2).

95. Keller to Visser't Hooft, May 8, 1941 (WCC 42.0042 2,1).

96. Keller, "Concerning enlargement of the American Committee for the Central Bureau," April 24, 1941 (PHS NCC RG 18 12/8).

97. Keller to Visser't Hooft, May 4, 1942 (WCC 42.0042 2,1).

98. "Letter" of the Federal Council, December 16, 1939 (PHS NCC RG 18 3/12).

99. Leiper, presumably 1941 (PHS 99-0728, Henry S. Leiper Papers, 2/3, "Antisemitism").

100. Leiper to Visser't Hooft, March 18, 1965 (WCC 301.43.31/6).

101. Freudenberg to Keller, October 31, 1940 (WCC 42.0042 1,3).

and educated . . . The refugee need is not very popular because many are afraid of the 5th columnists.[102]

In regard to refugees, the situation is rather desperate . . . a certain interest has been weakened by the magnitude of the problem, partly by . . . governmental restriction which cannot be overrun . . . Having gone through the country I see how difficult it is to find jobs for the refugees or affidavits which are considered as being sufficient by the Government. We are all in despair about this situation.[103]

Lack of knowledge and a certain indifference which must be stirred up found expression in the budget of the ridiculously small sum of 50,000 Dollars for the suffering churches of Europe as the Joint Appeal Committee put it down in my absence [1940]. I protested against this neglect and quoted that Switzerland alone raised nearly double that sum.[104]

Keller pressed all emotional buttons to rouse the Americans:

A caravan of despair has been moving along the roads of Europe during these last years. Hundreds of thousands who have lost everything are seeking a new home somewhere, Jews mostly, but also thousands of Christians, Protestant and Catholic, who have a Jewish grandfather or grandmother or a Jewish wife . . . America once wrote the beautiful verses on the Statue of Liberty:

> Give me your tired, your poor,
> Your huddled masses yearning to be free,
> The wretched refuse of your teeming shore,
> Send these, the homeless, tempest-tossed, to me.
> I lift my lamp beside the golden door.

American labor is afraid of rival labor and the government has closed the door . . . Thousands are shivering and starving in horrible refugee camps like Gurs in poor France, or are trying to hide themselves on their bitter pilgrimage from country to country . . . Since May, 1933, I have spoken with men and

102. Keller to Visser't Hooft (and to Koechlin, Barth, and Brunner), November 17, 1940 (WCC 425.1.006).

103. Keller to the Central Bureau in Geneva, December 23, 1940 (NLAK C 2,2). See also Keller to Freudenberg, February 10. 1941 (WCC 42.0042 1,3).

104. Keller to Visser't Hooft, April 17, 1941 (NLAK C 2,2).

women who climbed over the glaciers of the mountains at the frontiers and arrived scratched and torn by underbrush in the woods, or by jagged rocks, sick and hungry. I saw others who were kicked over the frontier by the police, after having been hunted from place to place for months, or having lived in prison . . . I saw refugees who had swum across the Rhine during the night, and were nearly drowned or shot by the guards. I saw children who with their mothers crept nightly through the forests of Schaffhausen in order to reach a free land [Switzerland]. I saw how a psychology of fear, of bitterness, of suicide, of a neurosis was developing . . . I saw families whose fathers had to remain in a concentration camp in Germany while the mothers lived in Italy and the children, perhaps, in England . . . The Jewish community accomplished a praiseworthy work of solidarity. But the Christian refugees are . . . a stigma on the Christian conscience.[105]

Keller made an essential contribution to the increase in American funding: while funds amounted to only 11,680 Swiss francs in 1941 (compared to 66,000 in Switzerland and 20,000 in Sweden),[106] they totaled 44,000 in 1942 (compared to 81,000 in Switzerland, and 46,000 in Sweden).[107] Freudenberg transmitted the major share to southern France, often in the form of foodstuffs.[108] In 1943, America's contribution rose to 241,000 Swiss francs. But this assistance came too late for those imprisoned in southern France—in the summer of 1942, deportations to the extermination camps in Eastern Europe commenced. Instead, the funds were used to help war refugees.[109] One was "extremely grateful" to Keller in Geneva.[110] Freudenberg informed him, however, that expenditure for France alone ran to $1,700 per month. The Geneva Committee therefore requested Keller to

105. Keller, *Christian Europe Today*, 121–22.

106. "The Provisional Committee of the World Council of Churches: Special Account for Relief Work among Refugees, 1941 (WCC 425. 1.029 Department of Refugees, Financial Reports). Elisa Perini, Keller's secretary at Inter-Church Aid, wrote: "It is probably owing to the work of the Central Bureau that we are receiving so many donations for the refugees in France," June 9, 1942, (WCC 425. 1.029).

107. Comité Oecuménique pour les Réfugiés, "Rapport financier 1942" (WCC 425.1.029).

108. Freudenberg to Keller, October 31, 1940 (WCC 42.0042 1,3).

109. Comité Oecuménique pour les Réfugiés, "Rapport financier 1943" (WCC 425.1.029).

110. Freudenberg to Keller: "We are extremely grateful for the $750 . . . , and we are very glad, that you have found other $1000 for the Ecumenical Refugee work," March 20, 1941 and December 23, 1941 (WCC 42.0042 1,3 u. WCC 425.1.006)

"reiterate our concerns, once again, and that you may continue to lend us your support as best as possible."[111]

In late 1940, Freudenberg asked Keller to enter a plea on behalf of Robert Liefmann, an economist and lawyer who had been dismissed from his professorship at the University of Freiburg in 1933 due to his Jewish ancestry, and also on behalf of his sisters, Martha Liefmann, an art historian, and Else Liefmann, a pediatrician. They had been arrested on October 22, 1940, and deported to Gurs: "We hope that these new human tragedies will at least guide the conscience and the actions of American Christians."[112] Keller was asked to contact the writer Thomas Mann.[113] "I did what was possible and was given hope of help," Keller wrote, and "I tried to interest people in Washington personally for this case . . . , but everything goes very slow."[114] On March 20, 1941, he reported that his endeavors had succeeded. The Liefmanns were granted permission to leave Gurs immediately.[115] Robert Liefmann, however, died of an infection one day after their release. He had been offered a position as professor of political science at New York University![116] Martha Liefmann managed to reach Geneva, where she was taken in by the Keller family.[117] Soon afterwards, Else Liefmann also succeeded in fleeing to Switzerland.[118]

In late 1941, Keller noted that since 1933 he had personally attended to around 2,600 refugees, mostly "Jewish Christians," in personal meetings, correspondence, or telephone conversations, conducted in Switzerland, France, Germany, Italy, Austria, Hungary, Romania, and the United States.[119] In 1942, he informed the Americans about the existence of concentration camps in Poland.[120] Until the summer of 1942, Freudenberg was able to support a small "Jewish Christian" congregation in Warsaw. In

111. Freudenberg to Keller, June 17, 1942 (WCC 425.1.006).

112. Freudenberg to Keller, October 30, 1940 and November 4, 1940 (WCC 42.0042 1,3).

113. Freudenberg to Keller, October 31, 1940 (WCC 42.0042 1,3). Thomas Mann had emigrated to the United States in 1939, shortly before the outbreak of war.

114. Keller to Freudenberg, February 10, 1941 (WCC 42.0042 1,3).

115. Freudenberg to Keller, March 20, 1941 (ibid.).

116. Liefmann, Helle Lichter auf dunklem Grund.

117. Freudenberg to Keller, June 10, 1941, and November 6, 1941 (WCC 425.1006).

118. Paul Vogt, "Liefmann, Martha und Else, Lebenslauf" (Archiv für Zeitgeschichte Zürich 3.4.1.14).

119. Keller, "Twenty Years Central Bureau for Relief of the Evangelical Churches of Europe," November 1941 (NLAK C 2,2).

120. Keller, Christian Europe Today, 96.

late 1942, he informed the Americans that since the summer 7,000 Jews and many "Jewish Christians" had fled to Switzerland, and that "conditions in Poland must be terrific."[121] Freudenberg had contact with Gerhart Riegner, director of the Geneva office of the World Jewish Congress, who was among the first to learn about the extermination camps in Poland.

We can thus turn to the fiercely debated entry into the war of the United States. Following the Japanese attack on Pearl Harbour in December 1941, the United States entered World War II. While Keller approved of this decision,[122] he also maintained: "I could not share a conviction which simply ridiculed the pacifist cause . . . Nor could I in spite of my British sympathies consider the present war simply as a crusade which would, more or less, identify the cause of a worldly empire with the Kingdom of God."[123]

Prisoners of war camps were now erected in the United States. The Federal Council appointed Keller a member of the American branch of the World Chaplaincy Commission for Prisoners of War of the Ecumenical Council, which closely cooperated with the YMCA.[124] Visser't Hooft requested Keller to furnish a report on the prison camps.[125] After lengthy efforts, he gained admission to two camps:[126] he visited one hundred and fifty German prisoners of war in Fort Forrest, Tullahoma (Tennessee):

> Some of the internees . . . are in the hospital which makes an excellent impression . . . After supper, which I had with the interned, I saw nearly all the barracks which have two or three beds . . . The Chaplain had brought together quite a library of good books . . . German bibles are available. While visiting these baracks I had ample opportunity for individual contacts . . . The next day, a Sunday, . . . a German Evangelical service took place in the club room of the camp. The Chaplain opened the service in English and I continued in German with prayer, scripture

121. Freudenberg to Samuel McCrea Cavert, December 9, 1942 (PHS NCC RG 18 5/16).

122. Keller to John A. Mackay, June 16, 1941 (John Mackay Collection, Princeton Theological Seminary).

123. Keller, "What does the slogan 'Let the Church be the Church' mean in the present world crisis? 20 Theses on the Church and War," June 10, 1941 (NLAK C 2,2). The slogan "Let the Church be the Church" had originally been phrased by Mackay! Cf. Mackay, *Ecumenics: The Science of the Church Universal*, 5.

124. Keller, *Amerikanisches Christentum*, 358.

125. Visser't Hooft to Keller, April 1, 1942 (WCC 42.0042 2,1).

126. Keller's endeavors to visit the Japanese internees were in vain; see "Activity of Doctor Keller during January 1942" (NLAK C 2,2).

> lesson and sermon. About two-thirds of the interned were present . . . When I stressed the necessity for a Christian to put his trust in God, even if he does not understand Him, one of the interned, in the discussion afterwards, challenged the audience to put their trust in their national philosophy and in their leader. The Christian group, on the other hand, gave witness to their Christian faith.[127]

Keller made several requests: the establishment of Bible groups, choirs, and orchestras; events in the native languages of the prisoners; a parcel service (to be organized by the YMCA); the discharging of seriously ill prisoners; and "family camps" for married internees.[128]

THE ECUMENICAL SEMINAR IN THE UNITED STATES

Keller was flooded with lecturing requests.[129] Among other speeches, he addressed an audience of one thousand delegates at the Presbyterian General Assembly in Milwaukee,[130] and spoke at conferences of the western section of the World Alliance of Reformed Churches, whose eastern section he served as president. He gave talks at Yale, Union Theological Seminary, George Washington University, Andover Newton Seminary, Wellesley College near Boston, Stanford University in California, and Princeton Theological Seminary. In a letter to Keller, John A. Mackay, president of Princeton Theological Seminary, wrote: "The Hromadkas[131] and ourselves are most eager to have you as our guest, and we shall decide between us who is to have the honor."[132] Keller discussed "'The Defense of the Christian Heritage on the Continent,' which would allow me to speak also of the theological background."[133] His address attracted great

---

127. Keller, "A Report on Visits to Prisoners of War Camps," New York, September 28, 1942, pp. 2ff. (WCC 303.003.8.1).

128. Ibid., 6ff.

129. Keller to Koechlin, July 2, 1941 (NLAK C 2,2).

130. Keller to Elisa Perini, May 31, 1942 (WCC 42.0042 2,1).

131. Josef L. Hromàdka, a scholar of systematic theology in Prague, emigrated to the United States in 1939. He served as a guest professor at Princeton Theological Seminary.

132. Mackay to Keller, December 16, 1940 (John Mackay Collection).

133. Keller to Mackay, December 9, 1940 (ibid.).

interest.[134] In Princeton, he met Thomas Mann, who was actively helping German refugees, for at least the second time.[135] At Harvard Divinity
School, Keller delivered the Lowell Lectures on "The Present Religious
Crisis in Europe" and "A Vision of Reconstruction."[136] He donated his
speaker's fees to Inter-Church Aid, which had been paying his salary since
1940.[137]

Adolf Keller and Henry Van Dusen (archive Dr. Pierre Keller)

Essentially, Keller's lectures were in fact ecumenical seminars, just as
the seminars that he had given before at the National Christian Mission.
In Hartford, Connecticut, he ran his Carew Lectures expressly as an Ecu-
menical Seminar.[138] The six-day program covered a wide range of themes:
"The Una Sancta in the Bible and Church History," "The Recent World
Conferences," "Comparative Study of the Main Problems of the World

134. Mackay to Keller, Princeton, January 31, 1941 (ibid.).

135. Keller to Mackay, January 5, 1941 (ibid.); see also Mann, *Tagebücher*, 368.

136. Leaflet published by the Lowell Institute, Free Lectures in King's Chapel: "The
Present Religious Crisis in Europe" (Adolphe Keller, D.D., LL.D.), December 1, 4, 8,
11, 15, and 18, 1941 (PHS NCC, RG 18, 12/8).

137. "Résumé of sums paid to Dr. Adolf Keller by the Central Bureau," (NLAK C
2,1).

138. On Keller's Ecumenical Seminar, see above pp. 145–57.

Conferences," "Comparative Study of the Ecumenical Messages and the Papal Encyclicals," and "The World Council of Churches and the Outlook for the Ecumenical Movement."[139] Reviewing the event, the *Hartford Echoes* observed: "Suffice it to say that [Keller's] Carew Lectures on The History and Theological Problems of the Ecumenical Movement, together with the two guest lectures by Dr. Leiper and Dr. Ferré, and the discussion seminars, gave to students, faculty, alumni and friends a far more lively interest and understanding concerning the church at large."[140] Keller ran another Ecumenical Seminar within the Moore Lectures, delivered at the San Francisco Theological Seminary in San Anselmo, and one within the Earl Lectures, held at Pacific School of Religion in Berkeley; he also ran various seminars for women actively involved in the church.

Keller's lectures in the United States were reflected in his book *Christian Europe Today*.[141] His *Church and State on the European Continent* (1936) was out of print, and therefore he returned to the subject but included the latest developments: "The main question treated in this book is: What do need, persecutions, the war, the suffering of refugees and prisoners of war, the attack of a pagan secularism mean for the Christian church?"[142] William A. Brown considered the book "the most authoritative work of its kind."[143] Much of its content was new to Keller's American readership. He described the concentration camps as "a hotbed of sadistic instincts. Enough information and witness have slipped through the barbed wires and pores of these camps to inform the civilized world of the psychology of terror, of brutal humiliation, of corporal and mental tortures which are evidently not simply the execution of orders, but a manifestation of the pathological instincts of the guards."

The Nazi euthanasia program practiced murder "as an administrative measure." Furthermore, he observed, "What makes the solution of this problem in Germany so horrifying is the absence of a deeper reflection or moral scruples, of any reverence for life itself. Hypnotized by the biological and racial ideas, shortsighted men play destiny . . . Here was an attack on the sacredness of life."[144]

139. Keller, "Syllabus for the Carew Lectureship at the Hartford Theological Seminary" (John Mackay Collection).

140. *Hartford Echoes*, December 1941, published by the Hartford Seminary Foundation (NLAK C 2,2).

141. Keller, *Christian Europe Today*.

142. Keller, "Memorandum 8," 4–5 (NLAK C 2,2).

143. Brown, *Toward a United Church*, 246.

144. Keller, *Christian Europe Today*, 85–86 and 144.

He also wrote a book titled *Amerikanisches Christentum—Heute* (American Christianity Today).[145] This was an updated, expanded edition of his earlier *Dynamis*. It offers an exhaustive account of the influence of dialectical theology on American theology. John A. Mackay wrote: "Not less theology, but more! Not general ideas or social programs . . . but insights, truth from God, leadership by means of avowal, and by means of responsibility for the clearly recognized gift of mercy—therefore theology!"[146] Only very few theologians voiced such "dialectical" standpoints.[147] However, William A. Brown, Walter Horton, George Richards, Henry Sloane Coffin, and John Van Dusen had also returned to a "Theology of Revelation."[148] Various theologians who had emigrated to America— Paul Tillich, Otto Piper, and Josef Hromàdka—reinforced this tendency. Reinhold Niebuhr was the actual spokesman of the American dialectical group.[149] It demanded from the Church "sharper thinking, a more committed creed, and an emancipation from the world, which must first of all start from the recognition of the radical opposition between the world empire and the Kingdom of God."[150] However, the group was keen to work out the impulses received from Europe on its own. It did not endorse Karl Barth's strict rejection of natural theology. Emil Brunner's notion of the relationship between the Church and the world appealed better to current American needs.[151] Notably, all the theologians mentioned by Keller were ecumenists, and they had all been involved in Keller's Ecumenical Seminar in Geneva, including Reinhold Niebuhr.

Barth's response to Keller's book was most favorable:

> The enervating "ecumenical" style is absent. Owing to a broad and profound knowledge of the subject, the reader learns a great deal about issues, persons, and circumstances that should have long been interrelated . . . You will no doubt recall that I once accused you of your dual nationality in "our" theological world and in that of Harnack, Troeltsch, etc. You didn't like to hear that at the time. But if there were some truth to what I said, then I would now add that that dual nationality reveals itself in the

145. Keller, *Amerikanisches Christentum*.

146. Ibid., 156.

147. Ibid., 158.

148. Ibid., 171–72; see also Keller, *Christian Europe Today*, 239.

149. Keller, *Amerikanisches Christentum*, 172.

150. Ibid., 174.

151. Ibid., 182. Brunner had been guest professor in the United States several times.

most fortunate manner in your book, insofar as the historical love and breadth of our fathers is combined most fortunately with the theological judgment without which we can neither talk about the Church and churches nowadays, nor wish them to be discussed.[152]

BIDDING FAREWELL TO INTER-CHURCH AID AND THE ECUMENICAL SEMINAR

"Les absents ont toujours tort" (Those absent are always in the wrong): Keller made this painful experience during his stay in the United States. Against his wish, he was replaced as secretary of the Federation of Swiss Protestant Churches. Moreover, several leading figures of the ecumenical movement began contemplating the future of Inter-Church Aid above his head. Their move was correct insofar as the end of the war was expected to cause massive distress. But they partly failed to include Keller in their deliberations. It is worth recalling that at the time Inter-Church Aid stood under the auspices of the Federal Council of the Churches of Christ in America and the Federation of Swiss Protestant Churches. The latter, moreover, assumed a supervisory role. During the war, the international Executive Committee of Inter-Church Aid could not meet *in corpore*. Eugène Choisy served as president of the Executive Committee and at the same time of the Federation. Keller had always been convinced that affiliating Inter-Church Aid to Life and Work made sense. However, he was unable to find majority support for this proposal in the Executive Committee, with the exception of the Americans.[153]

In the summer of 1941, Alphons Koechlin, who had succeeded Choisy as president of the Federation of Swiss Protestant Churches, informed Keller that Inter-Church Aid could not simply be left in the hands of Choisy and his secretary, and that therefore an emergency committee had been appointed.[154] Keller's impression was that neither the Executive Committee nor he were respected any longer.[155] In principle, he understood that, at the age of sixty nine, he would eventually have to step down,

152. Barth to Keller, December 11, 1943 (KBA 9243.167); see above, p. 58 and p. 118.

153. Keller to Choisy, Visser't Hooft, Koechlin, July 16, 1941 (NLAK C 2,2); see above, p. 73, 82, and 134.

154. Koechlin to Keller, June 13, 1941 (NLAK C 2,2).

155. Keller to the Central Bureau in Geneva and to Henriod, June 23, 1941 (ibid.).

and "that the Central Bureau has to undergo certain transformations if it is to meet the tremendous tasks which the war and post-war situation is placing before the churches."[156]

In the summer of 1942, Choisy notified Keller that there was no need for the emergency committee to convene. Matters were taking their usual course.[157] In 1942, Inter-Church Aid transmitted funds and food parcels to Bohemia, Moravia, Poland, Romania, Hungary, Norway, Finland, Southern France, Spain, Denmark, Holland, the Greek Protestant and Orthodox churches, and to students and professors of theology in Warsaw. With the assistance of the Red Cross, hundreds of French children were brought to Switzerland for a three-month vacation. When this was no longer possible, sponsorships for 458 children were organized; this number grew to over 900 in the years 1944 and 1945. Inter-Church Aid also supplied pastors active in German, American, and Canadian prison camps with bibles and theological literature.[158]—Between 1922 and 1941, Inter-Church Aid distributed a total of twelve million Swiss francs; Protestant Switzerland contributed approximately one half of this amount, the United States almost the other, while the rest came from different European countries.[159]

Now, however, Samuel McCrea Cavert, general secretary of the Federal Council of the Churches of Christ in America, devised a plan to create a Department of Relief and Construction within the Ecumenical Council. He informed Keller about this plan.[160] In October 1942, Cavert traveled to Geneva to present the idea to Visser't Hooft, who immediately embraced it with such enthusiasm that he felt he needed "to soften the hard line he had taken."[161] Cavert also set out his plan before the board of the Federation of Swiss Protestant Churches, where it was greeted with surprise. Its approval, which it eventually brought itself to give, meant the loss of "its" relief agency.

156. Keller, "Memorandum 8" (1942), 1–2. (NLAK C 2,2).

157. Choisy to Keller, June 21, 1942 (ibid.).

158. Keller, Annual Reports of the Central Bureau for 1940–1943, 5, and for 1943–1944, 8 (BAR J.2.257 1243/132).

159. Keller, "Memorandum 8," 1 (NLAK C 2,2). According to Professor Dr. Alfred Meier from the University of St Gallen, the sum of 12 million Swiss francs would correspond to at least 120 million francs today. Personal communication with author, October 8, 2006.

160. Keller, "Tatsachen und Gedanken zur Prüfung der christlichen Hilfsarbeit und der Zukunft der Europäischen Zentralstelle," June 26, 1943, 5 (BAR J.2.257 1243/132).

161. Letters from Visser't Hooft to Cavert, July 22, 1942, and Cavert to Visser't Hooft, October 20, 1942, quoted in Schmidt, *Architect of Unity*, 141.

Eugène Choisy, the acting president of Inter-Church Aid, approved the plan only on the proviso that Keller was involved in the transition. A few weeks later, in November, Keller returned to Switzerland, just ahead of the German occupation of southern France. He requested a meeting of the Executive Committee of Inter-Church Aid, which was rejected by Cavert, Visser't Hooft, and Koechlin, since the decision in favor of Cavert's plan had already been taken, thereby demonstrating that they had taken over the reins.[162] The British members of the Executive Committee and Leiper approved Cavert's proposal after the fact, but they demanded that they be consulted and that Keller's great experience be rendered useful.[163] The latter subsequently formulated seven theses on future ecumenical relief:

> 1. The general tasks of spiritual and material reconstruction as actual relief policy and planning should be distinguished from relief operations in a narrow sense. 2. Church relief operations must set themselves clearly apart from general humanitarian reconstruction plans and the work of neutral relief agencies, and should be restricted to church assistance in a narrow sense. ... 3. The church relief agency should ensure in all respects that it conducts its operations with the consent of and in cooperation with the legitimate church authorities in the respective country ... 4. The relief agency can be expected to exert an ideal effect where central, coordinated cooperation nevertheless allows for individual and denominational initiative ... and for the freedom of charismatic inspiration. 5. ... : Human beings take precedence over things ... In church relief, proclamation, ministry, the pastoral care of congregations, take precedence over institutions and social welfare; educational tasks *over* organizational and administrative ones ... 7. Close cooperation with the Ecumenical Council should be aspired to [...] either in terms of a) well-ordered cooperation ... or b) the creation of a special department within the Ecumenical Council, or indeed c) a complete merger.[164]

In 1944, an agreement was reached, according to which Inter-Church Aid would be incorporated into the Provisional World Council of Churches.[165]

162. "Minutes of the Board of the Federation of Swiss Protestant Churches, November 5, 1942" (BAR J.2.257 2193/286).

163. "A meeting of the members of the Central Bureau ... ," London, April 29, 1943 (WCC 425.1.006).

164. Keller, "Bericht über die Tätigkeit der europäischen Zentralstelle für kirchliche Hilfsaktionen von Ende Juli 1940 bis Juli 1943," 9–10 (BAR J.2.257 1243/132).

165. "Agreement," April 19, 1944, English version (WCC 42.0042 2,1).

Although Visser't Hooft initially rejected them, Keller's seven theses were largely accepted. In the summer of 1945, he transferred the remaining $100,000 to the World Council. On October 12, 1945, the merger between Inter-Church Aid and the recently established Department of Reconstruction and Inter-Church Aid was completed. Keller found leaving difficult. At the farewell ceremony, Visser't Hooft at least mentioned Keller's pioneering role, and called on him to continue serving the common cause.[166] The Swiss Alphons Koechlin became Department chair, while the Scotsman J. Hutchinson Cockburn was appointed director.

After the war, the Department received funds in abundance. John D. Rockefeller Jr. donated half a million dollars. Work was now undertaken on a grand scale. The Department soon had a hundred and forty staff members. Under its roof, a special committee responsible for refugee aid was formed, on which Adolf Freudenberg continued his work. In a letter dated June 7, 1948, Cockburn expressed his gratitude to Keller for his valuable advice and support.[167] Twenty years later, the information officer of the Department wrote about Keller, who had meanwhile passed away: "His counsel can still be read with benefit by all those engaged today in Inter-Church Aid. It is astonishing to what extent his principles continue to guide and animate those currently involved in ecumenical sharing."[168]

The APIDEP (Association Protestante Internationale de Prêts), which had also been established by Keller, had been incorporated into the World Council of Churches as early as September 18, 1944.[169] Marc Sauter retained his post as director; moreover, he was appointed as treasurer responsible for the Department of Reconstruction and Inter-Church Aid of the Ecumenical Council as a whole.

But let us return to the war years: in the spring of 1943, Keller convened the last Ecumenical Seminar to be held in Geneva. It attracted more than a hundred students, theologians and non-theologians, including Swiss nationals and foreigners studying in Switzerland, as well as several women enrolled at the École Sociale de Genève and many guests. Among

166. "Joint Statement of members of the Executive Committee of the European Central Office for Inter-Church Aid and the Department of Reconstruction and Inter-Church Aid of the World Council of Churches," October 12, 1945 (WCC 42.0042 2,1).

167. Cockburn to Keller, June 7, 1948 (WCC 42.0042 1).

168. Geoffrey Murray, Information Officer DICARWS (Department Inter Church Aid, Refugee, and World Service), "Adolf Keller and his work for Refugees," (written after 1966), 15 (WCC 301.43.25/7).

169. Marc Sauter to Freudenberg, September 14, 1944 (WCC 425.1001 Doss. APIDEP). See above, pp. 144–46.

the new lecturers were Roger Schütz (later the founder of Taizé) and Susanne de Dietrich, from France, who later lectured at Bossey.[170] Naturally, the future of the Ecumenical Seminar greatly preoccupied Keller. He therefore discussed the matter with Visser't Hooft: "We should take over and assimilate what has been successfully introduced and has become established."[171] He hoped, moreover, that his longstanding wish for a permanent institution could become a reality.[172] John D. Rockefeller Jr., who had granted Keller's "leadership programme" substantial assistance on several occasions, donated a large sum for the purchasing of a castle on Lake Geneva. In a letter to Keller, he noted that it gave him satisfaction to be able to help the courageous Christians in Europe.[173] In October 1946, the Ecumenical Institute at the Château de Bossey was inaugurated. At the opening ceremony, Marc Boegner recalled the Ecumenical Seminar.[174] Keller held one of the first courses on "Glimpses from the Growth of the Ecumenical Movement."[175]

The Bossey program booklet for the year 2005–2006 reads: "The Ecumenical Institute's mission is to educate and form church leaders, both clergy and lay, for service in parishes, classrooms, and ecumenical centres around the world. The Ecumenical Institute plays a major role in shaping ecumenical thought through intercultural and interconfessional encounter, through academic study in residential programmes and through common worship and life in community."[176] This resembles a summary of what Keller had initiated with the Ecumenical Seminar and with his "leadership programme." He had also harbored the dream of a building devoted to the institute.[177] Great emphasis was now placed on training the "laity," and

170. "Semaine d'Etudes Oecuméniques," March 29 to April 4, 1943, list of participants (NLAK C 9).

171. Keller to Visser't Hooft, Geneva, January 28, 1943 (WCC 42.0042 2,1).

172. Keller to the World Council of Churches, January 17, 1946 (WCC 42.0042 2,1).

173. Rockefeller Jr. to Keller, February 11, 1946 (WS Ms Sch 153/39).

174. Keller, "Das Ökumenische Institut," newspaper cutting from *Basler Nachrichten*, October 1946 (WCC 42.0042 2,1).

175. Keller to Visser't Hooft, July 10, 1946 (ibid.).

176. The Ecumenical Institute at Château de Bossey. Academic program for 2005/2006, 2.

177. See above, p. 149 and n. 173. Visser't Hooft insisted that something entirely new be established at Bossey: "The *General Secretary* [Visser 't Hooft] reported on the ecumenical Institute [Bossey]. He underlined the fact that the work which it sought to accomplish had no precedent in ecumenical history." Minutes and reports of the Meeting of the Provisional Committee of the World Council of Churches, Buck Hill

Asia and Africa attracted growing interest.[178] Keller donated more than two thousand books related to ecumenism, as well as numerous documents and photographs. His gift laid the foundation for the library and archive at the headquarters of the World Council of Churches in Geneva.

Amsterdam, 1948. From left to right: Adolf Keller, Alphons Koechlin, Karl Barth and Emil Brunner (archive Dr. Pierre Keller, newspaper cutting)

Keller attended the meetings held in preparation of the founding conference of the definite World Council of Churches in Amsterdam. In 1947, he traveled to Egypt, where he visited his former congregation and presented the Coptic Patriarch with an invitation to the Amsterdam conference. At the conference, which took place from August 22 to September 4, 1948, he served as a consultant. Karl Barth's spectacular lecture and Emil Brunner's both pleased him. After all, he had made an essential contribution to the fact that, as he put it, the "most important and most influential theologians of our time," had found their way to the ecumenical movement.[179]

By contrast, Henry Smith Leiper, who had served as one of three general secretaries since 1938, was frustrated: "At Amsterdam in 1948,

Falls, Penn., April 1947, Geneva 1947, 30. See also Visser't Hooft to Keller, November 6, 1952 (WCC 42.0042 3,2).

178. Weber, *A Laboratory for Ecumenical Life*, 12ff.

179. Keller, "Ökumenische Portraits."

the leadership of the World Council decided to drop him from the core work."[180] Notably, Leiper's commitment to the ecumenical movement had been unwavering; moreover, he had raised the majority of funds for Amsterdam, for Bossey, and for the new Inter-Church Aid! And Paul Tillich received no invitation to Amsterdam, although he had played an important role at Oxford in 1937.[181] He, too, took offence. Brunner also felt ousted after Amsterdam.[182] It appears as if Visser 't Hooft endeavored to remove those theologians who failed to unconditionally represent Barth's line.[183] Keller, however, remained "Honorary Lecturer" and "Consultant" within the movement. He made his last appearance at the conference of the Ecumenical Council in Evanston in 1954. At the age of eighty-two, he was now a patriarch! In a letter to Keller, John D. Rockefeller Jr., who would have loved to have attended the proceedings, wrote: "That men and women throughout the world who believe in things of the spirit are increasingly finding in the simple platform of love for God and a desire to follow in Christ's footsteps, a common basis for their religious lives, is most gratifying and encouraging. What a satisfaction it must be to you to have had so important a part in bringing about this broader spirit of Christian unity. I rejoice in what you have accomplished."[184]

INITIATING THE RECONSTRUCTION OF THE WORLD[185]

At the end of World War II, Keller reaffirmed the political commitment that he had demonstrated in the aftermath of World War I. At the Amsterdam conference, he actively contributed to the work of the Committee for Reconstruction. Already in 1942, during his stay in the United States, he had been involved in a committee of the Federal Council of the Churches of Christ in America dedicated to reconstruction.[186] America planned to

180. Schmidt, "Henry Smith Leiper: Ecumenical Pioneer," 79.

181. Pauck, *Paul Tillich*, 200; Tillich dined in Geneva "with his old friend Adolf Keller" (ibid., 218).

182. See Jehle, *Emil Brunner*, 456.

183. See William J. Schmidt and Eduard Quellette, "Henry Smith Leiper," typescript, before 1986, unnumbered pages (PHS99–0728 Henry S. Leiper Papers Box 1 of 3): Visser't Hooft had been brilliant, but he was nevertheless "an enigma, exhibiting a 'shortsightedness regarding human relations.'"

184. John D. Rockefeller Jr. to Keller, August 23, 1954 (WS Ms Sch 153/39).

185. Keller, "We must rebuild the world" (1915). See above, p. 34

186. Keller, "Bericht über die Tätigkeit der Europäischen Zentralstelle für

make a great effort on behalf of Europe.[187] While this pleased Keller, he could not conceal a certain unease: the Americans envisioned a new kind of "missionary task," namely, the rebuilding of entire continents, saving the lives of whole peoples, combatting anti-Christian powers, and reclaiming the Christian world. They were much more enthusiastic about erecting a gargantuan "new edifice from scratch" than for modest, long-term enterprises like Inter-Church Aid: "Here, we encounter that characteristic peculiarity of constructive, optimistic idealism, which . . . undertakes tremendous ventures of faith . . . However, it is not unusual for these to collapse, suddenly and miserably, no sooner have they been forged, owing to a lacking sense of reality, a lacking understanding of the limitations of planning . . . , and a neglect of unforeseen obstacles."[188]

America was constantly devising plans for world improvement. The absence of a sense of history had resulted in the continuous repetition of what had long been said, and in an impatience that stifled that ripening of plans.[189] Keller commented thus on the future of the churches:

> The Church of faith has a future, because she believes in the victory of God . . . The church looks at her past with repentance and into her future with faith . . . Repentance means a break with the past . . . But there is memory which maintains a continuity and allows men to learn the lessons of the past.
>
> I believe that the present war, although it may sound paradoxical, means the purification of the world from hatred. There is less hatred in the world today, in spite of more horrors, than during the last war, because men understand better that hatred is absolutely meaningless and destructive. What comes out of the human soul today as revenge and hatred is the last vestige of pus which must be pressed out of a wound. Only when it is completely drained, can the healing process begin.[190]

The churches needed to advocate the partnership of nations: "Whether such fellowship is understood as a rejuvenation of the League of Nations, a European union . . . , the suggestion programs are unanimous in urging a closer living and working among nations in the future . . . The League

---

kirchliche Hilfsaktionen von Ende 1940 bis Juli 1943," 7 (BAR J.2.257 1243/132).

187. "Delaware Principles," in Keller, *Christian Europe Today,* 222ff.

188. Keller, *Amerikanisches Christentum,* 436 and 460.

189. Keller, "Tatsachen und Gedanken," June 26, 1943, p. 9ff. (BAR J.2.257 1243/132).

190. Keller, *Christian Europe Today,* 199ff.

of Nations is dead—long live the League of Nations!"[191] At that time, one knew far better than after World War I that without an ethos the world "was doomed." Keller was also forward-thinking in another respect: "In practical terms, the endeavor to rebuild the world can not rely on Christianity alone, since all great peoples must have their say, whose mental presupposition lay not in Christianity but instead in Islam, Buddhism, or Confucianism." Keller suggested conferences of the great religions, where a new ethos should be established on the basis of freedom, social justice, and the will to community.[192] "God's freedom is absolute, ours no more than relative," he maintained; those who believed that they possessed the absolute, became intolerant.[193] Keller joined the World Brotherhood, whose members included Christians, Jews, and members of other religions. As he explained, the Brotherhood "proposes a program for *justice, amity, understanding,* and *cooperation* among all men of good will."[194] At the 1952 Brotherhood Conference of 1952 in America, he met Martin Buber.[195]

Keller also returned to the relationship with Bolshevist Russia. He suggested that this be revised according to prevailing conditions, that is, from the perspective of the war experience.[196] Two years later, he qualified this cautiously-worded positive stance as follows: "Today, it [Russia] acts imperiously. It does not wish to engage in a dialogue with the West, but instead to take its seat [like a stumbling block] among Western democracies."[197] But he also called for a balanced, differentiated judgment: "Russia's friends only see the good side, while the enemies of communism see the bad one. Only a small number of critical observers appears to preserve the inner independence and the freedom of judgment necessary to see and report on matters in a truly critical light."[198]

191. Ibid., 213.

192. Keller, *Wiederaufbau der Welt,* 60 and 41.

193. Ibid., 20 and 28.

194. "Outline of purpose, policy and program" (of the World Brotherhood) (Archiv für Zeitgeschichte der ETH Zürich, Juna-Archiv 1.7.3); italics original.

195. "World Brotherhood. The National Conference of Christians and Jews," 1952 (NLAK D Graue Mappe, "Reise Amerika 1952").

196. Keller, *Wiederaufbau der Welt,* 39–40.

197. Keller, *Zeit-Wende,* 120 (bracketed material added by translator).

198. Ibid., 121–22; Barth tended to play down the postwar Soviet Union, whereas Emil Brunner was a decided anti-Communist.

As far as Germany was concerned, Keller, like Barth, advocated forgiveness.[199] In *Zeit-Wende* (Turn of Time), published in 1946, he observed: "The extent of collective responsibility cannot be fully measured. It is a fact, however, that the German people not only allowed this fate to occur, but also that its best part endured bloody and grating suffering, in its own concentration camps, in the early death of its children, in the ignominy that the world heaps on this people." Not only did one need to recall the downfall of Sodom and Gomorrha, but also Abraham's haggling with God over the doomed and condemned city.[200] The—relatively unsullied— bishops of Württemberg and Berlin, Theophil Wurm and Otto Dibelius, wished to discuss the (re)education of the Germans with Keller; they were also keen for him to hold lectures at theological faculties and assist their efforts at renewing ties with faculties and seminaries in America.[201] Keller thus became active in Germany once again.

A pressing concern after the demise of National Socialism was Germany's accounting for its own history. This was the subject of a conference in Tyrol, which was held within the "Austrian Forum," where Keller addressed an audience of three hundred students. In 1950, moreover, he became the first European theologian after the war to deliver a sermon at evening service at St Paul's Cathedral in London: "They wished to honor my long and deep relationship with the ecumenical movement and service."[202]

Amid the postwar hustle and bustle, Keller thus wrote to Leiper in August 1949:

> I made the second journey to Germany where upon invitation from the British Government, Education Branch, I gave some lectures in German Universities in the British zone as I did in May . . . I am enjoying the new liberty of having little to do in committees and conferences and can give more time to teaching, writing and human relations. I saw Thomas Mann here and had supper with Albert Schweitzer . . . Just now I am giving an English course at the "Summer School for European Studies" on the transatlantic dialogue between America and Europe going [on] in the field of cultural relations . . . I am enjoying Zurich

---

199. Keller to Barth, September 27, 1945 (KBA 9345.755).
200. Keller, *Zeit-Wende*, 81–82.
201. Keller to Leiper, August 20, 1945 (NLAK C 26).
202. Keller to Leiper, October 1, 1950 (ibid.).

very much where I still give my course at the University and do
a lot of writing.[203]

As observed, Keller's stance on postwar America was both benevolent
and critical: "The world is much more complex than optimistic mor-
alists think, and it cannot be reduced that easily to good and evil."[204]
On the one hand, he categorically rejected what he referred to as an
American "management of the world."[205] On the other, he considered
American-European dialogue absolutely necessary: "On my proposal
the University of Zurich has already created an Institute for Foreign
Studies with a section on cultural relations with America where I am
constantly consulted."[206] Keller had already suggested the founding of
such an institute to Emil Brunner, the then President of the University,
in late 1942.[207] Founded on June 24, 1943, it marks another of Keller's
achievements that has survived to this day.

The Keller family had made Zurich its home again since 1948. Keller
often traveled to the United States. On his eightieth birthday, in 1952, he
received a congratulatory note from Thomas Mann: "But how you bustle!
It is most admirable!"[208] "Do you happen to know," Emil Brunner queried
Max Huber, "that Adolf Keller will be celebrating his eightieth birthday on
February 7, during his lecture tour in the United States? Such vitality is
quite extraordinary."[209]

Owing to his susceptibility to bronchitis, from 1950 Keller would
spend the winter months in California, where he remained indefatigably
active. In 1957, he decided to make California his home. Notwithstanding his reservations about America, he felt at ease there, and was still
highly regarded. Henry Leiper had already written in 1942: "Just as on his
many previous visits to America, Dr. Keller was by no means a stranger
to us on this occasion, but one of us. His insights, knowledge, Christian
love, profound empathy, and prophetic vision were a constant source of

203. Keller to Leiper, Zurich, August 18, 1949 (NLAK C 2,3).

204. Keller, "Furcht vor Amerika."

205. Keller, *Wiederaufbau der Welt*, 20.

206. Keller to Leiper, March 5, 1945 (NLAK C 26). Emil Brunner was appointed
first president of the Swiss-American Society for Cultural Relations; see Jehle, *Emil
Brunner*, 475.

207. Keller to Brunner, November 19, 1942 (StAZ W I 55,25), and Brunner to
Keller, Zurich, November 20, 1942 (WS Ms Sch 152/83).

208. Mann to Keller, March 31, 1952 (WS Ms Sch 153/19).

209. Brunner to Max Huber, January 10, 1952; a copy of this letter is held by the
Emil Brunner Foundation in Zurich.

help and inspiration. His friendly nature and personal charm made him sympathetic to all kind of people."[210] By contrast, Keller considered both Europe's weather and its moral climate cold.[211] The "conservative 1950s" were not to his taste. Tina Keller thus went about dissolving their Zurich household and made preparations to leave Switzerland to join her husband in America. Her mother was deceased, the children grown up. Their sons were living in America anyway. Then, in early 1958, Keller suffered a stroke, from which he never recovered. Cared for lovingly by his daughter Margrit and his wife Tina, he died on February 10, 1963, three days after his ninety-first birthday.

Tina and Adolf Keller in Zurich (ca. 1955)
(archive Dr. Pierre Keller)

210. Leiper, "An die schweizerischen Brüder!" October 1942, in Keller, ed., *Auswahl einiger Äusserungen,* 3 and 6.

211. Keller to Visser't Hooft, May 18, 1957 (WCC 42.0042 3,2).

Adolf Keller

FRIENDSHIP

Following her husband's death, Tina Keller-Jenny remained in California for several more years. Working at a psychiatric clinic, she collaborated with Trudi Schoop, a fellow Swiss, on developing a revolutionary new breathing and dance therapy for the mentally ill.[212] She had emancipated herself from her mentor C. G. Jung to become an extraordinarily independent and distinguished woman by standards at the time. Throughout his life and work, Adolf Keller had advocated university education for women, the introduction of the right to vote for women, and a cooperative arrangement between husband and wife.

It was Keller who rekindled the friendship with C. G. Jung. He sought to approach the latter not as a student, as which he had often felt treated, but instead as Jung's equal.[213] Thus, he wrote: "Dear friend! . . . once again, one reaches out to those who form part of our destiny and join us on our journey. You have been one of these fateful influences for *us*, and I call you a friend . . . I would like to see you more often, in a relationship that befits the apprentices of dying."[214]

Keller intended to discuss the oppositions and points of contact between theology and psychology with Jung. Jung agreed to become involved, albeit reluctantly. In February 1951, however, he wrote to Keller: "I would very much like to discuss a subject close to your heart, because I have few opportunities to talk to men. I have had some friends over the years, but they have died. Conversations with others . . . are very difficult because they have no relationship with my intellectual world and therefore feel out of their depths."[215] Thus, a "genuine meeting of minds" occurred, "even where no single language suffices."[216] Keller resigned himself to the fact that they could not agree on substance.[217] Keller's theology of a transcendent God and Jung's concept of an inner God were not compatible. They did, however, strike a chord in human terms. In late 1951, Keller departed for the United States, but not without bidding farewell: "Since we are both mortals, we should say 'Hail and Farewell, my friend,' just

212. Trudi Schoop was a dancer, cabarettist, and theater director.
213. Keller to Jung, February 6, 1951 (NL C. G. Jung Spezialsamml. ETH Hs 1056: 16'793).
214. Keller to Jung, Muzot ob Siders, May 21, 1943 (ETH Hs 1056: 10'500).
215. Jung to Keller, February 12, 1951 (ETH Hs 1056: 17'960).
216. Keller to Jung, May 29, 1951 (ETH Hs 1056: 17'619).
217. Keller to Jung, July 11, 1955 (ETH Hs 1056: 22'025).

in case."[218] Following Keller's stroke in early 1958, Jung wrote to him: "I am very shaken and distraught by your news . . . But at our age, we have learned, after all, to face all kinds of fate . . . and to entrust everything good and helpful to higher powers . . . Your old and faithful friend, C. G. Jung."[219]

Despite occasional friction, the early ecumenists were a community of fellow travelers, animated by idealism for a great cause. Without them, Keller would have been unable to accomplish his life's work, all the more because this was the first half of the twentieth century, a period of extreme political and economic difficulty. Among the early ecumenists, Keller's closest friends were Marc Boegner, Charles Macfarland, Robert Speer, Henry S. Leiper, Nathan Söderblom, Wilfred Monod, Adolf Deissmann, and William A. Brown. The latter four were no longer alive when World War II ended. As he grew older, Keller cultivated old friendships more intensively, and also met John Mott[220] and Reinhold Niebuhr on numerous occasions.[221] His association with Leiper was particularly warm. He also made new friends, including Henry Van Dusen, who had been President of Union Theological Seminary since 1946. On his visits to UTS, Keller would stay at the Prophets Chamber, where Bonhoeffer had also resided during his time in New York.[222] Here was a network of friends that stuck together!

Keller's relationship with Visser't Hooft had been tense at times. All the more, then, did he appreciate the latter's conciliatory and rueful stance in later years: "It gives me particular pleasure that, with the exception of brief periods of misunderstanding, our relationship was and remains one of mutual trust," Visser wrote in a letter to Keller in 1950.[223] In 1957, he addressed Keller as his "dear friend": "Now that I have served the ecumenical movement for thirty-three years, I, too, belong to the older generation and can consider the entire ecumenical development somewhat better in its context. This also renders meaningless any thought of an opposition between the generations. My concern is for the older generation to remain

218. Keller to Jung, November 27, 1951 (ETH Hs 1056 17'622).

219. Jung to Keller, April 3, 1958 (ETH Hs 1056: 26'303a).

220. Mott to Keller, October 16, 1951 (WS Ms Sch 153/27).

221. Keller to Visser't Hooft, March 7, 1947 (WCC 42.0042 3,2).

222. Van Dusen to Keller, January 22, 1957 (UTS Presidential Papers 25/ Keller, Prof. Adolph Keller II).

223. Visser't Hooft to Keller, November 10, 1950 (WCC 42.0042 3,2).

involved for as long as possible, because we shall otherwise lose our good relationship with our history."[224]

For decades, Eugène Choisy had stood by Keller's side in the Federation of Swiss Protestant Churches and in his capacity as president of Inter-Church Aid. Shortly before his death in 1949, Choisy wrote to Visser't Hooft: "How touched I am, and mindful of your thoughtfulness, in inviting me to the banquet yesterday evening in honor of the 75th birthday of our friend Adolf Keller! You will understand what a joy it was to spend the evening in the company of this dear collaborator, pioneer of every aspect of the ecumenical movement, with whom I worked so long and so happily!"[225] Keller grieved for his "unforgettable" friend for many years.[226] Alfred Jörgensen, vice-president of Inter-Church Aid from 1922 to 1945, was also one of Keller's most loyal companions. He described their friendship as "one of the best experiences" of his life.[227] He would not have begrudged Keller the Nobel Prize, but instead it was awarded to John Mott.[228]

Bishop George Bell had been aware of Keller's outstanding qualities ever since 1933. They worked hand in hand against National Socialism, and for ecumenism and the refugees. When Bell denounced the bombing raids of German cities in the House of Lords in 1944, and faced harsh criticism in response, Keller expressed his solidarity with the beleaguered bishop: "This Christian voice was answered with a deep inner relief because it was expected that the Christian conscience would not simply suffer silently what the necessity of war may command but would at least express its sympathy with the innocent victims. What you said has even a political effect in so far as those for whom politics and war is not simply a sheer manifestation of violence, see that the voice of humanity is not entirely suffocated [. . .]."[229]

In 1960, Bell wrote that the Department of Reconstruction and Inter-Church Aid of the Ecumenical Council had inherited "a great work and a noble tradition [. . .] which emerged under the pioneering leadership of Dr. Adolf Keller."[230]

224. Visser't Hooft to Keller, February 27, 1957 (WCC 42.0042 3,2).

225. Choisy to Visser't Hooft, February 7, 1947 (WCC 42.0017 1).

226. Keller to d'Espine, June 28, 1954 (NLAK D Prof. D. Adolf Keller. Corr. 1949–1954, grüne Mappe).

227. Jörgensen to Keller, July 15, 1947 (NLAK C 23).

228. Jörgensen in *Kirchenblatt für die reformierte Schweiz* (October 16, 1941), 336.

229. Keller to Bell, Geneva, February 20, 1944 (LPL Bell 21 f. 384).

230. Bell, *Die Königsherrschaft Jesu Christi*, 45.

Barth's theology continued to fascinate Keller. In a letter to Leiper, he wrote: "I am just reading his second volume of 'Dogmatics' mostly between midnight and one in bed."[231] Barth observed: "Perhaps we shall enjoy a heart to heart over tea or another mild drink sometime soon—however, a true and honest alcoholic beverage, for instance, from the vineyards of the Vaud or Neuchâtel, would serve this purpose even better—and if you so wish, I could tell you more, eye to eye."[232] "What you lack," he added bluntly in another letter, "is some of the thick skin, which I acquired already thirty years ago during my battles with the political right wing [. . .]."[233] Thick skin would have served Keller well. Since he was more or less the figurehead of ecumenism, he was particularly exposed to criticism of the movement, even though he was often the wrong target. Sometimes, he took offence quickly. He was, after all, a sensitive person. What is striking, however, is what Barth emphasised toward Visser't Hooft: "I think highly of Adolf Keller, whom I have been acquainted with for quite some time."[234] Barth compared Keller to Martin Bucer, the great ecumenist of the Reformation, and that is saying a lot.[235] In 1956, *This Is My Faith: The Convictions of Representative Americans Today* was published in New York.[236] Besides Albert Einstein, Keller was the only non-American who wrote an article. He asked: "Where can we find the principles to guide us in the new orientation of human life in a universe which we can no longer understand in terms of our traditional beliefs?"[237]

Keller was convinced that "individual and collective progress" could not be achieved "by resort to humanistic self-redemption," but only by "that spiritual help and cooperation provided by the personalistic influence of Jesus Christ and the inspiration and belief in the never-ending challenge of the Holy Spirit." Hope consisted for him in "a turning to that total otherness of the transcendent God whom man may meet through a personal encounter."[238]

231. Keller to Leiper, March 21, 1940 (NLAK C 2,3).

232. Barth to Keller, July 21, 1944 (KBA 9244.110).

233. Barth to Keller, Basel, July 8, 1944 (KBA 9244.100).

234. Barth to Visser 't Hooft, Basel, March 3, 1943, in *Karl Barth–W. A. Visser't Hooft. Briefwechsel 1930-1968*, 165.

235. Göckeritz, ed., *Friedrich Gogartens Briefwechsel*, 200–201.

236. Cole, Stewart Grant, ed., *This Is My Faith: The Convictions of Representative Americans Today* (New York: Harper & Brothers, 1956).

237. Ibid., 161.

238. Ibid., 169–70.

The elderly Adolf Keller and Emil Brunner would attend each other's lectures in Zurich— an unusual sign of trust among fellow professors.[239] In his letter congratulating Brunner on his sixtieth birthday, Keller wrote that the grain sown by Brunner had fallen into his "deepest furrows" and flowered.[240] When Keller departed for California in late 1951, he wrote to Brunner: "I shall now be cheerfully on my way [. . .]." Given the "ubiquitous officialdom," he found it less difficult "to travel to the country of expansive breath and of great possibilities [. . .]. We are both mortal, but we live in the cheerful certainty that we are in God's hands, you and I, and must do our work for as long as the day lasts."[241]

In early 1957, Keller traveled to Lambarene, and thus a long-harbored dream came true. Celebrating his eighty-fifth birthday there, he was delighted when Albert Schweitzer played Bach's Prelude in G Minor. Speaking in honor of Keller, Schweitzer said: "Well, God has led you [. . .] into the world of churches and conferences, while He led me into the great solitude of the primeval forest with its millions of underdeveloped and suffering people. Each of us had his tasks."[242] On his safe return home, Keller wrote to Schweitzer: "I am deeply moved that at our age we can see each other at work and discuss what matters to us. [. . .]. At our age, one is prepared to soon entrust oneself to the highest mercy, which sustains us all."[243]

239. Keller to Brunner, July 6, 1946 (StAZ W I 55,25).

240. Keller to Brunner, December 21, 1949 (ibid.).

241. Keller to Brunner, November 28, 1951 (ibid.).

242. Quoted from an article that Keller contributed to the journal *Wisdom* (archive of Pierre Keller).

243. Keller to Schweitzer, February 23, 1957 (WS Ms Sch 152/53).

Conclusion

The Significance of Adolf Keller

ADOLF KELLER ENJOYED A long, eventful, and fulfilled life. His interests ranged widely, his intellectual horizon was broad, and his activities manifold. Cosmopolitanism, tolerance, and a sense of responsibility are the outstanding features of his character. His pioneering spirit became evident already at a young age, in his interest in the Arabic language, his courage to accept a ministry in Cairo, his original activities as a pastor in Switzerland, his commitment to social justice and peace already during World War I, and his innovative work in the fledgling Federation of Swiss Protestant Churches.

On entering the ecumenical movement after World War I, conveying its core message became his guiding principle. It marked the beginning of his passionate, worldwide commitment to promoting reconciliation among the nations and peoples of Europe, to fostering dialogue between America and Europe, to the rapprochement between the Christian denominations, to assisting others in finding a spiritual home, to combatting hunger and misery, and to the protection of minorities and refugees. Never wavering in his commitment, he pursued it by means of ecumenism, the Council of the League of Nations, the United Nations, and European unification. He was realistic enough to question the development of these organizations.

In 1954, the World Brotherhood conferred upon Keller "its honorary award, in recognition of and admiration for 'his life of devotion to the service of God and humanity, his utter devotion to great moral and intellectual causes, his indefatigable efforts in promoting Christian unity, the tenacity and enthusiasm with which he pioneered cooperation among people of different races, religions, and nationalities, above all in relations between the peoples of Europe and America.'"[1]

"Keller proved himself to be a visionary," a later member of staff of the World Council of Churches asserted.[2] Not only was he visionary, but he was also actively involved in carrying his ideas into practice. Mention of the "prophetic beginning" of the ecumenical movement, which served as a "laboratory of fruitful ideas and plans," was closely related to Keller's work.[3] Numerous organizations and ventures—Inter-Church Aid, the Association Protestante Internationale de Prêts, the International Christian Social Institute, comparative ecclesiology, the Ecumenical Seminar, the aid for so-called "non-Aryan" refugees—either arose directly from his impetus or largely involved his initiative. He propagated dialectical theology as the spiritual binding agency and backbone of ecumenism and as a remedy against National Socialism. While Keller never occupied center stage at the world conferences, he was not only the most active but also the most creative figure among the early ecumenists. An expert on Keller's work thus commented: "It is recognised widely that you [Keller] maintained the work of this Movement almost single handed, and that you have left a legacy which the World Council of Churches has gratefully inherited, and to which it feels itself constantly indebted."[4]

Keller unselfishly took upon himself a considerable number of arduous journeys, since he placed utmost emphasis on personal encounters. He was a masterful networker. Only thus, he was convinced, could the seed of ecumenical thinking be planted. He became a world citizen. At social events and congresses, he exuded kindness and cosmopolitanism. He was a colorful, stimulating figure—which might come as some surprise, since he saw himself as introverted. He needed his "piece of solitude." He was not necessarily passionate about conferences.[5] But he was aware "that the human being can attain his highest value only in the community" and that "one must live with others and for them."[6] Tina Keller confirmed his

1. Fraternité Mondiale, "Le professeur Adolphe Keller à l'Honneur," May 18, 1954, press release (Archiv für Zeitgeschichte der ETH Zürich, Juna-Archiv 1.7.3).

2. G. Murray, "Adolf Keller and his Work for Refugees" (written after 1966), 7–9 (WCC 301.43.25/7).

3. Ehrenström, "Die Bewegungen für Internationale Freundschaftsarbeit und für Praktisches Christentum," 194.

4. J. Robert Nelson to Keller, January 22, 1957 (WCC 42.0042 3,2).

5. Keller, "Aus meinem Leben," 273; see also Keller to Doris Keller, June 16, 1937 (Sulzberg-Archiv Winterthur, NLDSK).

6. Keller, "Aus meinem Leben," 273.

view of himself: "There was a side to him that needed solitude . . . But it is just as true, that he liked people and people enjoyed him."[7] Macfarland wrote: "I know him to be frugal," which probably had to mean "modest."[8]

Keller was compelled to be an all-rounder, just like the other early ecumenists.[9] He committed ideas to paper swiftly, and was therefore accused at times of being superficial. He realized that he "ventured too far in an academic field that only appreciated meticulousness." But he consoled himself: "If theologians refuse to take me seriously, then others will."[10] Keller's task was not that of a specialized professor of theology undertaking strictly scholarly work, but instead that of someone conveying information about the ecumenical movement and its theological questions, and rendering these accessible to a wider audience. His tasks were enlightenment, reconciliation, and assistance. And therein lay his charisma.

Tina Keller observed: "Adolf had a wide Christianity. It was very real, but it had nothing of narrow sectarianism. It was a feeling-relation to a worldwide God, he would express this in saying that he felt himself 'safe in the everlasting arms.' This was not something he just said, but one felt it was deeply experienced."[11] On this solid foundation, he was able to deal with the spiritual and religious tendencies of his time in an unbiased manner. With Gandhi, for instance, whom he once heard speak.[12] While he advocated the rapprochement of the world religions with a view to resolving the large problems facing the world, he also believed that Christianity would need to make a considerable contribution, since it rested upon biblical realism.[13] Thus, he also proved to be a philanthropist in this respect.

Keller realized that one's "life's work is piecework and ultimately concealed in God."[14] "My entelechy has always been rather that of the inspirer and pioneer," and he admitted that it lacked roundedness.[15] He enjoyed citing 1 Corinthians 3:6–7: "I have planted, Apollos watered; but God gave

---

7. Tina Keller, *Adolf Keller* (1973) (NLTK).

8. Macfarland to Sloane Coffin, May 14, 1932 (UTS Presidential Papers, 25/3).

9. D'Espine, *Alphons Koechlin*, 144.

10. Keller to Brunner, Los Angeles, December 16, 1957 (StAZ W I 55,25).

11. Tina Keller, "In Memoriam."

12. Keller, *Am Fusse des Leuchtturms*, 53ff. Keller does not mention where and when he heard Gandhi speak.

13. Keller, *Am Fusse des Leuchtturms*, 61.

14. Keller to Emil Brunner, December 21, 1949 (StAZ W I 55/25).

15. Keller to Brunner, Los Angeles, December 16, 1957 (ibid.).

the increase. So then neither is he that planteth anything, neither he that watereth; but God that giveth the increase" (KJV).

"Just as I always returned to an innermost home, I have always emigrated from within myself . . . It was mostly by way of assignment or occupation, pursuant to a duty, and yet it was somehow also a mysterious call: 'Go forth from your country and your people to a country that I shall show you.' I was shown a field of work, a task. It was the work in another parish, a great church. The whole great theater of the world opened up before me." Keller had witnessed "human greatness and misery (grandeur et misère de l'homme)." "So I find all the more pleasing . . . the real experience of a great, indissoluble community that I was blessed to experience among many peoples and their churches."[16] "All those who did great work among men and women were ardent," he once wrote.[17] And ardent he was.

16. Keller, *Am Fusse des Leuchtturms*, 33–35. The French expression alludes to Blaise Pascal's *Pensées*, chapters 2 and 3 in part 1.

17. Ibid., 135.

Chronology

February 7, 1872	Born in Rüdlingen, Canton of Schaffhausen, Switzerland
1888–1892	Attends the Humanistisches Gymnasium Schaffhausen
1892–1896	Studies theology in Basel und Berlin
1896–1899	Auxiliary pastor in Cairo
1899–1904	Pastor auf Burg, Canton of Schaffhausen
1904–1909	Pastor in Geneva; studies psychology; Karl Barth becomes Keller's auxiliary pastor
From 1909	Pastor at St Peter's Church in Zurich
January 1912	Marries Tina Jenny. The couple starts a family and goes on to have five children.
1918	Journey to Paris and first journey to Great Britain
1919	First journey to the United States of America
1920	Founding member of the Federation of Swiss Protestant Churches
1920	Founding member of the ecumenical movement known as the Universal Christian Conference on Life and Work
1922	Founding member and director of the European Central Bureau for Relief (Inter-Church Aid); Keller's book *Dynamis* (about the churches in America) is published

1923	Two long journeys to America
End of 1923	Retires from his pastorage at St Peter's
1925	Conference of Life and Work in Stockholm; Keller is appointed second associated general secretary
1926	Appointed director of the International Christian Social Institute in Geneva. Keller starts the "leadership programme."
1927	Publication of *Protestant Europe*; receives honorary doctorate from Yale University
1928	Appointed editor of the journal *Stockholm*
1930	Receives honorary doctorate from the University of Edinburgh
1931	Publication of *Der Weg der dialektischen Theologie*
1933	Hitler is appointed German chancellor; Keller organizes relief operations for German refugees and travels to the United States to lecture at Princeton Theologcial Seminary.
1934	Publication of *Religion and Revolution*; lecture tour in Great Britain
1934	First Ecumenical Seminar in Geneva
1936	Publication of *Church and State on the European Continent*
1937	World conferences of Life and Work and Faith and Order
1939	Outbreak of World War II; establishes contact with the Catholic Church.
1940–1942	Stimulates relief operation for German refugees and Ecumenical Seminar in the United States
1943	Publication of *Amerikanisches Christentum—Heute*

1945	Inter-Church Aid becomes part of the provisional Ecumenical Council
1946	The Ecumenical Institute at Bossey is established as the successor of the Ecumenical Seminar
1948	Definite founding of the World Council of Churches
1957	Journey to Lambarene
1958	Suffers stroke in California
February 10, 1963	Dies in Santa Monica, California

List of Persons

Ainslie, Peter (1867–1934), American ecumenist

Althaus, Paul (1988–1966), professor of theology at the University of Erlangen

Ammundsen, O. Valdemar (1875–1936), Bishop of Hadersleben, Denmark

Arseniew, Nikolaj (1888–1977), professor at the Russian Orthodox Academy St Serge in Paris

Atkinson, Henry A. (1877–1960), American theologian; General Secretary of Life and Work

Bach, Johann Sebastian (1685–1750), German composer

Barot, Madeleine (1909–1995), General Secretary of CIMADE (Comité Intermouvements Auprès Des Evacués) in southern France, 1940–1956

Barth, Karl (1886–1968), Swiss theologian

Barth-Hoffmann, Nelly (1893–1976), wife of Karl Barth

Bauhofer, Oskar (1897–1975), Swiss theologian; studied at UTS, Keller's assistant

Baumann, Johannes (1874–1953), Swiss federal counsellor 1934–1940

Beach, David Nelson (1848–1926), American theologian

Beethoven, Ludwig van (1770–1827), German composer

Bell, George Kennedy Allen (1883–1958), from 1929 Bishop of Chichester; from 1932 a leading figure of Life and Work

Bergson, Henri (1859–1941), professor of philosophy at the Collège de France

Besson, Marius (1876–1945), Catholic Bishop of Lausanne, Geneva, and Freiburg

Billing, Einar (1871–1939), Bishop of Västeras, Sweden

Blau, Paul (1861–1944), general superintendent of the United German Church in Poznań (Poland)

Bleuler, Eugen (1857–1939), chief physican at the Burghölzli Psychiatric Clinic in Zurich

Bodelschwingh, Friedrich von (1831–1910), founder of the Bethel hospices

Bodelschwingh, Friedrich von Jr. (1877–1946), director of Bethel; appointed Reichsbischof in 1933

Boegner, Marc (1881–1970), from 1929 President of the Federation of French Protestant Churches

Böhl, Franz Marius Theodor (1882–1976), professor of theology in Groningen, Netherlands

Bonhoeffer, Dietrich (1906–1945), German pastor and theologian

Bovet, Ernest (1870–1941), professor of romance studies at the Swiss Federal Institute of Technology (ETH Zurich)

Brahms, Johannes (1833–1897), German composer

Brent, Charles H. (1862–1929), bishop of the Episcopal Church of the United States; founder of Faith and Order

Brown, Arthur Judson (1856–1963), President of the Federal Council

Brown, Ralph W. (1885–1981), American theologian

Brown, William Adams (1865–1943), professor of theology at Union Theological Seminary (UTS), ecumenist

Brunner, Emil (1889–1966), professor of theology at the University of Zurich

Buber, Martin (1878–1965), Jewish philosopher and theologian

Bülow, Otto von (1859–1915), member of the International Court at Cairo

Bülow-Schriecker, Elsa (1874–1949), wife of Otto von Bülow

Burckhardt, Jacob (1818–1897), professor of art history in Basel

Bursche, Julius (1862–1942), bishop of the Lutheran-Polish Church in Warsaw

Bychak (Butschak/Biczak), Lev (–1963), Protestant pastor in Galicia; arrested in 1939; exile in the United States

Cadman, Samuel Parkes (1864–1936), President of the Federal Council 1924–1928

Calvin, John (1509–1564), Swiss theologian and reformer

Carlyle, Thomas (1795–1871), Scottish writer, historian, social policymaker

Cassian, Sergei Bezobrazov (1892–1965), priest and monk at the Academy of St Serge in Paris; later Bishop of Romania

Cassirer, Ernst (1874–1945), professor of philosophy in Hamburg, dismissed in 1933; based at Yale from 1941

Cavert, Samuel McCrea (1888–1976), General Secretary of Federal Council from 1930

Choisy, Eugène (1866–1949), professor of church history at the University of Geneva; 1928–1945 President of Inter-Church Aid; 1930–1941 President of the Swiss Federation of Protestant Churches

Cockburn, J. Hutchinson (1882–1973), from 1945 director of the Department of Reconstruction and Inter-Church Aid of the World Council of Churches

Coffin, Henry Sloane (1877–1954), from 1904 professor of practical theology at UTS in New York; 1926–1946 President of UTS, professor at Yale and Princeton

Cramer, Jan Anthony (1864–1952), professor of theology in Utrecht, Netherlands

Cuendet, William Eugène (1886–1958), 1911–1924 pastor at the French Church in Zurich

Curtius, Ernst (1814–1896), professor of Hellenistic studies and archaeology in Berlin

Curtius, Ernst Robert (1886–1956), son of Friedrich Curtius, professor of romance studies in Heidelberg

Curtius, Friedrich (1851–1933), son of Ernst Curtius; lawyer; President of the Lutheran and Reformed Church of German-speaking Alsace-Lorraine before and during World War I

Deissmann, Adolf (1866–1937), professor of New Testament in Berlin; ecumenist

Dibelius, Martin (1883–1943), professor of New Testament in Heidelberg; ecumenist

Dibelius, Otto (1880–1967), from 1945 Bishop of Berlin

Dietrich, Suzanne de (1891–1981), a native Alsacian; lecturer at Bossey

Dilthey, Wilhelm (1833–1911), German philosopher

Duhm, Bernhard (1847–1928), professor of Old Testament in Basel

Dumas, Frédéric Charles (1848–1933), French pastor

Ehrenström, Nils (1903–1984), Swedish professor of ecumenism in Lund; from 1930 member of staff at Life and Work

Eidem, Erling (1880–1972), 1931–1950 Archbishop of Uppsala

Escher-Bürkli, Jakob (1864–1939), President of St Peter's Parish in Zurich

Eulogios (Guéorguievski) (1868–1946), Russian-Orthodox Metropolitan for Western Europe; founder of the Academy of St Serge in Paris in 1925

Faber, Wilhelm (*1858), pastor; head of a "Mohammedan Mission"

Fatio, Edmond (1871–1959), architect; committed Protestant in Geneva

Faulhaber, Michael (1869–1952), Archbishop of München-Freising; Cardinal; opposed to Hitler

Ferre, Nels (1908–1971), professor of theology at Andover Newton Seminary and Vanderbilt University

Feuchtwang, David (1864–1936), 1933–1936 Chief Rabbi of Vienna

Fleming, John Robert (1858–1937), theologian in Edinburgh

Fliedner, Fritz (1845–1901), German pastor; founder and leader of the Protestant hospices and schools in Madrid

Fliedner, Theodor Carl Johannes (1873–1938), son of Fritz Fliedner; his successor in Madrid 1901–1934

Flournoy, Théodore (1854–1929), professor of psychology at the University of Geneva

Freud, Sigmund (1856–1939), Austrian physician and psychotherapist

Freudenberg, Adolf (1894–1977), lawyer and theologian; 1939–1947 director of Refugee Aid at the provisional Ecumenical Council in Geneva

Frick, Wilhelm (1877–1946), German Minister of Home Affairs, 1933–1943

List of Persons

Froendt, Antonia, executive director of the Inter-Church Aid office in New York

Fuog, Theophil (–1910), President of the German Protestant Church in Geneva

Galen, Clemens August Graf von (1878–1946), Catholic Bishop of Münster

Gandhi, Mohandas (1869–1948), Indian lawyer and reformer

Gardner, Lucy (1863–1944), executive secretary of the British Conference on Christian Politics, Economics, and Citizenship; member of staff at Life and Work

Garvie, Alfred Ernest (1861–1945), President of the National Council of Free Churches in England; ecumenist

Gerstenmaier, Eugen (1906–1986), studied liberal arts and theology; 1936 collaborator of Bishop Heckel's; from 1942 member of the Kreisau Circle; 1954–1969 President of the German Parliament

Gide, Charles (1847–1932), professor of economics in Paris; President of the Mouvement du Christianisme Social

Goebbels, Joseph (1897–1945), German Minister of Propaganda, 1933–1945

Goethe, Johann Wolfgang von (1749–1832), German author

Gogarten, Friedrich (1887–1967), professor of systematic theology

Goodrich, Chauncy W. (1836–1925), director of the American office of Inter-Church Aid

Gounelle, Elie (1865–1950), pastor in Paris; editor of the journal *Le Christianisme Social*; ecumenist

Grimm, Hermann (1828–1901), historian of art and literature in Berlin

Grüber, Heinrich (1891–1975), pastor; director of the aid center for "non-Aryan" Christians in Berlin; 1940–1943 concentration camp prisoner; became a chaplain after the war

Guardini, Romano (1885–1968), German Catholic theologian and philosopher of religion

Häberlin, Heinrich (1868–1947), Swiss federal counsellor 1920–1934

Hadorn, Friedrich Wilhelm (1869–1929), professor of church history in Bern; 1920–1921 President of the Swiss Federation of Protestant Churches; ecumenist

Harnack, Adolf von (1851–1930), professor of church history in Berlin

Hasselbach, Carl (1849–1932), German businessman in Cairo

Hasselbach-Sommer, Olga (1872–1949?), wife of Carl Hasselbach; lived as a widow in Martin Niemöller's parish in Berlin-Dahlem

Heckel, Theodor (1894–1967), 1934–1945 Director/Bishop of the Foreign Office of the Evangelical Church of Germany (Reich Church)

Heimann, Eduard (1889–1967), professor at the Foreign Policy Institute in Hamburg

Henriod, Henry-Louis (1887–1970), Swiss theologian; 1920–1931 General Secretary of the World Student Christian Federation and later of the World Alliance; 1933–1938 General Secretary of Life and Work

Hentsch, Gustave (1909–1962), private banker in Geneva; actively involved in APIDEP and ECLOF

Herold, Otto (1848–1945), 1910 President of the Church Council of Zurich; 1921–1930 President of the Swiss Federation of Protestant Churches; 1922–1928 President of Inter-Church Aid; ecumenist

Hirsch, Emanuel (1888–1972), professor of theology in Göttingen

Hitler, Adolf (1889–1945), 1934–1945 German chancellor

Homringhausen, Elmer George (1900–1992), professor of theology in Princeton

Horton, Douglas (1891–1968), American theologian; translator of the works of Karl Barth; ecumenist

Hossenfelder, Joachim (1899–1976), bishop; Reichsleiter (leader for the Reich) of the "German Christians"

Hromàdka, Josef L. (1889–1969), professor of systematic theology in Prague; emigrated to 1939 Princeton, and returned to Prague after the war

Huber, Max (1874–1960), Swiss expert on international law; 1922–1930 Judge at the Permanent Court of International Justice in The Hague; 1928–1945 President of the International Committee of the Red Cross

Hug, Walther (1898–1980), lawyer and economist, lecturer at Harvard; from 1931, professor in St Gallen, Switzerland

Ibsen, Henrik (1828–1906), Norwegian playwright

List of Persons

Ihmels, Ludwig (1858–1933), professor of theology; from 1922 Bishop of Saxony

Innitzer, Theodor (1875–1955), Archbishop of Vienna; Cardinal

Jäger, August F. Ch. (1887–1949), "Rechtswalter" (state commissar) of the Evangelical Church of Germany (Reich Church) from 1934

James, William (1842–1910), American philosopher and psychologist

Jenny, Conrad Jr. (1888–1944), Tina Keller-Jenny's brother; diplomat

Jenny, Conrad Sr. (1848–1928), father of Tina Keller-Jenny

Jenny-Jenny, Albertina (1863–1957), mother of Tina Keller-Jenny

Jenny Alice (1890–1943), Tina Jenny's sister, married to State Counsellor Paul Lachenal

Jézéquel, Jules (1870–1942), general secretary of the French Protestant Church

Jörgensen, Alfred Theodor (1874–1954), Danish theologian; vice-president of the Executive Committee of Inter-Church Aid 1922–1945

Jud, Leo (1482–1542), pastor at St Peter's Church in Zurich; supporter of Zwingli; Bible translator

Jung, Carl Gustav (1875–1961), Swiss physician and psychotherapist

Jung, Emma (1882–1955), wife of C. G. Jung; psychotherapist

Kaftan, Julius Wilhelm Martin (1848–1926), professor of dogmatics and ethics in Berlin

Kagawa, Toyohiko (1888–1960), "The Evangelist of Japan"; ecumenical social reformer

Kapler, Hermann (1867–1941), lawyer; chairman of the Federation of German Protestant Churches until 1933

Keller, Doris (1912–2003), eldest daughter of Adolf and Tina Keller; pianist; married to Hans Sträuli

Keller, Esther (b. 1923), third daughter of Adolf and Tina Keller; married to Pieter Putman Cramer

Keller, Johann Georg (1841–1917), Adolf Keller's father; teacher

Keller, Margrit (1916–1997), nurse; second daughter of Adolf and Tina Keller

Keller, Paul (1914–1998), elder son of Adolf and Tina Keller; lived in California

Keller, Pierre (b. 1927), younger son of Adolf and Tina Keller; married to Claire-Jeanne de Senarclens; diplomat and banker

Keller-Buchter, Margaretha (1847–1929), Adolf Keller's mother

Keller-Jenny, Tina (1887–1985), Adolf Keller's wife; psychiatrist

Kirschbaum, Charlotte von (1899–1975), friend of and theological assistant to Karl Barth

Köcher, Otto (1884–1945), German ambassador in Bern 1937–1945

Koechlin, Alphons (1885–1965), Swiss theologian; 1936–1969 President of the Basel Mission; 1941–1954 President of the Swiss Federation of Protestant Churches; from 1945 Chair of the Department of Reconstruction and Inter-Church Aid of the Ecumenical Council of Churches

Künzler, Jakob (1871–1949), Swiss citizen, based as a nurse and church social worker at Urfa hospital in Turkey from 1899; witnessed the persecution of the Armenians; later served as the director of the charitable organization for Armenian refugees on behalf of the Near East Relief in Beirut

Kusiv, Basil (1887–1958), Ukrainian citizen; Presbyterian pastor in Newark, New Jersey; 1935–1939 superintendent of the Reformed wing of the Ukrainian Protestants in Galicia

Kutter, Hermann (1963–1931), cofounder of the religious social movement in Switzerland in 1906

Lavater, Johann Caspar (1741–1801), pastor at St Peter's Church in Zurich; author of *Physiognomical Fragments*

Leiper, Henry Smith (1875–1975), American theologian; from 1930 responsible for the American office of Inter-Church Aid and member of the Executive Committee; executive secretary of the American Section of Life and Work; 1938–1952 associate general secretary of the Ecumenical Council

Lieb, Fritz (1892–1970), Swiss theologian; lecturer in Eastern Christendom in Bonn; from 1937 professor of dogmatics and the history of theology in Basel; ecumenist

Liefmann, Else (1881–1979), paediatrician; interned in Gurs in 1940 before fleeing to Switzerland

Liefmann, Martha, (1876–1952), art historian; interned in Gurs in 1940 before fleeing to Switzerland

Liefmann, Robert (1874–1941), economist and lawyer, dismissed from his professorship at the University of Freiburg im Breisgau in 1933; deported to Gurs in 1940 where he died as a result of imprisonment

Lilje, Hanns (1899–1977), Lutheran theologian; from 1947 Bishop of Hannover

Lunn, Henry Simpson Sir (1859–1939), British physician; publicist and ecumenist

Luther, Martin (1483–1546), German theologian and reformer

Maas, Hermann (1877–1970), German pastor; protected Jews and Christians of Jewish descent

Macfarland, Charles Stedman (1866–1956), American lawyer and theologian; 1912–1930 general secretary of the Federal Council of Churches of Christ in America; along with Söderblom the key early protagonist of Life and Work and promoter of Inter-Church Aid

Mackay, John Alexander (1889–1983), Scottish professor of theology; from 1936 President of Princeton Theological Seminary

Madariaga y Rojo, Salvador de (1886–1978), Spanish writer and diplomat

Maksumujk, A. (1908–1945), Protestant pastor in Galicia; murdered by the Soviets

Mann, Thomas (1875–1955), German writer; emigrated in 1933 and lived in the United States from 1939–1952, and in Zurich from 1952

Maritain, Jacques (1882–1973), French philosopher; 1945–1948 French ambassador to the Vatican; later moved to Princeton; one of the stimulators of the Second Vatican Council

McCormick, Harold (1872–1941), chairman of the board of Harvester Company in Chicago, husband of Edith Rockefeller McCormick

McGiffert, Arthur Cushman (1861–1933), professor of church history at Union Theological Seminary; became UTS President since 1917

Mendelssohn Bartholdy, Albrecht (1874–1936), director of the Foreign Policy Institute at the University of Hamburg; emigrated to Great Britain in 1934

Mendelssohn Bartholdy, Felix (1809–1847), German composer

Michelangelo Buonarroti (1475–1564), Italian artist

Moffat, James (1870–1944), professor of New Testament in Glasgow

Monod, Wilfred (1867–1943), professor of theology in Paris; president of the Union des Eglises Reformées de France; the most important early French protagonist of Life and Work

Morel, Emil (1858–1935), president of the Federation of French Churches

Mott, John Raleigh (1865–1955), American Methodist; held leading positions at the YMCA and the World Student Christian Federation, and at the World Mission Conference of 1910 in Edinburgh and the Life and Work Conference of 1937 in Oxford

Motta, Giuseppe (1871–1940), Swiss federal counsellor 1912–1940

Müller, Felix von (1957–1918), German General Consul in Cairo 1897–1903

Müller, Ludwig, (1883–1945), "Reichsbischof" (bishop for the whole Reich) of the Evangelical Church of Germany (Reich Church) from the autumn of 1933 until the end of 1934

Mussolini, Benito (1883–1945), Italian prime minister

Naumann, Friedrich (1860–1919), socially committed German theologian

Neurath, Constantin von (1973–1956), German foreign minister 1932–1938

Niebuhr, Reinhold (1892–1971), professor of practical theology at UTS

Niemöller, Martin (1892–1984), pastor in Berlin–Dahlem; founder of the "Pfarrernotbund" (Pastors' Emergency League) in 1933; member of the Bekennende Kirche ("Confessing Church"); 1937–1945 concentration camp prisoner

Nietzsche, Friedrich (1844–1900), German philosopher

Nightingale, Thomas (1867–1934), British citizen; 1920–1931 general secretary of the National Council of the Evangelical Free Churches; ecumenist

Nuelsen, John L. (1867–1946), German-American citizen; from 1912 Methodist bishop in Europe, based in Zurich

Oldham, Joseph Houldsworth (1874–1969), Scottish theologian; 1934–1938 chairman of the Research Department of the provisional Ecumenical Council; responsible for overseeing preparations for the Life and Work Conference of 1937 in Oxford

Orelli, Conrad von (1846–1912), professor of Old Testament at the University of Basel

Overbeck, Franz Camille (1837–1905), 1870–1897 professor of New Testament at the University of Basel

Paton, William (1886–1943), General Secretary of the International Missionary Council; from 1938 associated general secretary of the provisional Ecumenical Council of Churches

Pauck, Wilhelm (1901–1981), German church historian; from 1926 professor at Chicago University; from 1953 at Union Theological Seminary in New York; from 1967 at Vanderbilt University in Nashville

Perini, Elisa (1897–1966), Swiss, secretary of Inter-Church Aid in Geneva

Pestalozzi, Johann Heinrich (1746–1827), Zurich-born pioneer of modern pedagogy

Peter the Venerable (1092/94–1154), scolastic theologian; Abbot of Cluny

Pfister, Oskar (1873–1956), from 1902 pastor at the Predigerkirche in Zurich

Piper, Otto F. (1891–1982), professor of theology in Münster; dismissed from his post in 1933; from 1937 professor at Princeton Theological Seminary

Pius XI (1857–1939), pope 1922–1939

Pius XII (1876–1958), pope 1939–1958

Pribilla, Max (1874–1956), German Jesuit; pioneer of ecumenical dialogue

Ragaz, Leonhard (1868–1945), cofounder of the religious social movement in Switzerland in 1906; 1908–1921 professor of theology in Zurich, thereafter freelance

Ravasz, Laszlo (1882–1950), Protestant Bishop in Budapest

Richards, George W. (1869–1955), professor of church history; president of Lancaster Theological Seminary USA

Riegner, Gerhart M. (1911–2001), lawyer, from 1936 director of the Geneva office of the World Jewish Congress; sent telegram to the president of the World Jewish Congress concerning the "Endlösung" der Judenfrage ("Final Solution" of the Jewish Question)

Rihner, Hans Oskar (1893–1950), Swiss theologian; founder of the Protestant Welfare Association of Jugoslavia in 1922; established church welfare institutions of the Inner Mission in Novi Vrbas

Rockefeller McCormick, Edith (1872–1932), sister of John Rockefeller Jr.; married to Harold McCormick; lived in Zurich from 1913 to 1921

Rockefeller, John Davison Sen. (1839–1937), cofounder of Standard Oil Company

Rockefeller, John D. Jr. (1874–1960), businessman and philanthropist

Rolland, Romain (1866–1940), French writer and peace activist

Rosenberg, Alfred (1893–1946), 1933–1945 Reichsleiter (Leader of the Foreign Policy Office) of the NSDAP

Runestam, Arvid (1887–1962), professor of theology in Uppsala; from 1937 Bishop of Karlstadt

Sarasin, Alfred (1865–1953), banker in Basel; chairman of the Board of APIDEP

Sauter, F. Marc (1881–1961), director of APIDEP (International Protestant Association for Loans); from 1945 treasurer of the Department of Reconstruction and Inter-Church Aid of the Ecumenical Council

Schaible, David (1903–1989), from 1929 pastor at the Reformed church in Odessa, arrested and banished in 1930; returned to Germany in 1974

Schlatter, Adolf (1852–1938), Swiss professor of New Testament in Greifswald, Berlin, and Tübingen

Schleiermacher, Friedrich Daniel Ernst (1768–1834), professor of theology in Berlin

Schönborn, Christoph von (*1945), archbishop of Vienna; cardinal

Schönfeld, Hans (1900–1954), German theologian and economist; from 1929 Keller's collaborator in Geneva; 1931–1946 director of the Research Institute of the Provisional Ecumenical Council; confidant of Bishop Heckel; from 1942 Member of the Kreisauer Circle

List of Persons

Schumacher, Hermann (1868–1952), German economist and professor, first in Bonn, from 1917 in Berlin

Schutz, Roger (1915–2005), Protestant theologian from the Swiss Canton of Vaud; founder and director of the Taizé community in Burgundy

Schweitzer, Albert (1875–1965)

Schweizer, Eduard (1913–2006), professor of New Testament at the University of Zurich

Seippel, Paul (1858–1926), professor of romance studies in Zurich, fought for the unity of Switzerland during World War I

Semeniuk, Fylymon (1912–2011), Protestant, Ukrainian-speaking pastor in Galicia; imprisoned in Siberia for eleven years; once more active in the Ukraine up to his death

Shaw, George Bernhard (1856–1950)

Shimun, Mar (Lord) Eshai (1908–1975), patriarch of the Assyrian Christians, 1940 forced to emigrate into the United States

Siegmund-Schultze, Friedrich (1885–1969), cofounder of the World Alliance; editor of the journal *Die Eiche*; professor of social ethics in Berlin; forced to emigrate in 1933 for providing assistance to Jews; student pastor in Zurich, attended to German refugees

Söderblom, Nathan (1866–1931), from 1914 archbishop of Uppsala, active in the World Alliance; dominant figure during the first ten years of Life and Work, Nobel Peace Prize 1930

Sommerlath, Ernst, (1889–1983), 1924–1959 professor of systematic theology in Leipzig

Sorel, Georges (1847–1922), French sociologist

Speer, Robert E., (1867–1947), 1920–1924 president of the Federal Council of Churches; responsible for the Board of Foreign Missions of the Presbyterian Church in the U.S.A.

Spengler, Oswald (1880–1936), German philosopher of culture and history; principal work: *Der Untergang des Abendlandes* (The Decline of the West)

Spitteler, Carl (1845–1920), Swiss epic and lyric poet, essayist; delivered an important speech propagating the unity of Switzerland in 1914 "Unser Schweizer Standpunkt" (Our Swiss Standpoint)

Staehelin, Ernst (1899–1980), from 1924 professor of modern church history in Basel; chief editor of the *Kirchenblatt für die reformierte Schweiz*

Stalin, Josef W. (1879–1953)

Stewart, George (1892–1972), American theologian: coauthor of Keller's *Protestant Europe*

Straub–Bachofner, Jakob (1871–1953), treasurer of Inter-Church Aid 1925–1945

Strenopoulos, Germanos (1872–1951), Greek-Orthodox professor of theology; 1920–1951 most important spokesman of Orthodoxy in the ecumenical movement; metropolitan; often referred to simply as "Germanos"

Temple, William (1881–1944), Archbishop of York, then of Canterbury; president of Faith and Order from 1929; from 1938 chairman of the Provisional Committee of the Ecumenical Council

Thélin, Georges (1890–1963), lawyer; staff member at the International Labor Organization (ILO) of the League of Nations

Thurneysen, Eduard (1888–1977), 1927–1959 pastor at Basel Minster; Associate professor of practical theology; close friend of Karl Barth's

Tillich, Paul (1886–1965), theologian and philosopher; professor in Marburg, Dresden, and Frankfurt a. Main; emigrated to the United States in 1933 and appointed professor at Union Theological Seminary

Tippy, Worth M. (1870–1961), Methodist; member of staff at the research department of the Federal Council

Titius, Arthur (1864–1936), adjunct professor in Berlin; professor of systematic theology in Göttingen; initiator of the ecumenical journal *Stockholm*; later became a National Socialist

Tolstoy, Leo (1828–1910), Russian novelist

Tour, Elvine de La, née Freiin v. Zahony (1841–1916), dedicated Protestant; founder of the welfare institutions in Russitz (now Russiz near Gorizia, Friuli), Villach, and Trieste

Treitschke, Heinrich von (1834–1896), professor of history in Berlin

Troeltsch, Ernst (1865–1923), theologian and philosopher; from 1914 professor in Berlin

Van Dusen, Henry Pitney (1897–1975), professor at UTS; from 1946 President of UTS

Vischer, Lukas (1926–2008), Swiss theologian; 1965–1979 director of Faith and Order at the Ecumenical Council; from 1980 associate professor of ecumenical theology in Bern; 1982–1989 chair of the Department of Theology at the Reformed Alliance

Visser't Hooft, Willem A. (1900–1985), Dutch theologian; 1924 secretary of the YMCA; from 1931 secretary of the World Student Christian Federation; 1938–1948 general secretary of the provisional Ecumenical Council of Churches, and from 1948 to 1966 of the definite Council

Vycheslavtseff, Boris (1877–1950), professor of philosophy at the Academy St Serge in Paris

Webster, James Macdonald (*1870), Scottish theologian; 1922–1945 committed member of the Executive Committee of Inter-Church Aid

Wernle, Paul (1872–1939), New Testament scholar; from 1900 professor of church history in Basel; his publications earned him international acclaim

Wilhelm II (1859–1941), German emperor

Wilson, Woodrow (1856–1924), president of the United States 1913–1921

Wipf, Jakob (1871–1947), Dr. theol. h.c.; from 1911 pastor in Buchthalen (Canton of Schaffhausen)

Woods, Frank Theodor (1874–1932), bishop of Peterborough; from 1924 bishop of Winchester; most important early Anglican protagonist of Life and Work

Wünsch, Georg (1887–1946), from 1931 professor of ethics, social ethics, and apologetics in Marburg; dismissed in 1945 (for alleged National Socialist leanings); rehabilitated in 1950

Wurm, Theophil (1868–1953), from 1933 bishop of Württemberg

Zankow, Stefan (1881–1965), Orthodox Professor of Theology and for Church Law in Sofia; active in the World Allliance, in Faith and Order, and in Life and Work

Zilka, Františšek (1871–1944), professor of New Testament at the Jan Hus Faculty of Theology in Prague

Zöckler, Martin (1911–1987), theologian; son of Theodor and Lilly Zöckler

Zöckler, Theodor (1867–1949), 1890–1939 Bishop of the United German-speaking Churches in Galicia

Zoellner, Wilhelm (1860–1937), director of Kaiserswerth hospices; from 1935 President of the Board of the Evangelical Church of Germany (Reich Church)

Zwingli, Huldrych (1484–1531), leader of the Reformation in Zurich

Bibliography

WORKS BY ADOLF KELLER (in chronological order)

Keller, Adolf. "Curriculum vitae, 1896." StAZ T 30a, 16.

————. *Der Geisteskampf des Christentums gegen den Islam bis zur Zeit der Kreuzzüge.* Leipzig: Verlag der Akademischen Buchhandlung, 1896.

————. *Eine Sinai-Fahrt.* Frauenfeld: Huber, 1901.

————. "Ein Traum." *Gemeinde-Blatt* 1, no. 1 (November 5, 1904). Archive of Geneva University Library.

————. "The Healing of the Paralytic." Mark 2:3–12, January 29, 1905. NLAK A 3 Early Sermons.

————. "Die heutige äussere und innere Lage des Protestantismus." *Gemeinde-Blatt für die Glieder und Freunde der St. Petersgemeinde* 2/5 (October 5, 1912).

————. "Von der Macht des Alkohols." *Gemeinde-Blatt für die Glieder und Freunde der St. Petersgemeinde* 4/1 (January 31, 1914).

————. *Eine Philosophie des Lebens: Henri Bergson.* Jena: Diederichs, 1914.

————. "Die Rüstung des Herzens." In Johannes Sutz and Adolf Keller, *Gotteshilfe in Kriegszeit: Sechs Predigten.* Zurich: Orell Füssli, 1914.

————. "Einer trage des andern Last." In Johannes Sutz and Adolf Keller, *Gotteshilfe in Kriegszeit: Sechs Predigten,* 44–53. Zurich: Orell Füssli, 1914.

————. "Dein Wille geschehe." In Johannes Sutz and Adolf Keller, *Gotteshilfe in Kriegszeit: Sechs Predigten.* Zurich: Orell Füssli, 1914.

————, and Eugène Cuendet. *Wir wollen sein ein einzig Volk von Brüdern: Vaterländische Ansprachen in einem gemeinsamen deutsch- und welschschweizerischen Gottesdienst am 9. Sept. 1914 im St. Peter.* Zurich: Orell Füssli, 1914.

————. "Der Glaube des Alltags." *Gemeinde-Blatt für die Glieder und Freunde der St. Petersgemeinde* 5/5 (November 18, 1915) 14–17.

————. *Von der inneren Erneuerung unseres Volkes: Eine Bettagsbetrachtung.* Zurich: Rascher, 1915.

————. "Evangelium und Christentum." Typescript article, 1918. Archive of the Psychologischer Club, Manuscripts section, 1 M 12.

————. "An der Schwelle des fünften Jahres. Dennoch! Die feineren Stimmen. Eindrücke eines Schweizers im christlichen England und Schottland." In

Bibliography

Deissmann, Adolf, editor. *Evangelischer Wochenbrief 75/76* (July 31, 1918).

————. "Der internationale Kitt." *Wissen und Leben* 18/19 (1918).

————. "Tiefenpsychologie." In *Kunstwart und Kulturwart*, edited by Ferdinand Avenarius. Vol. 32/14 (1919).

————. *Der Völkerbund und die Kirchen.* Zurich: Orell Füssli, 1919.

————. "Ist Gott für uns, wer mag wider uns sein. Röm. 8,31." Basel: Separatdruck, 1919.

————. "Die Schweizerische Delegation an das Federal Council der Kirchen Christi in Amerika: Kurzer Bericht der schweizerischen Kirchenkonferenz erstattet." Bern, 1919.

————. "American Churches as Seen by an European." New York, 1919. (PHS NCC RG 18 12/8).

————. "Der Idealismus als praktisches Problem." In Ernst Bovet, ed. *Wissen und Leben* 14/16 (January 1, 1921).

————. "Vom religiösen Jugendunterricht." *Gemeinde-Blatt für die Glieder und Freunde der St. Petersgemeinde* 12/4 (April 18, 1922).

————. *Dynamis, Formen und Kräfte des amerikanischen Protestantismus.* Tübingen: Mohr/Siebeck, 1922.

————, editor. *Zur Lage des Europäischen Protestantismus: Übersicht über Notstände und Hilfswerke im Gebiet der europäischen evangelischen Kirchen.* Zurich: Sekretariat des Schweizerischen Evangelischen Kirchenbundes, 1922.

————. *Evangelisches Zusammenwirken: Kurze Darstellung der Notlage im europäischen Protestantismus und der allgemein evangelischen Hilfsaktion.* Zurich: Europäische Zentralstelle für kirchliche Hilfsaktionen, 1923.

————. *Von protestantischer Not und Hilfe: Erster Bericht der Europäischen Zentralstelle für kirchliche Hilfsaktionen vom Sept. 1922–Mai 1924.* Zurich: Europäische Zentralstelle, 1924.

————. "Eine britische religiös-soziale Konferenz in Birmingham, 5.–12. April 1924." *Neue Wege* (1924).

————. "Das Ergebnis von Stockholm," *Neue Zürcher Zeitung*, September 6, 1925.

————. "A Theology of Crisis." *The Expositor*, 9th series, vol. 3 (1925) 164–75 and 245–60.

————. "The Crisis of European Protestantism." *Hands across the Sea: Bulletin of the European Central Bureau for Relief to the Protestant Churches* 2 (February 1925)

————. "Poland." *Hands across the Sea: Bulletin of the European Central Bureau for Relief to the Protestant Churches* 2 (February 1925).

————. "A Visit to America." *Hands across the Sea: Bulletin of the European Central Bureau for Relief to the Protestant Churches* 2 (February 1925).

————. "From the Roman Catholic field." *Hands across the Sea: Bulletin of the European Central Bureau for Relief to the Protestant Churches* 3 (June 1925).

————. "A Journey to the East." *Hands across the Sea: Bulletin of the European Central Bureau for Relief to the Protestant Churches* 3 (June 1925),

————. "Our New Programme." *Hands across the Sea: Bulletin of the European Central Bureau for Relief to the Protestant Churches* 3 (June 1925).

————, "Der amerikanische Protestantismus." In Gotthilf Adolf Schenkel and Emil Brunner, eds. *Der Protestantismus der Gegenwart*. Stuttgart: Verlag Friedr. Bohnenberger, 1926.

————. "Die soziale Erneuerung der Menschheit durch das Christentum." *Die Eiche* 3 (1926)

————. *Die Kirchen und der Friede, mit besonderer Berücksichtigung ihrer Stellung zum Völkerbund*. Berlin: Furche, 1927.

————, and George Stewart. *Protestant Europe: Its Crisis and Outlook*. New York: Doran, 1927.

————. "Vorbemerkungen zur Lausanner Konferenz." *Kirchenblatt für die reformierte Schweiz* 31 (August 4, 1927).

————. *Die Kirche und die soziale Arbeit: Bericht des Generalsekretärs des Sozialwissenschaftlichen Instituts an den Fortsetzungsausschuss für seine Sitzung in Winchester, Juli 1927*. Zurich: Sonneggstrasse 16 [s.n.], 1927.

————. "Die Weltkirchenkonferenz in Lausanne I." *Kirchenblatt* 32 (August 11, 1927).

————. "Die Weltkirchenkonferenz in Lausanne." *Basler Nachrichten* (Tuesday, August 16, 1927).

————. "Die Schweiz an der Weltkirchenkonferenz in Lausanne, Teil 2." *Kirchenblatt für die reformierte Schweiz* 35 (September 1, 1927).

————. "Die Weltkirchenkonferenz in Lausanne II." *Kirchenblatt* 36 (September 8, 1927).

————, editor. *Stockholm: International Review for the Social Activities of the Churches* (Internationale kirchliche Zeitschrift; Revue Internationale d'Etudes sociales). 4 vols. Göttingen: Vandenhoeck & Ruprecht, 1928–1931. (WCC Archive).

————. "Der kirchliche Ausdruck einer neuen sozialen Gesinnung." *Stockholm* 1 (1928).

————. "The Dialectic Theology." *The Congregational Quarterly* (London, January 1928) 56–68.

————. *Bericht über die Tätigkeit des Internationalen sozialwissenschaftlichen Instituts pro 1927/28*. Geneva: Selbstverlag, 1928.

————. *Der Schweizerische Evangelische Kirchenbund und die internationalen kirchlichen Einigungsbewegungen: Im Auftrag des Kirchenbunds dargestellt*. Zurich: Wanderer, 1928.

————. *Religious Revival in the Ukraine and the Religious Problem of Eastern Europe*. London: Continental Society, 1928.

————. *Die Europäische Zentralstelle für kirchliche Hilfsaktionen*. Geneva: Selbstverlag, 1928.

————. "Notes." *Bulletin Life and Work* 6 (December 1928).

————. "Wesen und Form der kirchlichen Gemeinschaft." Inaugural lecture delivered at the Faculty of Theology of the University of Zurich. Special reprint of *Monatsschrift für Pastoraltheologie zur Vertiefung des gesamten pfarramtlichen Wirken* 1 and 2. Göttingen: Vandenhoeck und Ruprecht, 1928.

———. *Das Internationale Sozialwissenschaftliche Institut in Genf,* 1928–29.
Geneva: Selbstverlag, 1929.

———. *Auf der Schwelle: Einsichten und Ausblicke in die tiefere Wirklichkeit.*
Zurich:Wanderer, 1929.

———. *Die Fortsetzungsarbeit der Stockholmer Weltkirchenkonferenz Life and Work.*
Studien und Dokumente 1. Zurich: Wanderer, 1929.

———. *Die Sozialen Programme der Kirchen und freier religiöser Organisationen:*
Studien und Dokumente 2. Zurich: Wanderer, 1929.

———. "Nordische Reise IV." *Neue Zürcher Zeitung,* Wednesday, November 13,
1929 (lunchtime edition).

———. "Notizen." *Stockholm* 2 (1930).

———. "Die Lambeth-Konferenz." *Neue Zürcher Zeitung,* Sunday July 6, 1930.

———. *Das Christentum und der heutige Wirtschaftsmensch.* Zurich: Wanderer,
1931.

———. *Der Weg der dialektischen Theologie durch die kirchliche Welt: Eine kleine*
Kirchenkunde der Gegenwart. Munich: Kaiser, 1931.

———. "Soziale Probleme im Balkan." *Neue Zürcher Zeitung,* July 12, 1931.

———. "Denkschrift" (confidential, early 1932) (NLAK C 30).

———. "Le rapprochement des Eglises et la théologie dialectique de Karl Barth."
Etudes théologiques et religieuses. Revue trimestrielle publiée par la faculté de
Théologie Protestante de Montpellier (May-June 1932): 191–223.

———. "Memorandum IV (confidential). Zur Lage und zukünftigen Gestaltung
der Ökumenischen Bewegung." Typescript. Geneva, May 25, 1932 (EZA 51/o
III 1 @m)

———. "Die Europäische Zentralstelle für kirchliche Hilfsaktionen 1922–1932."
Reprinted from *Die Eiche,* no. 1 (1933).

———. *Karl Barth and Christian Unity: The Influence of the Barthian Movement*
upon the Churches of the World. Translated by Manfred Manroat and A. J.
Macdonald. New York: Macmillan, 1933.

———. *Vom Unbekannten Gott: Not und Hoffnung der Gegenwart.* Gotha: Klotz,
1933.

———. "Abrüstung." In *Vom Unbekannten Gott. Not und Hoffnung der Gegenwart.*
Gotha: Klotz, 1933.

———. "The Position of Protestantism in Relation to Faith and Order." *The*
Churches in Action: Newsletter of the Ecumenical Council 3 (October 1933).

———. "Protestantismus und deutsche Revolution," *Kirchenblatt für die reformierte*
Schweiz 9 (May 4, 1933).

———. "Der reformierte Weltbund in Belfast." *Kirchenblatt für die reformierte*
Schweiz 15 (July 27, 1933).

———. *Die europäische Zentralstelle 1922-1932.* Gotha: Klotz, 1933.

———. *Von Geist und Liebe: Ein Bilderbuch aus dem Leben.* Gotha: Klotz, 1934.

———. *Religion and Revolution: Problems of Contemporary Christianity on the*
European Scene. New York: Revell, 1934.

———. *Religion and the European Mind.* The L. P. Stone Lectures, Princeton

Theological Seminary 1933. Lutterworth Library 4. London: Lutterworth, 1934.

———— et al. ""Eine interkonfessionelle Hilfskonferenz für die Hungernden in Russland." *Evangelischer Pressedienst* 1 (January 3, 1934) 197.

————. "Eine Demarche des Federal Council bei der Deutschen Evangelischen Kirchenleitung. Bericht über ein Gespräch in Berlin mit Reichsbischof Ludwig Müller, Ministerialdirektor Dr. Jäger, Rechtswalter der Deutschen Evangelischen Kirche, und Bischof D. Heckel, Vertreter des Aussenamtes," May 14, 1934 (WCC 301.43.19/5).

————. "Streitgespräch zwischen Emil Brunner und Karl Barth (Emil Brunner: Natur und Gnade, Tübingen 1934)," *Der Bund* 251 (June 3, 1934).

————. "Der ökumenische Rat und der deutsche Kirchenkonflikt. Fanö, 30. August." *Neue Zürcher Zeitung*, September 4, 1934. Morning edition no. 1578.

————. "Der Schweizerische evangelische Kirchenbund und die ökumenische Bewegung." In *Ekklesia*: Eine Sondersammlung von Selbstdarstellungen der christlichen Einigungsbewegungen. Edited by Friedrich Siegmund-Schultze. Vol. 3, Die Mitteleuropäischen Länder, 1935.

————. "Analytische Psychologie und Religionsforschung." In Psychologischer Club Zürich, ed. *Die kulturelle Bedeutung der komplexen Psychologie, Festschrift zum 60. Geburtstag von C.G. Jung,* 1935. Berlin: Verlag Julius Springer, 1935, 271–297.

————. "Schicksalsfragen des Europäischen Protestantismus." *Rufe in die Zeit.* Bern: Evangelische Gesellschaft Bern, 1935.

————. "L'influence des Révolutions continentales sur le Protestantisme." *Oecumenica* (Paris, July 1935) 156–67.

————. "Die Flüchtlingsfrage." *Kirchenblatt für die reformierte Schweiz* (December 26, 1935).

————. *Church and State on the European Continent: The Social Service Lecture (Beckly Lecture).* London: Epworth, 1936.

————. "Kurzer Bericht über die Tagung des Internationalen Komitees (Zentralstelle)." Geneva, August 2–September 1, 1936 (BAR J.2.257 1245/133).

————. "Geist und Dämonie in der Geschichte." *Neue Schweizer Rundschau* 4 (April 1937).

————. "Europe's Regret at Lack of Virile Leadership." *British Weekly* (September 30, 1937) (WCC 42.0042 3,1).

————. "Bericht der Europäischen Zentralstelle, 1937" (actually 1937/38) (BAR J.2.257 1247/133).

————. "Wege zum religiösen Frieden." In Gottfried Guggenbühl and Charly Clerc, eds. *Kultur- und Staatswissenschaftliche Schriften* no. 17 (1940).

————. *Am Fusse des Leuchtturms.* Zurich: Wanderer, 1940.

————. "Aus meinem Leben." Typescript 1940, 281 pages (NLAK).

————. *Christian Europe Today.* London and New York: Harper Brothers, 1942.

————, ed. *Auswahl einiger Äusserungen amerikanischer Organisationen und Persönlichkeiten zur kirchlichen Mission von Prof. D. Adolf Keller in Amerika.* Bern: F. Pochon-Jent, 1942.

————. *Amerikanisches Christentum—Heute.* Zollikon: Evangelischer Verlag, 1943.

————. *Wiederaufbau der Welt: Geistige Voraussetzungen.* Zurich: Schulthess, 1944.

————. *Zeit-Wende.* Zurich: Wanderer, 1946.

————. "Furcht vor Amerika." *Neue Zürcher Zeitung,* September 17, 1947, editorial.

————. "Ökumenische Portraits." *Neue Zürcher Zeitung,* September 11, 1948.

————. "Aus den Anfängen der Tiefenpsychologie," *Neue Zürcher Zeitung* (July 24, 1955, Sunday edition).

————. "Aus der Frühhzeit der psychoanalytischen Bewegung." Reprinted from *Schweizerische Zeitschrift für Psychologie und ihre Anwendungen* 15:2 (1956). Unpaginated.

————. "This Is My faith." In *This Is My Faith: The Convictions of Representavie Americans Today,* edited by Stewart Grant Cole, 161–71. New York: Harper & Brothers, 1956.

TEXTS BY TINA KELLER

Keller, Tina. "Soziale Arbeit in Ost-London." *Neue Wege* 6, no. 1 (January 1912), 22–33.

————. "In Memoriam" (1972). NLTK.

————. *Wege inneren Wachstums für eingespannte Menschen: Aus meinen Erinnerungen an C. G. Jung.* Erlenbach ZH; Bad Homburg: Bircher-Benner, 1972.

————. "Zusatz" to Adolf Keller's "Aus meinem Leben." NLTK.

————. "Autobiography" (version of summer 1981). Typescript. NLTK.

Swan, Wendy K. *The Memoir of Tina Keller-Jenny: A Lifelong Confrontation with the Psychology of C. G. Jung.* New Orleans: Spring Journal Books, 2011.

TEXTS BY OTHER AUTHORS

Adam, Karl. "Die Theologie der Krisis." *Hochland, Monatsschrift für alle Gebiete des Wissens, der Literatur und Kunst* 23 (April–September 1926) 271-86.

Ainslie, Peter. Book Review of *Dynamis,* by Adolf Keller. *The Christian Union Quarterly* 12/4 (1922–1923).

Algner, Caren, editor. *Karl Barth–Eduard Thurneysen. Briefwechsel.* Vol. 3, 1930–1935. Gesamtausgabe 34. Zurich: TVZ, 2000.

Avenarius, Ferdinand, editor *Kunstwart und Kulturwart.* Vol. 32/14. Munich: Callway, 1919.

Barth, Karl. *Der Götze wackelt: Zeitkritische Aufsätze. Reden und Briefe von 1930.* Edited by Karl Kupisch. Berlin: Vogt, 1961.

————. *Die Kirchliche Dogmatik: Die Lehre vom Wort Gottes. Prolegomena zur Kirchlichen Dogmatik.* Munich: Kaiser, 1932.

————. "Nein! Antwort an Emil Brunner." *Theologische Existenz heute* 14 (Munich, 1934).

———. "Die Not der evangelischen Kirche." *Zwischen den Zeiten* 2 (1931) 89–117.

———. "Reformation als Entscheidung." In *Dokumente der Begegnung Karl Barths mit dem Pfarrernotbund in Berlin*, edited by Eberhard Busch, 35–56. Zurich: TVZ, 1998.

———. "Der Römische Katholizismus als Frage an die Protestantische Kirche." *Zwischen den Zeiten* (1928) 274–302. Collected in *Karl Barth: Vorträge und kleinere Arbeiten 1925–1930*. Gesamtausgabe 24. Edited by Hermann Schmidt, 308–43. Zurich: TVZ, 1994.

Bell, G. K. A. *Die Königsherrschaft Jesu Christi: Die Geschichte des Ökumenischen Rates der Kirchen*. Translated by Rudolf Dohrmann. Hamburg: Reich, 1960.

Besson, Marius. "Vers la paix religieuse." In Gottfried Guggenbühl and Charly Clerc, eds. *Kultur- und Staatswissenschaftliche Schriften* no. 17 (1940).

Bethge, Eberhard. *Dietrich Bonhoeffer: Theologe, Christ, Zeitgenosse*. Munich: Kaiser, 1967.

Blet, Pierre et al., editors. *Actes et Documents du Saint Siège Relatifs à la Seconde Guerre Mondiale*. Vol. 6, *Le Saint Siège et les Victimes de la Guerre. Mars 1939–Décembre 1940*. Rome: Editrice Vaticana, 1972.

Boegner, Marc. *L'Exigence Œcuménique: Souvenir et Perspectives*. Paris: Michel, 1969.

Boyens, Armin. *"Ökumenische Bewegung und Bekennende Kirche in Deutschland 1933 bis Kriegsausbruch 1939."* PhD diss., University of Geneva. Munich: Kaiser, 1969

Brown, William Adams. "General War-Time Commission of the Churches. Its Organization and its Purpose" (1917). UTS, Presidential Papers 47/37, 1903–43.

———. *Toward a United Church: Three Decades of Ecumenical Christianity*. New York: Scribner, 1946.

Brunner, Emil. "Adolf Keller, Der Weg der dialektischen Theologie durch die kirchliche Welt." *Zwischen den Zeiten* 11 (1933).

———. "Der Staat und das christliche Freiheitsverständnis." In *Totaler Staat und christliche Freiheit*, edited by Forschungsabteilungdes Provisorischen Ökumenischen Rats der Kirchen, Genf 1937.

———. *Theology of Crisis*. New York: Scribner, 1929.

Busch, Eberhard, editor. *Einleitung zum Reformationstag 1933: Dokumente der Begegnung Karl Barths mit dem Pfarrernotbund in Berlin*. Zurich: TVZ, 1998.

———. *Karl Barths Lebenslauf: Nach seinen Briefen und autobiographischen Texten*. Munich: Kaiser, 1975.

———. *Karl Barth, His Life from Letters and Autobiographical Texts*. Translated by John Bowden. 1993. Reprinted, Wipf & Stock, 2005.

Busch, Eberhard et al., editors. *Karl Barth: Briefe des Jahres 1933* Zurich: TVZ, 2004.

Cavert, Samuel McCrea, editor. *Twenty Years of the Church Federation, Report of the Federal Council of the Churches of Christ in America*. New York: Scribner, 1929 (PHS NCC RG 18 79/17).

———, editor. *United in Service: Report of the Federal Council of the Churches of*

Christ in America, 1920-1924. New York: Federal Council of Churches, 1925 (PHS NCC RG 18 79/14).

Cole, Stewart Grant, editor. *This Is My Faith: The Convictions of Representative Americans Today.* New York: Harper & Brothers, 1956.

Deissmann, Adolf. *Die Stockholmer Weltkirchenkonferenz: Amtlicher Deutscher Bericht.* Berlin: Furche, 1926.

————. *Die Stockholmer Bewegung: Die Weltkirchenkonferenzen zu Stockholm 1925 und Bern 1926 von innen betrachtet.* Berlin: Furche, 1927.

D'Espine, Henri. *Alphons Koechlin: Pasteur et Chef d'Eglise, 1885–1965.* Geneva: Labor et Fides, 1971.

Drewes, Hans-Anton. *Bibliographie Karl Barth.* Vol. 1. Zurich: TVZ, 1984.

Ehrenström, Nils. "Die Bewegungen für internationale Freundschaftsarbeit und für Praktisches Christentum, 1925–1948." In Ruth Rouse and Stephen Neill, eds. *Geschichte der Ökumenischen Bewegung.* Part 2. Göttingen: Vandenhoeck & Ruprecht, 1958.

Feldges, Fritz. "Ökumenisches Seminar in Genf." In Karl Ludwig Schmidt and Hermann Strathmann, editors. *Theologische Blätter* 14 (Leipzig, 1935), col. 229–30.

Flournoy, Théodore, and Edouard Claparède, editors. *Archives de Psychologie de la Suisse Romande.*

Forschungsabteilung des Provisorischen Ökumenischen Rats der Kirchen, editors. *Die Kirche und das Staatsproblem in der Gegenwart.* Genf, 1935.

Frischmuth, Gertrud. "Adolf Deissmann: Ein Leben für die Una Sancta." In *Oekumenische Profile,* edited by Günter Gloede, 280–90. Stuttgart: Evangelischer Missionsverlag, 1961.

Gerlach, Wolfgang. "Zur Entstehung des Internationalen kirchlichen Hilfskomitees für deutsche Flüchtlinge 1933–1936." In *Aktiver Friede: Gedenkschrift für Friedrich Siegmund-Schultze (1885–1969),* edited by Hermann Delfs Soest: Mocker & Jahn, 1972.

Göckeritz, Hermann Götz, editor. *Friedrich Gogartens Briefwechsel mit Karl Barth, Eduard Thurneysen und Emil Brunner.* Tübingen: Mohr/Siebeck, 2009.

Göhring, Andreas. *75 Jahre deutschschweizerische reformierte Kirchgemeinde Genf, 1903-1978.* Typescript. Archive of the Geneva Church Parish.

Grotefeld, Stefan. *Friedrich Siegmund-Schultze: Ein deutscher Oekumeniker und christlicher Pazifist.* Heidelberger Untersuchungen zu Widerstand, Judenverfolgung und Kirchenkampf im Dritten Reich 7. Gütersloh: Gütersloher Verlag, 1995.

Herwig, Thomas, and W. A. Visser't Hooft, editors. *Karl Barth–W.A. Visser't Hooft: Briefwechsel.* Gesamtausgabe 43 Zurich: TVZ, 2006.

Jehle, Frank. *Emil Brunner: Theologe im 20. Jahrhundert.* Zurich: TVZ 2006.

Jehle-Wildberger, Marianne. *Adolf Keller (1872–1963): Pionier der ökumenischen Bewegung.* Zurich: TVZ, 2008.

————. "Karl Barth und Adolf Keller. Geschichte einer Freundschaft." *Theologische Zeitschrift* 66/4 (2010) 355–80.

————. *Das Gewissen sprechen lassen. Die Haltung der St. Galler Kirche zu*

Kirchenkampf und Flüchtlingsnot 1933–1945. Zurich: TVZ, 2001.

———. "Marius Besson und Adolf Keller. Ein frühes ökumenisches Gespräch." *Freiburger Zeitschrift für Philosophie und Theologie* 58, 2 (2011) 505–530.

Kaiser, Marcus Urs. *Deutscher Kirchenkampf und Schweizer Öffentlichkeit in den Jahren 1933 und 1934.* Zurich: TVZ, 1972.

Kerner, Hanns. *Luthertum und Ökumene: Bewegung für Praktisches Christentum, 1919–1926.* Die lutherische Kirche, Geschichte und Gestalten 5. Gütersloh: Mohn, 1983.

Kocher, Hermann. *"Rationierte Menschlichkeit": Schweizerischer Protestantismus im Spannungsfeld von Flüchtlingnot und öffentlicher Flüchtlingspolitik der Schweiz 1933–1948.* Zurich: Chronos, 1996.

Horn, Ewald. "Berlin, Universität." In *Religion in Geschichte und Gegenwart* 1:1041–54. Tübingen: Mohr/Siebeck, 1909.

Liefmann, Martha and Else. *Helle Lichter auf dunklem Grund: Erinnerungen.* Bern: Christliches Verlagshaus, 1966.

Lindt, Andreas, editor. *George Bell–Alphons Koechlin. Briefwechsel 1933–1954.* Zurich: EVZ, 1969.

Macfarland, Charles. *The New Church and the New Germany: A Study of Church and State* New York: Macmillan, 1934.

———. *Steps toward the World Council: Origins of the Ecumenical Movement as Expressed in the Universal Christian Council for Life and Work.* New York: Revell, 1938.

Mackay, John A. *Ecumenics: The Science of the Church Universal.* Englewood Cliffs, NJ: Prentice-Hall, 1964.

Mackintosh, H. R. "The Swiss Group." *Expository Times,* 36/2 (1924–1925) 73–75.

Maiwald, Birger. *Ökumenischer Kirchenkampf: Die "Berner Erklärung" des Schweizerischen Evangelischen Kirchenbundes von 1934.* Bern: SEK, 1997.

Mann, Thomas. *Tagebücher 1937-1939.* Frankfurt: Fischer, 1980.

Mattmüller, Markus. *Leonhard Ragaz und der religiöse Sozialismus.* Vol. 2. Basler Beiträge zur Geschichtswissenschaft 100. Zurich: EVZ, 1968.

Messenger, Jack, and Brigitte Lee. *The Story of the Ecumenical Church Loan Fund.* Geneva: ECLOF, 1996.

Pauck, Wilhelm, and Marion Pauck. *Paul Tillich. Sein Leben und Denken.* Vol. 1, *Leben.* Stuttgart: Evangelisches Verlagswerk, 1976.

Pribilla, Max. *Um kirchliche Einheit: Stockholm, Lausanne, Rom: geschichtlich-theologische Darstellung der neueren Einigungsbewegungen.* Freiburg: Herder, 1929.

Rauschning, Hermann. *Die Revolution des Nihilismus.* Zurich: Europa, 1938.

Rosenberg, Alfred. *Der Mythos des Zwanzigsten Jahrhunderts.* Munich: Hoheneichen, 1930.

Schmidt, William J. *Architect of Unity: A Biography of Samuel McCrea Cavert.* New York: Friendship, 1978.

———. "Henry Smith Leiper: Ecumenical Pioneer." *Ecumenical Trends* 15/5 (May 1986) 77–80.

Bibliography

Scholder, Klaus. *Die Kirchen und das Dritte Reich.* 3 vols. Frankfurt: Ullstein, 1977.

Schweizerischer Evangelischer Kirchenbund, editor. *Die Kirche und die Arbeitslosigkeit.* Bern: Selbstverlag, 1931.

Semmler, Kurt. *Kirche und Völkerbund: Das Verhalten der evangelisch-reformierten Kirchen der Schweiz gegenüber dem Völkerbund.* Zurich: Juris Druck, 1974.

Sträuli-Keller, Doris. „Erinnerungen—und jetzt." Typescript. Winterthur: Archiv Stiftung Sulzberg, 2000.

Sundkler, Bengt. *Nathan Söderblom: His Life and Work.* Lund: Gleerups, 1968.

Thurneysen, Eduard, editor. *Karl Barth–Eduard Thurneysen.* Briefwechsel. Vol. 2. Gesamtausgabe 4. Zurich: TVZ, 1974.

Vuletic, Aleksandar-Sasa. *Christen jüdischer Herkunft im Dritten Reich: Verfolgung und organisierte Selbsthilfe* 1933–1939. Veröffentlichungen des Instituts für Europäische Geschichte Mainz 169. Mainz: von Zabern, 1999.

Visser't Hooft, W. A. *Die Welt war meine Gemeinde.* Munich: Piper, 1972.

Wagner, Oskar. *Ukrainische Evangelische Kirchen des byzantinischen Ritus.* Oikonomia. Quellen und Studien zur orthodoxen Theologie 30. Erlangen: Lehrstuhl für Geschichte und Theologie des Christlichen Ostens, 1991.

Weber, Hans-Ruedi. *A Laboratory for Ecumenical Life: The Story of Bossey, 1946–1996.* Geneva: WCC Publications, 1996.

Weisse, Wolfram. *Praktisches Christentum und Reich Gottes: Die ökumenische Bewegung Life and Work* 1919-1937. Kirche und Konfession 31. Göttingen: Vandenhoeck & Ruprecht, 1991.

Wildberger, Marianne. "Die schweizerischen evangelischen Kirchen und der deutsche Kirchenkampf 1933–1939." MA thesis, University of Zurich, 1964 (BAR J.2.257 1288/137).

Zöckler, Christian. *Ein Leben für die Kinder: Das Bethel des Ostens, Theodor Zöckler und Lilly Zöckler.* Bergisch Gladbach: Edition Epb/Breuer, 2005.

Index of Names

Index of Groups and Organizations